THE PAGEANT
OF AMERICA

Independence Edition

VOLUME VII

THE PAGEANT OF AMERICA

A PICTORIAL HISTORY OF THE UNITED STATES

RALPH HENRY GABRIEL

EDITOR

PETER GUILDAY   JOHN CHESTER ADAMS

ASSOCIATE EDITORS

EDWIN MIMS, JR.

ASSISTANT EDITOR

<table>
<tr><td>CHARLES M. ANDREWS</td><td>ALLEN JOHNSON</td></tr>
<tr><td>HERBERT E. BOLTON</td><td>WILLIAM BENNETT MUNRO</td></tr>
<tr><td>IRVING N. COUNTRYMAN</td><td>VICTOR H. PALTSITS</td></tr>
<tr><td>WILLIAM E. DODD</td><td>ARTHUR M. SCHLESINGER</td></tr>
<tr><td>DIXON RYAN FOX</td><td>NATHANIEL WRIGHT STEPHENSON</td></tr>
</table>

ADVISORY EDITORS

DAVID M. MATTESON

INDEXER

From the painting by Eastman Johnson (1824–1906) in the Union League Club, New York

THE WOUNDED DRUMMER BOY

THE PAGEANT OF AMERICA

IN DEFENSE
OF LIBERTY

BY

WILLIAM WOOD

RALPH HENRY GABRIEL

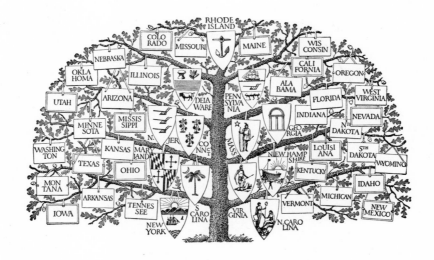

NEW HAVEN · YALE UNIVERSITY PRESS

TORONTO · GLASGOW, BROOK & CO.

LONDON · HUMPHREY MILFORD

OXFORD UNIVERSITY PRESS

TABLE OF CONTENTS

THE MILITARY FOLKWAYS OF RECENT AMERICA

ONE morning in the spring of 1861 a cannon boomed from the quiet shore of Charleston harbor and a shell shrieked toward Fort Sumter. The reverberations echoed through the nation. The shot was the signal that the American people had abandoned peaceful discussion in their efforts to solve a difficult problem and had resorted to the primitive arbitrament of arms. So began the greatest disaster in the history of the United States. Out of the communities of both North and South stepped thousands of volunteers offering themselves in support of the cause which they held dear. At home remained other sons who avoided the responsibilities of citizenship. There were some whom necessity prevented from entering the conflict and others who, for one reason or another, could not honestly bring themselves to participate in a fratricidal war. When, four years after the firing on Sumter, spring came with its verdure of trees and fields and its promise of new life, thousands of fresh graves dotted the cemeteries of the nation, and other thousands of maimed or invalid men faced with what energy they could muster the tasks of life. The dead and wounded of the first two years of the struggle were mostly from among those choice sons of the Republic who had sallied forth as volunteers and who left but the memory of a gallant fight and an ennobling sacrifice. Their graves made vivid the worst aspect of the tragedy of the Civil War. America, less than a century after the Declaration of Independence, had drenched its soil with its finest blood.

Careful students of the past have come to look upon the clash between the North and South as almost, if not quite, inevitable. Two civilizations of different and divergent ideals had appeared within the same nation. (See Vol. VIII, Introduction.) Climatic influences had caused the abandonment of slavery in the North, and had made that institution profitable for a considerable period in the South. The smaller section sought to become independent in order that it might develop in its own way; the patriots of the larger could not see their nation dismembered without doing everything in their power to prevent it. So war came. But there is one aspect, frequently ignored, which especially merits consideration. The Civil War was one of the fiercest and bloodiest wars of the nineteenth century. For these characteristics Americans must assume full responsibility, since no foreign nations were involved. It was fought out to an exhausting conclusion by a people who from the first year of their independence had proved themselves by their military policy and their persistent attitude toward military things a profoundly non-militaristic nation. William Graham Sumner has pointed out that there is no necessary connection between purposes and consequences. The high and unmistakable purpose of the American people was peace; yet war came, a peculiarly cruel and devastating war, which brought ruin and desolation to one of the fairest sections of the country.

This war, moreover, was in no way the result of that mutual fear which is sometimes engendered by large national armaments. Quite the contrary is true. By 1861 the lean years of the Regular Army had been so many that the South could and did largely ignore its existence. The navy was scarcely better off. As a result neither side saw beyond the dividing line any trained and organized military force that it would be impossible to combat. They saw only military weakness. Each side enjoyed that confidence in its own fighting ability which had characterized Americans since the beginning of their national history. Each believed that a few short months would see the adversary brought to terms. The fact cannot be gainsaid that this belief in easy victory, engendered by the obvious military weakness of the opponent, made both northerners and southerners more willing to commit the issue to the hazard of war. Had these non-militaristic Americans understood better the realities of war, they must have hesitated more than they did to enter upon armed conflict.

Such a situation was not new in American history. The apparent weakness of Canada in 1812, which had led Clay to predict a peace dictated at Montreal within a few weeks, played no small part in persuading the War Hawks to plunge the country into war. A generation later the weakness of Mexico, patent to all the world, was not without its influence in deciding the Polk administration to take up arms against the sister republic. In each case the military strength of the United States was very slight. War is engendered by weakness which invites as well as by strength which menaces. The question naturally arises whether a regular army and navy, strong and efficient, would have changed the crisis of 1861. Military service in the United States had always emphasized above all else the cardinal virtue of loyalty, particularly loyalty to the nation and to the flag which is its symbol. From the beginning of the nation's history the American army has been representative of the American people, although commissioned officers have tended to sympathize more with aristocratic than with democratic tendencies in American life. In 1861 the army divided as the people divided. But it divided significantly. Out of a total of about nine hundred commissioned officers two hundred and sixty-nine, less than one third, resigned to join the Confederacy and twenty-six were dismissed for sympathy with the South. Nearly one half the West Point alumni whose homes were in the South put their loyalty to the nation above that to their state. Among the enlisted personnel, between twelve and thirteen thousand in number, the merest handful joined the South. In the navy the proportion of resignations was smaller than in the army. Such was the response of services which had received anything but generous treatment at the hands of either the Government or the people.

These facts give point to the expressed conviction of Lord Wolseley of the British army, who accompanied Lee's battalions in the operations after Antietam, that at any time during the war a single corps of regular troops would have turned the scale in favor of either side. Writers on the Civil War have almost universally referred to Bull Run as an engagement between amateur armies, but they have usually failed to note that the forces which clashed during the next two years were also to a large extent amateur troops. Southerners, perhaps because of their aristocratic tradition and of the fact that the direction of large enterprises was an habitual part of the planter's life, adjusted themselves more quickly than northerners to the necessities of military life. Particularly in Virginia in 1862 and 1863 they were in general the more effective troops. A true picture of the armies on both sides during the first three years of the struggle, however, would reveal them as clumsy instruments of war. Neither in maneuvering nor in battle was the commanding general on either side ever sure that his orders would be obeyed exactly or completely. There was a consequent lack of cohesion which was fatal to decisive results. This military ineffectiveness was due in part to the fact that the regular officers had not had, since the days when they were lieutenants and captains in the Mexican War, opportunity to participate in the maneuvers of large units. The junior officers of the Civil War were for the most part civilians without training for their new responsibilities. Finally, until the latter phases of the conflict, neither combatant had provided for an adequate staff to assist the commanding general in his work. The evidence available suggests the conclusion that, had the United States possessed in 1861 a strong army properly equipped and trained, the war might have been avoided and would certainly have been shortened. Perhaps, as has been suggested, a larger army, because of the aristocratic tendencies of its officers, would have been an aid to the southern cause. The manner in which the army divided in 1861, however, does not support this contention. A military policy which was the clear expression of the will of the people, both North and South, was to a considerable extent responsible for that waste of the nation's finest citizens which characterized this national calamity. The primary function of the state is to defend its people from enemies without and to maintain peace at home. In 1861 the Government of the United States failed completely to meet the second obligation.

War, particularly a prolonged war, brings out the best and the worst in a people. Side by side it presents the brutality of the savage and the sacrifice of the martyr, corroding hatred and the fine devotion of comrades in arms. The Civil War raised many Americans to heights of idealism unattained since Valley Forge, and it plunged others into corruption so repellent that the years immediately preceding and following the celebration of the nation's Centennial have been aptly called "the nadir of national disgrace." The hatred engendered by the war found its full expression in that policy of vindictive reconstruction of the conquered South which has left scars not effaced after the lapse of more than half a century. Such was a part of the price paid to maintain the integrity of the nation.

Significant of the military characteristics of the American people is the fact that the lessons of the Civil War were no more heeded than those of the War of 1812. Following demobilization, the regular army was steadily reduced until it was but a shadow, and the navy of obsolete wooden vessels was allowed to rot at the wharves without being replaced by new ships. The depths were plumbed in the fiscal year 1877–78, when army officers borrowed money at interest in order to live, the Fifty-Fourth Congress having neglected to pass the appropriation bill for their pay. The navy was in one sense worse off than the army, for every naval officer knew that the wooden ships which he commanded could never be taken into battle. In both services, however, able and devoted men were working effectively, though in the face of great discouragements, for the progress of their professions. Outstanding among the army men was Brevet Major-General Emory Upton. After a tour of duty in Europe studying the armed forces in England and on the Continent, Upton devoted himself to an exhaustive investigation of the organization and management of armies in the history of the United States. His untimely death in 1881 found his work brought down only to the middle of the Civil War. The fate of the manuscript which he left is not without significance in displaying the military attitude of the American people a decade and a half after the conclusion of the Civil War. Upton's *Military Policy of the United States* is a plain-spoken book full of unpalatable truths. The work was pigeon-holed. For nearly a quarter of a century the policy of suppression was continued until Elihu Root as Secretary of War courageously published the book for the benefit of the American people.

The swift return after the Civil War to the military habits which preceded it made it clear that four wars fought in a little less than a century had not changed the military folkways of the American people. Among other evidence for this conservatism was the fact that in 1892 the Militia Act, basic to the defense program, completed a century of service without having been altered. There are several reasons for this extraordinary failure of a progressive people to profit by experience. Fundamental is the fact that down to and after the Civil War the United States was in what might be called an agricultural stage of culture. To be sure industry was developing and there was an important minority of seafaring folk along the coast. But the great bulk of the people, both North and South, derived their living from the land. These men of the mid-nineteenth century were not the scientific agriculturists of a later day. They still largely used the hand tools and the traditional methods which they had inherited from the past. Though they were vigorous individualists supporting their families on semi-self-sufficient farms, conservatism was woven through the fabric of their thought. The habits of the past, be they agricultural, religious, or military, were good enough for them. They had largely lost the eighteenth-century fear of a standing army, but they had no interest in one. In spite of the fact that, at one time or another, many of them had been soldiers, they had no conception of the needs of a military force or of the service both in peace and war which it is capable of rendering. The navy was quite beyond their ken. And the man of the soil was to the end of the second third of the nineteenth century the dominant power in American political life.

His conservatism in military matters was strengthened by the fact that the nation in its first four wars had not been defeated. The indispensable aid of France in the Revolution was largely forgotten. The lessons of the War of 1812 were lost in popular historical accounts which emphasized the useless frigate duels, the naval victories on the lakes, Jackson's triumph at New Orleans, and which largely ignored or laid at the door of individual incompetence the gross and inexcusable failures of the conflict. The North had won the Civil War; that fact alone was sufficient justification for the military policy which preceded it. Throughout the course of the development of the United States had appeared a series of men, beginning with Washington, who had been apprehensive that disastrous results would flow from the military policy which the American people were pursuing. The unnecessary waste of life in the Civil War was the grim justification for these prophets of warning. But it was not recognized as such by the common man of the time, who accepted the losses and suffering of the conflict with what amounted to fatalism. There were, in fact, throughout most of the nineteenth century no adequate means for disseminating the ideas of intelligent leaders among the masses of the voters, a majority of whom lived in the semi-isolation of the nineteenth-century rural community. The attitude of mind which had its origin in the colonial period did not change until an agricultural civilization began to give way to industrialism.

In the last decades of the nineteenth and the first of the twentieth centuries, industrialism transformed American life. The exploitation of unparalleled natural resources brought to the nation both wealth and transcendent economic power. Before the end of the nineteenth century an overseas empire had been acquired, and in the twentieth century American business interests began seeking throughout the world for raw materials and markets. That period of national isolation which started with the Treaty of Ghent in 1815, and during which practically the entire attention of Americans was focused upon domestic problems, began to disappear in 1898 and came to an end in 1917. After the World War the American people realized, as never before, the fact that their nation is one of a group of nations and that among their chief problems is that of living in peace with their neighbors. Industrialism has made the United States one of the small group of great powers and has forced upon Americans the responsibilities which accompany such a position. It has done more. The aggressive individualism of the independent farmer has been sharply modified as more and more Americans have become parts of increasingly complex commercial and industrial organizations. The people of the United States have learned the value of coöperative effort and have come to appreciate the importance of team work. They have also come to understand the significance of the specialist. As a consequence they have become more willing to listen to the advice of the man of the army or the navy. When he has spoken of the needs of his service in terms of organization, coöperation, technical equipment, specialists, discipline, and morale, he has used language which industrial America, in contrast with the agricultural America of the early nineteenth century, can understand. The swift rise of industrialism after the Civil War had hardly been in progress a decade and a half when the renaissance in both navy and army was well under way.

In each case this began with development within the service. In the army improvement dates from Upton who, besides his work on military policy, introduced changes of importance in drill regulations. In the navy the new day began with those investigations by naval officers of the problem of steel ships which led to the creation of a steel navy. That the changing public attitude affected the navy more quickly than the army is demonstrated by the fact that the brilliant work of the then Captain A. T. Mahan on the significance of sea power was widely read, while General Upton's chapters on military policy, written but a few years earlier, were suppressed. When, by 1898, the new navy had been practically completed, the United States became involved in a war with Spain as a result of the misgovernment of Cuba. The decisive events of this hundred days' war were the annihilation of two enemy fleets with a loss of life on the part of the Americans almost unbelievably small. The war demonstrated that the traditions of efficiency and devotion to duty established by officers like John Paul Jones, Perry, MacDonough, and Farragut permeated the spirit of the new navy. The record of the army was not so glorious. The Government had kept it too small to be effective. The outbreak of war brought the usual feverish efforts to create a fighting force over night. The result was pandemonium and dangerous impotence while volunteers were being recruited and organized. Then it became clear that the United States had called its young men to the colors only to see them sicken and die in the camps at home and in the campaigns in Cuba because no proper steps had been taken to improve the medical corps or the department of supply. In the end the army accomplished the missions on which it was sent but with much suffering and sacrifice that was quite unnecessary.

The Spanish-American War was followed by the pacification of the Philippines and by the international expedition into China following the Boxer uprising. In Cuba, meanwhile, the army showed what it could accomplish in the way of bringing order and health to a community which had suffered for many decades from the incompetence of its foreign rulers. Significant of the change which industrialism had brought to American life was the fact that the United States profited somewhat by the unhappy experiences of the war. Slowly but steadily the army increased in efficiency during the first decade and a half of the twentieth century. Congress began to take an intelligent interest in military matters that was quite at variance with its customary neglect of former years. The navy was increased in size and its efficiency was maintained at a high point. Its fighting power was vastly augmented by the construction of the Panama Canal, which made the development of two fleets unnecessary. All in all these were years of promise, when the establishment of a sound military and naval policy seemed not far distant. Before this occurred, however, the United States had been drawn into the maelstrom of the World War, quite unprepared to face the enemy on the field of battle.

A year and a quarter elapsed after the declaration of war before American troops appeared in important force upon the fighting front. During this time the war was almost lost. The German drive of 1918 came within a hair's breadth of smashing the exhausted French army and forcing France to make peace. Again, as in the War of 1812 and the Civil War, the people of the United States escaped by the narrowest margin paying the extreme penalty for lack of adequate preparedness. This time they were saved by the blood of their allied comrades in arms who were fighting on land and sea in the Old World. Yet the World War displayed the American people in one of their finest moods. Never in all their history had they been so united, never so filled with determination to fight for what they deemed the right. When the crisis was on them, they met it with profound idealism and with measures of high intelligence. Profiting by their own past mistakes and by those of the people by the side of whom they were about to fight, Americans at the very outset of their participation in the war established the principle that every son of the Republic who was physically fit and of the proper age should share in the burdens imposed by the emergency. The pernicious volunteer system was abandoned, and with it the equally pernicious officer who owed his commission to political preferment. An aroused public opinion lashed the "slacker" as in no previous conflict. In the end the war was won.

The years that have elapsed since the Armistice brought to a close the greatest and the saddest tragedy the world has suffered have seen a swift development in the thinking of the American people in military and naval matters. In 1920, after exhaustive study, the Government of the United States established a military policy adequate to the needs of the nation and in harmony with the genius of its people. Under its terms the Army of the United States is made up of three parts: a first line of defense consisting of the highly trained Regular Army; a second line of defense consisting of the National Guard, whose officers and men are civilians yet constantly in training and ready to be called out at a moment's notice; and a third line of defense made up of an officers' and an enlisted Reserve Corps. The latter are not an inchoate mass, but are organized into army corps, divisions, regiments, battalions, and even companies. They are ready to receive promptly the men selected by the draft and turn them speedily into soldiers. This army of defense is based upon traditions that go back to the very origin of the American people. As was the case in the days of the old militia system, twentieth-century Americans depend for their defense primarily upon themselves; but with the difference that, as a people, they have recognized the importance of organization and training.

The naval building program undertaken because of the necessities of the World War promised to give the United States in a few years the most powerful naval force in the world. The years following the cessation of hostilities witnessed a naval race into which the people of the United States together with those of Great Britain and Japan were unwillingly drawn. Then appeared a second aspect of the developing preparedness policy of the United States. A friendly conference of the leading naval powers resulted in the taking of the first steps toward the reduction and limitation of armaments. The United States, whether wisely or unwisely remains for the future to disclose, went so far in the limitation of its naval strength as to put itself into a position which makes the defense of its most distant possessions extremely difficult if not impossible. The principle upon which the Washington Conference was founded has become fixed in American foreign policy. The American nation, assuming that forces of evil which can only be curbed by force exist in human society, has armed itself to perform those ancient functions of a state, defense against enemies without and the maintenance of peace within. In the belief that national impotence breeds war the United States has declined to accept the policy of complete disarmament. At the same time the nation has inaugurated the practice of acting constantly in coöperation with other powers to the end that armaments may not threaten the peace of the world. America has sought a mean between undue military strength and excessive weakness.

The twentieth century has seen the growth of a new attitude toward the problem of national defense, that of the pacifists. The so-called peace movement stood out at the end of the first quarter of the twentieth century as one of the important phases of American thought. Pacifism, however, is not a new phenomenon in American life. Non-resistant sects appeared in the New World in the seventeenth century. A peace movement sprang up after the War of 1812. Between 1812 and 1828 peace societies under various names were established in many states. In the latter year a national organization assumed the name of the "American Peace Society." The appeal of these societies was primarily religious. Along with a large part of the American public they condemned the Mexican War. When faced, however, with the failure of the United States in 1861 to maintain peace within its own borders, the American Peace Society took a curious position. In its *Proceedings* of 1862 the statement was made that it was no part of the society's business "to inquire how murder . . . shall be punished; . . . and by what specific means government shall enforce its laws, and support its rightful and indispensable authority; how a people, deprived of their rights, shall regain and preserve them, or in what way any controversy between a government and its own subjects shall be adjusted. With such questions, however important, the cause of peace is not concerned, but solely with the intercourse of nations for the single purpose of abolishing the custom of war, or their practice of settling their disputes by the sword."

Though many of these mid-nineteenth-century societies persisted after the Civil War, the peace movement of the first quarter of the twentieth century was virtually a new one. It showed a rapid growth though one of its most striking characteristics was its tendency to divide. In 1927 some thirty-five organizations were going their separate ways and pursuing their separate objects while new ones were continuing to spring up. Though their programs vary all the way from conservative to radical, their general objective is the elimination of war from the affairs of men. In this respect they are in harmony with the dominant mood of the American people who in the Washington Conference demonstrated a willingness to make surprising sacrifices to ensure the peace of the world. At one extreme of the peace movement are endowed organizations, like the World Peace Foundation and the Carnegie Endowment for International Peace, whose soundly based scholarly activities are an excellent expression of that conscious will to peace which has characterized the thinking part of the American public since an almost complete absorption in their own domestic affairs has given place to a realization of their position in the society of nations. These organizations, beside investigating the causes of war, seek to build up a better understanding and to establish a truer sympathy among the peoples of the world. At the other extreme are the crusading nonresistant societies. Their activities are an interesting twentieth-century manifestation of that belief, so pronounced at the end of the eighteenth century, in the perfectibility of human nature. They emphasize, what is accepted by the intelligent elements of the American people, that war is a crude and ineffectual method of settling disputes, that it is bad economics and bad religion. The ultimate, though not the only, expression of their opposition to war is a refusal to fight in the event of an emergency. Like other organizations seeking to achieve definite objectives they take a keen interest in the teaching of history. They deplore any emphasis upon wars and particularly upon any glorious episodes or consequences that may have been connected with them. They desire to eliminate military training from schools and colleges. Their theory is that such training tends to develop in the individual a point of view which makes for war. They, unfortunately, ignore the fact that the trained man who understands the frightful realities of modern war as no civilian can is the least likely to bring unnecessarily either himself or his brothers face to face with that hell which is called "no man's land." In 1861 the people of the United States had a demonstration of the consequences that may flow from a virtually universal ignorance of the realities of armed conflict.

The peace movement in all its various aspects is an active expression of the idealism of the American people. There are other reasons, however, why the United States in the second quarter of the twentieth century offers unusually fertile soil for such developments. The Americans are a contented people largely because their nation is the wealthiest in the world and because in America the good things of life are widely diffused among the masses. What economic advantage accrued from the World War went largely to the United States, where the invader never set foot to burn or to destroy. With priceless natural resources at home, Americans covet no territory abroad. What they desire above all else is peace to enjoy the well-being which is theirs. As a people they do not know what it means to be bankrupt or hungry. Their shores are guarded by two oceans, and their nearest neighbors on land are vastly weaker than themselves. As has been true since the beginning of their history, no potential enemy lives near at hand who could pounce suddenly upon their populous cities. With a background made up of a sense of security, economic contentment, and a genuine idealism, the American Government has taken the lead in seeking to establish the world over that mean between excessive armaments and excessive weakness which at the present stage of civilization seems the surest guarantee of world peace. On May 30, 1927, this military policy was clearly set forth by the President of the United States: "However much we wish to pursue the paths of peace, however much we are determined to live on terms of good-will both at home and abroad, we cannot escape the fact that there are still evil forces in the world which all past experience warns us will break out from time to time and do serious damage to lawful rights and the progress of civilization unless we are prepared to meet such situations with armed intervention. We could no more dispense with our military forces than with our police forces. While we are firmly convinced that it is altogether practical and possible by international covenants to limit them in size, to consent to their abolition would be to expose ourselves first to aggression and finally to destruction."

RALPH HENRY GABRIEL

CHAPTER I

THE PLUNGE INTO CIVIL WAR

IN October, 1860, the Wide Awakes in caps and capes and bearing their flaming torches were parading for "Honest Abe." In November, after a three-cornered campaign, Lincoln was elected President by a minority of his fellow citizens. (See Vol. VIII.) In December the state of South Carolina repealed its ratification of the Constitution of 1787 and seceded from the Union. Georgia, Florida, Alabama, Mississippi, Louisiana, and Texas followed. In February, 1861, the Confederate States of America came into being with Jefferson Davis as President. In March the Confederate Congress made provision for a regular army; but outside of its staff departments and a few regiments of the line this army was never raised. The Confederacy depended for its military strength upon a provisional army formed at first from quotas of volunteers furnished by the several states and later by conscription. In the same month the Confederate Government called into the service thirty thousand men who were to be used to take possession of the coast defenses of the South.

The inauguration of President Lincoln found the nation filled with supressed excitement. The future of the American people depended to a considerable extent upon his decisions and actions. The uncertainty was increased by the fact that Lincoln was an untried man. In the face of secession President Buchanan had stood impotent, taking no effective measures to enforce the laws of the United States in the disaffected area. On March 4 he turned over the responsibilities of his high office to an Illinois lawyer. On that day, facing a crisis greater than any in the history of the people whose destinies had been placed in his charge, Lincoln addressed the nation. "I take the official oath today with no mental reservations, and with no purpose to construe the Constitution or laws by any hypercritical rules. I hold that, in contemplation of universal law and the Constitution, the Union of these States is perpetual. Perpetuity is implied, if not expressed, in the fundamental law of all national governments. It is safe to assert that no government proper ever had a provision in its organic law for its own termination. I therefore consider, that, in view of the Constitution and the laws, the Union is unbroken; and to the extent of my ability I shall take care, as the Constitution itself expressly enjoins upon me, that the laws of the Union be faithfully executed in all the States. Doing this, I deem it to be only a simple duty on my part, and I shall perform it so far as practicable, unless my rightful masters, the American people, shall withhold the requisite means, or in some authoritative manner direct the contrary. I trust this will not be regarded as a menace, but only as the declared purpose of the Union that it will constitutionally defend and maintain itself. . . . In your hands, my dissatisfied fellow-countrymen, and not in mine, is the momentous issue of civil war. You have no oath registered in heaven to destroy the Government; while I shall have the most solemn one to 'preserve, protect, and defend' it.

"I am loath to close. We are not enemies but friends. We must not be enemies. Though passion may have strained, it must not break our bonds of affection. The mystic cords of memory, stretching from every battlefield and patriot grave to every living heart and hearthstone all over this broad land, will yet swell the chorus of the Union when again touched, as surely they will be, by the better angels of our nature."

1   Second Reënforcement of Fort Pickens, Apr. 16, 1861, from *Harper's History of the Great Rebellion*, 1866–68

THE SURRENDER OF THE FORTS IN THE SOUTH

FROM time to time during the winter of 1860–61 the press of the North carried news of the surrender of Federal forts in the South to the seceding states. The stories, however, were not always of surrender. On January 8 the little garrison at Fort Pickens off Pensacola fired upon a small knot of state troops and dispersed them. It was the first shot of the war. Lieutenants Slemmer and Gilman held out with only eighty men until they were reinforced in April. Fort Pickens never fell. On February 18, however, General David E. Twiggs surrendered the army posts in Texas to the state. By March 1 all of the forts south of the entrance of Chesapeake Bay were in the possession of the state Governments except Fortress Monroe at the entrance of Hampton Roads, Fort Moultrie and Fort Sumter at the entrance of Charleston Harbor, Fort Pickens, and some fortifications on the islands at the entrance of the Gulf of Mexico.

2   Fort Wachita, Texas, from a sketch in *Harper's Weekly*, Mar. 16, 1861

3   Charleston Battery drilling, from a photograph by George S. Cook in the H. P. Cook Collection, Richmond, Va.

MILITARY PREPARATIONS IN THE SOUTH

PRESIDENT DAVIS was a West Pointer (see Vol. VI) and well knew the need for preparation for the impending struggle. In March he called for fifteen thousand volunteers to take charge of the Federal forts which had fallen into the possession of the Confederate Government. Five thousand of these, sons of South Carolina, he assigned to Brigadier-General Pierre G. T. Beauregard for the capture of Fort Moultrie and Fort Sumter. Already South Carolina had felt the stir of military activity. Men were leaving the pursuits of peace to learn the technique of the unfamiliar calling of arms. Companies and batteries were drilling. The air was charged with excitement. There was talk that a show of force was all that was necessary, for the North would never fight. Men worked with a zest at soldiering but, like their forefathers who had defied England in 1775, they had no conception of the terrible realities of war.

4   Evacuation of Fort Moultrie, from *Frank Leslie's Illustrated Newspaper*, Jan. 19, 1861

THE BOMBARDMENT OF SUMTER

A GRAY dawn was breaking over Charleston on the morning of April 12 when the boom of a cannon awakened the city. Quickly other cannon from both sides of the harbor opened fire. Shells shrieked above the gray-black water and burst against the walls of Sumter rising darkly in the dim morning light. Within the fort Major Anderson and sixty-five men stood beside the guns pointing through the embrasures awaiting the daylight before replying to the shore batteries. The Civil War had begun.

5   Major Anderson and his officers, from a photograph by George S. Cook in the H. P. Cook Collection, Richmond, Va.

FROM LEFT TO RIGHT. *Standing:* Captain Truman Seymour, Lt. S. W. Syduer, Lt. Jeff. C. Davis, Lt. R. K. Meade, Lt. Theo. Talbot. *Sitting:* Captain A. Doubleday, Major Robert Anderson, Asst. Surgeon S. W. Crawford, Major John C. Foster

An interesting story lay behind the firing of the first shot. Not long before, Anderson had abandoned Fort Moultrie and withdrawn to Sumter, his reasons being the smallness of his force and the shortage of his supplies. More than once he had notified Washington that the day must soon come when he would have to march out of the fort because of lack of provisions. The news had caused discussion in the National Capital but Lincoln had finally decided to send not only the needed supplies but reinforcements as well. In April Confederate agents in Washington had reported that Federal boats were actually on their way to the relief of Sumter. President Davis in Montgomery discussed the situation with his Cabinet. Toombs, Secretary of State, opposed aggressive measures but his voice did not prevail. The Confederate

Government sent orders to General Beauregard to demand the surrender of the fort. On April 11 Beauregard complied with the order. Major Anderson refused but observed that lack of supplies would compel him to surrender by the fifteenth. The reply left Beauregard undecided as to the wisest course. In the evening pilots came in from sea to report to the general that a Federal vessel lay off the mouth of the harbor. Then followed hurried consultations in Beauregard's hotel room. In the middle of the night a boat was rowed across the dark water to Sumter and four aides of the southern general confronted Anderson with a second demand to surrender. Again he refused but said that he would be compelled to surrender in three days. The aides then handed him a note dated 3:20 A.M. which said that the Confederates would open fire in an hour. Anderson busied himself with making preparations for the impending battle, perhaps little realizing that fortune had destined him to immortality. When dawn broke he was ready to resist the shore batteries.

6   House Tops in Charleston during the Bombardment of Fort Sumter, from *Harper's Weekly*, May 4, 1861

7   View of Terre-Plein of the Gorge of Fort Sumter, April 15, 1861, from a lithograph in the *Atlas to Accompany the Official Records of the Union and Confederate Armies,* Washington

THE SURRENDER OF SUMTER

ALL day on April 12 Charleston echoed with the artillery battle in progress in the harbor. All the following night a string of row boats kept watch along the bar to guard against surprise from the sea. By eight o'clock of the next morning the walls of the fort were crumbling and flames were shooting from the barracks. The fire was subdued and the garrison fought on. But the Confederates were firing red hot balls and fires broke out afresh in Sumter. Anderson's men worked feverishly throwing powder into the sea, for the magazine was threatened. About noon, according to the Charleston *Courier,* "flames burst out from every quarter of Sumter and poured from many of its portholes . . . the wind was from the west driving the smoke across the fort, driving the smoke into the embrasures where the gunners were at work." An hour more and the guns of the fort became silent. Beauregard made out a white flag floating above the walls. A little after two of the following day Anderson evacuated the fort amid a salute of fifty guns and started northward to report to the President.

VIRGINIA

To the time when the guns opened on Sumter Virginia had remained outside the Confederacy. President Davis had estimated that the outbreak of hostilities would compel the Old Dominion to make common cause with the other southern states. His forecast was correct. Virginia, North Carolina, Tennessee, and Arkansas were added to the Confederacy. Davis' policy of boldness seemed justified in its results. Yet neither Davis nor any other southern leader realized at the time that Virginia brought the sword of the greatest military chieftain of the war to the aid of the Confederate cause. Colonel Robert E. Lee of the Second Cavalry had been in Texas when Twiggs had surrendered the posts there. He had

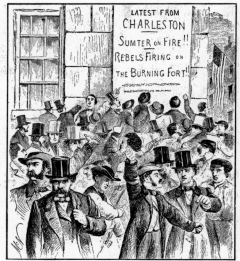

8   Scene around a Bulletin Board, from *Harper's Pictorial History of the Great Rebellion,* New York, 1866–68

been deeply moved when he heard the news, but had remained an officer in the Army of the United States, until Virginia seceded. Then he had resigned his commission and made his way to Richmond, the new

9   General Robert Edward Lee, 1807–70, from a photograph after a daguerreotype, about 1855

capital of the Confederacy. His feelings in that sad hour may be guessed from a letter that Mrs. Lee wrote to their old friend, General Winfield Scott, commander in chief of the Federal forces. "Arlington, May 5th [1861]. My dear General: Hearing that you desired to see the account of my husband's reception in Richmond, I have sent it to you. No honor can reconcile either of us to this fratricidal war, which we would have laid down our lives freely to avert. Nor can it ever terminate *now* till *every* heart in the whole South ceases to beat, or they obtain the justice they demand. Whatever may happen, I feel that I may expect from your kindness all the protection you can in honor afford. More I would not ask, or expect. Nothing can ever make me forget your kind appreciation of Mr. Lee. If you knew all you would not think so hardly of him. Were it not that I would not add one feather to his load of care, nothing would induce me to abandon my home. Oh, that you could command peace to our distracted country! Yours in sadness and sorrow, M. C. Lee." — BREVET MAJOR-GENERAL E. D. TOWNSEND, *Anecdotes of the Civil War,* 34.

LINCOLN'S PROCLAMATION, APRIL 15, 1861

"*WHEREAS*, the laws of the United States have been for some time past and are now opposed, and the execution thereof obstructed, in the States of South Carolina, Georgia, Alabama, Florida, Mississippi, Louisiana, and Texas by combinations too powerful to be suppressed by the ordinary course of judicial proceedings, or by the powers vested in the Marshals by law: Now, therefore, I, Abraham Lincoln, President of the United States, . . . have thought fit to call forth, and hereby do call forth, the Militia of the several States of the Union, to the aggregate number of seventy-five thousand, in order to suppress such combinations, and to cause the laws to be duly executed. . . . I appeal to all loyal citizens to favor, facilitate, and aid this effort to maintain the honor, the integrity, and the existence of our National Union and the perpetuity of popular government, and to redress wrongs already long enough endured. I deem it proper to say that the first service assigned to the force hereby called forth will probably be to repossess the forts, places, and property which have been seized from the Union, and, in every event, the utmost care will be observed

10　The Lincoln Memorial by Gutzon Borglum (1867-), Newark, N. J.

consistently with the objects aforesaid, to avoid any devastation, any destruction of, or interference with property, or any disturbance of peaceful citizens in any part of the country; and I hereby command the persons composing the combinations aforesaid to disperse and retire peaceably to their respective abodes within twenty days from this date. . . ."

11　The Seventh Regiment Marching down Broadway, New York, from *Harper's Pictorial History of the Great Rebellion*, New York, 1866-68

12　The Eleventh Indiana Volunteers swearing to remember Buena Vista, from a sketch by James F. Gookins in *Harper's Weekly*, June 12, 1861

THE MILITIA

PRESIDENT LINCOLN, when the nation faced its gravest crisis, called for seventy-five thousand militia. He had already in his first inaugural proclaimed to the world that the Union would defend itself; he now commanded the organizers of the Southern Confederacy to disperse. To give force to his brave words he had only the shadow of a regular army and that scattered over the nation. To enforce his commands and, as it quickly turned out, to defend the National Capital, he had to rely on the militia of the states. The militia had failed in the Revolution and again in the War of 1812. Since the latter conflict there had been no serious effort on the part of the National Government to increase the efficiency of the state troops. The last Federal militia law was the first, that of 1795, and Lincoln was compelled to fall back upon the authority provided by this ancient piece of legislation to get the troops he needed. Under the terms of the act he could hold them in service only three months. Washington had once called the militia a "broken reed." Yet in spite of the experience of two wars the Government was forced to depend upon it to meet the emergency of 1861. A few weeks later the President called for volunteers for three years' service and undertook the task of increasing the size of the regular army.

13   Yankee Volunteers Marching into Dixie, from a lithograph published by
                          C. F. Morse, Washington

NORTHERN FIRE EATERS

TWELVE days after President Lincoln's proclamation *Harper's Weekly* expressed one aspect of the feeling in the North. "War is declared. . . . The die is now cast, and men must take their sides, and hold to them. No one who knows anything of the Southern people supposes for a moment that, having gone so far as to bombard a United States fort and capture it, they will now succumb without a fight. No one who has seen the recent manifestations of popular sentiment in the North can doubt that the Northern blood is up, and that they will listen to no more talk of compromise, truce, or treaty until they are fairly beaten. Let us then forbear puling, and look the situation in the face. There are some among us who still whine about the evils of Civil War. These are they who, with a burglar in their house, his hand on the throat of their wife or daughter, would quote texts on the loveliness of Christian charity." Unfortunately the determination expressed by the editor of *Harper's Weekly* was mixed in some quarters with an absurd confidence born of ignorance in military matters. The *New York Times* wrote: "Let us make quick work. The 'rebellion,' as some people designate it, is an unborn tadpole. . . . A strong active 'pull together' will do our work effectually in thirty days. We have only to send a column of twenty-five thousand across the Potomac to Richmond, and burn out the rats there; another column of twenty-five thousand to Cairo, seizing the cotton ports of the Mississippi; and retaining the remaining twenty-five thousand included in Mr. Lincoln's call for seventy-five thousand men, at Washington, not because there is need for them there, but because we do not require their services elsewhere." The *New York Daily Tribune* added: "The nations of Europe may rest assured that Jeff. Davis & Co. will be swinging from the battlements at Washington, at least by the 4th of July. We spit upon a . . . longer deferred justice." — Quoted in EDWARD A. POLLARD, *The Lost Cause*, 127, 1886.

14   A Northern Conception of Enthusiastic Troops going to the Front, from a contemporary sketch
          by W. T. Troze in the Prints Division, Library of Congress, Washington

15   Second Mississippi Regiment Passing along Main Street, Winchester, Virginia, from a sketch in
Harper's Weekly, August 3, 1861

A SOUTHERN VIEWPOINT

THAT outspoken Virginian, Edward A. Pollard, remarked in 1866 that in the South "there was also very imperfect appreciation of the impending crisis, and of the extent and solemnity of the adventure in which the Confederate States were to embark. In the first stages of the dispute the southern leaders had declared there would be no war; that the mere act of secession would exact from the North all that was claimed, and prove in the end a peaceful experiment. Heated orators in Charleston exclaimed that there would be no conflict of arms, and that they would be willing to drink all the blood shed in the contest. Again, when the Confederate Government was established at Montgomery the idea still prevailed that secession had the countenance of a large party in the North, and that the Black Republicans would find it impossible to get up a war in front of hostile States and in face of a partisan opposition at home. . . . But no sooner did these silly prospects of amicable association with Northern Democrats end and war blaze out at Sumter, than a new delusion took possession of the Confederate leaders. This was that the war would be decided speedily, and its history be compassed in a few battlefields. It had been a theme of silly declamation that 'the Yankees' would not fight; and so-called statesmen in the South expounded the doctrine that a commercial community, devoted to the pursuit of gain, could never aspire to martial prowess, and were unequal to great deeds of arms." — *The Lost Cause*, 128–30, New York, 1866.

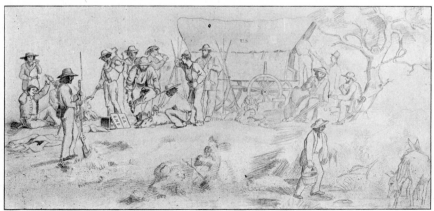

16   Camp at Las Moras, Texas, retouched from an original sketch in the Prints Division,
Library of Congress, Washington

Address.

Fly to the South, come fly to me,
In Richmond there's a home for thee;
But oh! the choice, what heart can fear
Submission at home, or *Freedom* here!

If wounded, thy true love will be,
A Florence Nightingale to thee;
If killed, above thee, she will pour
Of pearly tears, full many a shower.

Then fly to me, if thou dost claim,
Thy Southern rights and Southern name
And foremost 'mid our ranks show forth,
Thy hatred of the oppressing North!

But if like some in deep contrition,
You hope for Maryland's submission
And like a dastard calmly kneel,
And cringe to the usurper's heel.

Then fare thee well! I'd never own,
My locks were on a coward thrown;
Love to a poltroon I'd ne'er give,
But rather bid him *die* than live!

M. F. Q.

RICHMOND, May 3, 1861.

17   From a song in the Division of Manuscripts,
Library of Congress, Washington

THE SPIRIT OF THE SOUTH

VASTLY different from those offensive sentiments that sometimes crept into the press or filled the discourses of demagogues were the reactions of the sober-minded, God-fearing folk who were the strength of both North and South. No one has expressed more thoughtfully the spirit of the southern people than a young officer of the regular army stationed at an isolated post in the Northwest. Weeks passed before he got the news of war and the call of his native state. On the day after his return to Virginia he wrote to his fiancée: "I, of course, have always strenuously opposed disunion, not as doubting the right of secession, which was taught in our text-book at West Point, but as gravely questioning its expediency. I believed that the revolutionary spirit which infected both North and South was but a passing phase of fanaticism which would perish under the rebuke of all good citizens. . . . You know, my little lady, some of those cross-stitched mottoes on the cardboard samplers which used to hang on my nursery wall, such as, 'He who provides not for his own household is worse than an infidel' and 'Charity begins at home,' made a lasting impression upon me; and while I love my neighbor, i.e., my country, I love my own household, i.e., my state, *more*, and I could not be an infidel and lift my sword against my own kith and kin, even though I do believe . . . that the measure of American greatness can be achieved only under one flag, and I fear, alas, there can never again reign for either of us the true spirit of national unity, whether divided under two flags or united under one." The writer of these lines was George E. Pickett. *The Heart of a Soldier*, 34–36, Seth Moyle Inc., New York, 1913.

THE BAY STATE SONG

LONG before Pickett was able to get back to Virginia the Sixth Massachusetts had fought its way through a hostile mob at Baltimore six days after the surrender of Sumter and had hurried on to the defense of the capital. These men had been trained and prepared for war as few of the militia had been. Their spirit is reflected in a song they sang to the tune, "There is Rest for the Weary."

'Tis the Old Bay State a-coming,
With the Pine Tree waving high,
Foremost where the fight is thickest,
Freedom still her battle cry.
From the rocky shore of Plymouth,
From the plains of Lexington,
From beneath the shaft of Bunker,
Every hero sends a son.

To the fray comes the Bay State!
Clear the way for the Bay State!
Trust you may in the Bay State!
She will do or die.

On the anniversary of the death of John Brown this regiment stood in formation beside his grave and sang a song which had been written by James E. Greenleaf, organist of Harvard Church, in Charlestown, Massachusetts, and which became an immediate favorite of the Glee Club of the Boston Light Infantry.

John Brown's body lies a mouldering in the grave
But his soul goes marching on.

18   The Sixth Massachusetts Regiment firing in Baltimore, from *Frank Leslie's Illustrated Newspaper*, Apr. 30, 1861

"A GENTLEMAN'S WAR"

GENERAL MCDOWELL'S reply to a letter from Mrs. Lee throws light on one aspect of this sectional conflict which continued to the end. The traditions of courtesy to the enemy which had their origins for the American army in the Revolutionary War marked many an interchange in the hostilities of 1861–65. The letter was written from Arlington, the former home of Robert E. Lee, on May 30, 1861. "With respect to the occupation of Arlington by the United States troops, I beg to say that it has been done by my predecessor with every regard for the preservation of the place. I am here temporarily in camp on the grounds, preferring this to sleeping in the house, under the circumstances which the painful state of the country places me with respect to these properties. I assure you that it will be my earnest endeavor to have all things so ordered that on your return you will find things as little disturbed as possible. . . . Everything has been done as you desire with respect to your servants, and your wishes, so far as they have been known or could have been understood, have been complied with. When you desire to return every facility will be given you for doing so. I trust, madam, you will not consider it an intrusion when I say that I have the most sincere sympathy for your distress, and, so far as compatible with my duty, I shall always be ready to do whatever may alleviate it." — J. W. JONES, *Life and Letters of Robert Edward Lee*, 143, Neale Publishing Co., New York, 1906. McDowell's letter reflects

19   Mrs. Robert E. Lee, 1806–73, from a photograph in the possession of H. P. Cook, Richmond

the peculiar hardship which the war brought to officers of the regular army. The very smallness of the establishment before the conflict made strong and intimate the social ties developed among its members. The war developed bitter hatreds but these found their extreme expression in civilian populations of both North and South. Soldiers, particularly professional soldiers, were less affected by them. The same phenomenon manifested itself in America in 1917–18.

United States Volunteers Throwing Up Intrenchments at Arlington, from *Harper's Weekly*, June 15, 1861

21 General Pierre Beauregard, 1818–93, from a
photograph by Gutekunst, Philadelphia

22 General Samuel Cooper, 1798–1876,
from an engraving, after a photograph,
in the Print Room, New York Public
Library

23 General Joseph E. Johnston, 1809–91, from
a photograph by H. P. Cook, Richmond

24 Jefferson Davis, 1808–89, from a photograph,
1851, by Brady

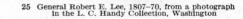

25 General Robert E. Lee, 1807–70, from a photograph
in the L. C. Handy Collection, Washington

THE FIRST LEADERS OF THE SOUTHERN ARMY

By July 1, 1861 the Confederacy had a hundred thousand men present for duty. They were lacking, however, in arms and equipment. On May 16 Samuel Cooper was commissioned general, the highest possible military rank. Since 1852 he had been Adjutant-General of the United States Army and was promptly made Adjutant-General of the Confederate Army. Fourteen days later Albert Sidney Johnston was given the rank of general. He had been a colonel in the cavalry. On June 14 Robert E. Lee, also a cavalry colonel, was made a general. The commission as general of Joseph E. Johnston was dated July 4. He had been Quartermaster-General. Finally on July 21 Beauregard became the fifth of the full generals. He had been a captain of engineers. He owed his rank to his fame as the captor of Sumter. President Jefferson Davis, himself a graduate of West Point, never rendered better service to his people than when he chose these trained and experienced soldiers, all of them West Pointers, to lead the soldiers of the Confederacy. Each had resigned his commission to offer his sword to the southern cause. The problem of creating an effective army quickly from a civilian population was well on the way to solution with the appointment of the first five generals.

26   Maj.-Gen. Nathaniel P. Banks, 1816–94,
from a photograph by Brady

27   Maj.-Gen. George B. McClellan, 1826–85,
from a photograph by Brady

28   Maj.-Gen. John C. Frémont, 1813–90,
from a photograph by Brady

29   Maj.-Gen. John A. Dix, 1798–1879, from an engraving
by J. C. Buttre after a photograph by Brady

THE FIRST LEADERS OF THE NORTHERN ARMY

When the war broke out, Major-General Winfield Scott was the ranking officer and commander in chief. He was, however, too old for service and soon retired.   The same was true of Brigadier-General John E. Wool. Brigadier-General David E. Twiggs left the Union service to join the Confederacy and Brigadier-General William S. Harney, being a southerner, did not wish to participate actively in the conflict.   In May, 1861, President Lincoln appointed five new major-generals to command the regular and volunteer forces.   George B. McClellan had graduated from West Point in 1846 and had served until 1857 in the engineers and cavalry. In April, 1861, he had been called from civilian life by the Governor of Ohio to organize and train the volunteers from that state and had been given the rank of major-general in the militia.   John C. Frémont had been an officer in the regular army for ten years from 1838 to 1848, having been a lieutenant-colonel of mounted rifles in the Mexican War.   He owed his selection, however, to his political prominence, having been the first candidate of the Republican party for President.   John A. Dix had been in the regular army from 1814 to 1828. He was selected also because he was a political leader, having been Senator from New York from 1845 to 1849 and Secretary of the Treasury under Buchanan in 1861.   Nathaniel P. Banks was a man without any military experience.   He was, however, a prominent Republican, had been speaker of the House of Representatives in 1856 and Governor of Massachusetts from 1858 to 1861.   In the latter office he had been active in the organization and training of the state militia in anticipation of war.   Benjamin F. Butler was a political leader of lesser importance who held a commission as brigadier-general in the Massachusetts militia.   These men, only one of whom was a West Pointer and four of whom owed their commissions to politics, were selected to lead the young men who volunteered from the North against the trained chieftains of the South.

30   Camp on the Battery, New York, from a sketch in *Harper's Weekly*, May 11, 1861

RECRUITS FOR THE NORTHERN ARMIES

LINCOLN'S calling of the militia to service was only an emergency measure. A volunteer army was to be the main force upon which the Government would depend for the preservation of the Union. Universal conscription was, at the outset of the war, both impossible and unthought of. The Civil War revealed the worst aspects of the system of volunteering. The delusion that the war would be of short duration brought a great variety of recruits into the military forces. Men of high purpose and sacrificial spirit found themselves standing in ranks side by side with the worst sort of idlers and adventurers. This did not necessarily make for inefficiency. Under proper leadership the adventurer type frequently makes soldiers of fine quality, and even idlers can be turned into useful men. Efficient leadership was sadly lacking.

UNION OFFICERS

THE manner of choosing officers for the Federal armies is perhaps the most amazing aspect of the Civil War. The methods that had proved so ineffective in the Revolution were repeated, evidence that the people of the North had learned few military lessons in the intervening three quarters of a century. Men were recruited by companies and regiments. The pernicious practice of electing officers was almost universal. Ohio affords an excellent illustration. In April and May, 1861, a regiment was being formed, to command which became the aspiration of a member of the Ohio senate. Yet James A. Garfield had had no military experience and knew nothing of training, tactics, or strategy. His own comments give an insight into the spirit of the times. "I do not feel about this matter as I do about ordinary offices. To seek a place of usefulness in the army seems to me rather meritorious than otherwise. When I hear that Ben Wade, John Sherman, A. G. Riddle, and other men of that character have enlisted in the ranks, I say it is done for buncombe and is an unmanly piece of demagogism. I know the time may come when it might be the duty of all men of every class to go into the ranks . . . but that time has not yet come. I looked the field over and thought I ought to have at least as high a position as staff officer. My friends thought so likewise and generously offered to aid me in obtaining such a position. The Governor would have given me one still higher if he had had one in his gift. I went to Cleveland . . . to see whether I could honorably obtain the colonelcy. . . . I would have been elected before now, but for my absence to Illinois. The Governor of his own accord delayed giving the order for the election 'til my return. While I was gone, Tyler of Ravenna, whom I had aided in various ways and who had told me that he would aid me in the election, turned in and offered himself as a candidate and by bargains and brandy got an informal ballot by which he was elected. But the regular election has not yet been held." — THEODORE CLARKE SMITH, EDITOR, *Life and Letters of James Abram Garfield*, Vol. I, 163–64, Yale University Press, New Haven, 1925. Before the election took place various newspapers, notably the Ravenna *Sentinel*, were accusing Garfield of all sorts of intrigues. In the end the election went to Tyler, five hundred and eighty to two hundred and forty-three. So were transferred to the army that was to fight for the preservation of the Union the political habits of the American people.

31   Volunteer Troops drilling at Cairo, Illinois, from a sketch in *Harper's Weekly*, June 15, 1861

A FORMER REGULAR OFFERS HIS SERVICES

ON May 24, 1861, Ulysses Simpson Grant who had seen service in the Mexican War but who had retired to private life sent the following letter to the Adjutant General. "Having served for fifteen years in the regular army, including four years at West Point, and feeling it the duty of every one who has been educated at Government expense to offer their services for the support of that Government, I have the honor, very respectfully, to tender my services, until the close of the war, in such capacity as may be offered. I would say, in view of my present age and length of service, I feel myself competent to command a regiment, if the President, in his judgement, should see fit to entrust one to me. Since the first call of the President I have been serving on the staff of the Governor of this State [Illinois], rendering such aid as I could in the organization of our state militia and am still engaged in that capacity." Grant has commented on the letter as follows. "This letter failed to elicit an answer from the Adjutant-General of the Army. . . . I felt some hesitation in suggesting rank as high as the colonelcy of a regiment, feeling somewhat doubtful whether I would be equal to the position. [What a contrast to Garfield!] But I had seen nearly every colonel who had been mustered in from the State of Illinois, and some from Indiana, and felt that if they could command a regiment properly, and with credit, I could also. [Meanwhile Grant got a week's leave of absence to go to

32 Grant's Letter offering his Services to the War Department, from the original in the War Department, Washington

Cincinnati.] General McClellan had been made a major-general and had his headquarters at Cincinnati. In reality I wanted to see him. I had known him slightly at West Point, where we had served one year together, and in the Mexican war. I was in hopes that when he saw me he would offer me a position on his staff. I called on two successive days at his office but failed to see him on either occasion, and returned to Springfield." — *Personal Memoirs of U. S. Grant*, Vol. I, 239–41, New York, 1886. Grant finally got into the army as colonel of the twenty-first Illinois Infantry. He was appointed by the Governor because the regiment had refused to go into service with the colonel whom it had elected.

33 Brig.-Gen. Ulysses S. Grant, 1822–85, from a photograph taken in 1861

GRANT'S COMMENT ON HIS REGIMENT

"MY regiment was composed in large part of young men of as good social position as any in their section of the state. It embraced the sons of farmers, lawyers, physicians, politicians, merchants, bankers and ministers, and some men of maturer years who had filled such positions themselves. There were also men in it who could be led astray; and the colonel, elected by the votes of the regiment, had proved to be fully capable of developing all there was in his men of recklessness. It was said that he even went so far at times as to take the guard from their posts and go with them to the village near by and make a night of it. When there came a prospect of a battle the regiment wanted to have someone else to lead them. I found it very hard work for a few days to bring all the men into anything like subordination; but the great majority favored discipline, and by the application of a little regular army punishment all were reduced to as good discipline as one could ask." — *Personal Memoirs of U. S. Grant*, Vol. I, 243.

34   General Winfield Scott, 1786–1866, from
              a photograph by Brady, 1861

REGULAR OFFICERS IN THE FEDERAL ARMY

In the American army which participated in the World War practically all the senior officers were men from the regular service who had been temporarily commissioned for the emergency. Only a few of the officers recruited from civilian life went beyond the rank of lieutenant-colonel, and almost never in the fighting branches. In the Civil War the troops of the United States were divided into a Regular Army, small but larger than it had been before the outbreak of hostilities, and a

35   Maj.-Gen. Irvin McDowell, 1818–85, from
              a photograph by Brady, 1861

Volunteer Army which was the main dependence of the Government. In the regular units promotion was in accordance with the custom of the service, but in the volunteer army generals commanding in the field had to apply to the proper Governor before an officer from a particular state could be promoted. There were no officers' training schools where men from civilian life or from the ranks could learn the rudiments of the military profession. This was a serious lack. The evils which resulted from having untrained officers in high command were augmented by the Governmental policy with respect to the officers of the old Regular Army. Out of something more than five hundred and fifty officers of the Regular Army who remained faithful to the Union, only one hundred and forty-two rose to the rank of general officer. The rest, with the exception of one hundred and six colonels, were kept in subordinate positions, and the full value of their training and experience was lost to the nation. The policy of the Confederacy was in sharp contrast. Early in the war provision was made that officers of the old Regular Army who joined the Confederacy should retain their relative rank. Out of two hundred and fifty who threw in their lot with the South one hundred and eighty-two rose to the rank of general officer. Such figures help materially to explain the relative efficiency of the armies of the North and South. The policy of the Lincoln administration which in the matter of the use of the regular officers contrasted so sharply with that of the Davis Government may have been due, in part, to the political exigencies of the situation in which the Republican President found himself.

36   Grand Review of McDowell's Army Corps, from a sketch in *Harper's Weekly*, July 6, 1861

37   Crossing Manassas Gap Railroad, from a sketch in *Harper's Weekly*, Sept. 28, 1861

MILITIA OFFICERS IN THE SOUTH

A CONSIDERABLE part of the Confederate forces called to arms in the spring of 1861 were militia whose officers owed their commissions to election or appointment by the Governor. Almost immediately upon the resignation of his commission in the United States Army General Lee had been placed in command of all the Virginia forces. On his advice an ordinance had been promulgated decapitating every militia officer above the rank of captain, and authorizing the Governor and his military council to fill the vacancies. The then Captain John D. Imboden has described the result of this order in the Confederate force that in April had been sent up the Shenandoah Valley to seize and hold Harper's Ferry. "Militia generals and their brilliant 'staff' were stricken down, and their functions devolved, according to Governor Letcher's order of April 27th, upon Thomas J. Jackson, colonel commandant . . . who arrived during the first week of May. This was 'Stonewall' Jackson's first appearance at the theatre of the war. I spent one day and night in Richmond, and then returned to camp, arriving about 2 P.M. What a revolution three or four days had wrought! I could scarcely realize the change. The militia generals were all gone, and the staff had vanished. The commanding colonel and his adjutant had arrived. . . . Jackson and his adjutant were at a little pine table figuring upon the rolls of the troops present. They were dressed in well-worn dingy uniforms of professors in the Virginia Military Institute, where both had been recently occupied. Colonel Jackson had issued and sent to the camps a short, simple order assuming the command, but had had no intercourse with the troops. The deposed officers had nearly all left for home or for Richmond in a high state of indignation. . . . I . . . found the men of the Fifth Virginia regiment, from my own county, in assembly, and greatly excited. They were deeply attached to their field-officers, and regarded the ordinance of the convention as an outrage on freemen and volunteers, and were discussing the propriety of passing denunciatory resolutions." — R. U. JOHNSON AND C. C. BUEL, EDITORS, *Battles and Leaders of the Civil War*, Vol. I, 121, The Century Co., New York, 1884–88. The affair quickly blew over but it is significant of the fact that the point of view of the southern volunteer was much like that of the northerner.

38   Lee's Resignation from the United States Army, from the original
in the War Department, Washington

39   Review of the Clinch Rifles at Augusta, Ga., from *Campfire and Battlefield*, Desmond Publishing
Company, Boston, 1896

DISCIPLINE IN THE SOUTHERN ARMY

TIME was required in the South as well as in the North to inculcate in the minds of men fresh from civilian life the soldier's point of view. But the work was carried on more swiftly there partly because of the southern aristocratic tradition which had trained men in a certain deference to their superiors and partly because of the importance of old Regular Army officers in the Confederate armies. These men given high command used their authority to expedite the creation of an efficient fighting force. The mingling of gaiety and seriousness which characterized the southern troops at the beginning of the war stands out in an account of the experiences of one of Stonewall Jackson's enlisted men. He belonged to a Richmond company which, late in April, 1861, was ordered northward as a result of an alarm about Aquia Creek. "We went to bed that night in regular military order, had a camp guard, lights out by taps, etc. Some of the boys, during the day, had purchased whistles, tin horns, and other noisy things, and as soon as lights were out, the fun commenced. One blew a horn, another in a distant part of the building answered on a whistle. This went on for a few minutes. When the officers commanded silence, no attention was paid to them. When the officers said to the sergeant, 'Arrest those men,' the sergeant would strike a light, and go where he thought the noise originated; but each man looked so innocent that he could not tell who it was. By this time another would blow. Soon there were four sergeants, running here and there, trying to catch the delinquents. This was kept up until the perpetrators became tired, not one being detected. . . . The following letter was written while we were in this camp [near Fredericksburg about a month later] and explains itself: 'George W. Peterkin, Esq.: Dear Sir — We, the undersigned comrades in arms with yourself, have been struck with the propriety of evening prayer, and desire, if agreeable to you, that you, from this time, and so long as we may remain together, conduct that service.' . . . This gallant young soldier and truly good man conducted the service each night, and by his Christian example won the respect and affection of every member of the company; and when he left us in 1862, to take a staff appointment, it was like breaking up a household." — JOHN H. WORSHAM, *One of Jackson's Foot Cavalry*, 17–18, 22–24, Neale Publishing Co., New York, 1912. Early in 1861 a Federal soldier wrote from Washington: "Such a feeling pervades the minds of the soldiers that discipline is played out."

40   Tennessee Riflemen on their way to join the Virginia Army, from a sketch in
Harper's Weekly, July 6, 1861

JULY, 1861, IN VIRGINIA

MILITIA regiments which had been called out for three months were hurried to Washington until pandemonium reigned within the capital. Their time would be up in July. They were to be offered the opportunity of reënlisting for three years. As the end of the three months approached rumor began to confuse the soldiers with conflicting reports. Some said that the Government had not decided what would be done with the three months' men. Report had it that they would be discharged and also that they would be taken into the service. Meanwhile the newspapers raised the cry, "On to Richmond" and the Government was about to yield to the pressure. Under the illusion that the war would be a short one both the Federal and Confederate Governments had amassed troops, Lincoln about Washington and Harper's Ferry and Davis in the region of Manassas Junction and in the Shenandoah Valley. Northern papers demanded a swift blow at Richmond

AN AFFECTIONATE TESTIMONIAL TO THE PENNSYLVANIA FOURTH, AND TO VARIAN'S (N. Y.) FIELD BATTERY.
41   From a cartoon in *Harper's Weekly*, May 19, 1861

which would end the war. Winfield Scott, still commander in chief, called upon McDowell, field commander of the Federal troops south of the Potomac, to formulate a plan for the advance on the Confederate capital. McDowell, knowing well that his troops because of inadequate training were not ready for an actual campaign, complied with reluctance.

He proposed that Major-General Patterson should use his fourteen thousand men at Martinsburg in the Shenandoah Valley to prevent General J. E. Johnston, who had ten thousand five hundred men, from reinforcing General Beauregard at Manassas. McDowell then with superior numbers would turn Beauregard's flank, threaten his line of communications, and force him from his positions south of Bull Run. The plan was approved and orders were issued to McDowell and Patterson. McDowell moved southward on July 16 with more than thirty thousand men. Beauregard had but eighteen thousand near Manassas. Beauregard learned at once of the Federal movement, estimated that its objective was Manassas, and notified Richmond. Orders were sent to concentrate the Confederate troops in front of McDowell. The Confederate leaders were as anxious over the outcome of the impending engagement as their Federal opponents. They had at their disposal only raw and partly trained troops. Both Confederate and Federal leaders hoped and half expected that the oncoming battle would decide the war.

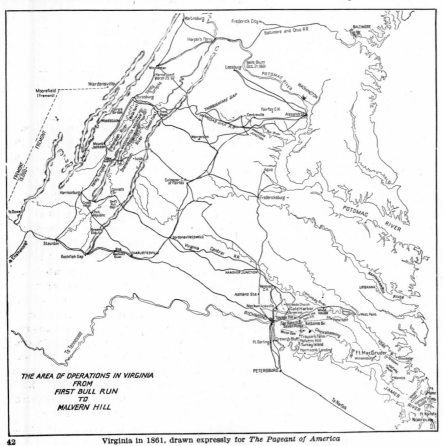

THE AREA OF OPERATIONS IN VIRGINIA FROM FIRST BULL RUN TO MALVERN HILL

Virginia in 1861, drawn expressly for *The Pageant of America*

10,613

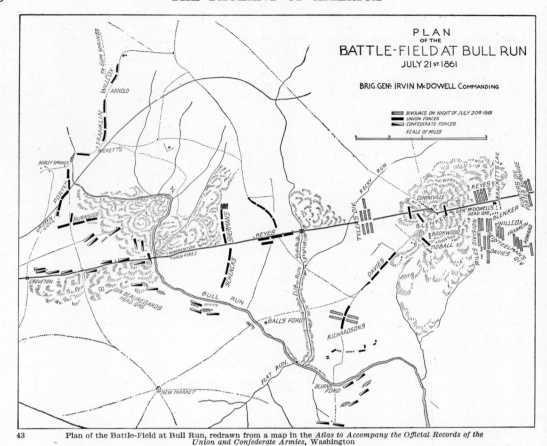

43   Plan of the Battle-Field at Bull Run, redrawn from a map in the *Atlas to Accompany the Official Records of the Union and Confederate Armies*, Washington

THE BATTLE OF BULL RUN

JOHNSON was called in from the Valley and a small force on the Potomac twenty miles east of Bull Run was ordered to join Beauregard. The Confederates completed their concentration at noon of July 21 in the middle of the Battle of Bull Run. They then outnumbered McDowell by more than a thousand men. The weakness in the Federal plan was in assuming that Patterson with raw troops and inadequate transportation could keep Johnston from slipping out of the Valley. Patterson blundered and Johnston virtually ignored him. On the afternoon of July 18 McDowell reached Centerville on the Warrenton road and was four miles from his enemy, whose eighteen thousand men were extended along a six mile front on the south bank of Bull Run between the railroad and the Warrenton pike. Had he struck Beauregard the following morning he would have had greatly superior numbers and might have won a victory. McDowell, virtually in contact with the enemy, waited two days, however, for his trains to come up, to complete the concentration of his "loosely organized force," and to study the terrain. On July 21, he ordered a feint at the stone bridge where the Warrenton road crosses Bull Run while with his main force he made a long march to the ford at Sudley Springs. McDowell then delivered his main blow against Beauregard's left. The Confederate commander, however, massed his troops in front of McDowell and Stonewall Jackson won his famous nickname when his brigade stood fast and checked the Federal advance. The battle was decided late in the afternoon when Beauregard with fresh troops, the last of Johnston's force, that had reached the field of battle at noon turned the Federal right. The Confederate commander at the same time pressed against McDowell's center. The effect was decisive. The Federal troops without any show of panic broke ranks and started for home in spite of the efforts of their officers to stop them. Their action was the result of lack of discipline and training. Such men were not capable of a finish fight unless protected by breastworks. The same phenomenon occurred among Washington's troops at Germantown during the Revolution. The panic began when the retiring soldiers, guns, wagons, and Congressmen in their carriages who had come out to see the victory were fired on while crowding the Warrenton road east of Bull Run.

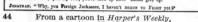

44 From a cartoon in *Harper's Weekly*,
Aug. 10, 1861

45 Panic of the Union Troops at Bull Run, from the painting by
Walter Russell (1871–)

LINCOLN AND THE SOLDIERS AFTER BULL RUN

COLONEL WILLIAM T. SHERMAN commanded a brigade at Bull Run and spent several difficult days in reorganizing and disciplining it after the battle. About July 26 Sherman, whose camp lay on the south bank of the Potomac, recognized the President and Secretary Seward crossing the river in a carriage on the Georgetown ferry. Lincoln took the colonel into the carriage. "As we slowly ascended the hill," says Sherman, "I discovered that Mr. Lincoln was full of feeling and wanted to encourage our men. . . . I asked him then to please discourage all cheering, noise, or any sort of confusion; that we had had enough of it before Bull Run to ruin any set of men, and that what we needed were cool, thoughtful, hard-fighting soldiers — no more hurrahing, no more humbug. He took my remarks in the most perfect good nature. Before we had reached the first camp, I heard the drums beating the 'assembly,' saw the men running for their tents, and in a few minutes the regiment was in line, arms presented, and then brought to an order and 'parade rest.' Mr. Lincoln stood up in the carriage, and made one of the neatest, best and most feeling addresses I ever listened to, referring to our late disaster at Bull Run, the high duties that still devolved on us, and the brighter days yet to come. At one or two points the soldiers began to cheer, but he promptly checked them, saying: 'Don't cheer, boys. I confess I rather like it myself, but Colonel Sherman here says it is not military; and I guess we had better defer to his opinion.' In winding up, he explained that, as President, he was commander in chief; that he was resolved that the soldiers should have everything that the law allowed; and he called on

46 The Battle of Manassas, from the *Confederate War Journal*, Lexington, Kentucky, and
New York, 1893

one and all to appeal to him personally in case they were wronged. The effect of this speech was excellent. We passed along in the same manner to all the camps of my brigade; and Mr. Lincoln complimented me highly for the order, cleanliness, and discipline, that he observed. Indeed he and Mr. Seward both assured me that it was the first bright moment they had experienced since the battle." — WILLIAM T. SHERMAN, *Memoirs*, 189–90, New York, 1886.

47   Confederate Jubilations at Richmond — firing a salute of one hundred guns on receiving news of the Battle of Bull Run, from a sketch by a Confederate officer in *Frank Leslie's Illustrated Newspaper*, Oct. 5, 1861

THE SIGNIFICANCE OF BULL RUN FOR THE SOUTH

POLLARD has left a vivid picture of the reaction of the southern people to the Battle of Bull Run. "The victory at Manassas proved the greatest misfortune that could have befallen the Confederacy. It was taken by the Southern public as the end of the war, or, at least, its decisive event. Nor was this merely a vulgar delusion. President Davis, after the battle, assured his intimate friends that the recognition of the Confederate States by the European Powers was now certain. The newspapers declared that the question of manhood between North and South was settled forever; and the phrase of 'one Southerner equal to five Yankees' was adopted in all speeches about the war — although the origin or rule of the precise proportion was never clearly stated. An elaborate article in *De Bow's Review* compared Manassas with the decisive battles of the world, and considered that the war would now degenerate into mere desultory affairs, preliminary to a peace. On the whole, the unfortunate victory of Manassas was followed by a period of fancied security, and of relaxed exertions on the part of the Southern people highly dangerous and inauspicious. The best proof of this inactivity is to be found in the decrease of enlistments by volunteers." — *The Lost Cause*, 152–53. A southern song developed after the battle expresses well the point of view of the time.

> I come from old Manassas, with a pocket full of fun —
> I killed forty Yankees with a single-barrelled gun;
> It don't make a niff-a-stifference to neither you nor I,
> Big Yankee, little Yankee, all run or die.

McCLELLAN IN WEST VIRGINIA

TEN days before the Federal disaster at Bull Run McClellan had brought to an end the first phase of the West Virginia campaign. At the outbreak of the war West Virginia had been part of the Old Dominion. The people of this mountainous region, however, were divided on the question of secession and a majority favored the Union. The purpose of the Federal campaign which began scarcely a month after the firing on Sumter was to drive all Confederate troops from the region so that it could be organized as a separate state. On July 11 McClellan won a small victory at Carrick Ford as a result of which he found himself in possession of the greater part of the present state of West Virginia. In August he was called to the command of the Department of the Potomac. He contented himself with holding the bridgehead at Washington and guarding the crossings of the Potomac. Meanwhile General Rosecrans commanded in West Virginia.

48   View on the James River Canal — Confederate troops going from Lynchburg to Buchanan on their way to western Virginia from a sketch in *Harper's Weekly*, Sept. 28, 1861

THE DEPARTMENT OF SOUTH-EAST VIRGINIA

In May, 1861, General Butler was sent with a Federal division to reinforce Fortress Monroe and occupy the outlying territory which became the Department of Southeast Virginia. On June 10 at Big Bethel a Union force was repulsed by a much smaller Confederate force under Colonel Magruder. In August General Wool assumed command of the department but Butler retained command of the volunteer troops. In the latter part of this month Butler with the coöperation of Flag Officer Silas

49   Battle of Big Bethel, from a sketch in *Harper's Weekly*, June 29, 1861

H. Stringham captured two small forts at the mouth of Hatteras Inlet where a brigade was left for a permanent garrison. In September Butler was sent to New England to organize a force for service on the coast of the Gulf of Mexico.

50   *Battle of Wilson's Creek*, from the mural by N. C. Wyeth (1882–) in the Missouri State Capitol, Jefferson City, Mo., courtesy of the St. Louis *Globe-Democrat*

THE STRUGGLE FOR MISSOURI IN 1861

Kentucky remained neutral. At the outset of the war the Confederate Government wished to avoid operations in that state and thought that the interests of the South would be best served by an attempt to win military control of the slave state, Missouri. Such a position would put the Confederate forces on the flank of Illinois. If Missouri could be won and held, the success would have a vital bearing on the Federal military operations in the Mississippi valley. On August 1 three small and independent Confederate forces were preparing for the task of winning the state. (See map, No. 142.) Some ten thousand volunteers from Missouri, Arkansas, and Louisiana under Generals Price and McCulloch were at Cassville in southwestern Missouri near the Arkansas line and were advancing on Springfield. At Pocohontas in northeastern Arkansas General Hardee was organizing five thousand Arkansas volunteers. General Pillow commanded a force of six thousand Tennesseeans at New Madrid on the Mississippi. He had fortified Island Number Ten to protect his line of communications. At the same time a Union force of six thousand under General Lyon was stationed at Springfield. There were some other Federal troops at Ironton on the Mississippi. Upon receipt of intelligence that Price and McCulloch were moving against him Lyon went out to meet them. On August 10 he attacked at Wilson Creek. He underestimated the strength of his opponents who greatly outnumbered him. He, moreover, divided his force on the day of the battle and attempted to attack his adversaries in both front and rear. The result was a defeat for his army while Lyon himself was killed. His troops were compelled to fall back along the mail route to Rolla.

51   Battle of Belmont, Missouri, from a sketch in *Frank Leslie's Illustrated Newspaper*, Dec. 14, 1861

THE END OF THE YEAR IN MISSOURI

McCULLOCH refused to invade Missouri and fell back to Arkansas but Price with his Missouri volunteers took possession of Springfield and then pushed northward as far as the Missouri River where on September 20 he captured a Federal brigade at Lexington. The Federal Government threw new troops into Missouri, the possession of which was thus threatened. General Frémont who since July had been in command of the Western Department, which included everything from the Mississippi River to the Rockies, took the field against Price in October at the head of twenty thousand troops. By threatening his line of communications with Arkansas Frémont forced Price back to southwestern Missouri and recaptured Springfield. At this city Frémont was relieved of command of the Western Department by General Hunter, who had fought at Bull Run. Hunter fell back to Rolla and Price spent the winter near Springfield. In November the Western Department was broken up. General Halleck took over the command of the new Department of Missouri, which comprised all the states bordering the Mississippi, while Hunter assumed command of the Department of Kansas. The last engagement of the year in this region occurred on November 7 when Grant, now a brigadier-general, basing his operations on Cairo, made an unsuccessful attack upon a Confederate camp at Belmont, Missouri, across the Mississippi from Columbus, Kentucky.

McCLELLAN'S TASK AT WASHINGTON AFTER BULL RUN

BULL RUN is one of the most extraordinary episodes in the military history of the American people. The two opposing armies, for want of training, were little better than armed mobs, and one, after showing what was, under the circumstances, extraordinary bravery, ran away. This battle taught the generation which fought the Civil War the importance of military training in waging war. McClellan was called to turn into an army the miscellaneous units that were crowding Washington. Adjutant-General E. D. Townsend gave him some good advice as McClellan left the office of General Scott on reporting to Washington. "I had just time to say: 'I want to give you a hint about the state of things here. You will find splendid material for soldiers sadly in need of discipline. You will be beset on all sides with applications for passes, and all sorts of things, and if you yield to the pressure your whole time will be taken up at a desk, writing. You can from the outset avoid this; another officer can do it as well in your name. The troops want to see their commanding general,

and to be often inspected and reviewed by him. Another thing: there is here a fine body of regulars; I would keep that intact, as a sort of "Old Guard." It may some time save you a battle.' He took what I said kindly. Perhaps he never thought of it again but it is certain that he pursued exactly that course. His splendid military evolutions while organizing and equipping his army will not soon be forgotten. . . . Meantime, McClellan went on acquiring more and more popularity as the 'young Napoleon of our army.'" — ADJUTANT-GENERAL E. D. TOWNSEND, *Anecdotes of the Civil War*, 60–61, 66, New York, 1884.

52   Grand Review of the Army in Washington by the President, McClellan and a portion of the Cabinet, Sept. 24, 1861, from a sketch in *Frank Leslie's Illustrated Newspaper*, Oct. 5, 1861

THE VOLUNTEERS OF 1861

"Some of the volunteer regiments came to Washington admirably provided. There were, especially, two from New Hampshire. They had complete clothing, arms and accoutrements, and tents. Their wagons were arranged like storerooms, with boxes for their various supplies. They had also very good bands of music. Their religious services were very impressive. The regiments were drawn up in a hollow square, with the chaplain in the middle, and, while the bands played hymns which he gave out, the men

53   Camp Curtin, near Harrisburg, Pa., from a sketch in *Harper's Weekly*, May 11, 1861

sang them. Their rendering of *Old Hundred* was truly grand. But with all this excellent material, the want of military instruction was apparent in such incidents as this: It was no unusual thing to see a sentry, when an officer in uniform passed his post, seated on a stone, with a musket between his feet. On the approach of the officer, aware that some complimentary recognition was expected, he would awkwardly raise his hand to his cap, while he continued sitting. General McClellan was not long in changing all this, and in forming a thoroughly disciplined army." — TOWNSEND, 61. The Adjutant-General gives a measure of the official standards of discipline early in the war. That McClellan transformed a miscellaneous host into an army is true. It was a great achievement. But to say that this army was imbued with the discipline which would give it the highest efficiency is incorrect. It remained, after the training of the fall and winter of 1861 was completed, an amateur army, a clumsy and sometimes unwieldly instrument of war. Lieutenant-Colonel Henderson of the British army has made a keen analysis of these American volunteers. "The *morale* of the armies,

54   Soldiers Washing Clothes, from *Harper's Weekly*, July 20, 1861

leavened by the presence of men of intelligence and high principle, was necessarily good. Crime was practically unknown; of insubordination there was very little, but, at the same time, the standard of discipline was never a very high one. It appears to have depended altogether on the personal character and capacity of the commanding officers, and even in the best regiments it seems to have been impossible to exact the same strict regard for duty as in a professional army. The truth is that neither officers nor men possessed the *habit* of obedience. They were willing enough, patriotic enough, and plucky as soldiers ever were, but they could not be depended on to obey under every circumstance, no matter by whom the order was given. Obedience was not an instinct, and good will did not prove an efficient substitute for the machine-like subordination of the regular. . . . In the first place it seemed that the men wanted a deal of humouring, and the regimental officers also. Mistakes had to be overlooked and ignorance excused. Marks of respect to rank and the ordinary etiquette of an army had often to be dispensed with, and it was injudicious to interfere between regimental officers and their men. Freedom of speech could not be checked, and there was much familiarity between even the generals and the privates. Still, taking into consideration the democratic institutions of the States, it is possible that these things might have existed, and 'the thinking bayonets,' as their leaders were so fond of calling them, have been as reliable soldiers as the best of European troops." — HENDERSON, *The Science of War*, 243.

55   Camp Recreations, Just After Dress Parade, from *Harper's Weekly*, July 20, 1861

56   Camp Recreations, From Tattoo to Taps, from *Harper's Weekly*, July 20, 1861

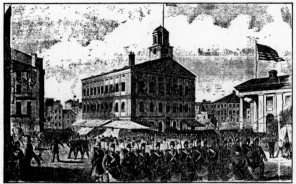

57 A New Regiment of Massachusetts Volunteers passing Faneuil Hall in Boston, from a sketch in *Harper's Weekly*, Aug. 17, 1861

THE COMPOSITION OF THE ARMIES

"THE private soldiers on both sides were drawn from all classes of society. Men of the best breeding and culture in America, of high education and great wealth, marched shoulder to shoulder with small farmers and clerks, with mechanics and labourers. In the North there was a proportion of men who enlisted merely for the sake of high bounties, and a number of foreigners. . . . The number of foreigners in the Federal armies has been greatly exaggerated, but there were whole divisions of Germans, and on both sides there were battalions and brigades of Irish. It may be interesting to mention that whilst the Irish were everywhere counted as excellent soldiers, the Germans fell short of such a reputation." — HENDERSON, 242–43. A song of an Irish outfit expresses the spirit of these soldiers, many of whom had come to America but a few years before.

Ye boys of the sod, to Columbia true,
Come up, lads, and fight for the Red, White, and Blue!
Two countries we love, and two mottoes we'll share,
And we'll join them in one on the banner we bear:
    Erin, mavourneen!   Columbia, agra!
    E Pluribus unum.   Erin go bragh.

Upon them, my lads! and the rebels shall know
How Erin can fight when she faces the foe;
If they can't give us arms, sure we needn't delay;
With a sprig of shillelagh we'll open the way.
    Erin, mavourneen!   Columbia, agra!
    E pluribus unum.   Erin go bragh.

58 Federal Troops in Camp, from a photograph by Brady in the United States Signal Corps, War Department, Washington

DEFECTS OF THE "THINKING BAYONETS"

"1. THE very prevalent habit of straggling from the ranks on the line of march which seems to have existed certainly for the first three years, and to have existed unchecked, and we can understand how much the generals must have been hampered in their operations by their uncertainty as to the number of men they could count on to reach a fixed place at a fixed time. 2. The very indifferent manner in which the infantry outpost duties were carried out, at least for the first two years of the war. Instances of surprises, not of small parties, but of whole armies, were numerous. Of course in the forests of the South outpost duty was most exacting, but that more than one great battle should have been begun by the rush of a long line on troops surprised in the act of cooking, or asleep in their tents, seems a proof that sentries and patrols were not so vigilant as they should have been. 3. The absolute want of control over the fire of the men. The only symptom of fire discipline was that the men could generally be induced to reserve their fire to short range where they were well sheltered and the enemy was advancing without firing. Directly the bullets began to fly the men 'took charge.' These shortcomings bear out Lord Wolseley's opinion that the presence of a single army corps of regular soldiers would have turned the scale in favour of either side." — HENDERSON, 244. Henderson's comment suggests some of the results of the military policy of the United States before 1861.

59   Federal Troops on the March, from a photograph by Brady in the United States Signal Corps, War Department, Washington

THE OFFICERS OF THE OPPOSING ARMIES

"As a rule they were young. Very few of those who made great names for themselves were more than fifty. Stuart and Sheridan, the two great cavalry leaders, were under thirty when the war broke out, and several of their most distinguished lieutenants had not more than four or five years' service. The most dashing Horse Artilleryman in the Confederacy was twenty-three when he was killed; and one of the best cavalry divisional commanders on the Federal side, General Mackenzie, did not even leave West Point until the war was nearly half over. . . . Some of the volunteer officers, moreover, who joined without any previous military knowledge whatever, made dashing and skillful leaders, notably General Terry on the Northern side, and Forrest on the Southern. The latter, who proved himself a most able tactician, would certainly have failed in any written examination for promotion. . . . Longstreet, one of the very ablest officers in the South, came from the pay department. Grant had been regimental quartermaster, had left the army and been

60 General Nathan Bedford Forrest, 1821–77, from a photograph in possession of the publishers

employed as a clerk in a tannery. Sherman had only thirteen years' army service, and had since been lawyer, banker, and professor in a military school; D. H. Hill had been professor in a university, and afterwards a lawyer; McClellan, president of a railway company; and Stonewall Jackson, perhaps the greatest soldier of them all, had served but four years in the Artillery, and for the ten years preceding the war had been Professor of Mathematics and Artillery in the Military Institute of Virginia. Another Confederate was at the same time a bishop. . . . Lee's chief of artillery, General Pendleton, was an Episcopal clergyman, who, it is said, condoned his relapse by always prefacing the command to fire with the words, 'The Lord have mercy on their souls!'" — *The Science of War*, 241–42.

SONGS OF THE UNION TROOPS

GEORGE F. ROOT was the most prolific writer of northern songs that were sung alike by soldiers and the people at home. One of the best and most widely used of the war songs, though now almost forgotten, was by Root and was first given to the public in the Chicago Court House Square by the Lombard Brothers, a popular singing pair of the day.

Just before the battle, Mother,
I am thinking most of you
While upon the field we're watching
With the enemy in view.
Comrades brave around me lying
Filled with thoughts of home and God,
For well they know that on the morrow
Some will sleep beneath the sod.

Farewell, Mother, you may never
Press me to your heart again,
But O you'll not forget me, Mother,
If I'm numbered with the slain.

The Americans of the mid-nineteenth century were to a marked degree a sentimental people. Naturally many of the songs of the Civil War reflected this characteristic. Root was responsible for one of the best remembered.

61 The Uprising at the North, from *Harper's History of the Great Rebellion*, New York, 1866–68

Yes, we'll rally round the flag, boys,
We'll rally once again
Shouting the Battle Cry of Freedom.
We will rally from the hillside,
We'll gather from the plain
Shouting the Battle Cry of Freedom.

The Union forever, hurrah, boys, hurrah,
Down with the traitor and up with the
    stars
While we rally round the flag, boys,
Rally once again,
Shouting the Battle Cry of Freedom.

SOUTHERN WAR SONGS

EARNEST HALPHIN wrote the words and C. W. A. Ellerbrock the music of one of the most stirring of the southern songs. It was published early in the war and was the national hymn.

God save the South,
God save the South,
Her altars and firesides,
God save the South,
Now that the war is nigh,
Chanting our battle-cry,
Freedom or death.

Now that the war is nigh,
Now that we arm to die,
Chanting the battle-cry,
Freedom or death.

Dixie was, of course, the song of the South and the greatest song of the war. Written by Daniel D. Emmet for a minstrel company playing in New York in 1859 it became the immediate favorite of the southern people. The version most commonly sung by the Confederate soldiers differed somewhat from Emmet's original. These are the soldier words.

Away down South in the fields of cotton,
Cinnamon seed and sandy bottom;
Look away, look away,
Look away, look away.
Den 'way down South in de fields of cotton,
Vinegar shoes and paper stockings;
Look away, look away,
Look away, look away.
Den I wish I was in Dixie Land
Oh-oh! Oh-oh!
In Dixie Land I'll take my stand,
And live and die in Dixie Land,
Away, away, away,
Away down South in Dixie.

ORDNANCE OF THE CIVIL WAR

"AT the outbreak of the war, the infantry arms in the possession of the government consisted of five hundred and sixty thousand smooth-bore muskets and forty-nine thousand rifles. Of these three hundred thousand muskets and twenty-seven thousand rifles were in northern arsenals: the remainder were in the southern arsenals. Though the musket was at this time an obsolete arm, one hundred and eighty thousand of these were imported by the United States. In addition about five hundred and fifty thousand rifles of various calibers and patterns were also imported. The muzzle-loading Springfield rifle became the standard arm of the infantry, and the national factory at Springfield, Massachusetts, was enlarged and private factories were equipped for its manufacture. In the year ending June 30, 1864, over six hundred thousand of these rifles were manufactured and the foreign arms were wholly replaced. A limited number of regiments of sharpshooters used breech-loading rifles. The standard carbine for cavalry was a breech-loader. At the beginning of the war about ten thousand were imported; these were gradually replaced by those of American manufacture. . . . In 1864, many of the cavalry regiments had repeating carbines. The repeating revolvers supplied to the cavalry and artillery were also of private manufacture. The standard field guns were the bronze muzzle-loading smooth-bore twelve-pounder Napoleon gun and the three-inch muzzle-loading rifle. Two types of rifles were used: the cast-iron gun with a wrought-iron reinforcing breech ring (Parrott rifle) and the wrought-iron gun. In the Confederate service a few breech-loading Whitworth guns were employed." — COLONEL GUSTAV J. FIEBEGER, *Campaigns of the American Civil War*, 6, West Point, 1914.

ALL! CALL ALL!

THE perennial shortage of guns under which the Confederate armies labored is reflected in one of the most interesting of the war songs of the southern soldiers.

Whoop! the Doodles have broken loose,
Roaring round like the very duce!
Lice of Egypt, a hungry pack:
After 'em boys, and drive 'em back!

Want a weapon? Gather a brick!
Club or cudgel, or stone or stick;
Anything with a blade or butt;
Anything that can cleave or cut.

Want a weapon? Why, capture one!
Every Doodle has got a gun,
Belt and bayonet, bright and new,
Kill a Doodle, and capture two!

Shoulder to shoulder, son and sire!
All! Call all! To the feast of fire!
Mother and Maiden, and child and slave
A common triumph, or a single grave!

64   From the painting *Spring*, by Charles Hoffbauer (1875–), in the Confederate
Memorial Museum, Richmond. © 1921

THE MAN POWER OF THE SOUTH

THE population of the North vastly outnumbered that of the South. In the spring of 1862 the illusion of security which followed Manassas was completely dispelled when the Confederacy faced invasions on both the eastern and western fronts. As a result, in April, 1862, was passed a conscription act which directed every male citizen between the ages of eighteen and thirty-five to enroll himself. In September, 1862, the age limit was extended to forty-five and in February, 1864, the limits were again enlarged to take men from seventeen to fifty. These conscription acts contained substitution clauses by which an individual could purchase exemption by sending a substitute. During the war slaves also were taken into the military service for the performance of certain duties. Somewhere between six hundred thousand and one million five hundred thousand men were enrolled in the Confederate armies during the war. The strength of the southern forces at various periods of the war is given in the War Records approximately as follows:

	ENROLLED	ABSENT PER CENT	PRESENT	SPECIAL DUTY ETC., PER CENT	PRESENT FOR DUTY
December 31, 1861	327,000	21	259,000	19	210,000
June 30, 1862	328,000	31	224,000	24	170,000
December 31, 1862	449,000	23	304,000	17	253,000
June 30, 1863	473,000	33	307,000	15	261,000
December 31, 1863	465,000	40	278,000	16	234,000
June 30, 1864	316,000	40	195,000	17	161,000
December 31, 1864	400,000	51	196,000	21	155,000
April 1, 1865	359,000	56	160,000	22	126,000

65   Group of Confederate Prisoners at Fairfax Court House, from a photograph
by Gardner, Washington

The column headed "special duty" is composed of men detailed as teamsters, ambulance drivers, hospital attendants, etc., and the men on sick report, in arrest, or in confinement. The column headed "present for duty" includes the armed and equipped officers and men, the non-combatants such as administrative and supply staffs, bands, etc., and the temporarily unarmed and unequipped combatants. Figures are quoted from FIEBEGER, *Campaigns of the American Civil War*, 3.

66   Recruiting Office in New York City Hall Park, from *Frank Leslie's
Illustrated Newspaper*, Mar. 19, 1864

MAN POWER OF
THE NORTH

THE North depended upon volunteering to recruit its armies until the adoption of conscription in March, 1863. Volunteering was still encouraged, however, by the bounty system. Under the act of July, 1861, every volunteer who enlisted for two or more years received one hundred dollars. After June, 1863, the veteran who reenlisted for the duration of the war was given four hundred dollars. Later a bounty of three hundred dollars was paid to each volunteer who enlisted in any three-year regiment. Whenever volunteering failed to fill up the state quotas recourse was had to the draft act of March, 1863, which provided for the enrollment of all men between twenty and forty-five inclusive. This measure also had the pernicious substitution clause. The figures for the Union armies form a striking contrast to those of the South.

	ENROLLED	ABSENT PER CENT	PRESENT	SPECIAL DUTY ETC., PER CENT	PRESENT FOR DUTY
December 31, 1860	16,000	6	15,000	—	108,000
June 30, 1861	152,000	17	130,000	17	108,000
December 31, 1861	528,000	10	477,000	11	425,000
June 30, 1862	624,000	20	502,000	13	433,000
December 31, 1862	868,000	24	664,000	18	556,000
June 30, 1863	848,000	25	636,000	17	530,000
December 31, 1863	837,000	30	601,000	17	497,000
June 30, 1864	1,002,000	30	683,000	19	555,000
December 31, 1864	937,000	35	605,000	18	496,000
April 30, 1865	1,052,000	30	734,000	15	622,000

The Confederate armies reached their greatest strength in June, 1863, on the eve of Gettysburg; the Federals reached their greatest power in April, 1865.
Figures are quoted from FIEBEGER, 5.

ECONOMIC ORGANIZATION

AT the time of the outbreak of the Civil War the South was almost wholly an agricultural section and one, moreover, dependent upon a single staple, cotton. Arms, munitions, and clothing had to be obtained from abroad. The Davis administration made a fatal blunder at the outset of the war in not transferring the cotton in southern warehouses to Europe while the southern ports were still open. Upon this cotton and the expectation of southern victory depended the credit abroad of the Confederacy. The belief that Bull Run had ended the war seems to have been one of the reasons for this failure in statesmanship. Davis also seems to have believed that the cutting off of the supply of cotton would force European nations to recognize the Confederacy. In the North were to be found the financial power and the manufacturing resources of the nation. The mobilization of both of these assets presented problems of considerable difficulty. In the end, however, the North proved itself to be a self-sufficient section capable of wearing down the power of its opponent.

67   Filling Cartridges at the United States Arsenal at Watertown, Mass., from *Harper's Weekly*, July 20, 1861

THE PROBLEM OF WINNING THE WAR

THE disadvantages of the South in man power and economic resources were, to a considerable extent, offset by the nature of the military problem which the southern leaders faced. The Confederacy was fighting for independence. To win, the South had only to hold off the Federal armies until the North grew tired of fighting, or until a foreign nation

68   A Fire Zouave relating his experience of the Battle of Bull Run, from a sketch in *Harper's Weekly*, Aug. 17, 1861

interfered. To that end southern agents labored persistently at Paris and London. In fighting off the northern invader the southern armies had the advantage of interior lines and of fighting among a friendly population. This latter factor was of the greatest importance in gaining information about the enemy and in making unnecessary the detachment of large forces from the field armies to defend lines of communications. The North, on the other hand, could only secure victory by destroying completely the military power of the South. As the event proved this was a task of extreme difficulty.

69   Coast Guard recruiting poster, from the original in the Division of Manuscripts, Library of Congress, Washington

70   Army recruiting poster, from the original in the Division of Manuscripts, Library of Congress, Washington

THE
ENISLEMENT
OF THE
SOUTH

APPROXIMATE LINE OF DIVISION
BETWEEN **NORTH** AND **SOUTH**
NAVIGABLE FOR LARGE VESSELS
"   "   " SMALL "
CANALS
RAILROADS
×   BATTLEFIELDS
BLOCKADE BY UNION VESSELS

MILES
50 0 50 100 150 200

71   Drawn expressly for *The Pageant of America* by Gregor Noetzel, American Geographical Society,
New York

THE ENISLEMENT OF THE SOUTH

THROUGHOUT the whole history of American warfare the side that ruled the water ruled the land. Armies did much, but fleets did more, to win the French and Indian Wars. It was the change in the balance of sea power that did most to settle the fate of Cornwallis' army at Yorktown. The War of 1812 preponderantly turned upon questions of relative sea power; witness the iron blockade of the coast, in favor of the British, and the countervailing advantages won by the American flotillas on Lakes Erie and Champlain. The Mexican campaign, though fought almost exclusively on land, owed a very great deal to the fact that all the odds in naval force and water transportation were overwhelmingly in favor of the Union states. When we reach the Spanish War and the World War we shall again find sea power of fundamental and determining importance all through. There is, therefore, nothing unusual about the decisive influence of sea power throughout the Civil War. The Union navy, taken as a whole, exerted greater pressure on the South than even the British navy succeeded in exerting on the United States toward the end of "1812," for though the final blockade of 1814 was as severe as the Union blockade of 1864, the British hold on inland waters was weak, while the Union hold on all the navigable rivers became as decisive as its hold upon the sea. When it is remembered that freight could be transported vastly more easily by water than by rail or by road, the advantage which the ultimate control of the sea and inland waters gave to the North is evident. The Federal navy not only starved the Confederate armies by stopping the import of supplies but blighted Confederate finance by preventing the export of its great staple, cotton. The map not only shows the almost complete enislement of the South by waters that became eventually hostile, but also shows how the Union folk of West Virginia and eastern Tennessee made a dangerous northern salient threatening to split asunder the southern territory and extending practically to Chattanooga.

CHAPTER II

VIRGINIA, 1862

THE spring of 1862 brought war in deadly earnest to the communities of old Virginia. McClellan, studying his map of the region with the eye of a trained soldier, observed that this state, where Washington had lived and where he had forced Cornwallis to surrender, was, for military purposes, divided into three sections. East of a line which would run from Washington southward through Fredericksburg, Richmond, and Petersburg was the flat and swampy country of the tidewater. Here sluggish rivers, like the James and York, broadened into estuaries. The roads were bad and but two railroads crossed the region in the neighborhood of Richmond. One of these ran from the capital of the Confederacy to West Point and the other from Petersburg to the chief Virginia port, Norfolk. The country was unfavorable for offensive military operations in all respects except that the York and James rivers provided excellent lines of supply to the western edge of the Tidewater country.

Beyond the Tidewater the Piedmont stretches its broad and hilly expanse as far as the Blue Ridge. McClellan noted that it was divided into two parts by the Bull Run mountains, parallel with the Blue Ridge. In the Piedmont the Federal armies could find fords by which to cross the east-flowing rivers which lay athwart any advance on Richmond from the north. McClellan observed, however, that just south of the Rapidan and the Rappahannock was a densely wooded area known as the Wilderness. The principal railway line of the region ran from Alexandria through Charlottesville and Lynchburg. From this were important branch lines running to the east and west. Railroad junctions of strategic importance were Manassas, Gordonsville and Lynchburg.

Beyond the Piedmont lies the Valley section between the Blue Ridge and the Alleghany mountains. In the north of this the low Shenandoah range separates the valleys of the South Branch of the Potomac and the Shenandoah. The Valley section is the most fertile part of Virginia. McClellan observed that through the farm land of the Shenandoah Valley ran an excellent turnpike extending from Lexington to Martinsburg. An inferior road paralleled the South Branch. There were also two short railroad lines, from Harper's Ferry to Winchester, and from Strasburg to Mt. Jackson. Beyond the Valley section lay the mountainous country of what was soon to be the state of West Virginia. Since June 1861 this region had been in the control of Federal troops. The mountains, in fact, presented a great barrier, peopled with Union sympathisers, which separated the Virginia front from that of the Mississippi Valley.

Virginia was, therefore, a vast bastion susceptible of attack from three sides, the east, north, and west. On December 31, 1861, McClellan commanded the Department of the Potomac with one hundred and seventy-four thousand men; General Wool commanded the Department of Southeast Virginia with ten thousand men; and General Rosecrans commanded the Department of West Virginia with twenty thousand men. McClellan, commander in chief, gave much study during the winter of 1861–62 to the military problems confronting him. On February 3 he submitted his plan of campaign to the President. In the following month was fought a ship duel of the utmost consequence for the outcome of the war. The conflict between the *Monitor* and *Merrimac* had a vital bearing on McClellan's scheme of maneuver.

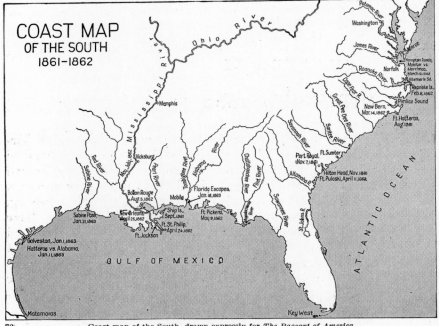

72   Coast map of the South, drawn expressly for *The Pageant of America*

COAST MAP OF THE SOUTH, 1861–1862

THE coast map makes clear how the strangling influence of sea power took effect on the comparatively shipless South; how Fortress Monroe was a perpetual coign of vantage for the North on the Virginian flank; how the capture of Hatteras and Roanoke Island struck two numbing blows at North Carolina; what South Carolina suffered through the loss of Port Royal; Georgia, through the fall of Fort Pulaski; the Gulf States through the loss of Pensacola, Ship Island, and New Orleans; and all Confederate naval hopes through the *Monitor's* arrival on the scene to checkmate the *Merrimac* in Hampton Roads, well within range of Fortress Monroe. A hundred and sixty-three vessels of all kinds were added to the United States navy in 1862. But real warships were still very scarce, and with the taking of New Orleans, in April, 1862, the Federal victories ceased for that year.

PORT ROYAL, SOUTH CAROLINA, NOVEMBER 7, 1861

ADMIRAL DuPONT'S finely fought action off Hilton Head, against both ships and forts, together with the whole management of the Port Royal expedition, is deserving of all praise. This was the crowning naval action of 1861. The Confederate forts at Hatteras Inlet had been taken by Flag-officer Stringham and General Benjamin F. Butler in August. Ship Island had been occupied in September as a dominant strategic point between New Orleans and Mobile. Now, in November, the Confederate sea flank was struck a heavy blow at Port Royal, where the coöperating troops were well led by General Thomas W. Sherman (not to be confused with the much greater William T. Sherman).

73   Admiral Samuel Francis DuPont, 1803–65, from a photograph by Brady

74 Plan of Attack for the Bombardment and Capture of Forts Beauregard and Walker, from *Frank Leslie's Illustrated Newspaper*, Nov. 30, 1861

PLAN OF ATTACK AT PORT ROYAL

THIS plan clearly shows how well the ships maneuvered so as to bring a maximum of fire upon the stationary forts while making the most of their own mobility.

75   Bombardment and Capture of Forts Walker and Beauregard, from an engraving made in 1861 by George E. Perine, after a drawing by Charles Parsons

PORT ROYAL, SOUTH CAROLINA, NOVEMBER 7, 1861: THE BOMBARDMENT

AN enthusiastic "Jackie" aboard the U. S. S. *Vandalia* burst into a rhymed "Port Royal Dance" over this victory in general and the *Vandalia* in particular:

> Each ship advanced in order, each captain wore a smile,
> Until the famed *Vandalia* brought up the rear in style,
> And as our guns were shortest we balanced to the right,
> And brought us to the enemy the closest in the fight.
>
> Then round the room (Port Royal Bay) we took a Highland Fling,
> And showed them in Fort Walker what loud music we could sing,
> And then we poured in broadsides that brought their courage low,
> And o'er the rebel batteries our Union flag did flow.

Fort Forrest   Piles in the Sound   Rebel Flotilla   National Gunboats   Fort Bartow   Landing National Troops

76   Bombardment of Fort Bartow, from a sketch by B. Marshall in *Frank Leslie's Illustrated Newspaper*, March 1, 1862

ROANOKE ISLAND, NORTH CAROLINA, FEBRUARY 8, 1862

THE joint naval and military expedition against Roanoke Island and Newbern was called the Burnside Expedition, from the name of the general in command. The navy's work, as usual, attracted less public attention, though Flag-officer Louis M. Goldsborough and his whole force did their very important part well. The effect of taking Roanoke Island was to shut Albemarle Sound against North Carolina; while taking Newbern (March 14) meant shutting up Pamlico Sound. When Fort Pulaski also fell (April 11) Georgia lost the outpost of Savannah.

THE *MONITOR* LAUNCHED AT NEW YORK, JANUARY 30, 1862

WHILE the South was suffering the loss of point after point on her coast, the North was building a new kind of warship against the makeshift southern ironclad *Virginia*, which never lost her old Union name of *Merrimac*. The innovating *Monitor* was launched on January 30, 1862, the hundredth day from the laying of her keel-plate. This was very fine work on the part of her Swedish naval architect, Ericsson, and of her builder, C. S. Bushnell. She was only one hundred seventy-two feet over all, with forty-one foot beam, ten foot draught, and had a crew of fifty-

77   Lieutenant (later Captain), John L. Worden, 1818–97, from a photograph by Elias Dexter, New York

78   John Ericsson, 1803–89, from a photograph by Brady

eight, under Captain John L. Worden. She carried only two guns; but they were cannon of eleven-inch bore. She looked like "a tin can on a shingle" or "a cheesebox on a raft." She was of not nearly half the tonnage of the *Merrimac*, and had not a quarter as many men in her crew. But all her men were naval experts, and all her plating, battery, and engines were the very best the country then could build. Commodore Franklin Buchanan of the *Merrimac* did all that a very gallant and skillful commander possibly could do with his ship, but though he was admirably seconded by several excellent naval officers, his vessel was a lubberly makeshift whose ten guns, however bravely served, were no match for Worden's two.

THE *MERRIMAC* ATTACKING THE *CUMBERLAND*, MARCH 8, 1862

THE *Merrimac* had been sunk and abandoned at the Norfolk Navy Yard at the beginning of the war. But the Confederates raised her, cut her down to a mere razee, plated her over with iron at an angle of thirty-five degrees, clamped a four-foot ram on her bows, mounted ten guns, and put her under the very competent command of Commodore Franklin Buchanan. With her wheezy old engines, with guns she had never yet fired, and with a crew mostly of landsmen, the *Merrimac* made for Newport News at a bare five knots

an hour. But the Confederate garrison cheered her to the echo, and she did take the Federal frigates by surprise. They, however, quickly opened fire, but she rammed and sank the gallant *Cumberland*, which went down with every gun aboard her firing to the last, and her colors waving "No Surrender" even as she sank. An hour later the overmatched *Congress* surrendered; while the big *Minnesota* lay grounded and equally helpless when the deep-draught *Merrimac* was forced to retire. March 8 was a day of crisis. The *Merrimac* had demonstrated that the wooden-sided frigates of the old navy could not prevent the ironclad from winning and holding the command of Chesapeake Bay. The *Merrimac* single handed seemed able to defeat McClellan's plan.

79   The *Merrimac* ramming the *Cumberland*, from the painting by Warren Sheppard (1859–). © 1897

THE *MONITOR* GOES SOUTH

MEANWHILE the *Monitor* had been hurrying down from New York. She was none too seaworthy, and nearly foundered on the way. But every man aboard her knew what to do and exactly how to do it — in marked contrast to the equally brave, but comparatively inexperienced, men aboard the *Merrimac*.

MONITOR AND *MERRIMAC*, MARCH 9, 1862

WHEN the *Merrimac* came back with the next tide to finish the helpless *Minnesota* she found the *Monitor* on guard. So here, in Hampton Roads, on March 9, 1862, the lists

80   Crew on deck of the *Monitor*, from a photograph by Brady in the L. C. Handy Collection, Washington

were set for this great tourney and all the world looked on because of the strange character of the vessels.

81   The Battle between the *Monitor* and the *Merrimac*, from an engraving after the sketch by Sergeant Charles Worret, in *Harper's Weekly*, April 12, 1862

MONITOR AND *MERRIMAC*, MARCH 9, 1862

BROADSIDE to broadside, the two better and heavier guns aboard the *Monitor* shook the makeshift *Merrimac* worse than the ten smaller guns of the *Merrimac* shook the far stauncher *Monitor*. Once head on to the *Monitor's* broadside, the *Merrimac* tried hard to ram. But her wretched old engines could give her no speed, while the far nimbler *Monitor* simply steered clear. The actual fight was, in a certain sense, a draw, though the damaged *Merrimac* put back into the James River. The *Monitor* had won command of the Chesapeake. The duel, however, is one of the most famous in all naval history for it marked the beginning of the era of the steel battleships. The *Monitor* was a primitive form that developed into the dreadnaught.

82   From the painting *The Monitor and Merrimac Fight*, by William F. Halsall (1841–1919) in the Capitol, Washington

83   From a cartoon "*Masterly Inactivity*," or *Six Months on the Potomac*, in *Frank Leslie's Illustrated Newspaper*, Feb. 1, 1862

FEBRUARY 22, 1862

THE people of the North grew restive under the prolonged inaction in Virginia which followed the Battle of Bull Run. Ignorant of the time required for the training of an army and critical of their military commanders, they demanded that the advance on Richmond be resumed. The President yielded to the pressure and issued a general order directing all the Union armies to advance on February 22. The most important result of this movement was the placing of General Banks in the Shenandoah Valley with an army corps. On March 10, acting under explicit orders from Lincoln, McClellan advanced with the Army of the Potomac toward Manassas. The Federal advance cavalry soon discovered that the Confederates had withdrawn from this region and had taken up a position south of the Rappahannock River. McClellan, who did not intend to attack Richmond from this direction, then retired toward Washington leaving two divisions in the neighborhood of Manassas. On March 11, he was relieved as commander in chief and retained only the control of the Army of the Potomac. From that day until July 11, 1862, Lincoln, with Secretary of War Stanton as his aide, was the actual as well as titular commander in chief. As such he has to bear the major responsibility for the operations of the Peninsular Campaign. In West Virginia Rosecrans was relieved by Frémont who was assigned to the command of what was now called the Mountain Department.

McCLELLAN'S PLAN

McCLELLAN proposed to attack Richmond by the shortest possible land route. His plan called for the transportation of the Army of the Potomac by water to Urbana, Virginia, whence he would march on Richmond via West Point. The advantage of the scheme was that it would compel the Confederates to retire from Manassas because of the threat to their communications. It would also cause the enemy to abandon the fortified position that had been constructed at Yorktown on the peninsula between the York and James rivers. The President was unwilling to permit such a movement while General Joseph E. Johnston, commanding the Army of Northern Virginia, was at Manassas. Lincoln feared for the safety of the capital. This is the explanation of his specific order directing McClellan to capture Manassas. After the occupation of this railroad junction Lincoln approved McClellan's plan with the proviso that it be modified in such a way as to provide a reserve force in northern Virginia strong enough to hold Manassas, and also an adequate garrison in the Washington defenses. McClellan's original plan was strategically correct. The Federal general perhaps did not take fully into account the difficulties of the terrain. The greatest weakness of the plan was that the President gave his consent reluctantly. As Lincoln was ultimately responsible for the conduct of the war his doubt as to the advisability of the proposed move was a matter of serious consequence.

84   Federal Occupation of Confederate Fortifications at Manassas, March 1862. from a
photograph by Gardner, Washington

McCLELLAN AND STANTON

On January 11, 1862, Lincoln in a curt note had dismissed his Secretary of War, Simon Cameron, Republican boss of Pennsylvania, and had appointed him ambassador to Russia. Cameron had proved incompetent. In his place Lincoln had appointed an energetic and outspoken lawyer, Edwin Stanton, who had won a good reputation by his sturdy patriotism while a member of Buchanan's cabinet. McClellan's comment gives a suggestion of the atmosphere in Washington on the eve of the Peninsular Campaign. "I was unaware of his appointment as Secretary of War until after it had been made, whereupon he called to ascertain whether I desired him to accept [McClellan was at the time commander in chief of the Union armies] . . . saying that to do so would involve a total sacrifice in his personal interests, and that the only inducement would be the desire to assist me in my work. Having no reason to doubt his sincerity, I desired him to accept, whereupon he consented and with great effusion exclaimed: 'Now we two will save the country.'. . . The more serious difficulties of my position began with Mr. Stanton's accession to the War Office. It

85   Edwin McMasters Stanton, 1814–69, from a photograph by Brady, in the United States Signal Corps, War Department, Washington

at once became very difficult to approach him, even for the transaction of ordinary current business, and our personal relations at once ceased. The impatience of the Executive immediately became extreme, and I can attribute it only to the influence of the new Secretary, who did many things to break up the free and confidential intercourse that had heretofore existed between the President and myself. . . . [A few weeks later the President called McClellan into conference relating to a 'very ugly matter' which he desired to talk about, and that was the movement by the lower Chesapeake.] He said that it had been suggested that I proposed this movement with the 'traitorous' purpose of leaving Washington uncovered and exposed to attack. I very promptly objected to the coupling of any such adjectives with my purposes, whereon he disclaimed any intention of conveying his own opinion, as he merely repeated the suggestions of others. — R. U. Johnson and C. C. Buel, Editors, *Battles and Leaders of the Civil War*, Vol. II, pp. 165–66, The Century Co., New York, 1888.

STARTING THE PENINSULAR CAMPAIGN

With the modifications which Lincoln proposed regarding the security of Washington, McClellan's plan was approved on March 13. McClellan promptly ordered Banks to bring five of his six brigades from the Shenandoah to Manassas leaving one to protect the Valley. This force together with the strong Washington garrison would be sufficient to meet the President's requirements for troops in northern Virginia. McClellan then planned to take four army corps, about one hundred and fifty thousand men, to Fortress Monroe. The base of operations had been changed from Urbana probably because of the better landing facilities at the fort and because the success of recent joint naval and military operations in the Carolinas had seemed to indicate that the fortifications at Yorktown could be easily reduced. In March opened a campaign which for numbers engaged and losses suffered surpassed any previous operation in North America.

86   General McClellan and his staff, from a photograph by Brady, in the United States Signal Corps, War Department, Washington

87   The Battle of Winchester, from a drawing in *Frank Leslie's Illustrated Newspaper*, Apr. 26, 1862

JACKSON IN THE SHENANDOAH VALLEY

THEN, on March 23, Stonewall Jackson struck the first blow of the campaign which was to result in wrecking McClellan's enterprise. Making a forced march down the Shenandoah Valley, in which his troops suffered greatly, he attacked Banks' subordinate, Shields, at Kernstown near Winchester. He was repulsed, but he was successful in his purpose of keeping Banks in the Valley. The result of Kernstown was that Banks, acting with McClellan's consent, sent only one brigade to Manassas and with the other five began a hot pursuit of Jackson. The sending of Banks in pursuit of Jackson was a grave blunder. McClellan by so doing failed to comply with the explicit orders of his chief and left an insufficient force at Manassas. When the War Department became aware of the activities of Banks, McClellan was on the water en route to Fortress Monroe. On April 4 the President detached McDowell's corps from McClellan's army and ordered it to cover Washington. Lincoln then ordered McDowell and Banks detached from McClellan's command. The former was given the command of the Department of the Rappahannock and the latter of the Department of the Shenandoah. Both were to be under the direct orders of the Secretary of War. At the very outset of the campaign, therefore, McClellan lost control of four of the twelve divisions of his field army and the two divisions of Banks' force.

THE CONFEDERATE DEFENSE OF VIRGINIA

SUPERIOR numbers gave the offensive to the North in the spring of 1862. The problem of the Confederates, therefore, was to hold an extended line awaiting the Union attack and then concentrate to meet it. General Joseph E. Johnston was in command of the Army of Virginia. General Lee had been brought to the War Department in March and was in general charge of all operations in Virginia. The Confederate right rested on the sea at Norfolk. It was strengthened by the ironclad *Virginia* (*Merrimac*), which prevented the Federal fleet from ascending the James. On the Peninsula between the James and the York Lee had caused strong fortifications to be constructed the year before. These faced Fortress Monroe and prevented a swift thrust from that base. The main army of defense was stationed on a line which ran from Aquia Creek along the Rappahannock and the Rapidan. A small detachment under Stonewall Jackson was operating in the Shenandoah Valley. When Lee was informed of the landing of a considerable number of troops at Fortress Monroe, he was at first undecided as to whether McClellan's plan was an attack on Richmond or on Norfolk. Awaiting further information he held the main Confederate army along the Rappahannock bringing only one brigade back. This he placed at Petersburg whence it could go by rail to Norfolk or by water to Yorktown. At Yorktown General Magruder held a line eight miles long with between fifteen and seventeen thousand men.

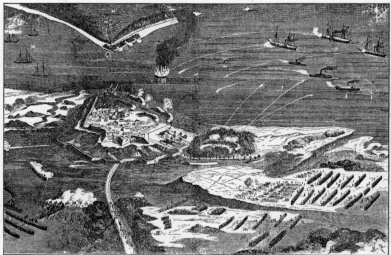

88   First Day's Firing at Yorktown, April 1862, from a sketch in *Harper's Weekly*, Apr. 26, 1862

McCLELLAN AT YORKTOWN

McClellan on April 1 reached the Peninsula, where sixty thousand men had already been concentrated. With these he advanced on April 4 but was stopped by the Yorktown fortifications. Not until he learned of this movement was Lee certain that McClellan's objective was Richmond. Lee at once ordered the transfer of the major part of Johnston's army to Yorktown. Such a movement required time. Meanwhile McClellan used

89   Arrival of McClellan at Yorktown, from a sketch by E. S. Hall in *Frank Leslie's Illustrated Newspaper*, May 3, 1862

April 5 and 6 to make a reconnaissance of Yorktown, after which he concluded that the line was too strong to be forced. This decision was McClellan's second error. On April 5 Magruder, realizing that he was vastly outnumbered, reported to Lee: "I have made arrangements to fight my small force, but without the slightest hope of success." Had McClellan assaulted Yorktown on this day or the next, he would have suffered heavy losses but he must almost certainly have won. He could then have pushed rapidly on to Richmond before his enemy could complete his concentration to defend the capital. Even more important, determined action at Yorktown would have renewed the President's confidence in McClellan and might very well have resulted in his regaining control of McDowell and Banks. As it was McClellan decided on regular siege operations and lay in front of Yorktown for a month. When at last his siege cannon had arrived and been put into position, Johnston, who had concentrated sixty thousand men at Yorktown, evacuated the place and fell back on a prepared position in front of Richmond.

THE SIGNIFICANCE OF YORKTOWN

McClellan's handling of the Yorktown problem should be contrasted with the operations in the World War of the Second Division at Belleau Wood and at Mont Blanc, or of the First Division in the drive of July 18, 1918, toward Soissons (see page 311). His delay robbed his offensive of the element of surprise and gave his opponent time to concentrate all his troops in the east to the defense of the capital and at the same time the opportunity to strengthen the works about Richmond. Early in May Lee made a decision that had a vital bearing on the outcome of the campaign. Although Johnston was greatly outnumbered by McClellan and McDowell, Lee ordered Jackson to continue his operations in the Valley instead of drawing him in to the defense of Richmond. Such a course was accompanied by grave risks. Jackson's mission in the Valley was to carry on such a vigorous campaign that Federal troops would be detached from the Richmond front to aid in defeating him. Jackson, meanwhile, must hold himself in readiness to abandon the Valley at a moment's notice and to hasten to the defense of Richmond. The plan and the willingness to assume the risk involved were the first demonstrations of Lee's military caliber.

90   Inspection of troops at Cumberland Landing, from a photograph by Gardner, Washington

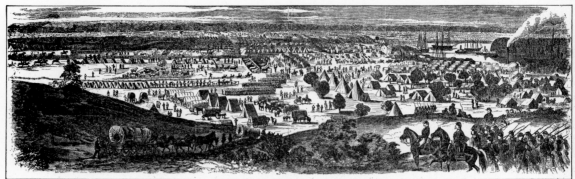

91   The Army of the Potomac in camp at Cumberland Landing, from a sketch by Mead in *Harper's Weekly*, June 21, 1862

MAY, 1862

JOHNSTON evacuated Yorktown on May 3 and Norfolk was promptly abandoned.   This opened the James River to the Federal fleet as far as Drewry's Bluff, seven miles below Richmond.   The *Merrimac* was destroyed to prevent its capture.   On May 24 McClellan was close to Richmond with his army astride the Chickahominy River.   Meanwhile, Lincoln, observing that McClellan's threat had drawn most of the Confederate troops to the protection of the southern capital, decided that he had too many men for the defense of Washington.   As a consequence he took a brigade away from Banks in the Valley and gave it to McDowell.   He also gave that officer some of the Washington garrison.   The President then ordered McDowell to concentrate his four divisions at Fredericksburg and move southward along the railroad to coöperate with McClellan. At Fredericksburg McDowell had forty thousand men less than fifty miles (three days' march) from McClellan's right flank on the north bank of the Chickahominy.   McClellan had taken up a defensive position in front of Richmond because after the Yorktown delay he was not strong enough to defeat his opponent without McDowell's aid.   The Chickahominy River seriously weakened the position of the Army of the Potomac by making it difficult to transfer reserves from one part of the line to another in the event of a battle.   McClellan found it necessary, however, to keep part of his army north of the river in order to protect his base at White House near the York estuary.   He must maintain this base, moreover, so long as McDowell was under orders to coöperate with him.   On the morning of May 24 the speedy fall of Richmond seemed inevitable.   When

McDowell and McClellan should unite in the next few days, their joint army, outnumbering that of Johnston, must drive the Confederates from the capital.

JACKSON IN THE VALLEY

ON May 24 the attention of Washington was suddenly riveted on Jackson in the Shenandoah Valley.   For more than three weeks his task had been one of great difficulty.   After Kernstown Banks had driven him as far south as Harrisonburg, from which place Jackson had retired eastward with his small force to Swift Run Gap in the Blue Ridge to put himself in a position to defend Gordonsville if necessary.   Then on May 1 Banks received orders from Lincoln to fall back to Strasburg and to send a brigade to McDowell.   Meanwhile Frémont in the valley of the South Branch on the western side of the Shenandoah mountains was concentrating a force to destroy Jackson.

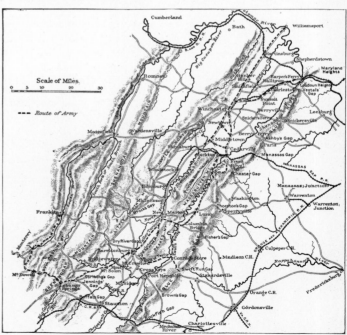

92   Route of Jackson's Army in the Valley, redrawn from the *Atlas to Accompany the Official Records of the Union and Confederate Armies*, Washington

JACKSON DEFEATS MILROY AND BANKS

FRÉMONT pushed a brigade under Milroy eastward into the Shenandoah mountains as far as the village of McDowell and was planning to reinforce him with his entire command as soon as possible. Jackson, realizing his danger, suddenly plunged into the mountains with his army, defeated Milroy at McDowell on May 8 and pursued him as far as Franklin in the valley of the South Branch. Jackson had, for the time being, checked Frémont. Eleven days later the swiftly

93   Arrival of Frémont's Vanguard above Strasburg in view of Jackson's trains, from a sketch made at the time, in *Battles and Leaders of the Civil War*, New York, 1888

moving southern leader was back in the Shenandoah Valley marching against Banks. Jackson was now reinforced so that his army numbered between seventeen and eighteen thousand. Banks was at Strasburg with an outlying brigade at Front Royal. On the afternoon of May 23 Jackson fell upon the detached brigade and practically destroyed it. Banks fled precipitately to the Potomac which he crossed at Williamsport. Jackson pursued him as far as Winchester and then turned east to Harper's Ferry. The victorious Confederates, therefore, were between Banks and Washington. Terror seized the National Capital.

McDOWELL SENT TO THE VALLEY

ON the morning of May 24 Washington learned of the disaster at Front Royal and the start of Banks' retreat. Orders were rushed to McDowell to suspend the movement against Richmond which he was just ready to begin and to send half of his forty thousand men to the Valley to assist in the capture of Jackson. So Lee's plan of defending Richmond by operations in the Shenandoah Valley was justified. Jackson had relieved the pressure on the Confederate capital. Johnston was quick to take advantage of the opportunity presented by the changed aspect of affairs. On May 31, the day after the advance guard of McDowell's detachment hurrying to catch Jackson had reached the Blue Ridge, Johnston struck McClellan while his army was still weakened by being astride the Chickahominy River. On that day and the next the Battle of Seven Pines or Fair Oaks was fought. Johnston's orders were not well carried out (see p. 54) and he was repulsed. Meanwhile Jackson, learning of McDowell's movement against his rear, fell back from Harper's Ferry to Winchester. On June 1 he passed through Strasburg just as the jaws of the Federal trap were about to close. On that day McDowell's advance guard under Shields was at Front Royal and Frémont's advance guard but five miles to the west of that village; Jackson's cavalry was skirmishing with that of Frémont. The Federal plan to have McDowell and Frémont come together at Strasburg and bag Jackson had failed by a hair's breadth.

94   Charge of General Sickle's Brigade at the Battle of Fair Oaks, from a sketch in *Frank Leslie's Illustrated Newspaper*, June 21, 1862

95   Attack on Jackson near Harrisonburg, June 7, 1862, from *Frank Leslie's Illustrated Newspaper*,
June 28, 1862

JACKSON AT STRASBURG

JOHN H. WORSHAM has left an account of Jackson's retreat from Winchester as viewed from the ranks. "On the 31st of May Jackson sent all his captured stores and his wagon train up the Valley pike, and our regiment with the prisoners followed in the afternoon. We marched to Cedar Creek, and stopped for the night; our guard line was around a large barn, in order to allow the prisoners to have the benefit of its shelter as it was raining. Some amusing scenes were witnessed the next morning. The barn had a large quantity of hay in it; we went to the door and ordered all out; we then called for those that were concealed to come out, or they would be punished when found. None came; so some of our men were ordered to go in, and see if they could find any. Two or three were pulled out of the hay, amidst the shouts of their comrades as well as our men. . . . At Strasburg we could see Ewell's division in line of battle on the right of the road, awaiting the advance of Frémont, whose skirmishers had made their appearance and were then engaged with Ewell's. Our prisoners became very much excited by this, and declared loudly that Jackson had met his match now, and would be badly whipped; and it would be only a few hours before they would be retaken. After all the wagons and prisoners had passed, Jackson waited for the Stonewall brigade to arrive, and as soon as it had passed Ewell was withdrawn and followed the column up the valley. Frémont made a big show at one time in Ewell's front, but hearing nothing from Shields, who for some reason had not made his appearance, he withdrew his men back into the mountain fastnesses, his skirmishers following Ewell a short distance. The plan to bag Jackson at Strasburg had failed; 'Old Jack' was too quick for them. . . ." — *One of Jackson's Foot Cavalry*, 89–90.

THE END OF THE VALLEY CAMPAIGN

BAD roads had delayed Frémont, and the difficulty of supplying his troops, due in part to the bad condition of the Manassas Gap railroad, had held up McDowell. The result was Jackson's escape. Frémont's column followed Jackson up the Valley pike. McDowell's men hurried southward along the eastern side of the Shenandoah Valley. Between Frémont and McDowell was a range of hills. Jackson would be overwhelmingly outnumbered if the two Federal armies effected a junction. After he had passed the southern end of the hills Jackson discovered that McDowell's force had gotten ahead of him and was holding the bridge at Port Republic. The Confederate commander therefore had an enemy both on his front and his rear. On June 8 Jackson stopped, attacked Frémont at Cross Keys, and drove him from the field. On the following day he turned on Shields at Port Republic and drove him down the valley. The Valley Campaign was over; Frémont was ordered to fall back to Harrisonburg, Shields to Luray, McDowell to concentrate once more at Fredericksburg, and Banks to advance from Harper's Ferry to Winchester. Colonel Fiebeger has remarked: "Never has a diversion had such important effects on the conduct of a campaign."

96   Frémont's Army on its March up the Valley, from a sketch by Edwin Forbes in
Frank Leslie's Illustrated Newspaper, July 5, 1862

JACKSON'S ACHIEVEMENT IN THE VALLEY

"In forty-eight days he had marched six hundred and seventy-six miles, fought five hard battles, accomplishing in each his purpose, baffled three Federal armies, his seventeen thousand matched against fifty thousand, brought off his prisoners and booty unmeasured, ruined the campaign of McClellan, and stricken the North with terror. He now stood, with army diminished, indeed, but trained, seasoned, superb in morale, and eager for new efforts, while his own reputation was forever fixed as one of the world's great captains." — J. K. Hosmer, *The Appeal to Arms*, 153, Harper Bros., New York, 1905.

97   Statue of Stonewall Jackson by Charles Keck
         (1874–) at Charlottesville, Va.

JUNE, 1862

Johnston had been wounded in the fighting of May 31 along the Chickahominy and Lee had assumed direct command of the army. Early in June it became clear that Jackson's diversion in the Valley had checked for the time being any offensive movement against Richmond from the north. Lee prepared to strike before McDowell's army could be collected. McClellan had entrenched his position and had thrown up obstacles. He was weak, however, in that one corps was still north of the Chickahominy and separated from the rest of the army by that river. Yet it had to remain there, for on June 8 Secretary Stanton had ordered McDowell to assemble his army, and McClellan's isolated corps was necessary to assist McDowell's advance when he should be ready to move on Richmond. The first three weeks of June saw Lee preparing for the final battles which were destined to end the Peninsular Campaign. Lee had no accurate maps of the region in the neighborhood of McClellan's right flank though this was within a few miles of Richmond. To secure the necessary information he sent his cavalry commander, General J. E. B. Stuart, to reconnoiter the country. About the middle of June Stuart with three regiments of cavalry not only accomplished his mission but rode entirely around McClellan's army, gaining a vast amount of information and destroying large quantities of supplies. Stuart's operation was at the same time a humiliation and a benefit to McClellan. It brought sharply to his attention the weakness in his position resulting from having his base at White House on the York and caused him to make preparations to transfer it to Harrison's Landing on the James. On the afternoon of June 26 the Seven Days' Battles opened.

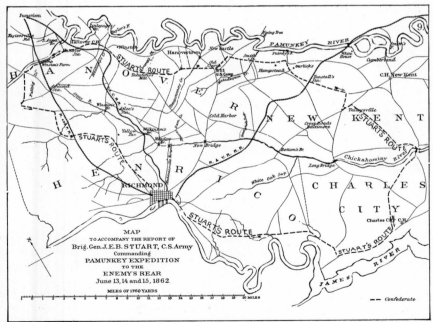

MAP
TO ACCOMPANY THE REPORT OF
Brig. Gen. J. E. B. STUART, C. S. Army
Commanding
PAMUNKEY EXPEDITION
TO THE
ENEMY'S REAR
June 13, 14 and 15, 1862

MILES OF 1760 YARDS

— — Confederate

98   Stuart's Route, redrawn from the *Atlas to Accompany the Official Records of the Union and Confederate Armies*, Washington

99   From the painting *The Rear Guard at White Oak Swamp*, by Julian Scott (1846–1901),
in the Union League Club, New York

THE SEVEN DAYS' BATTLES

LEE's plan of attack was marked by the audacity that characterized most of his maneuvers. Leaving the works in front of Richmond occupied by but a small force, he planned to envelop McClellan's right flank which lay north of the Chickahominy. Jackson had named the twenty-sixth as the day when his army from the Valley would be in readiness to attack. He was a day late however. As a result Lee made a bad start. McClellan did not attempt a decisive counter-attack. Had he ordered his right flank to hold Lee at any cost and thrown a strong force against Richmond, he could have marched into the city. Such a move would have been risky because Lee's attack was threatening to cut McClellan's communications with his base at White House. McClellan chose the conservative course. He withdrew his army with great skill toward the James and with equal skill effected a transfer of his base from White House to Harrison Landing. This latter operation involved driving some twenty-five hundred cattle across the Peninsula and taking a huge wagon train across. Lee was not able to interrupt either operation. Day after day, however, he attacked the retreating Federals, inflicting severe losses. When he found them drawn up at Malvern Hill in prepared positions and supported by a heavy concentration of artillery, he believed that the Union army was demoralized and that an assault would drive it from its position. The result was the bloody Battle of Malvern Hill in which the Confederates were repulsed with heavy losses. The names commonly given to the battles of the different days are, in order as follows: Beaver Dam or Mechanicsville, Gaines' Mill, Golding's Farm, White Oak Swamp, Savage's Station, Glendale, and Malvern Hill.

100   From the painting *Battle of Gaines' Mill*, by Prince de Joinville (1818–1900), in the United States Signal Corps,
War Department, Washington

STAFF WORK AT MALVERN HILL

THE Battle of Malvern Hill is an illustration of that lack of a proper staff which characterized both the Union and Confederate armies during the early years of the war. A staff officer is an assistant to the commander, charged with such duties as looking after the personnel of the unit, of getting information regarding the enemy, of aiding in formulating plans and seeing that they are carried out, and in looking after supply. The importance of a staff was not fully realized by the United States Army before the Civil War. At Malvern Hill Lee expected to mass his artillery in two great batteries at positions from which they could bring convergent and enfilade fire upon the Union batteries and lines of battle. Owing, however, to defects in the artillery organization and ignorance of the ground the artillery attack failed.

COMMENT ON THE CONFEDERATE PLAN

ABOUT noon of July 1 five Confederate divisions were in line near the base of Malvern Hill, most of them covered by woods. Two additional divisons were in reserve behind the Confederate right and one behind the left while still another division was well to the rear. D. H. Hill's division was in the front line second from the left, and on its right was Armistead's brigade of Magruder's division. After a long wait Hill with the other division commanders received the following attack order: "July 1st, 1862. General D. H. Hill:

101   Battle of Malvern Hill, from a sketch by William R. Waud, in *Frank Leslie's Illustrated Newspaper*, Aug. 2, 1862

Batteries have been established to act upon the enemy's line. If it is broken, as is probable, Armistead, who can witness the effect of the fire, has been ordered to charge with a yell. Do the same. R. H. Chilton, A. A. G." Colonel Henderson has commented: "The staff who considered . . . this order sufficient to ensure a combined attack in a wooded country must have been utterly incapable of directing the intricate movements devised by Lee to ensnare McClellan."

WHAT HAPPENED AT MALVERN HILL

GENERAL HILL observed that the Confederate artillery came up, a battery at a time, and was silenced almost as soon as it got into position. The contingency in the order was, therefore, not fulfilled. Hill sent a message to Stonewall Jackson, his corps commander, asking for instructions. Jackson replied, to advance when he heard shouting. Hill heard shouting in Armistead's brigade, perhaps due to the excitement of battle. Then Hill's division advanced alone. Jackson sent two divisions to Hill's assistance, but they were too late. Finally two other Confederate divisions assaulted and were repulsed. It was the worst kind of a piecemeal attack. The lack of proper coördination was due, in the first place, to the faulty attack order which violated almost every principle which should govern the formulation of such orders. The French observer, the Comte de Paris, has described the terrible price paid for the bungling of the attack. "Hill advanced alone against the Federal positions. . . . The woods skirting the foot of Malvern Hill had hitherto protected the Confederates, but as soon as they passed beyond the edge of the forest, they were received by a fire from all the batteries at once, some posted on the hill, others ranged midway, close to the Federal infantry. The latter joined its musketry fire to the cannonade when Hill's first line had come within range, and threw it back in disorder on the reserves. While it was re-forming, new Confederate battalions marched up to the assault in their

102   Battle of Malvern Hill — Confederates Repulsed by Union Artillery, from a sketch in *Harper's Weekly*, July 26, 1862

turn. . . . They try to pierce the line, sometimes at one point, sometimes at another . . . they are repulsed. The conflict is carried on with great fierceness on both sides, and, for a moment, it seems as if the Confederates are about to penetrate the very center of their adversaries and of the formidable artillery, which but now was dealing destruction in their ranks." Hill himself says: "Truly the courage of the soldiers was sublime! Battery after battery was in their hands for a few moments, only to be wrested away by fresh troops of the enemy. If one division could effect this much, what might have been done had the other nine coöperated with it!" — *Battles and Leaders of the Civil War*, 393–94, New York, 1888.

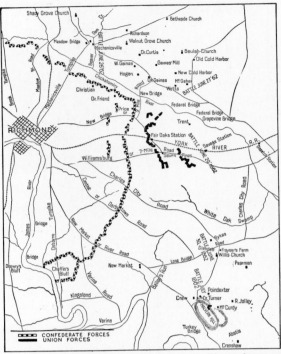

103 The Seven Days Battles, redrawn from *An Atlas to Accompany the Official Records of the Union and Confederate Armies*, Washington

CRITICISM OF THE SEVEN DAYS BATTLES

MAJOR MATTHEW FORNEY STEELE, former lecturer on military history at the Army Service Schools at Fort Leavenworth, has commented in part on the Seven Days Battles as follows: "In all the operations in the neighborhood of Richmond the plans of Johnston and Lee were bold and excellent. With a smaller army than their opponent's they did not hesitate to take the offensive; and their plans would have succeeded but for the inefficiency of their lieutenants. To be sure, Johnston lost a victory at Fair Oaks, partly by issuing a verbal instead of a written order, but mainly by Longstreet's mistakes and tardiness. . . . The first cause of Lee's failure to destroy McClellan's army was Jackson's tardiness on the 26th of June. Whatever excuses may be made for Jackson the fact stands that he failed to reach the ground on that day that he had agreed to reach; that Lee counted upon his reaching. He failed to turn the line behind Beaver Dam Creek and take it in reverse. . . . At Gaines' Mill Jackson was late, and he withdrew D. H. Hill's division from the battle at the critical moment; at Savage's Station Jackson did not arrive at all; and at White Oaks Swamp Creek, during the battle of Glendale, he made no apparent

effort to force a passage and get into the action. . . . In all these operations the 'Jackson of the Chickahominy' . . . was a different man from the 'Jackson of the Valley.' . . . On the part of the Federals it was a campaign of neglected opportunities. Perhaps McClellan's best opportunity fell to him on the day of Gaines' Mill. On that day Magruder with only twenty-five thousand men kept up a 'clatter' in front of Richmond; while McClellan had sixty thousand south of the Chickahominy, but made no effort to take the city. — *American Campaigns*, 215–16, The United States Infantry Association, Washington, 1922. "The credit of defeating the plan of McClellan must be awarded to Lee, who, as commander of the State forces of Virginia, ordered the construction of defenses at Yorktown in April, 1861; who, as directing general, assumed the responsibility of keeping Jackson and Ewell in western Virginia while McClellan and McDowell were threatening Richmond; and who, as commander of the Army of Northern Virginia, finally drove McClellan to the James River. He ran considerable risk in letting Jackson operate far from Richmond, but the events justified his conclusions that the moral effect of Jackson's movements on the authorities at Washington would warrant the risk. That Lee was not more successful in the Seven Days' battles must be attributed largely to Jackson's unexpected slowness in his operations during this week and to McClellan's foresight in preparing for his change of base to the James River." — COLONEL GUSTAV J. FIEBEGER, *Campaigns of the American Civil War*, 44, West Point, 1914.

104   Federal transports on the James River, from a photograph in the United States Signal Corps, War Department, Washington

LINCOLN AT THE HEIGHT OF THE SEVEN DAYS' BATTLES

As the news from the Chickahominy was flashed to Washington during those tense last days of June, 1862, the President became convinced that McClellan was suffering a terrible defeat. His reaction was characteristic of the man. When his hope had fled and before the news of Malvern Hill reached him, he sent Secretary Seward on a confidential mission to various state Governors. The written message which the Secretary carried ran, in part, as follows: "The evacuation of Corinth and our delay by the flood in Chickahominy have enabled the enemy to concentrate too much force in Richmond for McClellan. . . . Then let the country give us one hundred thousand new troops in the shortest possible time, which, added to McClellan, directly or indirectly, will take Richmond without endangering any other place which we now hold, and will substantially end the war. I expect to maintain this contest until successful, or till I die, or am conquered, or my term expires, or Congress or the country forsake me; and I would publicly appeal to

105 From the cartoon, *Another Federal Victory*, in Chatto and Whindus, *Cartoons*, London, 1874

the country for this new force were it not that I fear a general panic and stampede would follow, so hard it is to have a thing understood as it really is." — NATHANIEL WRIGHT STEPHENSON, *An Autobiography of Abraham Lincoln*, 297, 1926, used by special permission of the publishers, The Bobbs-Merrill Company. This document illustrated a fundamental weakness of the volunteer system. At a time of crisis when the President felt that the Federal fortunes were in a desperate plight, he dared not call for volunteers for fear of throwing the country into panic. Universal conscription, already in operation in the South, would have enabled him to call out immediately and quietly the number of men he needed.

LINCOLN AND McCLELLAN

ON July 9 Lincoln visited McClellan at Harrison's Landing to learn at first hand something of the conduct of the campaign. He no longer asked advice of McClellan. His temper and attitude were profoundly different from what they were in the conference with the generals on March 7 when the problem of the proper number of troops for the defense of Washington was under consideration. "The contrast in these two conferences cannot be over-emphasized. During the four months intervening Lincoln had passed through a transformation or something very near to that. The month of June is the turning point of his career. Some change in him was coming rapidly forward though just what the change was and how it was accomplished are matters of conjecture. The interview with Scott [in retirement at West Point on June 24, when Scott advised that the forces under Banks and Fremont were adequate to protect Washington, that those stationed at Fredericksburg were entirely out of position, and that a victory before Richmond would end the war] seems to form a crucial moment. It is to be noted that General Pope, who accompanied him to West Point, was placed in high command immediately upon their return. When Lincoln visited McClellan at Harrison's Landing all the timidity, the hesitation, that was conspicuous in him four months before had vanished.

106 Lincoln reviewing the Federal Army near Harrison's Landing, July 8, 1862, from a sketch by William Waud in *Frank Leslie's Illustrated Newspaper*, August 2, 1862

Previous to this time there is much in his attitude to life that is problematical. From this time forward there is very little. A great genius has found himself, has acquired confidence in himself, and henceforth will be master of his own house." — NATHANIEL WRIGHT STEPHENSON, *An Autobiography of Abraham Lincoln*, 301. In choosing Pope, however, the President erred grievously in judgment.

107   The Capitol Grounds at Harrisburg Turned into a Camp, from a sketch by Theodore R. Davis
in *Harper's Weekly*, Oct. 4, 1862

THE CALL FOR THREE HUNDRED THOUSAND MEN

LINCOLN's confidential message to the state Governors brought from the state executives support greater than he had anticipated. A further communication from the President to them expressed his satisfaction. "Fully concurring in the wisdom of the views expressed to me in so patriotic a manner by you . . . I have decided to call into the service an additional force of three hundred thousand men. I suggest and recommend that the troops should be chiefly of infantry." The spirit of the new volunteers was expressed in a song by James S. Gibbons published anonymously in *The Evening Post*, New York, which, when set to music, made an immediate and profound impression and was sung all over the country by thousands of men replying to Lincoln's call.

We are coming, Father Abraham, three hundred thousand more,
From Mississippi's winding stream and from New England's shore;
We leave our ploughs and workshops, our wives and children dear.
With hearts too full for utterance, with but a silent tear;
We dare not look behind us, but steadfastly before;
We are coming, Father Abraham, three hundred thousand more!

You have called us, and we're coming, by Richmond's bloody tide,
To lay us down, for Freedom's sake, our brothers' bones beside,
Or from foul treason's savage grasp to wrench the murderous blade,
And in the face of foreign foes its fragments to parade,
Six hundred thousand loyal men and true have gone before;
We are coming, Father Abraham, three hundred thousand more!

HALLECK IN COMMAND

Two days after the interview with McClellan the following order was sent General Halleck: "Ordered, That Major-General Henry W. Halleck be assigned to command the whole land-forces of the United States as general-in-chief and that he repair to this capital so soon as he can with safety to the positions and operations within the department now under his special charge." In a technical sense McClellan was not relieved of his command. His army was, however, taken from him to be merged with that of Pope. For the time being the defeated Federal officer was left without a command. Having lost confidence in McClellan's ability

108 Maj.-Gen. Henry Wager Halleck, 1815–72, from a photograph by Brady, in the United States Signal Corps, War Department, Washington

the President put the management of the Federal armies into the hands of Halleck, the only Federal officer charged with great responsibility whose command had been consistently successful in the fighting of 1862.

THE APPOINTMENT OF POPE

"JUST at the beginning of the Seven Days' Battles, President Lincoln had called from the West Major-General John Pope, and placed him in command of the three separate armies of Frémont and Banks, in the Valley of Virginia, and McDowell near Fredericksburg. The union of the three into one was a wise measure, but the selection of a commander was eminently unwise. One from the army in Virginia, other things being equal, would have possessed many advantages, and there was no lack of men of far sounder reputation than Pope had borne among his comrades in the old United States Army. . . . Pope arrived early in July and began to concentrate and organize his army. [Pope addressed his troops.]: — 'Let us understand each other. I come to you from the West where we have always seen the backs of our enemies; from an army whose business it has been to seek the adversary, and beat him when he was found; whose policy has been attack and not defence. . . . I presume I have been called here to pursue the same system, and to lead

109 Maj.-Gen. John Pope, 1822–92, from an ambrotype by Brady

you against the enemy. . . .' The arrogance of this address was not calculated to impress favorably officers of greater experience in actual warfare, who were now overslaughed by his promotion. McDowell would have been the fittest selection, but he and Banks, both senior to Pope, submitted without a word; as did also . . . all the Major-Generals of McClellan's army. But Frémont protested, asked to be relieved, and practically retired from active service." — ALEXANDER, *Military Memoirs of a Confederate*, 176–77, Charles Scribner's Sons, New York, 1907. Early in July Pope concentrated his army in Northern Virginia. By July 16 he had pushed his cavalry and a brigade of infantry forward and captured Culpeper on the main railroad from Alexandria to Charlottesville. Pope had a little more than fifty thousand men.

THE BEGINNING OF POPE'S CAMPAIGN

POPE hoped to advance south along the Alexandria-Charlottesville railroad, cross the Rapidan, capture the vital junction at Gordonsville and strike at Lee's communications south of the James. Lee, meanwhile, was held fast at Richmond watching McClellan who was still at Harrison's Landing. On learning of Pope's advance to Culpeper Lee hurried Jackson to Gordonsville. Pope was inactive during the last two weeks in July. He felt compelled to wait for the repair of the railroad as far south as Culpeper. He also wisely used his cavalry to make a thorough reconnaissance of the ground south of Fredericksburg and Culpeper and to locate the positions of the enemy. About August 1 the Washington authorities reached the decision to withdraw McClellan's army to Aquia Creek where it would be marched overland and joined with that of Pope. When the junction had been effected Halleck planned to assume command and lead this overwhelming force against the Confederates. The plan was sound although it involved the abandonment of an advanced position close to Richmond. The proper course of action for Pope while he was waiting for McClellan's troops was to have taken up a defensive position on the north bank of the Rappahannock where he could have threatened Richmond if Lee attempted to interfere with McClellan's withdrawal. Instead, the Union general on August 5 ordered his whole army to concentrate at Culpeper. He did this apparently because General Burnside who had been operating on the coast of the Carolinas was recalled and stationed at Falmouth at the mouth of the Rappahannock. This freed one of Pope's divisions and served to give a little protection to his left flank.

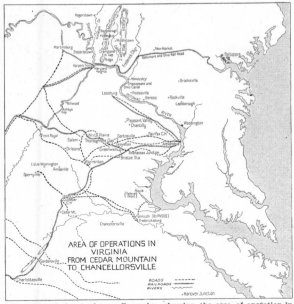

110 Map of the Antietam Campaign, showing the area of operation in Virginia from Cedar Mountain to Chancellorsville, drawn expressly for *The Pageant of America*

111   Battle of Cedar Mountain, Aug. 9, 1862, from a sketch by
A. R. Waud in *Harper's Weekly*, Aug. 30, 1862

THE BATTLE OF CEDAR MOUNTAIN

To concentrate at Culpeper Pope had to throw his army across the Rappahannock. While this maneuver, which began on August 7, was in progress the first detachments that arrived at Culpeper were in a dangerous position. As soon as Jackson at Gordonsville learned of Pope's movement he determined to strike and destroy the advance troops at Culpeper before the whole army could come up. The strategy was excellent but it was defeated by bad marching on the part of the Confederates. They had only twenty miles to advance to reach Culpeper. "But on the 8th, some little blunders and omissions in giving the orders to the three divisions of Jackson's army utterly confounded the march, and the head of the column only made eight miles, and the rear of it but two. . . . The whole incident shows that our staff service was poorly organized, and not efficient in its operations. The result of all this delay was that it was about 3 P.M. on the 9th before Ewell's division, and Winder's on the left, had formed line in front of Banks' corps, which had been encountered at Cedar Mountain, some seven miles south of Culpeper." — ALEXANDER, *Military Memoirs of a Confederate*, 180–81. Banks was covering the Federal concentration at Culpeper. Learning of Jackson's movement Banks boldly struck him, checked the Confederates until dark, and fell back on reinforcements who stopped Jackson's pursuit. After the failure of August 9 Jackson retired to Gordonsville. On August 12 the Army of the Potomac began a rapid march down the Peninsula to Fortress Monroe where transports were waiting to carry it to Aquia Creek. On August 13 Lee was sure that the pressure at Richmond had been relieved and he felt free to withdraw his troops. Two days later he was with Jackson at Gordonsville.

LEE'S PLAN

LEE had to act quickly for the uniting of the two Federal armies in Virginia would create a force that would heavily outnumber him. He had to defeat Pope at once. That general, lured on by Jackson's retirement after the battle of Cedar Mountain, had taken up a position on the north bank of the Rapidan. The Rappahannock, not easy to cross, was therefore in his rear. Pope's ill-advised position gave Lee such an opportunity as comes rarely in war, and he was quick to grasp it. He planned to turn Pope's left flank. Stuart with his cavalry was to cross the

112   The First Virginia Cavalry at a Halt, from a sketch by
A. R. Waud in *Harper's Weekly*, Sept. 27, 1862

Rapidan between Pope and Fredericksburg and to cut the railroads in the Federal rear. Meanwhile Longstreet was to crush the Federal left. Lee's plan was to put his army between that of Pope and Washington and overwhelm the Federal force before McClellan could unite with Pope. The orders were issued the day Lee reached Gordonsville. General Alexander who was with Lee's force through all this campaign has said that the Confederate army, "was not yet sufficiently well organized to be called a 'military machine,' or to be relied upon to carry out orders strictly." Two mistakes by subordinates foiled Lee's plan. General Stuart gave an order to one of his brigade commanders which was not sufficiently explicit with the result that Stuart's cavalry was not ready to open the action on the day that Lee had planned. When the night before Lee's original date for the attack Stuart discovered the absence of the brigade that had received the indefinite order from the point of rendezvous he sent his own adjutant-general, Major Fitzhugh, to search in the dark for the missing unit. Fitzhugh had in his pocket Lee's whole plan. He was the proper officer to carry this paper but he should have left it behind when dispatched on such a mission as that which Stuart gave him. He was captured by a Federal cavalry patrol. As a result Pope learned of the enterprise of his opponent and at once fell back behind the Rappahannock.

LEE'S STRATEGY

LEE estimated correctly that Pope would still expect an attack on the Federal left. The Confederates made a feint against it and threw Jackson against the Federal right. Jackson was stopped by a sudden freshet. On August 24 General Stuart handed Pope's dispatch book, and full copies of his correspondence to Lee. The capture was the result of a cavalry raid. Anxiously going through his opponent's files, Lee learned that the junction of the two armies of his enemy would begin in two days and be practically completed three days later, at which time Pope would command one hundred and thirty thousand men. There was not a moment to lose. Lee, having failed against his opponent's flanks, decided to attack his rear. Before dawn the following morning Jackson's "foot cavalry"

113 Jackson's Troops Pillaging Supplies at Manassas Junction, from *Battles and Leaders of the Civil War*, New York, 1888

was on the road in light marching order with orders to cover fifty miles at top speed, to make Manassas by a circuitous route, and to destroy Pope's base. Lee was playing a desperate game but he was not rash.

Lee had divided his army in front of an enemy who already outnumbered him. Pope's observers saw the gray column hurrying northward on the main road west of the Bull Run mountains and Pope tried to guess its destination. But he sent no cavalry to watch and follow it. He was surprised, therefore, to learn from a train crew which managed to escape that Jackson had reached Manassas on the morning of August 27, had taken what stores he could use, and had burned the great Federal depot there. Pope, undismayed, turned promptly to cut off his enemy's retreat.

THE SECOND MANASSAS

ON August 28 Jackson's movements were among his most brilliant and he succeeded in his object of confusing the Federals as to his exact whereabouts. The same was true of the morning of August 29. In the afternoon, however, Pope gained contact with Jackson and fought a battle with part of the Union force. The Federals were repulsed but the Confederates during the night withdrew to a previously selected position. This led Pope to think that Jackson's expected retreat had begun. At 3 P.M. on August 30 Pope with an army sadly lacking in cohesion because of the confused and hurried movements of the last few days advanced to

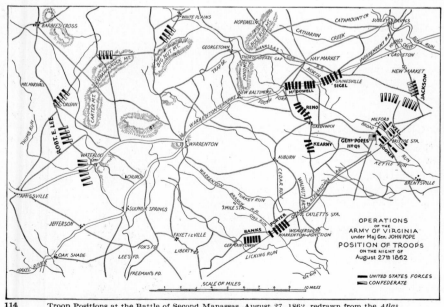

the assault on Jackson. Too late Pope discovered that he was facing Lee's entire reunited army. With movements swift and sure Lee turned Pope's left flank, got in his rear, and compelled him to seek safety behind Bull Run. On September 2 Lee threw Jackson against Pope's right wing. By this time the Federal army was so disorganized that Pope withdrew it within the defenses of Washington. Lee had brought one of his most dramatic campaigns to a successful conclusion.

114   Troop Positions at the Battle of Second Manassas, August 27, 1862, redrawn from the *Atlas to Accompany the Official Records of the Union and Confederate Armies*, Washington

115   Jackson's troop at Second Mansassas, from *Battles and Leaders of the Civil War*, New York, 1888

LEE'S ACCOMPLISHMENT

COLONEL FIEBEGER has commented concerning Pope that all "his orders were based on wrong hypotheses as to the position and intentions of Jackson, and as to the position of his own troops. This was due to the absence of Union cavalry in contact with Jackson, to the lack of a competent staff and intelligence bureau, and to his determination to adhere to his assumptions that Longstreet was still distant from the field and that Jackson was seeking to escape."

General Alexander has summed up Lee's accomplishment. "He had had the use of about eighty-five thousand men, and the enemy had had the use, in all, of fully two hundred thousand. At the beginning, the enemy had been within six miles of Richmond. He was now driven within the fortifications of Washington with a loss in the two campaigns of about thirty-three thousand men, eighty-two guns, and fifty-eight thousand small-arms." — ALEXANDER, *Military Memoirs of a Confederate*, 218. Lee's campaign against Pope was his best piece of offensive fighting. The coöperation between Lee and Jackson was perfect.

THE DEATH OF GENERAL PHILIP KEARNY

A LETTER of General Pickett's, dated July 15, 1862, gives an idea of the feeling which still persisted, in spite of war, between the officers of the old Regular Army. "The news came, too, this morning of the death of Kearny, one of the most brilliant generals of the Federal Army, a man whose fame as a soldier is world-wide. I knew him first in Mexico, where, as you know, he lost an arm in the siege of Mexico City. In Algeria he won the Cross of the Legion of Honor. He fought with the French in the Battles of Magenta and Solferino [in the Italian Wars of 1859] and received also from Napoleon Third the decoration of the Legion of Honor. I wish that we had taken him prisoner instead of shooting him. Marse Robert [General Lee], who was his old friend, sent his body to Pope under a flag of truce. I am glad he did that — poor old Kearny." — PICKETT, *The Heart of a Soldier*, 53.

116   General Philip Kearny, 1789–1862, from a photograph in the United States Signal Corps, War Department, Washington

BITTERNESS AFTER THE SECOND MANASSAS

"At the time I arrived in Alexandria, the greatest confusion prevailed, vast numbers of wounded had found their way back to Alexandria, and the hospitals were filled to overflowing. . . . The battlegrounds were occupied by the enemy, and access to our captured hospitals was in a general way cut off. Finally, Medical-Inspector Coolidge was allowed to pass within the enemy's lines,

117 Reception of Wounded Soldiers at Fortress Monroe, Virginia, from a sketch by J. H. Schell in *Frank Leslie's Illustrated Newspaper*, Aug. 16, 1862

with certain supplies. . . . Unfortunately, just at this time, a spirit of irritation existed among the Southern leaders, brought about possibly by unwise actions and orders of General Pope. The Confederate government had retaliated and issued orders, declaring that he or his commissioned officers were not entitled to be considered as prisoners of war, etc. The ordinary humane considerations as to the wounded were therefore unfortunately disturbed. . . . Our surgeons, it is true, had remained with their injured, but their medical supplies had been captured and largely used. In truth, one cannot blame the Confederate medical officers for laying hands on these hospital supplies, of which their own sick and wounded were so much in need. At last, by persistency and by personal influence, Medical-Inspector Coolidge did succeed in obtaining from the Southern commander an amelioration of the strictness of their order which for a while pressed so heavily upon our wounded of the 'Second Bull Run.'" — Major John H. Brinton, *Personal Memoirs of John H. Brinton*, 106–07, Neale Publishing Co., New York, 1914.

ALEXANDRIA AFTER THE SECOND MANASSAS

"It is almost impossible to convey an idea of the confusion and demoralization of everyone at or near Washington at that time. All had failed and defeat was everywhere; there seemed to be no one who could be trusted, no one who could make headway against our Southern enemy. From a military point of view there seemed to be little hope. And such odd things were being done. . . . The town of Alexandria at that time was in a most defenseless condition. At first the smallest force of the enemy could have captured it. Later the troops of General Franklin's division or corps arrived from the Army of the Potomac, and moved outwards on the Fairfax road. General McClellan's headquarters were for a short time in the town, and I saw something of the officers of his staff. There seemed then to be a very bitter feeling prevalent, antagonistic to General Pope, in fact, it almost appeared as if some were rather glad that he was being beaten, and there did not seem to be much activity in pushing forward to his assistance, nor much desire to do so . . . one morning a curious rumor passed around. It was that General Halleck had declared himself 'Dictator,' and that the army at Washington was satisfied that it should be so. As for those who were staying at Alexandria, or who were passing through, all seemed satisfied. I merely mention this idle rumor to show in what a state of doubt and want of confidence general opinion had lapsed. Halleck was often spoken of as the 'Tycoon,' but why, I cannot tell. He seemed big, he had a big head and a big hat, and was credited with brains." — Brinton, *Memoirs*, 196–97.

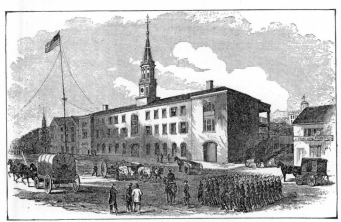

118 Town Hall and Market House, Alexandria, from a sketch in *Frank Leslie's Illustrated Newspaper*, Aug. 15. 1862

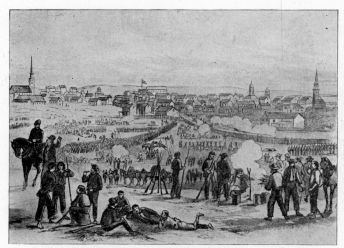

119   Hagerstown, Maryland, occupied by the Confederates, from a sketch by
       Theodore R. Davis in *Harper's Weekly*, Sept. 27, 1862

THE INVASION OF MARYLAND

ON September 2 Lee was reinforced and his army brought up to fifty-five thousand men. His success against Pope was not without disadvantages. "After the battle of the second Manassas, when the Federal Army had been driven into the intrenchments round Washington, the Confederate Army near Fairfax Court House was nearly one hundred and fifty miles from its base [Lee's line of communication at this time ran via Gordonsville to Richmond] and much further than that from the actual source of its supplies. The country around it within a compass of fifty miles had been stripped by both sides, and was wholly incapable of supporting an army. What was General Lee to do? His army could not be maintained where it was, and even if it could have remained there, as it was not possible to make a direct attack upon Washington, there was nothing to prevent the enemy as soon as he could recover from the present disasters from repeating General McClellan's plan and sending such a force by water to Richmond as must have taken General Lee back immediately to the place from which he set out on his Northern campaign. If he had returned to the line of the Rapidan after the second battle of Manassas, so as to place himself within reach of his base at Richmond, or if he had taken up the position that he assumed later in the season at Fredericksburg, his only alternative to an advance, what would have been the result? Such action on his part would have been taken as an admission that he was really unable to put Washington in serious danger, or to cross the Potomac river, and had no policy but to await such attacks as the Federals might make. . . . I must say again that General Lee's policy [in invading Maryland] was not to capture any portion of Federal territory, but to protract the war by breaking up the enemy's campaigns and so bringing about the pecuniary exhaustion of the North. At the same time he desired to increase the power of resistance of the South by keeping the enemy out of the Confederate territory." — SIR FREDERICK MAURICE, EDITOR, *An Aide-de-Camp of Lee*, 144–46, Little, Brown & Company, Boston, 1927.

LEE'S DECISION TO INVADE MARYLAND

ON September 3 Lee wrote to President Davis: "After the enemy had disappeared from the vicinity of Fairfax Court House and taken the road to Alexandria and Washington, I did not think it would be advantageous to follow him further. I had no intention of attacking him in his fortifications, and am not prepared to invest them. If I possessed the necessary munitions I should be unable to provide provisions for the troops. I therefore determined, while threatening the approaches to Washington, to draw the troops into Loudoun [county], where forage and some provisions can be obtained, menace their possession of the Shenandoah Valley, and, if found practicable, to cross into Maryland. The army is not properly equipped for an invasion of an enemy's territory. It lacks much of the material of war, is feeble in transportation, the animals being much reduced, and the men are poorly provided with clothes, and in thousands of instances are destitute of shoes. Still, we cannot afford to be idle, and, though weaker than our opponents in men and military equipments, must endeavor to harass them if we cannot destroy them. I am aware that the movement is attended with much risk, yet I do not consider success impossible, and shall endeavour to guard it from loss." — MAURICE, EDITOR, *An Aide-de-Camp of Lee*, 151. The problem of supply, therefore, played an important part in his decision to invade Maryland.

120   The Confederate Army Crossing the Fords of the Potomac,
       from *Harper's Weekly*, Sept. 27, 1862

LEE IN MARYLAND

On September 4 the population of Leesburg, Virginia, saw the columns of the Confederate army cross the Potomac, which formed the northern boundary of the Confederacy. Lee concentrated his army at Frederick and kept Stuart's cavalry as a screen between himself and Washington. The invasion of Maryland caused necessarily a change in Lee's line of supplies. They were now brought up through the Shenandoah Valley. Lee lived, to be sure, off the country, but the region could not supply his needs. The Federal force which still held Harper's Ferry menaced the Confederate communications. Lee had been disappointed in his justifiable expecta-

121   Harper's Ferry, from a photograph by Gardner, Washington

tion that it would retire when he put his army between it and Washington. His first task was, therefore, to take Harper's Ferry. On September 9 he decided to leave Frederick and retire west of South Mountain. He sent the greater part of his army under Stonewall Jackson to invest and take Harper's Ferry. The remainder, under Longstreet, was ordered to Hagerstown to intercept a detachment of Federal troops that were reported moving to the aid of Harper's Ferry from Chambersburg. The Confederate army was, therefore, widely scattered. After the fall of Harper's Ferry, it was to be concentrated either at Boonesboro or at Hagerstown.

McCLELLAN AGAIN IN COMMAND

When the Union troops withdrew into the defenses of Washington after the second Manassas, Lincoln directed Halleck to organize an army to take the field. Halleck gave this task to McClellan; Pope was assigned to duty in the West. About September 7 McClellan took personal command. With troops at his disposal which numbered some ninety-seven thousand, nearly twice as many as Lee commanded, McClellan advanced slowly and cautiously in the direction of the enemy. On September 13 McClellan had in his possession a copy of the order which Lee had given to Jackson and Longstreet for their respective operations. It had been found by chance by a Union soldier as it lay on a street in Frederick wrapped about three fragrant Virginia cigars. Great destinies sometimes turn on trifling things. The famous "Lost Order" was Order No. 191 and was dated September 9. Lee's staff wrote out three copies of it. One went to Longstreet who after he had read it chewed it up. A second went to Stonewall Jackson who pinned it to the inside of his coat. The third copy was intended for D. H. Hill who, having recently come up from Richmond, was not as yet attached definitely either to Jackson's or Longstreet's command. Jackson, however, assumed that Hill was under his orders and wrote out a copy of the order which he sent to Hill and which Hill received and produced as evidence after the war. The copy from Lee's headquarters that was destined for Hill was the one that was lost. Evidence that has recently come to light seems to demonstrate conclusively that Lee was unaware that McClellan had gained possession of the order until long after the Battle of Antietam.

122 General McClellan entering Frederick, Maryland, from a sketch by Thomas Nast (1840–1902), in *Harper's Weekly*, Oct. 4, 1862

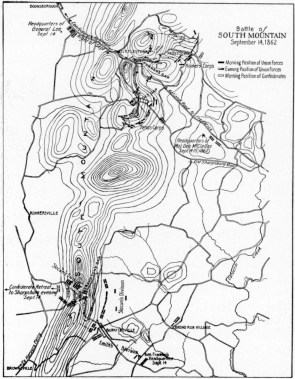

123   Battle of South Mountain, redrawn from the *Atlas to Accompany the Official Records of the Union and Confederate Armies*, Washington

FORCING SOUTH MOUNTAIN

LEE had not intended to fight a battle at South Mountain. His plan was to maneuver, avoiding a battle or accepting one only on his own terms. For the time being he was handicapped by the necessity of taking Harper's Ferry. McClellan's steady advance to Frederick caused Lee to decide on the very day that McClellan was reading Order No. 191 to establish a guard at the passes across South Mountain until Jackson could take Harper's Ferry. Then Lee would continue his policy of drawing his adversary as far from Washington as possible. The National Road (see Volume IV, p. 53) crossed South Mountain at Turner's Gap, a mile south of which was Fox's Gap through which passed the old Sharpsburg road. Five miles farther south is Crampton's Gap through which runs a road from Frederick to Harper's Ferry. On September 13 Lee sent D. H. Hill to help the cavalry hold Turner's Gap. On the afternoon of the same day McClellan, after reading the lost order, sent Burnside, who commanded the Federal right wing, early on September 14 to march with four corps on Boonesborough near the west end of Turner's Gap. During the forenoon of the fourteenth Lee learned of this movement and sent orders to Longstreet at Hagerstown to hurry to the aid of Hill at Turner's Gap. Longstreet arrived

late in the afternoon. Burnside did not make his main attack until five on this same afternoon. Then he assaulted and drove back the Confederates whom he outnumbered. That night Longstreet and Hill withdrew through Boonesborough. A strong Federal force sent against Crampton's Gap forced it also on the afternoon of September 14. On the morning of September 15 McClellan was in a position to put his army across South Mountain. The forcing of South Mountain was a decisive event in the campaign. Lee, unaware that his enemy knew his plans, apparently did not expect such immediate and vigorous action from his opponent. On

this same forenoon Harper's Ferry with its garrison of twelve thousand five hundred men was surrendered without waiting for a Confederate assault. Lee, therefore, on the eve of the Battle of Antietam was able to concentrate his army. A military court of investigation later found the Federal commander at Harper's Ferry incompetent. Had Harper's Ferry held a day or two longer, McClellan in all probability would have been able to catch Lee with his army seriously divided.

124   Battle of September 14 — The Confederates Driven from the Blue Ridge Pass, from a sketch by F. H. Schell in *Frank Leslie's Illustrated Newspaper*, Oct. 4, 1862

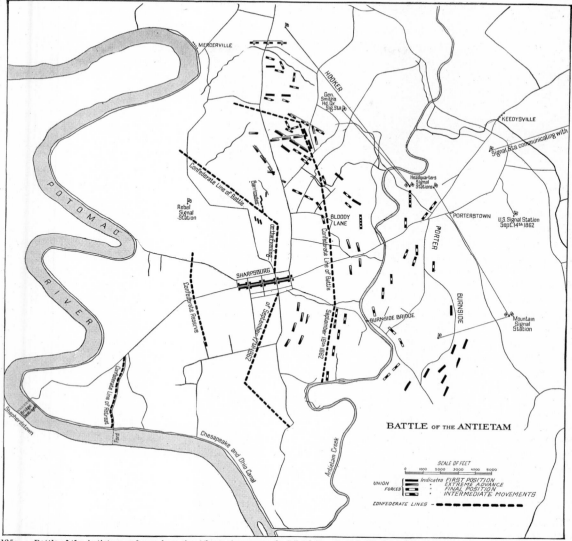

BATTLE of the ANTIETAM

125   Battle of the Antietam, redrawn from the *Atlas to Accompany the Official Records of the Union and Confederate Armies*, Washington

THE BATTLE OF THE ANTIETAM

On September 15 McClellan crossed South Mountain. The next day was spent in disposing of the Federal
army for attack. On September 17 was fought one of the bloodiest battles of the war. McClellan's general
plan was a frontal assault against the Confederate flanks and center. Major Steele has commented on the
tactics of the battle. "In the first place, no adequate reconnaissance was made to find out the position occupied by the Confederates; where the Antietam creek could be forded, etc. When the attack was made it
was made piecemeal; in fact there were five separate and distinct attacks by detachments, instead of one
single attack by the whole army with a general reserve held back to throw in at the critical moment. Strategically Lee's position in this battle was as bad as it could be. . . . The wages of defeat ought to have been
destruction. . . . McClellan claims to have defeated Lee in the battle; but it is hard to say which should
reflect least credit upon the Union commander, not to have defeated Lee's army or not to have destroyed it
if he defeated it. Truth to tell, McClellan did neither." — *American Campaigns*, 279–81. At the end of
the fighting of September 17 Lee's army remained on the field. On the next day both armies held their lines
though McClellan had eighty-seven thousand effectives as against less than forty thousand available for his
opponent. On the night of September 18 Lee crossed the Potomac without interference by McClellan.
The Confederate invasion had ended.

126   Burnside's troops at the Battle of Antietam, from a sketch in *Frank Leslie's Illustrated Newspaper*, Oct. 25, 1862

ANTIETAM AS SEEN BY A FEDERAL PRIVATE

"WE were getting ready now for the charge proper, but were still lying on our faces. . . . The discreet [Confederate] regiment behind the fence was silent. Now and then a bullet from them cut the air over our heads, but generally they were reserving their fire for that better shot which they knew they would get in a few minutes. The battery, however, whose shots at first went over our heads, had depressed its guns so as to shave the surface of the ground. Its fire was beginning to tell. I remember looking behind and seeing an officer riding diagonally across the field — a most inviting target. . . . While my eye was on him I saw, between me and him, a rolled overcoat with its straps on bound into the air and fall among the furrows. One of the enemy's grape-shot had plowed a groove in the skull of a young fellow and had cut his overcoat from his shoulders. He never stirred from his position, but lay there face downward — a dreadful spectacle. A moment after, I heard a man cursing a comrade for lying on him heavily. He was cursing a dying man. As the range grew better, the firing became more rapid, the situation desperate and exasperating to the last degree. Human nature was on the rack, and there burst forth from it the most vehement, terrible swearing I have ever heard. Certainly the joy of conflict was not ours that day. The suspense was only for a moment, however, for the order to charge came just after. Whether the regiment was thrown into disorder or not, I never knew. I only remember that as we rose and started all the fire that had been held back so long was loosed. In a second the air was full of the hiss of bullets and the hurtle of grape-shot. The mental strain was so great that I saw at that moment the singular effect mentioned, I think, in the life of Goethe on a similar occasion — the whole landscape for an instant turned slightly red. . . . We heard all through the war that the army 'was eager to be led against the enemy.' It must have been so for truthful correspondents said so, and editors confirmed it. But when you came to hunt for this particular itch, it was always the next regiment that had it. The truth is, when bullets are whacking against tree-trunks and solid shot are cracking skulls like egg-shells, the consuming passion in the breast of the average man is to get out of the way." — D. L. THOMPSON, *Battles and Leaders*, Vol. II, 661–62, Century Co., New York, 1888.

THE SOUTHERN SOLDIERS

"UNJUST criticism has been passed upon the Confederate soldiers in the Maryland campaign, based principally upon the great number of absentees. To those who have spent their lives near the ranks of soldiers and learned from experience that there is a limit to physical endurance, explanation is not called for; to those who look upon the soldier as a machine, not even needing oil to facilitate motive power, I will say, try to put yourselves in the soldiers' places. Another point to be noted was, that in the Confederate ranks were thousands of soldiers who had been wounded once, twice, and in some instances three times, who in any other service would have been on the pension-rolls at their comfortable homes. Sickness and weakness that creep into an army from irregular food, collected in the stress of march, were no trifling impediments to the maintainance of our ranks in vigorous form." — GENERAL JAMES LONGSTREET, *From Manassas to Appomattox*, p. 288, J. B. Lippincott Co., Philadelphia, 1896.

127   Confederate Prisoners and Deserters at the Guard-House, from a sketch by William R. Waud in *Frank Leslie's Illustrated Newspaper*, Mar. 15, 1864

128   Battle of Antietam, The Centre and Right Wing of McClellan's Army Engaged, from a sketch by Edwin Forbes in *Frank Leslie's Illustrated Newspaper*, Oct. 11, 1862

CRITICISM OF THE BATTLE OF ANTIETAM

"NEVER perhaps has any commander had a more favorable opportunity to win a decisive victory than had McClellan at Antietam. He had a full day to study the situation and rest his army and a full day in which to fight his battle. In front of him in an unfortified position was a force largely inferior to his own. Of the nine infantry divisions of Lee's army, one was far from the field and five others had just reached it after long and exhausting marches which must have reduced their numerical strength. At Lee's back was a wide and barely fordable river. That McClellan did not win a victory that would have rendered the surrender of Harper's Ferry a trifling incident was due to the fact that he held nearly one third of his infantry in reserve and sent his remaining troops into the battle in succession without adequate support. His cavalry, which might have been employed against Stuart, was not engaged. Lee on the contrary had no reserves. Every brigade of infantry and cavalry on the field was in the front line. His defense was greatly aided by his artillery which was well posted and well served. It will always be a marvel to military men that Lee was willing to accept battle under such adverse conditions. It is possible that he believed the Union troops were so demoralized by the preceding campaigns that he had a chance of winning a battle north of the Potomac which would bring to his army recruits from Maryland and strengthen the Confederate cause abroad." — FIEBEGER, *Campaigns of the American Civil War*, 75–76.

THE COMMENT OF GENERAL MAURICE

"THE loss of the campaign, so far as the Confederate army was concerned, was not due to any defect in the conception of it, but to an unforeseen accident, the loss of the order. . . . The one criticism of Lee's conduct of this campaign which Marshall did not foresee and therefore did not meet, was that Lee might have recrossed the Potomac on September 16, and so returned to Virginia with the prestige of the capture of Harper's Ferry, and have avoided the bloody, and for his purpose useless, battle of Sharpsburg. . . . It is generally said, in explanation of Lee's action, that having invaded Maryland he did not want to retreat without a fight, because to do so would affect the morale of his troops. But as Colonel Marshall says, and as his own statements show, he did not enter Maryland with the object of fighting a pitched battle, and that explanation does not therefore seem adequate. It is more probable that he wanted to gain time for the repair of

the railway bridges over the Rapidan and the Rappahannock, as he feared that if he reëntered Virginia before those bridges were restored he would have to fall back a long way to obtain supplies. The supply situation of the Confederate army is the key to the whole campaign." — MAURICE, 161–62.

129   Battle of Antietam, Burnside's Division, from a sketch by Edwin Forbes in *Frank Leslie's Illustrated Newspaper*, Oct. 11, 1862

130   Stonewall Jackson at Antietam, from a drawing by Sidney Riesenberg
in *Harper's Weekly*, Jan. 27, 1912

MEADE'S COMMENT ON ANTIETAM

GENERAL MEADE was a corps commander at Antietam. A letter to his wife dated September 20, 1862, gives an insight into the point of view of the Federal high command directly after that terrible engagement. "The battle of the day previous had been a very severe one, and our army was a good deal broken and somewhat demoralized — so much so that it was deemed hazardous to risk an offensive movement on our part until reinforcements arriving from Washington should reach the scene of action. . . . Whether the country will be satisfied with this or not I cannot say, but it ought to be, as I am free to confess I feared at one time the movement from Washington was a dangerous one, for if we were defeated and this army broken up, the country was gone. Now, if there is any common sense in the country, it ought to let us have time to reorganize and get into shape our new lines, and then advance with such overwhelming numbers that resistance on the part of the enemy would be useless. My command took a great many prisoners. They all concurred in saying that the Southern army was dispirited; that the great bulk were tired of the war and of fighting, and would be glad of any settlement that would terminate it. They were ragged, shoeless and half starved, and were certainly in a most pitiable condition." — G. G. MEADE, *Life and Letters of George Gordon Meade*, Vol. I, 311, Charles Scribner's Sons, New York, 1913.

THE AFTERMATH OF ANTIETAM

DURING the first three weeks of October, 1862, Lee and McClellan rested and watched each other on opposite sides of the Potomac. Lincoln urged McClellan to pursue vigorously but that general pleaded the excuse that his army must be reorganized and reëquipped. In October Stuart made a second raid about McClellan's whole force, doing little damage but gaining the information that Lee desired. Near the end of October McClellan finally crossed the Potomac and advanced into Virginia. By this time, however, Lincoln's confidence in him was gone. On November 7 he was relieved of the command of the Army of the Potomac and was never again assigned to active duty. The President was convinced that the war could not be won under McClellan's military leadership.

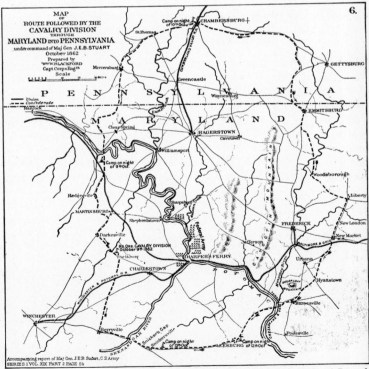

131   Map snowing the Route of Stuart's Cavalry Division through Maryland and Pennsylvania, from the *Atlas to Accompany the Official Records of the Union and Confederate Armies*, Washington

132   McClellan takes Leave of his Army, from a sketch by Theodore R. Davis in *Harper's Weekly*, Nov. 29, 1862

McCLELLAN'S FAREWELL, NOVEMBER 11, 1862

LATE at night on November 7, General C. P. Buckingham handed McClellan the Government's orders putting Burnside in his place. With all his faults in action McClellan was a very brave man, a good organizer, and a sympathetic father to his men, who warmly returned his affection with great personal devotion. There was one tense moment at the last farewell, when two thousand men broke ranks, uncoupled his car, and wildly cursed the Government. But McClellan stepped out on the front platform and nobly ended his very short farewell by asking all ranks to "stand by General Burnside as you have stood by me." On this the men recoupled his car and, with one long, mournful cheer, let his train pull out.

133   General Robert E. Lee, 1807–70, from a photograph by Brady, in the United States Signal Corps, War Department, Washington

LEE, THE FATHER

A PERSONAL bereavement that occurred a little more than a month after the Battle of Antietam gives an opportunity for a glimpse into the inner life of the man who led the Confederate armies. On October 26, 1862, he wrote to Mrs. Lee about the death of their daughter: "I cannot express the anguish I feel at the death of our sweet Annie. To know that I shall never see her again on earth, that her place in our circle, which I always hoped one day to enjoy, is forever vacant, is agonizing in the extreme. But God in this, as in all things, has mingled mercy with the blow in selecting that one best prepared to leave us. May you be able to join me in saying, 'His will be done!' When I reflect on all she will escape in life, brief and painful, at the best, and in all we may hope she will enjoy with her sainted grandmother, I cannot wish her back. I know how much you will grieve, and how much she will be mourned. I wish I could give you any comfort, but beyond our hope in the great mercy of God, and the belief that he takes her at the time and place when it is best for her to go, there is none. May that same mercy be extended to us all, and may we be prepared for His summons."
— JONES, *Life and Letters of Robert Edward Lee*, 198.

134   General McClellan surrendering the command of the Army of the Potomac to General Burnside, from a drawing by A. R. Waud in *Harper's Weekly*, November 22, 1862

BURNSIDE IN COMMAND

On November 7 General Burnside was elevated to the command of the Army of the Potomac. "The designation of Burnside to succeed McClellan was a great surprise to old army circles, both in the Federal and Confederate armies; and was, perhaps, an unpleasant one to Burnside himself. He was popular but was not generally esteemed as a general. He had commanded a brigade at Bull Run, but had in no way risen above, even if he reached, the average of the brigade commanders. He had later had the luck to command the expedition to the North Carolina Sounds, where his overwhelming force easily overcame the slight resistance that it met. This gained him the prestige, in newspapers and political circles, of successful independent command. As a commander of a corps, he was one of the four next in line for promotion — Burnside, Hooker, Sumner, and Franklin. The older officers dreaded Hooker's appointment. By many he was thought utterly unfit, though a brave man and a hard fighter. Moved by the wishes of his friends, Burnside was brought to accept the command rather than see it go to Hooker. . . . Burnside began his campaign with a blunder. He adopted Richmond as his objective, instead of Lee's army. The latter was within a day's march of him, and its wings were separated by two days' march. Here was an opportunity for a skilful commander, but Burnside decided to make Fredericksburg a base, and to move thence upon Richmond. On November 15, he turned his back upon Lee and marched for Fredericksburg." — Alexander, *Military Memoirs of a Confederate*, 283–84.

THE BATTLE FORMATION OF THE CIVIL WAR

To understand the Battle of Fredericksburg and its terrible losses it is necessary to know something of the peculiarities of the battle formation used in the Civil War. The organization at Fredericksburg was no different from that at Malvern Hill or Antietam. It was typical of the fighting of the times. The infantry organization was based on a regiment of ten companies. The number of privates in the latter might vary from sixty-four to eighty-two. A brigade was formed of two or more regiments. Several regiments were used in the later years when casualties had greatly reduced the size of these organizations. An infantry division consisted of from two to four brigades. In forming for an attack the usual method was the formation of the brigade in line of masses. Each regiment formed a mass with a two company front. Translated into non-technical language this meant that a regiment marched into battle with its ten companies advancing two abreast making a double column of five companies each. The regiments on either side advanced in the same formation. Eight paces was the normal distance between a company and the one in front of it while three paces was the normal interval between it and the next company abreast. The interval between regiments was about twenty-five paces. An assault, therefore, was a charge by men in dense, close-order formation. If the leading companies melted away before the artillery and musketry fire, the organizations in rear still carried on until they achieved their objective or were thrown back. When such tactical methods are understood the reasons for the frightful losses of the Civil War in spite of the fact that the artillery was still primitive and there were no machine guns become clear. The battle formation described was better adapted to a bayonet charge than to a fire fight.

135   Army of the Potomac — Bartlett's Brigade of Warren's Corps — Charging the Enemy, from a sketch in *Harper's Weekly*, May 28, 1864

ON THE EVE OF FREDERICKSBURG

THE interval between Antietam and Gettysburg had seen a marked change in both the Federal and Confederate armies. Burnside's force had been reorganized and increased to one hundred and eighteen thousand men and three hundred and seventy-four guns. He had fifty-one brigades of infantry and four of cavalry. Lee's army had been increased to seventy-eight thousand men, and two hundred and

136   Fredericksburg, Va., from a photograph by T. H. O'Sullivan and A. Gardner, Washington

fifty-five guns. Lee had forty-one brigades of infantry and three of cavalry. The increase in Lee's force was due in part to the recovery of a great number of stragglers who had been lost in the rapid advance into Maryland. By November 19 Burnside's army was in the neighborhood of Fredericksburg. At that time he could

137 Confederate Works at Marye's Heights, Fredericksburg, from a photograph in the United States Signal Corps, War Department, Washington

have taken and held the town with little opposition, as Lee had not yet concentrated in front of him. Burnside did not advance south of the Rappahannock because of a delay in the arrival of the pontoons which had been used to take that army across the Potomac. Because of this difficulty Burnside permitted Lee to take up a good defensive position south of the river. Like McClellan at Yorktown he robbed his campaign of the element of surprise. On December 9 Burnside decided to attack Lee and two days later six pontoon bridges were thrown across the river. On December 13 the attack began.

THE BATTLE OF FREDERICKSBURG

THE Battle of Fredericksburg must always remain an outstanding example of the unnecessary waste of human life which results from incompetent leadership. Fredericksburg was a frontal assault against an enemy skilfully posted in a terrain favorable for the defense. Lee's line was some six and a half miles long.

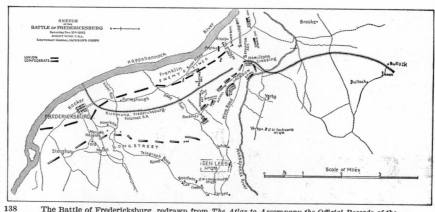

138   The Battle of Fredericksburg, redrawn from *The Atlas to Accompany the Official Records of the Union and Confederate Armies*, Washington

Burnside attempted to turn neither the right nor the left of his enemy's position. He had no scheme of maneuver in any real sense. The attack resolved itself into fourteen desperate, unsupported, successive assaults against the strongest point in Lee's line on the edge of the plateau known as Marye's Heights. Five miles away on the Confederate right another desperate assault was made. Here Meade made a penetration but was thrown back by Jackson's reserve. There was practically no fighting along a great part of the line and large numbers of the troops scarcely fired a shot. When night fell more than ten thousand Union soldiers had been killed or wounded while Lee lost but half as many. Burnside planned to renew the assault the following morning but his officers dissuaded him. Two days later he recrossed the Rappahannock. The Fredericksburg campaign was a failure and a deep gloom settled over the North.

139   Laying Pontoon Bridges Under Fire at Fredericksburg, from an artotype in *Prang's War Pictures* of the painting by T. de Thulstrup (1848–). © L. Prang & Co., Boston

THE IRISH AT FREDERICKSBURG

FROM the field at Fredericksburg Pickett, now a major-general, wrote with a heart full of emotion: "If war . . . is a necessity — and I suppose it is — it is a very cruel one. Your Soldier's heart almost stood still as he watched those sons of Erin fearlessly rush to their death. The brilliant assault on Marye's Heights of their Irish Brigade was beyond description. Why, we forgot they were fighting us, and cheer after cheer at their fearlessness went up all along our lines. About fifty of my division sleep their last sleep at the foot of Marye's Heights. I can't help feeling sorry for Old Burnside — proud, plucky, hard-headed old dog. I always liked him, but I loved little Mac [McClellan], and it was a godsend to the Confederacy that he was relieved." — PICKETT, *The Heart of a Soldier,* 65–66.

BURNSIDE AND LINCOLN

BURNSIDE was a gentleman if not a great commander. His preliminary report to Halleck of the defeat is a remarkable military document. "To the brave officers and soldiers who accomplished the feat of thus re-crossing in the face of the enemy, I owe everything; for the failure in the attack I am responsible, as the extreme gallantry, courage, and endurance shown by them were never

140   Battery D, 5th United States Artillery in Action at Fredericksburg, from a photograph by Sullivan and Gardner, Washington

exceeded, and would have carried the point had it been possible." Lincoln saw this dispatch and made a public reply to the army: "The courage with which you, in an open field, maintained the contest against an intrenched foe, and the consummate skill and success with which you crossed and recrossed the river,

141   Confederate dead behind a stone wall at Fredericksburg, from a photograph in the United States Signal Corps, War Department, Washington

in face of the enemy, show that you possess all the qualities of a great army, which will yet give victory to the cause of the country and of popular government." — TOWNSEND, *Anecdotes of the Civil War,* 85–86. Lincoln's message had not a suggestion of his anguish of spirit. Four days before he sent it he had become aware of the efforts of a cabal of Republican Senators to force out his cabinet and reconstitute it under the influence of Chase. On this day the President exclaimed: "We are on the brink of destruction. It appears to me that the Almighty is against us and I can hardly see a ray of hope." — STEPHENSON, *An Autobiography of Abraham Lincoln.*

CHAPTER III

THE MISSISSIPPI VALLEY, 1862 AND 1863

WEST of the barrier of the Appalachian mountains lay the broad and fertile valley of the Mississippi. Here for the most part the settlements were younger than those on the Atlantic coast. Arkansas and Texas were not far removed from the frontier stage. In these vigorous communities the primitive agricultural methods of slavery had not yet worn out the soil. Much of the strength of the Confederacy lay in the West. From this region came food and men. The Confederate West, moreover, bordered on Mexico, through which nation were smuggled quantities of stores from Europe which the Federal blockade excluded from southern ports. No railroad, however, reached westward from the Mississippi. But lines connected the Mississippi valley with the eastern states. The most important ran from Memphis through Corinth in northern Mississippi, Chattanooga in eastern Tennessee, to Lynchburg and Petersburg in Virginia. At Chattanooga this trunk line connected with the railway system of Georgia and southern Alabama. Let this line be cut anywhere and the Army of Northern Virginia would suffer a handicap. The fall of Chattanooga would be a disaster. When the Federal commanders in operating west of the mountains studied their maps, their eyes ran naturally to the railroad junctions, particularly to those at Corinth and Chattanooga. Even more obvious than these junctions, however, was the great Mississippi.

When the blight of the Civil War fell upon it, the steamboat traffic of the Mississippi was at its height. The evolution of the river steamboat, progressing with a swiftness born of great profits, had resulted in the production of a craft capable at the same time of making great speed and carrying heavy loads. The people of southern Illinois, Indiana, and Ohio still thought in terms of steamboats, and still looked to New Orleans as the natural port from which to export their products. Chicago had been connected with the Atlantic seaboard by railroad for only a few years. The organization of the Confederacy gave the control of the lower Mississippi into the hands of what would be a foreign nation if the South should be successful in the war. As at the end of the eighteenth century the frontier folk of Kentucky and Tennessee felt a bitter resentment at the Spanish control of New Orleans and demanded free navigation of the Mississippi, so the people of the Middle West in the Civil War made the demand that the Father of Waters be reconquered. At the outset of the war, therefore, the two great objectives of the armed forces of the North were the capture of Richmond and the opening of the Mississippi. The conquest of the Father of Waters required the coöperation of the army and navy, a fact which necessarily increased the difficulties in the way of solving the problem. In 1862 the task was begun and advanced well toward completion. In that year, so full of stirring events in Virginia, both army and navy won dramatic successes in the Mississippi valley.

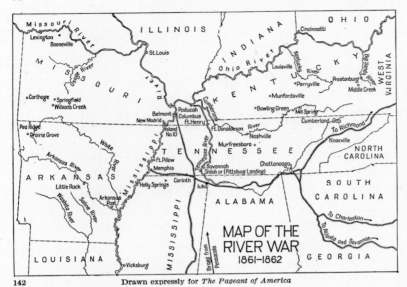

MAP OF THE RIVER WAR 1861-1862

142   Drawn expressly for *The Pageant of America*

THE CONFEDERATE LINE OF DEFENSE, JANUARY, 1862

IN January, 1862, the Confederate Government was planning to defend the Mississippi Valley country with troops divided into two departments. Department No. 1 embraced the state of Louisiana. Here General Lovell with seven thousand men was charged with the defense of New Orleans and the lower reaches of the river. Department No. 2 embraced the states of Tennessee, Arkansas, and the southern parts of Kentucky and Missouri. Here General Albert Sidney Johnston with some sixty-two thousand men sought to prevent invasion from the North. In addition to these two departments General Braxton Bragg with thirteen thousand men commanded the Department of Western Florida and Southern Alabama. His mission was the defense of Pensacola and Mobile. Far to the west General Hebert commanded the Department of Texas with three thousand men. At the same time Generals Price and Thompson were operating in the Department of Southern Missouri with eight thousand men. The first of these department commanders to come into serious collision with the enemy was General Johnston. In January, 1862, his right lay at the famous Cumberland Gap through which the Wilderness road had once run (see volumes II, and IV, 52). Johnston had fortified this important pass which was the natural route for an invasion of the valley of eastern Tennessee where Union sympathisers were in a majority. Farther to the west near the important road center at Somerset, Kentucky, General Crittenden was stationed with a small force to protect the upper waters of the Cumberland River. Johnston himself with a considerable force lay at the railroad junction at Bowling Green. Two forts, Henry and Donelson, within supporting distance of each other had been established to prevent the Federals from ascending the Tennessee and Cumberland rivers. Johnston's left lay on the Mississippi where Polk commanded at Columbus, Kentucky, and where Island Number Ten had been strongly fortified. A second line of defense on the Mississippi was Fort Pillow in western Tennessee.

THE BEGINNING OF OPERATIONS IN THE WEST

OPPOSING Johnston were two Federal department commanders. General Buell with some seventy-two thousand men commanded the Department of Ohio which comprised the states of Ohio, Indiana, Michigan, and Kentucky east of the Cumberland River. General Halleck with about ninety-one thousand men commanded the Department of Missouri which comprised the states along both banks of the Mississippi together with Arkansas and Kentucky west of the Cumberland River. The campaign in the West opened when General Thomas of Buell's army attacked Crittenden on January 19 at Logan Crossroads and drove him back to Mill Spring. Thomas promptly invested this place and Crittenden retreated precipitately in the night, abandoning his stores and artillery. Crittenden was severely criticized for his defeat, and General Kirby Smith was sent from the Army of Northern Virginia to attempt to repair the breach that Thomas had made in the Confederate line of defense.

143   Battle of Mill Spring, from a sketch in *Frank Leslie's Illustrated Newspaper*, Feb. 8, 1862

THE FALL OF FORT HENRY

By January, 1862, Grant, a brigadier-general, had won the confidence of Halleck. On the thirtieth of this month he received permission from his superior to attempt the capture of Fort Henry on the Tennessee in coöperation with Flag-officer Andrew H. Foote. The fort stood on the east bank of the river and was a closed fieldwork mounting seventeen

144   Bombardment of Fort Henry, from a sketch by Henri Loire in *Frank Leslie's Illustrated Newspaper*, Mar. 1, 1862

guns. It was on low ground near the river bank and on the day of the battle was partly under water. Immediately behind it on higher ground was an intrenched camp, the fortifications of which were not completed. General Tilghman with about a hundred artillerymen commanded at Fort Henry. With four ironclads and three other gunboats Foote ascended the Tennessee, skillfully avoided the drifting Confederate

145   Rear-Admiral Andrew Hull Foote 1806–63, from a photograph in the United States Signal Corps, War Department, Washington

torpedoes, and, on February 6, bombarded the Confederate fortification. The plan was that the bombardment should cover the landing of troops which would invest the fort. Foote was much stronger than his adversary in artillery power. As a result Tilghman, seeing that he could accomplish nothing, surrendered the fort and its surviving garrison. Immediately after the fall of Fort Henry, Foote hastened up the Tennessee destroying the railroad bridge a little above the fort and all the Confederate gunboats as far as the Alabama border. Meanwhile Grant was securing the stores captured at the fort and was preparing to march overland against Fort Donelson.

FORT DONELSON

THE fall of Fort Henry was a heavy blow to Johnston who decided, immediately he heard the news, to withdraw from Bowling Green to the neighborhood of Nashville on the southern bank of the Cumberland. He planned that Fort Donelson should hold at least until this movement was completed, to prevent Federal gunboats from interfering with it. He therefore reinforced Donelson, bringing up its strength to seventeen thousand men commanded by General Floyd. Donelson was a formidable fortification. It was a large inclosed fieldwork built on a high bluff overlooking the Cumberland. "An intrenched camp, of which the fort was the citadel, extended a mile along the river and three-fourths of a mile inland. The camp inclosed the town of Dover on the Cumberland. Except on the downstream side, where it was limited by an unfordable stream, the camp was inclosed by an almost continuous line of standing trenches of strong profile with good positions for artillery in and behind the line. The total length of the line to be defended was about four thousand yards. The river was commanded by an embrasure battery of heavy guns having a command of thirty feet. There was no bridge over the river; when the land front was fully invested there was no means of escape for the garrison except by boat." — FIEBEGER, *Campaigns of the American Civil War*, 91–92. On February 12 Foote's vanship, the *Carondelet*, fired the first shot. Meanwhile Grant's troops, slightly outnumbering the Confederates, were moving on the fort. The investment began on the next day.

146   Fortifications at Fort Donelson, from a contemporary photograph in the L. C. Handy Collection, Washington

147   From a painting *The Battle of Fort Donelson*, by Paul Phillopotaux.
       © O. R. Griffin, Lowell, Mass., 1914

SURRENDER

On February 14, when Grant's investment was complete, Foote attacked the river batteries. So terrible was the plunging fire from Donelson, however, that Foote was repulsed and had to withdraw for repairs. He had planned to get above the fort and cut off the Confederate retreat by boat. His defeat left this exit still open. At this point Floyd decided to abandon Donelson. His scheme of maneuver was to push back Grant's right flank which extended to the Cumberland and so open a road by which he could retire up the river. He began the execution of this plan on the morning of February 15. Pillow was in command of the troops who delivered the main blow. By noon he had accomplished his mission, driven back the Federal right, and opened the road up the river. Pillow at this point estimated that he had beaten the Federals so badly that there was no longer any need to retreat. Instead of escaping with the major part of the garrison he sent part of his troops to assist in the fighting in other parts of the fort. In the afternoon Grant by able use of his troops drove Pillow back into the fort and again closed the line of investment. That night Floyd turned over the command to Pillow and fled, using two boats. Pillow after telling Colonel Forrest to take his cavalry out by a flooded road turned the command over to Buckner and followed the example of Floyd. On February 16 Buckner surrendered unconditionally.

148   The Surrender at Fort Donelson, from a sketch by Henri Loire in *Frank Leslie's Illustrated Newspaper*, Mar. 15, 1862

THE AFTERMATH OF DONELSON

"Scarcely had the retreat [of Johnston] to Nashville been accomplished, when the news of the fall of Donelson was received. The state of feeling which it produced [in the South] is described by Colonel Munford, an aide-de-camp of General Johnston, in an address delivered in Memphis. 'Dissatisfaction was general. Its mutterings, already heard, began to break out in denunciations. The demagogues took up the cry, and hounded on one another and the people in hunting down a victim. The public press was loaded with abuse. The Government was denounced for intrusting the public safety to hands so feeble. . . . The Senators and Representatives from Tennessee, with the exception of Judge Swann, waited upon the President.' Their spokesman, Senator G. A. Henry, stated that they came for and in behalf of Tennessee to ask for the removal of General A. S. Johnston, and the assignment of a competent officer to the defense of their homes and people. . . . Painfully impressed by this exhibition of distrust toward an officer, whose place, if vacated, I was sure could not be filled by his equal, realizing how necessary public confidence was to success, and wounded by the injustice done to one I had known with close intimacy in peace and in war, and believed to be one of the noblest men with whom I had ever been associated, and one of the ablest soldiers I had ever seen in the field, I paused under conflicting emotions, and after a time merely answered, 'If Sidney Johnston is not a general, the Confederacy has none to give you.'" — Jefferson Davis, *Rise and Fall of the Confederate Government*, 37–38, D. Appleton & Company, New York, 1912.

THE OPENING OF THE CORINTH CAMPAIGN

BUELL had followed Johnston in his retreat to Nashville. Johnston retired to Murfreesboro and by the end of February the Federals controlled the capital of Tennessee. Meanwhile Halleck was following up the victory at Donelson by an advance up the Tennessee River. General C. F. Smith had charge of this and on March 5 he established an advanced base at Savannah on the east bank of the Tennessee River. Six days later, while Halleck was busy getting his expedition under way, McClellan was relieved as com-

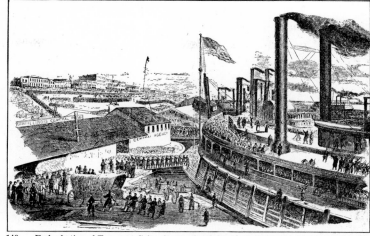

149   Embarkation of Troops at Cairo, from a sketch by Alexander Simplot in *Harper's Weekly*, Feb. 1, 1862

mander in chief and a new Department of Mississippi was created which included everything from the meridian of Knoxville, Tennessee, to the Great Plains. Halleck was given command of this, which brought Buell under his orders. On March 16 Halleck instructed Buell to move his army as rapidly as possible to Savannah. At this time Grant was at Fort Henry in charge of forwarding supplies to Savannah and W. T. Sherman was in command of the base at Paducah. Meanwhile news had come that the Federal General Curtis had defeated a superior Confederate force under Van Dorn at Pea Ridge in northwestern Arkansas on March 7 and 8, and that the Confederates, abandoning western Arkansas, were falling back to the defense of the Mississippi River (see map, No. 142).

150   General Earl Van Dorn, 1820–63, from a photograph in the possession of H. P. Cook, Richmond

THE EVE OF SHILOH

THE last two weeks in March were busy ones on the Tennessee River. Transports and freight boats were hurrying troops and supplies southward to Savannah. Soon the discovery was made that Pittsburg Landing seven miles south of Savannah was better suited to the needs of the Federals and the army was concentrated at that point. On March 17 Grant, now a major-general, was directed to resume command at the front, taking the place of Smith who fell ill. He made his headquarters at Savannah to be in closer contact with the disposition of supplies. At Pittsburg Landing the Federal encampment was not protected by trenches and only the routine outposts were established. Grant assumed that his force was overwhelmingly greater than any in the immediate vicinity and that the Confederates would wait at Corinth for an attack. He was not disturbed, therefore, to learn that Buell had been held up by floods in the Duck River and was not able to resume the march until March 29 on which day ninety miles still lay between his force and Savannah. On the same day McClellan was on Chesapeake Bay on his way to inaugurate the Peninsular Campaign. A little more than a week later Island Number Ten, the last position of Johnston's original line of defense, was destined to fall.

151   Railroad Yards in Western Tennessee, from a photograph in The Army War College, Washington

152   General Albert Sidney Johnston, 1803–62,
from a photograph by Cook, Richmond, in
the possession of H. P. Cook, Richmond

JOHNSTON AT CORINTH

MEANWHILE Johnston was executing a brilliant maneuver. Already Bragg had been ordered to evacuate Pensacola and go to Johnston's aid while Lovell in Louisiana had been ordered to send a part of his small force northward. By April 1 Johnston had concentrated his army at Corinth without arousing the suspicions of Grant. On the night of April 4 the Army of the Mississippi bivouacked at Mickey Crossroads. Six miles away Grant's army, ignorant of the enemy's concentration so near it, lay in camp. On this day a detachment from Sherman's brigade came into contact with enemy cavalry. Sherman reported this on April 5 but did not infer from the incident that an attack was impending.

THE BATTLE OF SHILOH

APRIL 5 was used by the Confederates in advancing about three miles and disposing their troops for the attack. At three A.M. the next morning a patrol of three companies was ordered to the front of Prentiss' Federal division. At five this patrol ran into a Confederate outpost. Sherman and Prentiss received, therefore, sufficient warning to form their brigades close to their camps. Johnston had, however, surprised his enemy. When the battle opened Grant was at Savannah to look after the receiving of Buell's troops and did not reach the field until the engagement had been in progress for about an hour and a half. His army was caught without a prearranged plan of defense, without intrenchments, and without a directing head. As a consequence Johnston drove the Federals from position to position. A part of the Federal left made a determined stand during most of the afternoon at a place known as "the hornet's nest." This force was finally practically surrounded and some two thousand men were captured before the position was given up. The affair at "the hornet's nest" so disorganized the Confederate army that Beauregard ordered the attack to cease at six. Johnston had been killed at two-thirty. The morale of Grant and his army had been sustained during this trying afternoon by the knowledge that Buell's troops would be available for the fighting of the next day. Grant also expected to have the use of General Lew Wallace's division which had been absent at the beginning of the battle and arrived at the end of the day. On April 7 Grant, reinforced by Buell's Army of the Ohio, began the attack at seven-thirty. The Confederates were driven back and at two in the afternoon gave up the fight and retired to Corinth. The Federals were so exhausted by forced marches, by the night movements of the sixth and the battle of the seventh that they were unable to pursue.

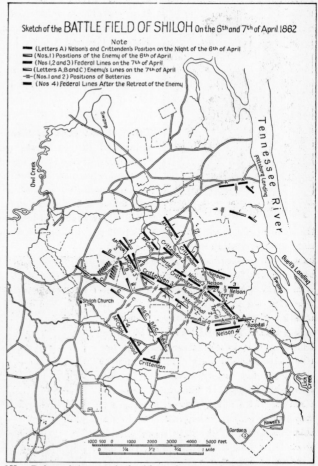

Sketch of the BATTLE FIELD OF SHILOH On the 6th and 7th of April 1862

Note

▬ (Letters A) Nelson's and Crittenden's Position on the Night of the 6th of April
▬ (Nos.1) Positions of the Enemy of the 6th of April
▬ (Nos 1,2 and 3) Federal Lines on the 7th of April
▬ (Letters A,B and C) Enemy's Lines on the 7th of April
▬ (Nos.1 and 2) Positions of Batteries
▬ (Nos 4) Federal Lines After the Retreat of the Enemy

153   Redrawn from a map in the *Atlas to Accompany the Official Records
of the Union and Confederate Armies*, Washington

A SOLDIER AT THE BATTLE OF SHILOH

"SUNDAY, 6th — The long roll sounded about half-past seven in the morning, and at once we formed a line of battle on the regimental parade ground. At about 8 o'clock we were ordered to the front, and marching out in battle line, about one-half mile, we met the rebels at Water Oaks Pond. . . . The rebels came up on our right, compelling us to fall back about eighty yards to our second position, where

154   From an artotype in *Prang's War Pictures*, after the painting *The Battle of Shiloh*, by Thure de Thulstrup. © Prang, 1887

we remained until we were again flanked when we fell back to within one hundred yards of our parade ground, where we lay down on the brow of a hill awaiting the approach of the rebels in front. While in this position, Thomas Hains of Company E took off his hat, placed it upon his ramrod, and holding it up, shouted to the boys along the line to see what a close call he had had while out in front, for a minie ball had passed through the creased crown of his hat making four holes. Before he could get his hat back on his head, a small shell burst over us and mortally wounded him. By this time the rebels were marching right oblique, just in front of us, in double line of battle with their two stands of colors flying. By order we waited until we could look them in the eye and then rose up and fired a volley at close range into their ranks, throwing them into great confusion. We then made a bayonet charge, capturing one of their standards. . . . In this charge Company E met its greatest loss of the day. . . ." — O. B. CLARK, *Downing's Civil War Diary*, 40–41.

GENERAL POPE

GRANT's advance toward Corinth was only one phase of Halleck's campaign to open up the Mississippi. While Grant was operating in the neighborhood of Donelson, Halleck recalled Pope from central Missouri and ordered him to mobilize a corps on the western bank of the Mississippi and attack New Madrid, Missouri. The fortification of this area had been begun in the preceding summer with the result that New Madrid and Island Number Ten had been developed into strong defensive positions. The Confederates attached great importance to the position for it was the left flank of Johnston's original line. When Pope was ready to begin active operations in this region the Confederate land batteries on both sides of the Mississippi contained some thirty heavy guns with nearly twenty more on Island Number Ten. An auxiliary defense was a flotilla of small gunboats. General McCown commanded the works.

155   Attack on Island Number Ten by Commodore Foote's Flotilla, from a sketch in
Harper's Weekly, Apr. 5, 1862

156   Gun and Mortar Boats on the Mississippi at the Bombardment of Island Number Ten, from an engraving by W. Ridgway after a drawing by C. Parsons, in possession of the publishers

THE ATTACK ON NEW MADRID

POPE, after studying the situation which confronted him, concluded that the most practicable way to take the place was by regular siege operations. On March 13 when his siege guns had been brought up and put in place Pope began his bombardment. Coöperating with him was Foote whose armored gunboats and mortar boats bombarded Island Number Ten and the shore batteries above New Madrid. McCown feared that he would be isolated and on the night of March 13 withdrew the garrisons from the fortifications at New Madrid across the river to the peninsula. The Confederates were off the west bank of the Mississippi. This action caused him to be relieved, General Mackall taking his place.

THE FALL OF ISLAND NUMBER TEN

THE capture of New Madrid marked the end of the first phase of Pope's operations. His next step was to get his force across the Mississippi south of Island Number Ten and turn the defenses of that place. Pope's transports were on the Mississippi above the fortified area. To get them below Island Number Ten the Federals cut a channel across the narrow neck of the ox-bow at the end of which was Island Number Ten. The channel was completed on April 4, the day that Johnston moved out of Corinth to attack Grant. On the same day the *Carondelet* ran the gauntlet of the Confederate batteries on Island Number Ten. On her exposed side was a barge containing coal and closely packed hay. Hoses were attached to her boilers to scald boarders. Going at full speed through a thunder storm as well as a terrific bombardment from the Confederate batteries she reached New Madrid by midnight. Two days later another armored gunboat came down. The two boats, aided by shore batteries which Pope had established, assisted the transports in taking Pope's force across the Mississippi. Four regiments were put over the river. Marching to Tiptonville they cut off the Confederate line of retreat. Then Mackall surrendered. Foote and Pope had opened the Mississippi as far as Fort Pillow. Pope was about to undertake the reduction of this fort when he was ordered by Halleck to unite with Grant and Buell in an advance on Corinth.

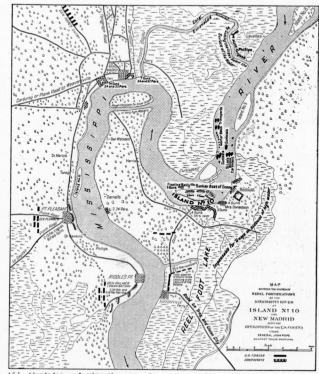

157   Confederate fortifications at Island Number Ten, redrawn from the *Atlas to Accompany the Official Records of the Union and Confederate Armies*, Washington

158   The 39th Ohio Regiment Embarking for Island Number Ten, from a lithograph in the Prints Division,
Library of Congress, Washington

THE CAPTURE OF CORINTH

In April Halleck took command in person of the army that he was assembling in the vicinity of Shiloh. When near the end of the month he began to move, he had a force of ninety thousand men which was increased to one hundred thousand before the campaign ended. Thomas commanded his right wing, Buell his center, and Pope his left wing. Grant was second in command. To oppose Halleck Beauregard had been able to concentrate sixty-six thousand men. So great was the importance of Corinth that the Confederates had turned it into an intrenched camp. They were determined to hold it if possible, for its fall meant that Fort Pillow and Memphis must also be abandoned. Halleck moved with extreme caution. He ordered his generals to intrench themselves daily. As a result he consumed a month in advancing a few miles but he gave his adversary no opportunity to attack. Beauregard realized that Corinth must fall. On the night of May 29, when Pope was within three miles of his line of retreat, Beauregard slipped quietly out of Corinth and took the road for Meridian. Pope was immediately ordered to follow him. On June 11 when the Confederates had retired well into Mississippi, the pursuit was abandoned. In it Colonel Philip Sheridan of the Second Michigan Cavalry distinguished himself. Following the evacuation of Corinth both Fort Pillow and Memphis were abandoned. The Mississippi was opened as far as Vicksburg which Beauregard had ordered fortified.

159   The Naval Battle before Memphis, June 6, 1862, from a sketch by Alexander Simplot in *Harper's Weekly*, June 26, 1862

160   Federal Schooners off Forts Jackson and St. Philip, from a sketch by William R. Waud, in *Frank Leslie's Illustrated Newspaper*, May 24, 1862

THE CAMPAIGN AGAINST NEW ORLEANS

WHILE Halleck was concentrating his army near Shiloh for the final advance against Corinth, Farragut was taking New Orleans. Gustavus Fox, Assistant Secretary of the Navy, conceived the plan which was approved by Secretary Welles and the President. Fox had several motives. The Federal navy, though undergoing rapid expansion, was as yet too small to maintain an effective blockade of the long and irregular coast line of the Confederacy. The capture of the greatest and most famous seaport of the South would prevent its use as a smuggling center and would free many Federal ships for service elsewhere. Such a capture would have, moreover, a profound moral effect in the North, in the Confederacy, and upon European nations. And, finally, it would greatly advance the project of securing control of the Mississippi River. After much consultation the enterprise was entrusted to Farragut, who had been in the naval service since the War of 1812. Fox planned that the expedition should run past the two forts, Jackson and St. Philip, which guarded the approach to New Orleans six miles below the city. He had been persuaded, however, to add a flotilla of mortar boats to the fleet which should bombard the forts before the attempt was made to pass them. Farragut entered into the execution of Fox's plan with enthusiasm but had little faith in the mortar boats. In April Farragut was off the mouth of the Mississippi. With him were twenty-four wooden vessels and gunboats carrying about two hundred guns and nineteen mortar boats each carrying a single thirteen-inch mortar. The flagship *Hartford* was a fine example of the warship built in the transition period between sail and steam. She was constructed in 1858 with full sail area and with auxiliary steam, making eight knots an hour. She carried what was then the very powerful battery of twenty-two nine-inch Dahlgren shell guns.

161   The flagship *Hartford* attacked by the ram *Manassas* and a fire raft, from a sketch in *Harper's Weekly*, June 14, 1862

162   Gustavus Vasa Fox, 1821–83, from a photograph in the Navy Department, Washington

163   Victorious National Fleet commanding the Surrender of New Orleans, from a sketch by William R. Waud in *Frank Leslie's Illustrated Newspaper*, May 24, 1862

THE BEGINNING OF THE ATTACK

ON April 18 the mortar boats began the bombardment of the forts. For two days shells were hurled upon Jackson and St. Philip without conclusive results. Farragut had given the mortars a trial; he now planned to run the forts. Many among his commanders did not agree with the wisdom of his course. It was new to naval tactics. For three days more the mortars pounded the forts while Farragut and his men completed their preparations for the impending struggle. "In the afternoon [of April 23]," wrote Farragut, "I visited every ship in order to know positively that each commander understood my orders for the attack

164   Farragut's Flagship *Hartford*, from the painting by E. Arnold in the United States National Museum

and see that all was in readiness. I had looked to their efficiency before. Everyone appeared to understand their orders well and looked forward to the conflict with firmness but with anxiety. . . . At about five minutes of 2 A.M. April 24 signal was made to get under way." Before Farragut moved to the attack one of his gunboats under the direction of Captain Bell had broken the chain which the defenders had slung on hulks across the river. Farragut went through the gap in double column under an intense cross fire from the forts which were but a thousand yards apart.

THE *HARTFORD* AGROUND

THE Confederates fought desperately with every resource at their disposal. They sent terrifying fire rafts against the Federal ships and attacked them with rams. The climax of the battle came when the *Hartford*, which was leading the way, ran aground in an effort to dodge a blazing raft. The then Lieutenant Kautz of the *Hartford* has told what followed. "No sooner had Farragut given the order, 'Hard-a-port,' than the current gave the ship a broad sheer, and her bows went hard up on a mud bank. As the fire-raft came against the port side of the ship, it became enveloped in flames. We were so near to the shore that from the bowsprit we could reach the tops of the bushes, and such a short distance above Fort St. Philip that we could dis-

tinctly hear the gunners in the casements give their orders; and as they saw Farragut's flag at the mizzen, by the bright light, they fired with frightful rapidity. Fortunately they did not make sufficient allowance for our close proximity, and the iron hail passed over our bulwarks, doing but little damage. . . . For a moment it looked as though the flagship was indeed doomed, but the firemen were called away. . . . As I crossed from the starboard to the port side of the deck, I passed close to Farragut, who, as he looked forward and took in the situation, clasped his hands high in the air, and exclaimed, 'My God, is it to end in this way!' Fortunately it was not to end . . . the sheet of flame succumbed to a sheet of water. . . . As the flames died away the engines were backed 'hard'. . . . The ship was again free. . . ."
— *Battles and Leaders of the Civil War*, 64.

165   Sketch Map of the forts at New Orleans, from Greeley, *The American Conflict*, Hartford, 1864–67

166   Panoramic View of New Orleans, with the National Fleet at Anchor,
         from *Frank Leslie's Illustrated Newspaper*, May 24, 1862

PANORAMA OF THE FLEET AND NEW ORLEANS, APRIL 25–28, 1862

THE battered fleet at last fought its way up-stream, where it was quickly joined by Butler's troops, which had been landed near the scene of action thus cutting off all communication down from New Orleans. The forts, completely isolated, surrendered. Meanwhile Farragut reached New Orleans on the twenty-fifth, and easily turned its defenses, which had been contrived only against an army, not a fleet; and the forts surrendered on the twenty-eighth. "The conquest of New Orleans and of its defenses . . . was wholly the work of the United States Navy," commented Admiral Mahan at a later time, "it was a triumph won over formidable difficulties by a mobile force, skillfully directed and gallantly fought." It made a profound impression in France and England where New Orleans was well known. Farragut's blow made Napoleon III waver in his desire to recognize the Confederacy, and it stayed the hand of Palmerston who had in mind joint action on the part of England and France to break the Federal blockade.

167   Captain Theodorus Bailey, 1805–77,
         from a photograph by Brady

CAPTAIN THEODORUS BAILEY

FARRAGUT'S second-in-command, Bailey, having led the line of attack in the *Cayuga* past the forts, now had the perilous honor of summoning New Orleans to surrender. He and Lieutenant Perkins landed there with a simple boat's crew. Carrying a flag of truce, these two naval officers then walked alone straight to the City Hall through a howling mob threatening their lives at every turn. Having delivered their message they returned unscathed. On May 1 Farragut turned over the command of the city to Butler who quickly occupied it with troops.

168   Maj.-Gen. Benjamin F. Butler, 1818–93, from an engraving by G. E. Perine after a photograph

BATON ROUGE, MAY AND AUGUST, 1862

FARRAGUT took Baton Rouge on his way up to Vicksburg, whither he was ordered to go by the Government, in spite of the uselessness of such a move, and of the risk and loss involved. Out of the Yazoo River came the Confederate ram *Arkansas*, fighting the *Carondelet*, and running through the fleet which lay in dangerously shoaling waters, till she stood clear for Baton Rouge. But her engines gave out, and her own crew destroyed her. The Confederates, however, still resolved to win back Baton Rouge. They attacked on August 5; but were repulsed.

169   The Battle of Baton Rouge, from a sketch in *Harper's Weekly*, Sept. 6, 1862

THE FIRST AMERICAN ADMIRAL

On July 16, 1862, four officers were commissioned as rear-admirals, the first time that that rank had ever been given in the United States Navy. Of these Farragut was the senior; so he may be fairly called the first of American admirals. On August 20 he arrived at Pensacola, where he hoisted his rear-admiral's flag as commander in chief in the Gulf.

170   Rear-Admiral David G. Farragut, 1801–70, from a photograph by Brady

OPERATIONS AFTER THE FALL OF CORINTH

While Farragut was still operating on the Mississippi above New Orleans, Halleck was reaching a decision as to the best solution for the problems pre-

171   The Guarded Capitol at Nashville, from a photograph by Brady, in the United States Signal Corps, War Department, Washington

sented by the situation in the West. His capture of Corinth and clearing of the Mississippi to Vicksburg were achievements of major importance. The whole of Tennessee west of the mountains was in his hands. This success won him his promotion as commander in chief at Washington. Halleck had conquered territory and had cut the main railroad connecting the Mississippi valley with Virginia. He had not, however, accomplished that most important object, the destruction of his adversary's army. Important as were his successes Halleck was not a great general. He was fortunate in his subordinates. With Corinth in his possession Halleck gave up the offensive and planned to strengthen the Federal grip on Tennessee. He distributed his army along the Memphis-Chattanooga railroad. Grant and Rosecrans were to hold the part west of Decatur and Buell the portion east of that point. Buell, moreover, was to capture Chattanooga. Halleck assumed that holding this vital railroad would keep the Confederate army in Mississippi and Alabama. Buell did not concur in all the judgments of his chief. He recommended the transfer of his army to Nashville which meant the abandonment of the eastern part of the Memphis-Chattanooga railroad (see map, No. 142). Nashville was the natural base for operations against Chattanooga. Buell, however, was overruled and kept in a position so far south that he found it impossible to protect his line of communications. As the campaign in eastern Tennessee and Kentucky developed, Grant's force in western Tennessee was depleted to reinforce Buell with the result that Grant was forced to remain on the defensive during the late summer and early autumn of 1862.

GENERAL BRAGG

When Buell had joined Grant at Pittsburg Landing in April on the eve of the Battle of Shiloh, he had left one small force in eastern Kentucky and another in central Tennessee. Across the mountains in the valley of the Tennessee River Kirby Smith was in command of an army of about ten thousand men. In June, shortly after the Confederate evacuation of Corinth, Buell's detached force in central Tennessee threatened Chattanooga, compelling Kirby Smith to concentrate his troops for the defense of the place. As a result the Federal troops in Kentucky took Cumberland Gap which they promptly fortified. Their purpose was to prevent an army in the Tennessee valley from invading Kentucky through this important pass. Meanwhile in June Beauregard was relieved of his command because of illness and Bragg took his place. Bragg decided to concentrate at Chattanooga, to take the offensive, and to force Buell to abandon Tennessee.

172   General Braxton Bragg, 1817–76, from a photograph by H. P. Cook, Richmond

173   Confederate Cavalry Attack a Federal Supply Train, from *Campfire and Battlefield*,
Desmond Publishing Co., Boston, 1896

MORGAN AND FORREST

WHILE Bragg was carrying out his concentration at Chattanooga two brilliant Confederate
cavalry raids alarmed the North and threw
Buell's plans into confusion. On July 4 Colonel
John H. Morgan with about eight hundred men
left Knoxville, Tennessee, made his way through
the Kentucky mountains, and swept through
the central and eastern part of the state. When
he slipped back into the mountain fastnesses
whence he had come, soon after July 22, he left
three of Buell's supply depots in ruins. The
moral effect of Morgan's raid was tremendous
for it occurred just after the Seven Days' Battles
in front of Richmond when Lee had driven

174   The Raid in Kentucky, from a sketch by Henri Loire in *Frank
Leslie's Illustrated Newspaper*, Aug. 16, 1862

McClellan back to the James River and brought the Peninsular Campaign to an end. While Morgan was
bringing terror to the small Federal detachments in Kentucky, Colonel
Nathan B. Forrest was operating in Tennessee. On July 9 with about
one thousand five hundred mounted men he slipped out of Chattanooga,
and surprised and captured a thousand men at McMinnville whose
mission was to guard the supply depot at Murfreesboro. Surprise can
always be avoided and reflects on the military capacity of the troops
concerned. The capture of the McMinnville detachment and the
resulting destruction of Buell's depot at Murfreesboro are examples
of how the plans of commanding officers are sometimes affected by failures of subordinates. On July 19 Forrest was off again from McMinnville and this time destroyed some important railroad bridges south
of Nashville interrupting thereby for seven days one of Buell's main
lines of communications and making it difficult for him to supply two
of his divisions. The Federal cavalry could not oppose these raids for
it was scattered in small detachments guarding vital lines of communications. The events of July demonstrated Halleck's lack of judgment in
requiring Buell to hold the Memphis-Chattanooga railroad.

175   General John H. Morgan, 1826–64, from
an engraving in the Prints Division, Library
of Congress, Washington

THE PLANS OF BUELL AND BRAGG

On July 11 Halleck was ordered to Washington (see page 56) leaving Buell in central Tennessee and Grant in the western part of the state in independent commands. Buell knew that Bragg was concentrating at Chattanooga and prepared to meet him. The Federal army remained on the defensive, disposed on a line, McMinnville-Decherd-Bridgeport. Buell assumed that his adversary would emerge from Chattanooga and attack one of these positions. In this assumption he proved to be in error.

176   Buell's Army Crossing Salt River, Kentucky, from a sketch by H. Mosler in *Harper's Weekly*, Oct. 25, 1862

Bragg planned, while completing his own concentration at Chattanooga, to send Kirby Smith into central Kentucky. In due course he would follow by a different route.

177   Battle of Champion Hills, Mississippi, from *Campfire and Battlefield*, Desmond Publishing Co., Boston, 1896

178   Buell's Army entering Louisville, from a sketch by H. Mosler in *Harper's Weekly*, Oct. 18, 1862

BRAGG AND SMITH IN KENTUCKY

In August Kirby Smith left Knoxville and made his way through a pass west of the Cumberland Gap. On August 30 he defeated a Federal force of five thousand men at Richmond, capturing four thousand of them. He penetrated as far as Lexington. His invasion caused the Federals to evacuate Cumberland Gap, threw the northern states in the Ohio valley into consternation, and brought his own promotion to a lieutenant-general. On August 26 Bragg left Chattanooga. He emerged from the mountains at Sparta, north of Buell's left flank. This was a complete surprise for the Federal general and put him in a difficult position. Bragg then made for central Kentucky. Buell retreated rapidly through Nashville, following his line of communications, crossed Kentucky, and on September 29 occupied Louisville, Kentucky, on the Ohio River, putting himself between Bragg and the North. Bragg's operations had begun brilliantly. Once in central Kentucky, however, his movements became aimless. He wasted time setting up a Confederate Government in that state. He did not fight Buell when the Confederate army was in high spirits as a result of the successes of the first phase of the invasion and when its enemy was correspondingly depressed. Bragg allowed Buell to reach Louisville without interference where he was reinforced by nearly fifty thousand raw troops. In short, Bragg allowed his enemy, whom he had so completely outmaneuvered, to take the offensive and march to battle.

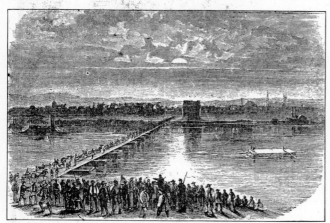

179   Volunteers crossing the Ohio to Covington, from a sketch by H. Mosler in *Harper's Weekly*, Sept. 27, 1862

180   Battle of Perryville, Ky., from a sketch by H. Mosler in *Harper's*
Weekly, Nov. 1, 1862

THE BATTLE OF PERRYVILLE

On October 8 the armies of Bragg and Buell met at Perryville. On the eve of the battle the Federal Government, dissatisfied with Buell's performance, had directed him to turn over his command to Thomas, but that officer had declined to supersede him with an engagement pending. From the Union point of view the battle was badly handled. Buell remained at his headquarters two and a half miles from the battlefield during most of the conflict because he did not get word until four in the afternoon that a battle was in progress. This was another illustration of the bad staff work which characterized the armies of both sides in the early years of the war. As a result of the failure of the staff to inform the commanding general of the situation only a part of Buell's army was engaged although it was all close at hand. The divisions of McCook and Sheridan bore the brunt of the fighting. Buell lost an opportunity to destroy Bragg's army, for Kirby Smith's force was not within supporting distance and, as a result, Bragg was greatly outnumbered. After the battle Bragg retreated into the valley of the Tennessee. On October 30 Buell was replaced by Rosecrans who up to this time had been with Grant. An investigating committee found only two points on which to criticize Buell. "The fact is that the Army of the Ohio was not at that time strong enough to do what was expected of it: to take and hold Chattanooga and at the same time protect Kentucky and its own line of communications." — FIEBEGER, *Campaigns of the American Civil War*, 132, West Point, 1914.

THE BATTLE OF STONE RIVER

In November Rosecrans was at Nashville and Bragg not far away at Murfreesboro. The two forces were now called respectively the Army of the Cumberland and the Army of Tennessee. The Confederate Government was disturbed by the defeat of Bragg's campaign and by a minor success which Grant had won at Corinth. In November President Davis visited both Murfreesboro and Vicksburg to observe the military

181   Battle of Stone River, from *Campfire and Battlefield*, Desmond
Publishing Co., Boston, 1896

situation at first hand. He had already ordered Joseph E. Johnston to exercise general supervision over the three Confederate armies now operating west of the mountains. These were the armies of Kirby Smith in the Tennessee valley, Bragg at Murfreesboro, and Pemberton in the region of Vicksburg. December was marked by more raids on the part of Morgan and Forrest but the Federals received no vital damage. Taking advantage of the absence from Bragg's force of these two cavalrymen Rosecrans left his position at Nashville on December 26 and moved toward Murfreesboro. On the last day of 1862 the battle of Stone River was fought. Though Rosecrans considerably outnumbered him, Bragg won a tactical success. He compelled the Federal right wing, commanded by McCook, to swing several miles to the rear, pivoting on the left wing, commanded by Crittenden. The Confederates, however, were unable to drive Rosecrans from the field. On January 2 the battle was renewed but the Confederate assault was repulsed mainly by the Federal artillery. On the night of January 3 Bragg began to retire on Shelbyville. He was not pursued. The engagement at Stone River was hailed as a victory by a government at Washington which was in despair as a result of the defeat of Burnside at Fredericksburg.

THE VICKSBURG CAMPAIGN

THE year 1863 opened with the dreary prospect of continued war. In Virginia the Army of the Potomac still lay on the banks of the Rappahannock recovering from the terrible defeat of Fredericksburg. In Tennessee Rosecrans and Bragg had gone into winter quarters to prepare for the arduous campaign that both knew the following summer would bring. Grant was on the Mississippi a little above Vicksburg, struggling to put himself into position to take that stronghold. Because of the nature of the terrain the taking of Vicksburg presented one of the most difficult military problems of the war. In some respects the Father of Waters was more difficult to conquer than the enemy. The lower Mississippi meanders through a flat country filled with a maze of swamps and bayous. A steep escarpment borders the eastern edge of the valley bottom on the edge of which Memphis and Vicksburg are built. Grant's plan called for an advance against Vicksburg by way of the river. On this broad stream he could transport his troops and bring up his supplies close to the Confederate citadel. But when he looked from a river boat to the towering cliffs bristling with cannon that rose above him, the task of taking Vicksburg must sometimes have seemed impossible. Obviously it was impossible to storm that steep escarpment against the base of which beat

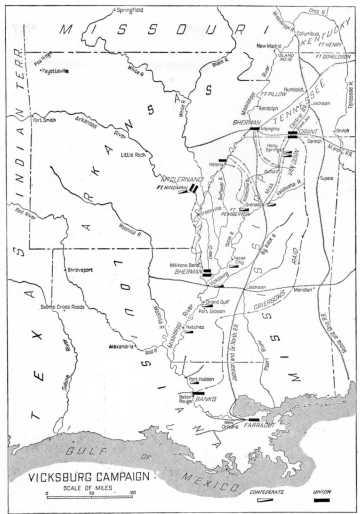

182   The Vicksburg Campaign, redrawn from Major Matthew Forney Steele, *American Campaigns*, The United States Infantry Association, Washington, 1922

the current of the Mississippi. Vicksburg and its batteries stood at the tip of a great ox-bow. Union gunboats attempting to run by the fortifications would be under fire as they approached the tip of the ox-bow and also on the opposite side of the bend as they sped away from the city. Grant was compelled to establish a base at a point where another meander of the Mississippi touched the escarpment as at Vicksburg. Otherwise his supplies could not be made available on the high ground east of the escarpment where his army must maneuver. The only feasible place for the establishing of such a base was south of Vicksburg. This explains the efforts of Grant's engineers in January and February to cut canals or open channels that would take Grant's transports and supply boats past Vicksburg out of range of the batteries. As early as January 30 Grant himself became convinced that there was little likelihood that the engineers would succeed and began to consider other possible plans. In the end three different attempted canals and channels ended in failure. Grant's army was busy but it was suffering greatly from disease brought on by its unhealthful surroundings. In the North a storm of criticism arose. But Lincoln, who strongly favored the canal plan, paid no heed to the popular disapproval of Grant. This northern reaction demonstrates the results of the absence of military censorship. The northern press was full of details, often exaggerated, that came in the dispatches of correspondents with the army or were gleaned from soldiers' letters. The depression among the people of the North was very great. The press had recounted many defeats for the Federal arms and had been filled with long casualty lists. The buoyant spirit of 1861 had passed and among the northern people the will to win the war was ebbing.

183 General William Starke Rosecrans, 1819–
98, from a photograph by Brady, in the
United States Signal Corps, Washington

GENERAL ROSECRANS

MANY Americans, despairing of Grant, thought that Rosecrans might be the chieftain who would bring victory. James A. Garfield, now a brigadier-general, returned in 1863 from a leave to the Army of the Cumberland. A letter to his wife describes an interview he had upon his arrival at camp with Rosecrans, whom he already knew. "I am greatly pleased with some features of Gen. Rosecrans' character. He has that fine quality of having his mind made up on all the questions which concern his work. In a military man this is a cardinal virtue. The whole texture of generalship is made up of theories which his mind must form of the position, force, and intentions of his enemy and he must shape his course, take his resolutions and act upon them in accordance with his theory. Hence a man who does not think decisively, and place full and implicit confidence upon his own judgment cannot act with confidence. Gen. R. thinks rapidly and strikes forward into action with the utmost confidence in his own judgment. In this he is perfectly unlike McClellan who rarely has a clear-cut, decisive opinion and dares not trust it when he has. The officers whom I have met since I came here seem to have the most unbounded confidence in Rosy and are enthusiastic in his praise. He is the most Spanish-looking man I know of — a kind of Don Menendez face — and though he swears fiercely, yet he is a Jesuit of the highest style of Roman piety. He carries a cross attached to his watch seal and as he drew his watch out of his side pants pocket his rosary, a dirty-looking string of friars beads, came out with it. There is much in his appearance that is striking and singular." — THEODORE CLARKE SMITH, *Life and Letters of James Abram Garfield*, Vol. I, 271–72, Yale University Press, New Haven, 1925.

FEDERAL TRANSPORT IN THE BAYOUS ABOVE VICKSBURG

THE picture, No. 185, done by an artist, later to become famous as a cartoonist, shows the tremendous difficulties under which Grant labored. When his engineers gave up, the Federal commander was faced with a difficult decision. The conservative thing to do was to abandon the approach to Vicksburg by way of the river, return to Memphis, and undertake a land campaign southward from that point. Grant's able subordinate, Sherman, advised this. Against it could be urged the inevitable effect of such a retrograde

184 Cutting away the dam at the head of the Vicksburg Canal, from a sketch by Theodore R. Davis in *Harper's Weekly*, Apr. 4, 1863

movement upon the North where the morale of the people had been lowered by the disastrous year of 1862 in Virginia. Grant chose to advance rather than to retreat. On the night of April 16 a part of Porter's flotilla ran past the Vicksburg batteries. Six days later six steamers, towing twelve barges of hay, corn, and provisions, made their way past the Confederate fortress ensuring the Federal army ample supplies for the maneuvers necessary before the east bank of the river could be reached. Meanwhile the army, concentrated on March 29 at Milliken's Bend, was making its way southward along a poor road which had dried up somewhat with the abatement of the high water. The feat of the navy in passing the Vicksburg forts was only surpassed in the river war by Farragut's exploit at New Orleans.

185 Transport in the bayous above Vicksburg, from an engraving after the drawing by Thomas Nast, in the possession of the publishers

GRANT AT THE CRISIS OF HIS CAREER

"WHEN General Grant had his army in its camps in the swamps across the Mississippi from Vicksburg, after failing in all his efforts to turn the town by way of bayous and canals, he was at the crisis of his military career. . . . He had already failed in five different projects for the capture of Vicksburg: first, in the combined movement in late autumn, 1862, in which he was to march a force overland from Northern Mississippi against the rear of the town, while Sherman moved by transports down the great river. This enterprise was brought to naught by the capture of Grant's advanced base at Holly Springs by Van Dorn's cavalry, by the breaking up of the railway in his rear by Forrest, and by Sherman's failure to defeat the Confederates at Chickasaw Bluffs. The second

186   General Grant and his horse, from a photograph by Brady, in the United States Signal Corps, War Department, Washington

effort was by way of the canal across the peninsula opposite Vicksburg; the third was by way of Lake Providence and bayous and rivers west of the Mississippi; the fourth was the expedition by way of the Yazoo Pass; the fifth was the expedition by way of Steele's Bayou. All of these projects had failed, and months of patient labor had been wasted upon them. The capture of Vicksburg seemed farther away than ever. A year before ten thousand men could easily have taken it; but within the last few months the Confederates had turned it into a fortress and placed twenty-two thousand men in its garrison. A large part of the public press had already declared Grant a failure, and Halleck and the Administration at Washington were about ready to try someone else in his place. . . . The stakes were larger, too, than he had reckoned them; they were not only Vicksburg, but Chattanooga, Appomattox, peace in the land, a general's commission, the White House, and a fame immortal." — STEELE, 416–17.

187   Military Bridge across the Tennessee built for the campaign of 1863, from a photograph by Brady in the United States Signal Corps, War Department, Washington

PORTER'S FLOTILLA AT THE BATTLE OF GRAND GULF, APRIL 29–30, 1863

AT Grand Gulf Porter secured an admirable position for concerted action between himself and Grant, who, on the 30th, landed twenty thousand men at Bruinsburg, some miles below. Grant was at last on the dry ground where the decisive action must be fought. He wired Washington that he considered the campaign half won.

VII—7

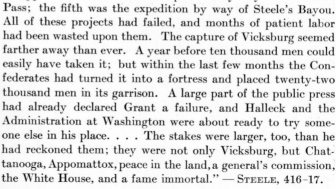

188   Porter's Bombardment of Grand Gulf, from an engraving by J. Rogers after the drawing by Thomas Nast

ADMIRAL DAVID DIXON PORTER

PORTER was a buoyant son of the sea, full of resourcefulness and adaptability, but likewise well versed in naval science. He had now cut Vicksburg off from all practical relief — north, south, and west. So Grant could devote his entire attention to the east. To this latter task Grant set himself with such vigor and ability that the Vicksburg campaign stands out as one of the most brilliant of the war. (See map, No. 182.)

189 Admiral David Dixon Porter, 1813–91, from a photograph by Brady, in the United States Signal Corps, War Department, Washington

GRANT'S ADVANCE ON VICKSBURG

ONCE the landing at Bruinsburg had been made, Grant, whose army numbered a little more than forty thousand, was forced to reckon with two opponents. Pemberton was in command of the Vicksburg area with about forty thousand troops, and Joseph E. Johnston was at Jackson, Mississippi, with a little

190 The Advance on Vicksburg, the Fifteenth Corps Crossing the Big Black River by Night, from *Campfire and Battlefield*, Desmond Publishing Co., Boston, 1896

less than fifteen thousand. Grant's first task was to prevent the uniting of these two forces. Abandoning his base and living off the country, he struck rapidly northeastward. In the swiftly moving campaign which followed he accomplished his mission. In the words of James Ford Rhodes: "In nineteen days, he had crossed the great river into the enemy's territory, had marched one hundred and eighty miles through a very difficult country, skirmishing constantly, had fought and won five distinct battles, inflicting a greater loss upon the enemy than he himself sustained and capturing many cannon and field-pieces, had taken the capital of the State and destroyed its arsenals and military manufactories, had been for ten days without communication with any base or with his government, and was now in the rear of Vicksburg." Lincoln, reading the dispatches from the Vicksburg front, realized that, at last, he had found his general. "The intrenched camp of Vicksburg proper extended along the river bank for a distance of nearly five miles and had a land front of over seven miles. Its greatest depth between land and river fronts was nearly two miles. Both fronts were well supplied with artillery. Finding that the place could not be taken by assault, Grant began a regular siege. To strengthen the besieging force and cover it from attack in rear, he drew from Memphis three divisions of the XVI Corps and called on Halleck for additional reinforcements. Halleck sent him Maj. Gen. Herron's division from Missouri, and the IX corps, under the command of Maj. Gen. John G. Parke, from the Department of the Ohio. His reinforcements began reaching him May 20, and by the middle of June he had over 70,000 men present for duty on the east bank of the Mississippi River and a small force on the west bank. As soon as his reinforcements arrived, Sherman was given command of a strong covering force which guarded the crossings of the Big Black River and protected the rear of the besieging force." — FIEBEGER, 199–200. See map, No. 196.

191   Troops Landing Near General Grant's Headquarters above Vicksburg, from *Campfire and Battlefield*, Desmond Publishing Co., Boston, 1896

APPROACH OF McPHER-SON'S SAPS AGAINST THE VICKSBURG WORKS

MANEUVERING gave place to siege operations with the doomed Pemberton shut up in the great fortress of the Mississippi. The closeness of the two sides led to many a desperate fight with bullets and bayonets. But it also led to some pleasant amenities of war, especially the fair exchange of Federal food for Confederate tobacco during the well-observed, but quite unofficial, market hour.

192   Approach of McPherson's Saps to the Confederate Works, from a sketch by Theodore R. Davis in *Harper's Weekly*, July 11, 1863

THE SIEGE OF VICKSBURG FROM THE VIEWPOINT OF THE RANKS

"WEDNESDAY June 24th — I was on picket today, each man going every other day, and the orders are very strict no one being allowed to go through the lines unless he can show a pass signed by General Grant. Our men are digging tunnels under the rebel forts and laying powder to blow them up. When a fort is blown up our forces are to make a charge at that point and capture the rebels. The report is that the rebels are planning to cut their way out through our lines. . . . Thursday, 25th — Everything on the outside is quiet as usual. Our engineers blew up one of the main rebel forts, and the infantry rushing in tried to hold the place, but on account of the fierce cross firing had to fall back to their rifle pits. A number of our forces were killed, including one colonel, and a number were wounded. Only a few of the rebels were killed . . . not many being in the fort at the time. . . . A negro in the fort blown up, was thrown high up in the air and came down on his head within our lines unhurt. . . . A photograph was taken of the negro and the boys had him on exhibition for a few days at five cents admission." — D. B. CLARK, *Downing's Civil War Diary*, 123–24.

193   The Fight in the Crater of Fort Hill, at the Siege of Vicksburg, from a photograph, after a drawing by A. E. Mathews, in the collection of L. C. Handy, Washington

194   From the painting *Surrender of Vicksburg* by Paul Philippoteaux.   © O. R. Griffin, Lowell, Mass.

UNDER THE VICKSBURG OAK

GRANT has described the surrender of Vicksburg.   "At three o'clock on July 3 Pemberton appeared at the point suggested in my verbal message, accompanied by the same officers who had borne his letter of the morning.   Generals Ord, McPherson, Logan and A. J. Smith, and several officers of my staff accompanied me. Our place of meeting was on a hillside within a few hundred feet of the rebel lines.   Near by stood a stunted oak-tree. . . . Pemberton and I had served in the same division during part of the Mexican War.   I knew him very well therefore and greeted him as an old acquaintance. . . . At the appointed hour on July 4 the garrison of Vicksburg marched out of their works and formed in line in front, stacked arms and marched back in good order.   Our whole army present witnessed this scene without cheering.   Logan's division, which had approached nearest the rebel works, was the first to march in; and the flag of one of the regiments of his division was soon floating over the court-house.   Our soldiers were no sooner inside the lines than the two armies began to fraternize.   Our men had had full rations from the time the siege commenced, to the close. The enemy had been suffering, particularly towards the last.   I myself saw our men taking bread from their haversacks and giving it to the enemy they had so recently been engaged in starving out.   It was accepted with avidity and with thanks.   During the siege there had been a good deal of friendly sparring between the soldiers of the two armies, on picket or where the lines were close together. . . . Often 'Johnny' would call: 'Well, Yank, when are you coming into town?'   The reply was sometimes: 'We propose to celebrate the 4th of July there.'   Sometimes it would be: 'We always treat our prisoners with kindness and do not want to hurt them'; or, 'We are holding you as prisoners of war while you are feeding yourselves.'   The garrison, from the commanding general down, undoubtedly expected an assault on the fourth.   They knew from the temper of their men it would be successful when made; and that would be a greater humiliation than to surrender. Besides it would be attended with severe loss to them.   The Vicksburg paper, which we received regularly through the courtesy of the rebel pickets, said prior to the fourth, in speaking of the 'Yankee' boast that they would take dinner in Vicksburg that day, that the best receipt for cooking rabbit was 'First ketch your rabbit.'   The paper at this time and for some time previous was printed on the plain side of wall paper.   The last number was issued on the fourth and announced that we had 'caught our rabbit.'" — *Personal Memoirs of U. S. Grant*, Vol. I, 563–64.

ON DIT.—That the great Ulysses— the Yankee Generalissimo, surnamed Grant—has expressed his intention of dining in Vicksburg on Sunday next, and celebrating the 4th of July by a grand dinner and so forth.   When asked if he would invite Gen. Joe Johnston to join he said "No! for fear there would be a row at the table." Ulysses must get into the city before he dines in it.   The way to cook a rabbit is "first to catch the rabbit," etc.

195   Extract from a newspaper printed on wall paper at Vicksburg, July 2, 1863, from the original in the Confederate Museum, Richmond, Va.

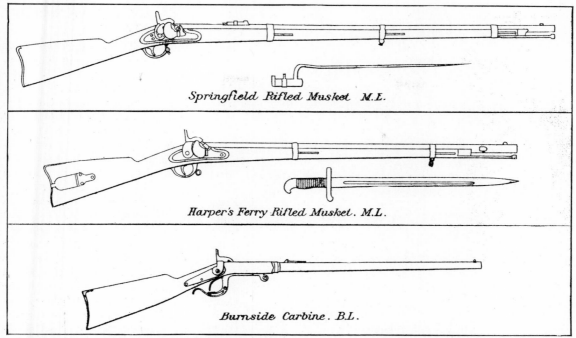

Springfield Rifled Musket. M.L.

Harper's Ferry Rifled Musket. M.L.

Burnside Carbine. B.L.

196   Muskets and Carbine used by the Federal Army, from the *Atlas to Accompany the Official Records of the Union and Confederate Armies,* Washington

ARMS OF THE NORTH AND SOUTH

"At Vicksburg thirty-one thousand, six hundred prisoners were surrendered, together with 172 cannon, about sixty thousand muskets and a large amount of ammunition. The small-arms of the enemy were far superior to the bulk of ours. Up to this time our troops at the West had been limited to the old United States flint-lock muskets changed into percussion, or the Belgian musket imported early in the war — almost as dangerous to the person firing it as to the one aimed at — and a few new and improved arms. These were of many different calibres, a fact that caused much trouble in distributing ammunition during an engagement. The enemy had generally new arms which had run the blockade and were of uniform caliber. After the surrender I authorized all colonels whose regiments were armed with inferior muskets, to place them in the stack of captured arms and replace them with the latter." — Grant, *Memoirs,* 572.

197   The Federal ram *Queen of the West* attacking the Confederate gun-boat *Vicksburg* off Vicksburg, from *Harper's Weekly,* Feb. 28, 1863

198   The United States gunboat *Indianola* running the blockade at Vicksburg, from *Harper's Weekly,* Mar. 7, 1863

GRANT'S TRIBUTE TO THE NAVY

"The navy under Porter was all it could be, during the entire campaign. Without its assistance the campaign could not have been successfully made with twice the number of men engaged. It could not have been made at all, in the way it was, with any number of men without such assistance. The most perfect harmony reigned between the two arms of the service." — Grant, *Memoirs,* 574.

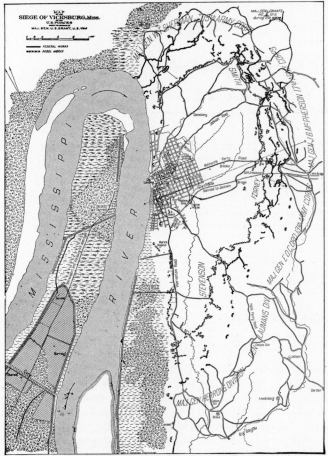

199   Siege of Vicksburg, redrawn from the *Atlas to Accompany the Official Records of the Union and Confederate Armies*, Washington

COMMENTS ON THE VICKSBURG CAMPAIGN

"IN his conduct of this campaign Grant proved himself to be a general of great ability. He was never dismayed by the difficulties of his position, but held firm to his purpose to land an army on one flank of the Confederate line of defense. . . . When Grant landed his army on the east bank of the Mississippi, he knew neither the strength nor the disposition of Pemberton's forces. With Napoleonic directness and decision he united all his available strength and attacked. . . ." — FIEBEGER, *Campaigns of the American Civil War*, 202. "If Pemberton had possessed the soldierly quality of obedience he might still have saved his army in spite of all the mistakes he made. If he had moved, — as Johnston ordered . . . he might have gained some advantage in coöperation with the Confederate troops at Jackson (under Johnston). He would thus at least have lessened the distance between the two Confederate forces, and made better their chances of uniting. Instead of obeying Johnston's order Pemberton called a council of war and . . . then started southward to cut Grant's communications, when Grant had no communications. Then later when Johnston, who saw that all hope of saving Vicksburg was lost, ordered Pemberton to evacuate the place, Pemberton by vigorous movement might still have saved the remnant of his

army, if he had obeyed Johnston's order. Instead of doing so Pemberton remained in Vicksburg, and lost his army as well as the town. . . . Johnston saved his little army at Jackson by slipping away with it across Pearl River, when Sherman had surrounded the town on the side away from the river. Johnston showed a far better judgment throughout the campaign than Pemberton showed; but he lacked the sort of bold-

ness and energy that might have delivered the Confederate army from the toils into which Pemberton had gotten it. — STEELE, *American Campaigns*, 420–21.

U.S.S. *RICHMOND* AT WORK AGAINST PORT HUDSON

THE navy kept steadily at work at Port Hudson. But when the truth was known the surrender of Port Hudson followed on the eighth. The Confederate General Gardner's sword was chivalrously returned to him, before his whole army, in acknowledgment of his heroic defense.

200   Surrender of Port Hudson, from a print published by Currier and Ives, New York, in the Prints Division, Library of Congress, Washington,

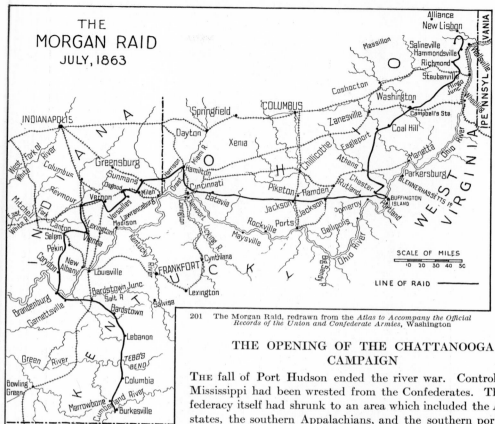

THE
MORGAN RAID
JULY, 1863

SCALE OF MILES
10 20 30 40 50

LINE OF RAID ———

201 The Morgan Raid, redrawn from the *Atlas to Accompany the Official Records of the Union and Confederate Armies*, Washington

THE OPENING OF THE CHATTANOOGA CAMPAIGN

THE fall of Port Hudson ended the river war. Control of the Mississippi had been wrested from the Confederates. The Confederacy itself had shrunk to an area which included the Atlantic states, the southern Appalachians, and the southern portions of Mississippi and Alabama. Three important seaports, Charleston, Savannah, and Mobile, remained as yet unconquered. In the meantime, ten days before Vicksburg surrendered, Rosecrans, who had remained at Murfreesboro since the Battle of Stone River, broke camp. On June 24 he started his army in motion along the roads that led to Chattanooga. Bragg fell back before him and again tried the tactics that had failed against Buell the year before. Before Rosecrans had started Morgan had obtained permission to make a raid in Kentucky with the twenty-six hundred men under his command. He was forbidden, however, to cross the Ohio as he had proposed. On his own in Kentucky Morgan decided to disobey his orders. July found him sweeping across Indiana and Ohio. Close on his heels was a Federal cavalry force. Morgan planned to cross the Ohio River by a ford at Ravenwood which he had examined before leaving Tennessee. When his tired horsemen reached it, they

found it protected by a redoubt. They rested during the night expecting to attack in the morning. The next day, July 20, however, found the pursuing Federals upon them. Morgan was defeated and the greater part of his command captured. A few Confederates got away across the river and Morgan with a small party escaped northward. He was captured a week later, however. Morgan ultimately escaped from the Ohio state penitentiary and made Tennessee in safety. His Ohio and Indiana raid, however, had destroyed his prestige. Rosecrans, meanwhile, was marching steadily on Chattanooga determined to wrest that vital railroad junction from his Confederate opponent, Bragg.

202 Entry of Morgan's Freebooters into Washington, Ohio, from a sketch in *Harper's Weekly*, Aug. 15, 1863

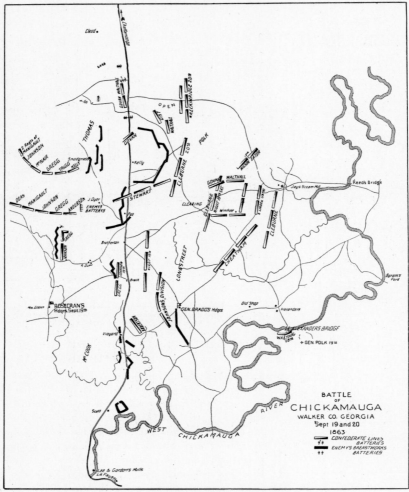

203   Battle of Chickamauga, redrawn from the *Atlas to Accompany the Official Records*
                  of the Union and Confederate Armies, Washington

CHICKAMAUGA, SEPTEMBER 20, 1863

ROSECRANS did his best work of the war in the brilliant campaign by which in the summer of 1863 he maneuvered Bragg back toward Chattanooga and finally out of the place. He had captured that most important
railroad junction without a battle. His success made him incautious. Chattanooga is in a narrow valley
above which high ridges lift their craggy slopes. Across these Rosecrans plunged in pursuit of Bragg, sending
his army through widely separated passes so that his units became so dispersed as to be beyond supporting
distance of one another. Then Bragg turned. Rosecrans sensed his error and spent several desperate days
in concentrating his army. When he had accomplished his task he was on the verge of exhaustion. As for
Bragg, he had let slip a priceless opportunity to destroy his enemy. Heavily reinforced, the Confederate
command outnumbered its opponent. On September 19 Bragg made an indecisive attack. On the next
day was fought the great Battle of Chickamauga. There is no space here to unravel the confusion of that
terrible day for the Federal troops. A mistaken order opened a gap in the Federal lines which the fiercely
fighting Confederates turned to full advantage. Rosecrans' right and center crumbled. The commanding
general was swept from the field and hastened some twelve or fifteen miles to Chattanooga to prepare for its
defense. Only the Federal left under Thomas stood fast. All the troops that Bragg could throw against
that "Rock of Chickamauga" could not drive him from his lines. That Rosecrans could have extricated
himself from the plight in which he was caught and returned to the field of battle is demonstrated by the
fact that his chief of staff, General James A. Garfield, requested permission to do this very thing and accomplished it. Thomas was later ordered to retire to Chattanooga. Bragg settled down to siege operations.

ROSECRANS RELIEVED

BEFORE the fight was over Rosecrans reported to Washington a terrible disaster. The affair had almost completely unnerved him. Thereafter he was of no military value. A council of war in Washington decided to send Hooker with two army corps from Virginia to Chattanooga. They arrived six days after departure, a very good record for those days. But the troops at Chattanooga were on the verge of starvation due to the difficulty of bringing up supplies over the rough country. Rosecrans was incapable of taking effective measures to meet the situation.

204   Thomas' men repulsing the attack of the Confederates at Chickamauga, from a sketch in *Harper's Weekly*, Oct. 31, 1863

Grant was then given the command of all the armies in the West save that commanded by Banks. One of the first acts of the conqueror of Vicksburg was to relieve Rosecrans and give his post to Thomas. At once order began to emerge from chaos, and by the time that Grant arrived to take command in person the army was well on the way toward the solution of its difficulties. Meanwhile Grant had ordered Sherman to Chattanooga. Bragg found himself confronted by four of the ablest generals that the Union cause produced: Grant, Sherman, Thomas, and Hooker.

DISSENSION IN THE CONFEDERATE RANKS

WHILE Thomas was bringing order to the Federals in the camp of the Confederates was bitterness and dissension. Bragg had no friends among his chief subordinates, whom he violently criticized. Longstreet, his chief aid, criticized him in turn for faulty tactics in the Battle of Chickamauga and for not cutting the Federal line of communications behind Chattanooga Jefferson Davis, made desperate by the reverses at Gettysburg and Vicksburg, visited the camp. His faith in Bragg remained unshaken. He did, however, listen to the complaints of the subordinate commanders. He even offered the command to Longstreet and to Hardee, both of whom declined. The former urged that he place Joseph E. Johnston in control but Davis refused. So Bragg was continued. Faced with a force menacing from the point of view of both numbers and leadership, Bragg made in November, 1863, a fatal blunder. Underestimating his opponent, he sent Longstreet northeast to Knoxville to drive out a Federal force under Burnside which had penetrated that region. On November 23, soon after Longstreet had left, Grant struck.

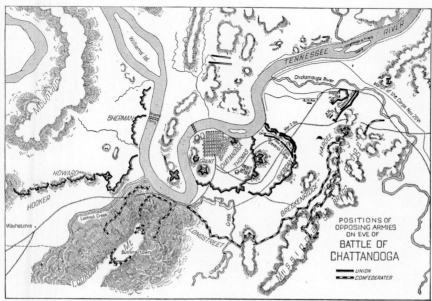

205   Battle of Chattanooga, redrawn from the *Atlas to Accompany the Official Records of the Union and Confederate Armies*, Washington

206   General George Henry Thomas, 1816–70, from a photograph by Brady, in the L. C. Handy Collection, Washington

BRAGG'S POSITION

BRAGG's right was at the end of Missionary Ridge where the Chickamauga River flows into the Tennessee; his center held the crest of the ridge to Rossville Gap; and his left, crossing the Chattanooga valley, was placed on Lookout Mountain. From this last position the troops of Longstreet had recently moved out leaving the upland lightly garrisoned. Grant sent Sherman against the Confederate right, Thomas against the center, and Hooker against the left.

CHATTANOOGA, GRANT'S HEADQUARTERS STAFF AT ORCHARD KNOB

GRANT began his three-day battle on November 23 with sixty thousand men against Bragg's thirty thousand. But Bragg's position on Missionary Ridge and Lookout Mountain was strong and tenaciously held. Thomas led the first day's fighting by taking the Confederate advanced works on the lower slopes of Missionary Ridge and cleverly using them against their old defenders. The second day Sherman reached the northern flank of the Ridge before Bragg knew he was on the way. Meanwhile Hooker, keeping touch with Thomas, who maintained contact with Sherman, felt the southern force on Lookout Mountain, and, finding it conquerable, fought his way up in the "Battle above the Clouds." All morning a mist had hung over the mountain and by two o'clock had become so dense as to render the fighting lines invisible. Because of the fog and lack of ammunition Hooker halted and intrenched. On the following day with fresh ammunition he scaled the summit.

207   From the painting *The Battle of Missionary Ridge* by Douglas Volk (1858–), in the State House, St. Paul, Minn.   © 1906 by the artist

CHAPTER IV

CHANCELLORSVILLE AND GETTYSBURG

DURING January, 1863, while Grant's army was toiling amid the bayous and oxbows of the Mississippi and Rosecrans was refitting his army at Murfreesboro, Burnside held the Army of the Potomac on the north bank of the Rappahannock across from Fredericksburg. The Virginia winter had settled down. The weather was cold and wet and the roads were channels of mud. In spite of these conditions, on the day after Christmas, 1862, the indefatigable Stuart made another of his raids behind the Federal lines. In the Army of Northern Virginia supplies of all kinds were desperately needed. On January 19 one of Lee's brigadiers reported that four hundred of his fifteen hundred men were without blankets. The meat ration was very much reduced. Difficulties of supply caused Lee to consent to send Longstreet to southwestern Virginia where that general involved himself in a siege operation which rendered him unavailable when Lee needed him. The absence of Longstreet reduced Lee's army by twenty thousand men. Yet with the first breath of spring the Confederate commander began to formulate plans for an offensive toward the Potomac. In the middle of March he wrote to Davis: "I think it is all-important that we should assume the aggressive by the 8th of May. . . . If we could be placed in a position to make a vigorous advance at that time, I think that the Valley could be swept of Milroy, and the army opposite [Hooker's] be thrown north of the Potomac." So he forecast the route which was later to be followed in the Gettysburg campaign.

Meanwhile Lincoln had replaced Burnside, who requested to be relieved, with Hooker. On January 26 the President addressed to Hooker one of the most remarkable documents in the annals of the American army. "I have placed you at the head of the Army of the Potomac. Of course I have done this upon what appears to me to be sufficient reasons, and yet I think it best for you to know that there are some things in regard to which I am not quite satisfied with you. I believe you to be a brave and skillful soldier, which, of course, I like. I also believe that you do not mix politics with your profession, in which you are right. You have confidence in yourself, which is a valuable if not an indispensable quality. You are ambitious, which, within reasonable bounds, does good rather than harm; but I think that during General Burnside's command of the army you have taken counsel of your ambition and thwarted him as much as you could, in which you did a great wrong to the country and to a most meritorious and honorable brother officer. I have heard, in such a way as to believe it, of your recently saying that both the army and the government needed a dictator. Of course it was not for this, but in spite of it, that I have given you the command. Only those generals who win successes can set up dictators. What I now ask of you is military success, and I will risk the dictatorship. The government will support you to the utmost of its ability. . . . I much fear that the spirit which you have decided to infuse into the army, of criticizing their commander and withholding their confidence from him, will now turn upon you. I shall assist you as far as I can to put it down. Neither you nor Napoleon, if he were alive again, could get any good out of an army while such spirit prevails in it; and now beware of rashness. Beware of rashness, but with energy and sleepless vigilance go forward and give us victories."

208 General Joseph Hooker, 1814–79, from a photograph by Brady, in the United States Signal Corps, War Department, Washington

GRANT'S OPINION OF HOOKER

"Of Hooker I saw but little during the war. I had known him very well before, however. Where I did see him, at Chattanooga, his achievement in bringing his command around the point of Lookout Mountain and into Chattanooga Valley was brilliant [see p. 100]. I nevertheless regarded him as a dangerous man. He was not subordinate to his superiors. He was ambitious to the extent of caring nothing for the rights of others. His disposition was, when engaged in battle, to get detached from the main body of the army and exercise a separate command, gathering to his standard all he could of his juniors." — *Personal Memoirs of U. S. Grant*, Vol. II, 539, 1895. Adjutant-General Townsend remarked on June 27, 1863, apropos of an order of the President replacing Hooker with Meade: "This is the first time I have drawn a long breath for several weeks."

HOOKER'S PLAN

Hooker planned to maneuver Lee out of his trenches and compel him to retreat southward. The Federal scheme of maneuver was elaborate. Its chief chance of success lay in the fact that Hooker greatly outnumbered his opponent who still did not have the use of Longstreet's troops. On April 13 Hooker sent his cavalry corps, which included practically all his mounted troops, up the Rappahannock with orders to cross that stream, make a raid southward to Gordonsville, turn east at that point against Lee's line of communications, and destroy bridges and depots. Hooker considered that such a raid would make Lee's anticipated retreat difficult and hazardous. Hooker, then, following the example of Lee himself, divided his army. He proposed to move the smaller part under the command of Sedgwick across the river below Fredericksburg. Hooker, himself, with the main army planned to march up the river, cross both the Rappahannock and Rapidan by fords and concentrate his troops at Chancellorsville on Lee's left flank. On April 29 Sedgwick crossed the river on two pontoon bridges to divert Lee's attention from the turning movement of the main

army. On April 30 Hooker himself was at Chancellorsville with fifty-two thousand men. His concentration would be completed by noon of the following day when a final detachment of eighteen thousand men would join him. He then planned to advance against Lee's flank. At Chancellorsville Hooker issued the following general order: "It is with heartfelt satisfaction the commanding general announces to the army that the operations of the last three days have determined that our enemy must either ingloriously fly, or come out from behind his defenses and give us battle on our own ground, where certain destruction awaits him." — Townsend, *Anecdotes of the*

209 General Hooker's Tent at the Headquarters of the Army of the Potomac, from a sketch by A. R. Waud in *Harper's Weekly*, Apr. 18, 1863

Civil War, 87. Meanwhile Hooker's cavalry had been delayed by high water in crossing the Rappahannock and did not get over until the main army crossed. The mounted troops then began their independent campaign and took no further part in the Chancellorsville operations.

210 Commissary's Department at Headquarters of the Army of the Potomac, from a sketch by A. R. Waud in *Harper's Weekly*, Apr. 18, 1863

211 Army Mail leaving Post Office at Headquarters of the Army of the Potomac, from a sketch by A. R. Waud in *Harper's Weekly*, Apr. 18, 1863

GENERAL MAURICE'S COMMENT ON HOOKER'S PLAN

"WHY, then, was what Lee did at the second Manassas right and what Hooker did at Chancellorsville wrong? Certainly not merely because the one succeeded and the other failed. In the first place, Hooker made, on a larger scale, the same mistake which Lee had made after Gaines' Mill [see page 54]. He sent his cavalry off on a distant raid when its absence would certainly be felt in the forthcoming battle. . . . In the second place, it was not safe to try against Lee methods which might well be taken against Pope. But the third and cardinal difference between Lee's maneuver before the second battle of Manassas and Hooker's at Chancel-

212   The Wilderness, from a photograph by Brady, in the United States Signal Corps, War Department, Washington

lorsville was the difference in the ground. Hooker had no friendly mountains to screen his march, which was not only fully known to Lee almost from its inception, but its purpose was obvious. Pope had been in doubt as to what Lee was doing, Lee was in no doubt as to Hooker's plan, and 'in vain is the net spread in the eyes of any bird.' Hooker took all possible precautions for secrecy . . . but this was all in vain unless he could conceal his purpose 'till he was ready to strike, and that was not, in the circumstances, possible. Then Hooker selected for his deployment the tangled woods of the Wilderness which would make control difficult at the time when control would be most needed. Calculations of time and space, the character of the opposing general and the quality of his troops, study of the ground and of obstacles which may be met, the chances of the object of the plan being discovered, these are all matters which must be weighed carefully before dividing forces in the presence of the enemy." — SIR FREDERICK MAURICE, *Robert E. Lee, the Soldier*, 177–78, Little, Brown & Co., Boston.

THE FIRST PHASE OF CHANCELLORSVILLE

THREE roads led eastward from Chancellorsville toward Fredericksburg. The southern two were separated by thick woods. About noon on May 1 a considerable part of Hooker's army in three detachments was marching east on these three roads. Hooker was beginning to move his army out of the dense wilderness to the open country about Tabernacle Church. At the same time large forces of Confederates under Stonewall Jackson were marching west on the two southern highways. In the afternoon the opposing armies met on the turnpike, the central road. When Hooker was informed of this he already had information from his observation balloon at Falmouth that large bodies of Confederate troops were moving west toward his army. Hooker estimated that Lee's whole army was on his front and promptly withdrew to Chancellorsville the columns advancing eastward. Here he intrenched his army and built abatis in front of it. Hooker placed implicit confidence in his plan which he was convinced would compel Lee to retreat. On the very first day of the battle, however, he passed from the offensive to the defensive. He badly needed cavalry to protect his flanks and to reconnoiter the enemy scattered through a vast forest.

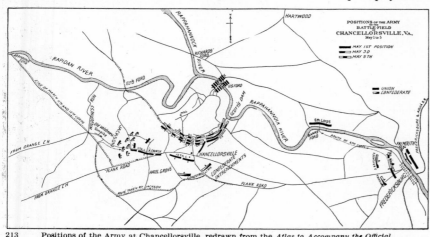

213   Positions of the Army at Chancellorsville, redrawn from the *Atlas to Accompany the Official Records of the Union and Confederate Armies*, Washington

214   Jackson's Troops Surprising Hooker's Right Flank, from a sketch by A. R. Waud
in *Harper's Weekly*, May 23, 1863

JACKSON TURNS THE FLANK

On the night of May 1–2 Lee and Jackson had their last conference. At its conclusion runners carried orders to the commanders of Jackson's corps to put their troops on the road. The night was clear and a white moonlight lay over the forest which had swallowed up two mighty armies. Before dawn broke Jackson's thirty thousand had passed the Federal flank marching by the Brock road. Lee and Jackson had decided that a frontal assault upon Hooker's intrenched position would be fatal. They had, therefore, decided upon the hazardous expedient of dividing the Confederate army and sending Jackson past the Federal right flank to strike the rear of Hooker's right wing. Hooker had no cavalry on the Brock road to inform him of such a movement. As dawn broke on May 2 outposts of General Sickles' corps discovered the gray column moving toward the west. Sickles estimated that the Confederates were retreating toward Gordonsville and asked permission to pursue. Hooker gave consent but told Sickles to proceed with caution. The only important operations of the morning and early afternoon was Sickles' pressure on Jackson's rear. The Federal general delayed two of the Confederate brigades and threatened Jackson's train but did not delay the main movement. Jackson's continued movement westward confirmed Hooker's belief that his enemy was retreating. Hooker had assumed from the outset of the campaign that Lee would have no other reasonable alternative. Hooker's failure, therefore, was the result of an incorrect estimate of the situation and his mistake seems to have been due to his holding tenaciously to his preconceived ideas as to what course the enemy would follow after the Federal army had crossed the Rappahannock and the Rapidan.

THE WOUNDING OF JACKSON

About four in the afternoon Jackson's column reached the Orange turnpike near Old Wilderness Tavern. Promptly the front was turned eastward and the troops were formed for the assault against Hooker's right wing. At six Jackson struck the Federal right flank three miles west of Chancellorsville. This part of Hooker's line was facing south when suddenly out of the forest on the west came Jackson's troops advancing in line of battle. The Federals, surprised, outflanked, outnumbered, and unsupported, made what resistance they could and fell back in a rout. As night was falling Hooker learned that his enemy had completely outmaneuvered him. The darkness of that same evening brought an irreparable loss to the Confederacy. Jackson with his staff was returning to his lines from a reconnaissance to the front when his party was mistaken for Federal cavalry and fired on by his own men. Jackson was mortally wounded. Soldiers thrown into confusion by the wooded nature of the terrain and by the maneuvers of a swiftly changing battle could easily make such an error. A. P. Hill, the next in rank, had been wounded also, so the mournful task of taking up the work of Lee's greatest lieutenant fell to the cavalry leader, Stuart.

215 Wooded Terrain in part of Battlefield where Jackson was shot, from a sketch by A. R. Waud in *Harper's Weekly*, May 23, 1863

THE FINAL PHASE OF CHANCELLORSVILLE

DURING the night of May 2–3 Sickles reoccupied his former position, a clearing on a hill since known as Hazel Grove. With battle lines as they stood on the morning of the third day Hazel Grove was a position of vital importance. Jackson's flank attack had bent Hooker's right flank so much that it was folded back upon itself. Two lines of Federals were deployed back to back astride the Orange turnpike, one fighting Lee on the east and the other Stuart on the west. Hazel Grove was at the very tip of the bend in the Federal line. Artillery placed on this eminence could enfilade Stuart's battle line. As night fell on May 2 the Battle of Chancellorsville was not lost by the Federals but when day dawned, the doom of Hooker's army had been sealed. Hardly had Sickles occupied Hazel Grove when orders came for his corps to fall back between the two Federal lines on the Orange turnpike and act as a reserve. The Confederates occupied the hill. Daylight brought assaults from Lee and Stuart on their respective fronts. In a short time Confederate batteries on Hazel Grove sent a cruel, enfilading fire along the Federal battle lines. Hooker himself was wounded by a ball from this position which he had abandoned. He was now completely defeated. By night he had withdrawn his army close to the Rapidan. On May 5 and 6 he retreated across the Rappahannock. Sedgwick, south of Fredericksburg, had advanced to the aid of his chief but had accomplished nothing decisive. When Hooker failed, he too withdrew his army to the north bank of the Rappahannock.

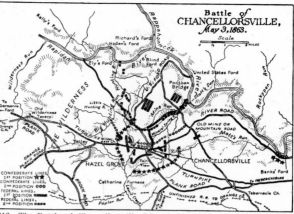

216 The Battle of Chancellorsville, May 3, 1863, drawn expressly for *The Pageant of America* from data in Major Matthew Forney Steele, *American Campaigns*, The United States Infantry Association, Washington, 1922

LEE AT THE CONCLUSION OF CHANCELLORSVILLE

"GENERAL LEE accompanied the troops in person, and as they emerged from the fierce combat they had waged in 'the depths of the tangled wilderness,' driving the superior forces of the enemy before them across the open ground, he rode into their midst. . . . The troops were pressing forward with all the ardor and enthusiasm of combat. The white smoke of musketry fringed the front of the line of battle, while the artillery on the hills in the rear of the infantry shook the earth with its thunder and filled the air with the wild shrieks of the shells that plunged into the masses of the retreating foe. To add greater horror and sublimity to the scene, the Chancellorsville house and the woods surrounding it were wrapped in flames. In the midst of this awful scene General Lee, mounted upon that horse which we all remember so well, rode to the front of his advancing battalions. The fierce soldiers, with their faces blackened with the smoke of battle, the wounded, crawling with feeble limbs from the fury of the devouring flames, all seemed possessed with a common impulse. One long, unbroken cheer, in which the feeble cry of those who lay helpless on the earth was mingled with the strong voices of those who still fought, rose high above the roar of battle and hailed the presence of the victorious chief. He sat in the full realization of all that soldiers dream of — triumph; and as I looked on him in the complete fruition of the success which his genius, courage, and confidence in his army had won, I thought that it must have been from some such scene that men in ancient days ascended to the dignity of the gods."
— Quoted in JONES, *Lee*, 238–39.

217 General Lee leading the troops at Chancellorsville, from a sketch by Warren B. Davis in *Frank Leslie's Popular Monthly*, July 1896

THE DEATH OF STONEWALL JACKSON

ON May 11, 1863, Lee issued General Orders, No. 61. "With deep grief the Commanding General announces to the army the death of Lieut.-Gen. T. J. Jackson, who expired on the 10th inst. at 3 P.M. The daring, skill, and energy of this great and good soldier, by the decree of an All Wise Providence, are now lost to us. But while we mourn his death we feel that his spirit still lives, and will inspire the whole army with his indomitable courage, and unshaken confidence in God as our hope and strength.

218   Cover of a song written in memory of Stonewall Jackson, from the original in the New York Public Library

Let his name be a watchword to his corps who have followed him to victory on so many fields. Let his officers and soldiers emulate his invincible determination to do everything in defense of our beloved country." On the same day Lee wrote his wife: "In addition to the death of friends and officers consequent upon the late battle, you will see we have to mourn the loss of the great and good Jackson. Any victory would be dear at such a price. His remains go to Richmond today. I know not how to replace him, but God's will be done. I trust He will raise some one in his place." Major Brinton, a Federal Surgeon, has left this comment. "I ought to say here that Jackson's wounds and expected death seemed to cause no elation in our army. All recognised how dangerous an enemy he was, how honorable and brave, how swift in his movements, how hard a striker, in fact, how great a military genius. Yet with all this, the feeling of the Northern army was one of pity, I might also say of regret, that so great a soldier was passing away." — *Personal Memoirs*, 233.

219   Jackson's Last Dispatch, from the original in the Virginia State Library, Richmond

220   General Richard Stoddert Ewell, 1817–72, from a photograph in the possession of H. P. Cook, Richmond

REORGANIZATION OF THE ARMIES

AFTER the Battle of Chancellorsville both armies returned to their positions of the previous winter to prepare for continued hostilities. Hooker had reorganized his army with great efficiency before the battle. After the conflict he had no important changes to make. The same was not true of Lee. In his judgment the fortunes of the Confederacy were at the crest. He was planning to strike the blow that he hoped would win the war. Both

221   General Ambrose Powell Hill, 1825–65, from a photograph in the possession of H. P. Cook, Richmond

Ewell and A. P. Hill had been promoted to the rank of lieutenant-general because of their efficient service.

THE SPIRIT OF THE ARMY

LEE now reorganized his army into three equal corps which were commanded by Longstreet, Ewell and A. P. Hill. The southern commander sent his depleted regiments to the south to be recruited and had them replaced with full units. He increased Stuart's cavalry and reorganized his artillery. Lee's army moving westward in June through Culpeper and Front Royal to the Shenandoah Valley was the most formidable weapon of war that the South ever produced. With infinite zest during these summer weeks Lee's dusty soldiers, turning their faces northward, sang one of the most widely known of the Confederate war songs.

222 General James Longstreet, 1821–1904, from a photograph in the possession of H. P. Cook, Richmond

Sitting by the roadside on a summer day,
Chatting with my messmates, passing time away,
Lying in the shadows underneath the trees,
Goodness, how delicious, eating goober peas!

Peas! Peas! Peas! Peas! eating goober peas!
Goodness, how delicious, eating goober peas!

Just before the battle the General hears a row,
He says "The Yanks are coming, I hear their rifles now,"
He turns around in wonder, and what do you think he sees?
The Georgia militia eating goober peas!

I think my song has lasted almost long enough,
The subject's interesting, but the rhymes are mighty rough,
I wish this war was over, when free from rags and fleas,
We'd kiss our wives and sweethearts and gobble goober peas.

Peas! Peas! Peas! Peas! eating goober peas!
Goodness, how delicious, eating goober peas!

MARCHING, MARCHING, MARCHING

"No one who has not had the experience, knows what a soldier undergoes on a march. We start off on a march some beautiful morning in spring; at midday slight clouds are seen floating about, which thicken with the appearance of a heavy storm soon to come; the instinct of home comes over us, and, instead of the merry chatter of the morning, stillness pervades the ranks. Each man is thinking of home and some place to shelter himself from the storm. The command, 'Close up!' awakens him from his reverie . . . and now the rain commences and soon pours down . . . he pulls down his hat, buttons up his jacket, pulls up his collar, and tries to protect his gun. . . . Now the water is slowly feeling its way down his back, and, as it gradually covers him, the courage goes out, and when his back gets completely wet, he for a few minutes forgets that he is a Confederate soldier . . . the storm within him breaks loose, resulting in his cursing the Confederacy, the generals, and everything in the army, and even himself! Then, with a new inspiration, he commences on the Yankees, is himself carried away, and is once more the good old Confederate soldier, marching along at a brisk rate in the pelting rain! . . . We went through equal trials in very dusty marches; when our eyes, our noses, our mouths, our ears, and in fact, our whole person became soiled with dirt. . . . Besides we had muddy days to march in! We soon got our shoes full, our pants wet to the knees. . . . At the commencement of the war, soon after starting on a march we were given the route step, on passing a village or town we were called to attention, and marched through with military precision; but toward the close of the war, we generally kept the route step throughout the march, as all had learned that the men got along so much better and could march much farther by being allowed to carry their guns as they chose, and take their natural step." — WORSHAM, *One of Jackson's Foot Cavalry*, 157–58.

223 The Equipment of a Confederate Soldier, from John H. Worsham, *One of Jackson's Foot Cavalry*, Neale Publishing Co., New York, 1912

224　Confederate field ambulance-wagon, from the *Atlas to Accompany the Official Records of the Union and Confederate Armies*, Washington

SICK CALL

"It is surprising how the Confederacy got along with such a small variety of medicines, which consisted, in the field, almost entirely of blue powders, one kind of pills and quinine. . . . Reaching the surgeon's quarters, the sick were lined up, and the surgeon with the hospital steward passed along. The first man accosted was asked, 'What is the matter with you?' The answer is sometimes like this: 'I don't know, doctor, but I have a terrible misery here,' designating the locality by placing his hands on his stomach. 'Put out your tongue,' says the doctor. After an examination, the doctor says to Blunt, the hospital steward of my regiment, 'Give him a blue powder.' The next is examined

in about the same manner, with instructions to Blunt to give him two pills; the next is given 10 grains of quinine. Occasionally some favored one was given a gill of whiskey; nearly every man thereafter developed

the same symptoms! Probably one of the men has an aching tooth; the doctor tells him to take a seat on some log near by. . . . When the doctor comes to him, he looks his mouth over and says, 'It must come out,' goes to his tent, gets a pair of forceps, and, on his return, straddles the log, inserts the instrument in the man's mouth, takes hold of a tooth, and by main strength, after a lengthy struggle, succeeds in pulling an excellent tooth!—but he cures the ache.

225　Confederate field litter, from the *Atlas to Accompany the Official Records of the Union and Confederate Armies*, Washington

This was about the daily routine in camp, and it was surprising how many cures were effected with this limited supply of medicines." — Worsham, *One of Jackson's Foot Cavalry*, 160–61.

FEDERAL SOLDIERS

Much may be learned by looking into the faces of the Federal soldiers about to enter upon the Battle of Gettysburg. The photograph shows a company, a part of the Sixth Maine Infantry, on parade. It was taken soon after the Battle of Fredericksburg but it typifies the Blue hosts which Meade led against Lee in Pennsylvania. The uniforms are clean and well kept though they fit in much the same way that the uniforms of private

soldiers are wont to do. Boys stand shoulder to shoulder with men of almost double their years. There are men whose faces suggest foreign birth. Such companies as this, no larger than modern platoons, were to meet and turn back Pickett's desperate charge on the last day of the great battle. By the time the signal corps took this picture the armies of the United States had ceased to be amateur and had been seasoned and trained by many campaigns.

226　The Sixth Maine Infantry on parade after the Battle of Fredericksburg, from a photograph in the United States Signal Corps, War Department, Washington

LEE BEGINS HIS INVASION OF PENNSYLVANIA

THE first days of June saw great activity in Lee's army. Troops were being moved toward the Shenandoah Valley and the heights above Fredericksburg were held by a small force. Stuart was at Brandy Station, a few miles north of Culpeper, inspecting and equipping his five cavalry brigades. Suddenly on June 9 Stuart was surprised by a Federal cavalry attack under Pleasanton. After a sharp battle the Confederate cavalrymen drove Pleasanton back upon his infantry supports. The Federal commander, however, had accomplished his mission and reported to Hooker the information he had gained. Hooker estimated correctly that Lee was concentrating on the Confederate left and was planning a move around the Federal right. He planned to check it by throwing an overwhelming force against Fredericksburg and, if successful at that point, to move against Richmond. Lee feared such a maneuver and ordered Ewell to hurry to Winchester in the valley, attack the Federal garrison there, and by so doing alarm Washington. This maneuver was unnecessary for the Federal authorities had already refused to approve Hooker's plan. Lincoln's dispatch to Hooker on the day after Pleasanton's raid shows a grasp of military matters quite unlike that of the year before. "Your long despatch of today is just received. . . . I think Lee's army, and not Richmond, is your true objective point. If he comes toward the upper Potomac follow on his flank and on his inside track, shortening your lines while he lengthens his. Fight him, too, when opportunity offers. If he stays where he is, fret him and fret him."

227   Charge of General Buford's Cavalry near a ford of the Rappahannock, from *Harper's Weekly*, July 4, 1863

STUART'S RAID

THE middle of June saw Lee's army advancing down the Shenandoah. It was not concentrated but occupied a long line in its progress northward. Ewell's troops led the way. In the Loudoun valley, east of the Blue Ridge, Stuart's cavalry screened the movements of the main body. Between June 17 and 21 Stuart and Pleasanton were engaged in a series of conflicts which resulted finally in the Confederate cavalry being driven from the Loudoun valley. Then Stuart reached a decision which vitally affected the succeeding campaign. He proposed another of his cavalry raids. He would ride through or around the American army and quickly rejoin Lee in Maryland or Pennsylvania. Lee's confidence in his great cavalry leader was so complete that he approved the plan, though apparently with misgivings. As a consequence of this fateful decision Lee was for some days ignorant of the position of Hooker's army and the battle of Gettysburg was joined before Stuart was again available. Stuart met with unexpected obstacles which delayed him so that he did not report to Lee until the last day of the battle which marked the turning point of the war. Had Stuart continued with the main army, screening its movements, guarding its flanks, and reconnoitering the enemy, the whole course of the Gettysburg campaign must have been different. Lee on the way to Gettysburg erred in his use of cavalry in the same way that Hooker had done at Chancellorsville.

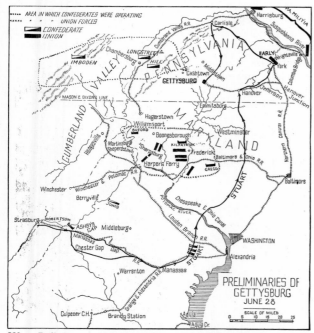

228   Preliminaries of Gettysburg, showing Stuart's Raid, drawn expressly for *The Pageant of America*

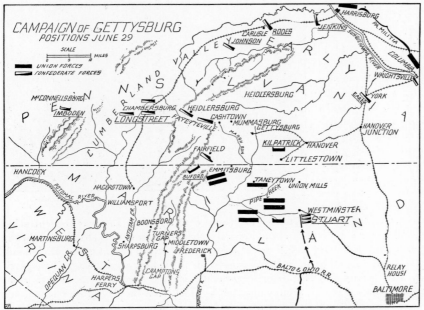

229   Positions of Opposing Forces at Gettysburg, June 29, drawn expressly for *The Pageant of America*

ON THE EVE OF GETTYSBURG

On June 28 Lee was at Chambersburg with the corps of Longstreet and A. P. Hill. Ewell's corps, far to the east, had divisions both at Carlisle and York. Ewell was threatening Harrisburg and capturing supplies. Between Ewell's corps and those of Longstreet and Hill lay the mountainous country which separates the Cumberland and the Susquehanna valleys. The best pass near at hand across these ridges debouched near Cashtown. On June 28 Lee was ignorant of the whereabouts of his enemy.

On the same day Stuart, whom Lee desperately needed, was at Rockville near Washington and was moving rapidly northward toward Harrisburg. On the night of June 28 a Confederate spy informed Lee that the Federal army was concentrated near Frederick. On the same night a staff officer from Washington awakened Meade to give him an order relieving Hooker and placing Meade in command of the Army of the Potomac. Meade was given an aggressive mission which included the covering of Washington and Baltimore. Meade knew the location of Lee's troops. He estimated that the Army of Northern Virginia would be concentrated at some points on the roads connecting York, Heidlersburg, and Chambersburg; but he had no information which would warrant an inference as to the exact locality. Meade, keeping his mission in mind, decided to advance northeastward to the Hanover-Gettysburg line. Such a movement would be an aggressive one and would cover Baltimore. Lee, meanwhile, when he learned that the Federal army was concentrated near Frederick, recognized the threat to his extended line of communications. He realized that he must concentrate his army promptly. The orders for concentration in the vicinity of Cashtown went out on June 29 and on June 30 the movement was well under way. On these two days Meade was advancing toward his new line from Hanover to Gettysburg and on June 30 Federal cavalry reached Gettysburg. Meade was uncertain as to the exact location of Lee's troops. He, therefore, ordered his engineers to survey a possible battle position at Pipe Creek near Taneytown in northern Maryland. Neither Meade nor Lee desired a battle on July 1 for on that day neither army was fully concentrated. The Battle of Gettysburg began by a chance collision between two small detachments of the armies which had now approached so close together.

WHY THE BATTLE WAS FOUGHT AT GETTYSBURG

On June 29 Heth's division of A. P. Hill's corps was in bivouac near Cashtown. On the next day Heth sent a brigade into Gettysburg to secure supplies, particularly shoes. This brigade found that Federal cavalry had just moved into the village and the brigade commander reported the fact to Hill. That general, not wishing to lose control of so important a road center, planned to move on Gettysburg on July 1 with two divisions and drive the Federals out. Buford, the Federal cavalry commander, had received orders from Pleasanton, his chief, to hold Gettysburg if possible. So the stage was set for the opening phase of the battle.

230 Brigadier-General John Buford, 1825–63, from a photograph in the United States Signal Corps, War Department, Washington

THE BATTLE OF JULY 1

ON July 1 the main body of Lee's army was moving eastward through the Cashtown pass toward Gettysburg and Ewell's corps was rapidly falling back from its advanced positions toward that town. At the same time Meade's left wing was moving leisurely northward with the expectation of reaching Gettysburg by night. Buford had taken up a position facing Cashtown on Seminary Ridge and had thrown out patrols on his front and flanks. Reynolds, commanding the left wing of the Federal army, was advancing to aid Buford. While still some distance from Gettysburg Reynolds received a message from Buford that the latter was about to be attacked. This caused Reynolds, who had not expected a battle that day, to hurry forward with one division to support the cavalry. On the morning of July 1 Hill struck the Federal line of defense with two brigades and was driven back. Reynolds who had come up and gotten into action was killed. In the very first fighting of the Battle of Gettysburg Meade lost his best corps commander. The death of Reynolds was a heavy blow. He was succeeded by Howard in command of the left wing. Meanwhile Hill, surprised at the strength of the Federal opposition, paused until afternoon. By that time Ewell's troops were arriving at Gettysburg and went into position north of the town. Meanwhile Howard had been rushing troops forward until, by

231 General John F. Reynolds, 1820–63, from a photograph, courtesy of W. B. Franklin, Ardmore, Pa.

two-thirty, the Federal line had been extended to face Ewell. The Union left was on the Hagerstown road and the right was on Rock Creek northeast of Gettysburg. The Federals were, however, outnumbered and outflanked. In spite of this they fought tenaciously and held their line until the Confederates assaulted and took a knoll which commanded the Federal right. Then the Union troops fell back through the town and reformed on Cemetery Hill to the south of the village. The Confederates were so disorganized that Ewell stopped the pursuit in the town. Hill's corps remained on Seminary Ridge and did not come to Ewell's aid. Lee riding to the battlefield after hearing the sound of cannon ordered Ewell to take Cemetery Hill if he thought advisable. Ewell did not consider it wise until his rear division came up from Cashtown. As this did not arrive before night, the fighting was ended for the first day.

232 General Winfield Scott Hancock, 1824–88, and members of his staff, from a photograph in the United States Signal Corps, War Department, Washington

GENERAL HANCOCK

ONE o'clock in the afternoon of July 1 came before Meade heard of the battle that was developing about Gettysburg and learned of the death of Reynolds. Meade knew that he had a considerable force, though not his entire army, within five miles of Gettysburg. His First, Third, Eleventh, and Twelfth corps were either at the village or close at hand. As Meade learned the news from the front, Hancock brought the Second Corps into Taneytown where for the time being were Meade's headquarters. The commanding general promptly sent Hancock to Gettysburg to study the situation and submit a report. Meade stayed at Taneytown which was an admirable location for headquarters if he decided to fall back and give battle at Pipe Creek. When Hancock reached the battle the Federal troops were falling back to Cemetery Hill. Dropping at once the rôle of observer, Hancock assisted Howard in forming line on this hill. The Federals were able to accomplish this because the Confederates did not assault. Hancock reached the conclusion that there was no further need of retreat and that the battle should be fought at Gettysburg. About six o'clock he left the battlefield to report to Meade. That general accepted his conclusions and at once began the concentration of his army at Gettysburg.

233   Assault of Brockenburgh's Brigade upon a stone barn, from *Battles and Leaders of the Civil War*,
New York, 1888

STEELE'S COMMENT ON THE FIRST DAY

"THE choice of Gettysburg as a battlefield was made wholly by chance. The first day's battle was an encounter. Neither army was at the time seeking the other to attack it. Neither Meade nor Lee had thought of Cemetery Ridge as a defensive position, or knew anything about the ground in the neighborhood. . . . The possession of Cemetery Hill was a decisive victory. Lee made a great mistake, therefore, in not following up the victory of Hill and Ewell promptly on the 1st of July, and in not making a vigorous effort to carry the hill as soon as the Union troops were driven back to it. True, the Confederate troops were well-nigh spent with marching and fighting, and their lines were in confusion. Yet this was apparently the only time during the battle when it would have been possible for them to carry the position. At that moment there were seventeen brigades of Confederate infantry on the ground and only thirteen brigades of Federal infantry and Buford's cavalry. General Lee, who arrived on the field, saw the importance of taking Cemetery Hill at once and sent Ewell an order to take it; but the order was not *positive* — it contained a condition — an *if*. Ewell took advantage of the conditional clause, and did not assault. Thus Lee's only chance of victory was thrown away." — STEELE, *American Campaigns*, 307–08.

COLONEL MARSHALL'S COMMENT ON THE FIRST DAY

"HAD Stuart been where he was ordered to be, he could have informed General Lee before June 29th that the Federal army had crossed the Potomac and left Virginia, and certainly the cavalry would have been able, as it marched along our right, to ascertain that the reported movement of the enemy from Frederick westward, — which induced General Lee to place his army east of the mountains [through the Cashtown pass] — was incorrect. As it was we were entirely ignorant until the afternoon of July 1st as to the whereabouts of General Stuart . . . we moved slowly on towards Gettysburg, believing that the enemy was yet in Maryland, to the south of us, moving from Frederick across our line of communication through Cumberland Valley, and with no other knowledge of his place and movements. That we came unexpectedly upon the Federal Army at Gettysburg may be inferred from the fact that, although our whole army could have been there on July 1st as easily as a part of it, only two of Ewell's and two of Hill's divisions were on the field during the engagement of that day, and the chief reason for not following up our success was the absence of Longstreet's corps and of one division of each of the other two. . . . Had all the army been up, there is no reason to suppose that there would have been any fighting at Gettysburg after the first day, to say nothing of the other consequences to General Meade's army that might have followed the crushing defeat or destruction of its advanced corps." — MAURICE, *An Aide-de-Camp of Lee*, 230–31.

234   The Town of Gettysburg, from a photograph in the United States
Signal Corps, War Department, Washington

MEADE'S POSITION

THE events of the second and third days of the battle were dependent upon the terrain. West of Gettysburg runs Seminary Ridge where General Lee had his headquarters. About a mile to the east of this eminence is a parallel rise of ground the most important features of which are Cemetery Ridge with Little Round Top and Big Round Top at its southern end and Cemetery Hill at its northern extremity. East of Cemetery Hill is Culp's Hill and northeast of this is Benner's Hill. Meade spent the night of July 1–2 in forming his line as his troops came up. He established his right on Culp's Hill. His center was the salient formed by Cemetery Hill. He ordered Sickles to establish the Federal left at Little Round Top. Sickles, however, acting on his own initiative, and without the knowledge of Meade, advanced to the Emmittsburg road in the vicinity of the peach orchard leaving the Round Tops unoccupied. Sickles' action offered Lee an unusual opportunity to envelop the Federal left.

THE BATTLE OF JULY 2

ON the afternoon of July 1 Lee decided that his main blow should be delivered against the Federal left. He planned to have Hill make a holding attack against Cemetery Ridge while Ewell and Longstreet should envelop the Federal left.

235   The Battlefield of Gettysburg, redrawn from the *Atlas to Accompany the Official Records of the Union and Confederate Armies*, Washington

Due to Sickles' ill advised action such a plan offered great prospects of success. Ewell, however, persuaded Lee to modify his plan. He informed the Confederate commander that Culp's Hill was unoccupied (a statement that was true at the time Ewell made it), and could easily be occupied on the morning of July 2. "By dawn of the following day (July 2) sufficient of the Federal army had arrived to occupy and fortify the heights. From where our battery was posted, a mile east of the town [Gettysburg], we had a full view of Cemetery Hill, with an arched gateway for an entrance. To the left of it and joined by a depressed ridge was Culp's Hill, steep and rugged as a mountain, all now held and fortified by the enemy. Jackson's old division, now commanded by Gen. Ed. Johnson, having arrived late in the night, formed at the base of Culp's Hill, and before an hour of daylight had elapsed had stirred up a hornet's nest in their front." — EDWARD A. MOORE, *The Story of a Cannoneer under Stonewall Jackson*, 189, Neale Publishing Co., New York, 1907. Lee, meanwhile, was developing his attack. He ordered Ewell to attack the Federal right and Longstreet the left. His scheme of maneuver called for the envelopment of both the hostile flanks. Under ordinary circumstances such an enterprise would be one of extreme difficulty. At Gettysburg Lee's front was a concave about the salient made by Cemetery Hill. The Confederate flanks were widely separated and troops moving from one part of the line to another had to cover great distances. Meade's position was just the reverse. His flanks were close together and he could move his reserves on interior lines. Lee's battle line was six miles long; Meade's was four.

236   From the painting *Gettysburg*, by P. F. Rothermel (1870–) in the Pennsylvania State Museum, Harrisburg, Pa.

237 Confederate Artillerymen at Dinner, from *Battles and Leaders of the Civil War*, New York, 1887

THE FEDERAL LEFT

HAD General Lee been able on the second day of Gettysburg to take the Round Tops and envelop the Federal left, the battle would have been his with results for the American people which no man can guess. His aide-de-camp, Colonel Marshall, has given the reason for the failure on this day. "General Lee slept that night (July 1–2) in a small house east of the Seminary Ridge and just north of the Chambersburg pike, his staff bivouacking in an orchard near by. Early on the 2nd, General Longstreet came to see General Lee and renewed his proposal that a movement could be made to turn the enemy's left, and to this General Lee answered that he was determined to attack the enemy where he was. General Longstreet then rode off to meet his troops. After waiting for some time for the expected development of General Longstreet's and expressing his surprise that it had not begun General Lee rode to the right to see General Ewell, to ascertain whether a reconnaissance made of Cemetery Hill in daylight showed that an attack on that position would be more promising. It was found that the enemy had strengthened his position greatly during the night, and that an attack on the enemy's right would have little prospect of success unless it was combined with other attacks on his left and center. General Lee thereupon returned to Seminary Ridge, and about 11 o'clock issued orders to General Longstreet to begin his attack upon the enemy's left as soon as possible. It was not, however, until 4 P.M. that Longstreet's batteries opened and soon afterward Hood's division on his extreme right moved to the attack." General Sir Frederick Maurice in a footnote to Marshall's account comments: "From what Colonel Marshall here says, it would appear that Lee in his conversation with Longstreet on the night of July 1st and the early morning of July 2nd expressed his intention of attacking as early as possible. Longstreet, who, as usual, considered his own plan the best, did not take this to be a definite order, and appears to have delayed in the hope of changing Lee's mind. The mistake made was in not committing the instructions to Longstreet to writing, and in not giving these orders in precise form. This mistake proved fatal. . . ." — MAURICE, *An Aide-de-Camp of Lee*, 233–34.

"It is hard to conceive of a worse conducted attack than that of July the 2nd. It ought to have begun at daybreak; and Lee's troops were all near enough to the field to have reached their position at that hour if they had received orders to do so and had exerted themselves. But the order did not issue until 11 A.M., and it was after 3 P.M. when the assault began. The plan of battle had in view successive attacks beginning at the right and progressing toward the left. . . . The result at Gettysburg was that Hood's division fought single-handed for more than an hour, and was brought to a stand-still; then two of McLaw's brigades took up the battle; after they had engaged for a half-hour or more the other two brigades of McLaw's division charged; and all were driven back. Then three brigades of McLaw's division charged; and all were driven back. Then three brigades of Anderson's division advanced, one at a time from right to left, and were driven back in the same order. . . ." — STEELE, 388–89. General Alexander commented that on July 2 the Federal army exhibited perhaps the best example which the war produced of active supervision and efficient handling of a large force on the defensive. — *Military Memoirs of a Confederate*, 403.

238   Slaughter Pen, foot of Round Top, Gettysburg, from a photograph by Gardner, Washington

239   A Harvest of Death at Gettysburg, from a photograph by Gardner, Washington

RESULTS OF THE FIGHTING OF THE SECOND DAY

By nightfall Meade's left had been driven back to the Round Tops which were still in Federal possession. Meade's right had stood firm; the Union positions on Culp's Hill had also held, but south of that hill the Confederates pushed forward until they were halted within thirty rods of the Baltimore turnpike. On this road lay Meade's trains and reserve ammunition. His enemy had almost gotten in his rear but the gray lines had been halted just before they reached a vital spot. That evening Meade telegraphed to Halleck. "The enemy attacked me about 4 P.M. this day and after one of the severest contests of the war was repulsed at all points."

THE CRISIS OF GETTYSBURG

"As soon as Longstreet's attack commenced, General Warren was sent by General Meade to see the condition of the extreme left. The duty could not have been entrusted to better hands. Passing along the lines he found Little Round Top, the key of the position, unoccupied except by a signal station. The enemy at the time lay concealed, awaiting the signal for assault, when a shot fired in their direction caused a sudden movement on their part which, by the gleam of reflected sunlight on their bayonets, revealed their long lines outflanking the position. Fully comprehending the imminent danger, Warren sent to General Meade for a division. The enemy was already advancing when, noticing the approach of the Fifth Corps, Warren rode to meet it, caused Weed's and Vincent's brigades and Hazlett's battery to be detached from the latter and hurried them to the summit. The passage of the six guns through the roadless woods and amongst the rocks was marvelous. Under ordinary circumstances it would have been considered an impossible feat, but the eagerness of the men to get into action with their comrades of the infantry, and the skillful driving, brought them without delay to the very summit, where they went immediately into battle. They were barely in time, for the enemy were also climbing the hill. A close bloody hand-to-hand struggle ensued, which left both Round Tops in our possession. Weed and Hazlett were killed, and Vincent was mortally wounded — all young men of great promise. . . . The enemy, however, clung to the woods and rocks at the base of Round Top, (and) carried Devil's Den and its woods." — GENERAL H. J. HUNT, in *Battles and Leaders of the Civil War*, New York, 1888.

240 General Gouverneur K. Warren, 1830–82, from a photograph by Brady, in the United States Signal Corps, War Department, Washington

241   *Home of a Rebel Sharpshooter*, from a photograph by Gardner, Washington

"HOME OF A REBEL SHARPSHOOTER"

GARDNER'S photograph of the "Home of a Rebel Sharpshooter" in Devil's Den depicts a characteristic of Civil War fighting. This infantryman, detached from his company, had established himself alone between two great rocks and had piled up a wall of stones in front. From his tiny fortress he picked off in comparative security the officers of the Federal troops. He was soon the object of an intense fire from muskets and artillery. The white spots on the stone to the right are bullet marks. The photographer found the stones on the outer side of the wall pitted in a hundred places. The trees in the vicinity were splintered and their branches cut off by the hail of lead. A fragment from a shell gave this brave Confederate lad a mortal wound in the head. He leaned his musket against the rampart he had built and lay down to die. The plan and accomplishment of this lone soldier are an example of that individual initiative and dogged determination that have characterized from the beginning the best American soldiers. The modern counterpart of this sharpshooter's stronghold may be found in the lone sniper and the deadly machine-gun nest.

THE FIELD OF GETTYSBURG ON THE THIRD AND FINAL DAY, JULY 3, 1863

LEE'S original plan on this third day was to feint against Meade's left, which held the Round Tops; while Elwell attacked Culp's Hill, so as to threaten Meade's right during the battle and smash it in case of Meade's retreat. Then, at Longstreet's word (as corps commander) Pickett's ten thousand first-rate shock troops were to drive their "desperation" wedge straight

242   Stewart's Brigade attacking Culp's Hill on the Third Day, from *Battles and Leaders of the Civil War*, New York, 1888

through the Federal center; whereupon all the central Confederate supports were to complete the victorious assault, while the remainder attacked the isolated flanks.

COLONEL MARSHALL ON PICKETT'S CHARGE

"THE result of this day's [July 2] operations induced the belief that with proper concentrated action, and with the increased support that the positions gained on our right would enable the artillery to give to the assaulting columns, we would ultimately succeed, and it was accordingly determined to continue the attack. The general plan was unchanged. Longstreet, reinforced by Pickett's three brigades, which arrived near the battlefield on the afternoon of the 2nd, was ordered to attack the next morning, and General Ewell

243   Repulse of Pickett's Charge, from *Prang's War Pictures.* © 1887

was directed to assail the enemy's right at the same time. . . . At an early hour on July 3rd General Lee met General Longstreet, who again proposed that a movement should be made round the enemy's left. General Lee however decided that the attack should be made as ordered. General Longstreet's dispositions were not completed as early as expected. [This resulted in Ewell's attack not being synchronous with that of Pickett thus losing its chief value.] . . . About 1 P.M., at a given signal a heavy cannonade was opened and continued for nearly two hours with marked effect on the enemy. His batteries replied vigorously at first, but toward the close their fires slackened perceptibly, and General Longstreet ordered forward the column of attack. . . . The troops moved steadily on under a heavy fire of musketry and artillery, the main attack being directed against the enemy's left centre; his batteries reopened as soon as they appeared; our own having nearly exhausted their ammunition in the protracted cannonade that preceded the advance of the infantry were unable to reply, or render the necessary support to the attacking party. The fact that the artillery ammunition had been so far reduced was known to General Longstreet, but was not reported to Lee. No order issued by General Lee justified the omission of notice of this important fact by General Longstreet. Owing to this fact, the enemy was enabled to throw a strong force of infantry against our left. . . . It finally gave way, and the right, after penetrating the enemy's lines, entering his advance work, and capturing some artillery, was attacked simultaneously in front and on both flanks, and driven back with heavy loss." — MAURICE, *An Aide-de-Camp of Lee*, 239–40.

PICKETT'S LETTER TO HIS BETROTHED ON THE EVE OF HIS CHARGE

244   Major-General George E. Pickett, 1825–75, from a photograph in the possession of H. P. Cook, Richmond

"AT early dawn [July 3], darkened by the threatening rain, Armistead, Garnett, Kemper and your Soldier held a heart-to-heart powwow. . . . Just as we three separated to go our different ways after silently clasping hands, our fears and prayers voiced in the 'Good luck, old man,' a summons came from Old Peter [Longstreet], and I immediately rode to the top of the ridge where he and Marse Robert were making a reconnaissance of Meade's position. 'Great God!' said Old Peter as I came up. 'Look, General Lee, at the insurmountable difficulties between our line and that of the Yankees — the steep hills, the tiers of artillery, the fences, the heavy skirmish line — and then we'll have to fight our infantry against their batteries. Look at the ground we'll have to charge over, nearly a mile of that open ground there under the rain of their canister and shrapnel.' 'The enemy is there, General Longstreet, and I am going to strike him,' said Marse Robert in his firm, quiet, determined voice. About 8 o'clock I rode with them along our line of prostrate infantry. They had been told to lie down to prevent attracting attention, and though they had been forbidden to cheer they voluntarily arose and lifted in reverential adoration their caps to our beloved commander as we rode slowly along. Oh, the responsibility for the lives of such men as these!" — *The Heart of a Soldier*, 95–96.

245   Third Day of the Battle of Gettysburg, from *Battles and Leaders of the Civil War*,
New York, 1888

PICKETT'S CHARGE, THE ADVANCE: 3:00 P.M., JULY 3, 1863

HUNT had stopped the Federal guns in the midst of Longstreet's artillery preparation so that they would be available for use at close quarters. When the Confederate guns ceased fire, as Pickett's three brigades advanced, both sides stood intently watching the fate of these devoted men. Three gallant lines of gray marched down the slope on the Confederate side. The blue ranks of Gibbon's division stirred a little, feeling their cartridge boxes and the jackets of their bayonets. "Steady, men, steady! Don't fire yet" came the calm warnings of the officers all down that waiting line.

THE SHOCK, 3:15 P.M.

FOR a very few tense minutes Pickett's division disappeared in an undulation of the ground. Then they rose into view again, not now in three successive lines, but in one consolidated mass of furiously charging gray. Instantly the Federal guns and rifles crashed out together, mowing down the front ranks as if with fiery scythes. But nothing could stay Pickett's undauntable survivors, who charged home, fighting the blue ranks hand to hand.

246   Pickett's Charge, from a sketch by S. Forbes in his *An Artist's Story of the Great War*, New York, 1890

HIGHWATER MARK, 3:30 P.M.

ONE stormy wave of desperate gray surged through the Federal front and broke in fury against the steadfast blue defense standing its ground upon the spot which was the last highwater mark of that invading tide. Then the fated ebb began. Back went the broken, but still undauntable, survivors, with not one single mounted officer left to lead. The battle was now lost, the campaign frustrated, and the whole war changed in favor of the North. For within this same momentous week the fall of Vicksburg and Port Hudson completed the enislement of the South.

247   From the painting *High Tide at Gettysburg*, by Thure de Thulstrup

THE HIGHWATER–MARK MEMORIAL

HERE, for all who love commemoration of brave deeds, stands this unique memorial, marking the farthest spot which Pickett's charging heroes reached, the spot, as well, where they were stopped by men quite worthy of their steel. Lee, the man, showed at his best when he rode out alone to meet the survivors of Pickett's gallant charge. Hat in hand and completely self-controlled he said: "All this has been my fault. It is I that have lost this fight."

248 The Highwater-Mark Memorial at Gettysburg, from a photograph reproduced in *The Gettysburg Memorial Pamphlet*

249   Pickett's Charge at Gettysburg, from a contemporary drawing by A. R. Waud in Joseph P. Derry, *Story of the Confederate States*, Richmond, 1895

PICKETT'S LETTER OF JULY 6

"ON the Fourth — far from a glorious Fourth to us or to any with love for his fellow-men — I wrote you just a line of heartbreak. The sacrifice of life on that blood-soaked field on that fatal third was too awful for the heralding of victory, even for the victorious foe, who, I think, believe as we do, that it decided the fate of our cause. No words can picture the anguish of that roll call — the breathless waits between responses. The 'Here' of those who, by God's mercy, had miraculously escaped the awful rain of shot and shell was a sob — a gasp — a knell — for the unanswered name of his comrade. There was no tone of thankfulness for having been spared to answer to their names, but rather a toll, and an unvoiced wish that they, too, had been among the missing. Even now I can hear them cheering as I gave the order, 'Forward!' I can feel the thrill of their joyous voices as they called out all along the line, 'We'll follow you, Marse George. We'll follow you — we'll follow you.' Oh, how faithfully they kept their word — following me on — on — to their death, and I believing in the promised support, led them on — on — on — Oh, God! I can't write you a love letter today, my Sally, for . . . the overpowering thought of those whose lives were sacrificed — of the broken-hearted widows and mothers and orphans." — *The Heart of a Soldier*, 101–02.

MEADE'S LETTER HOME ON JULY 5

"I HARDLY know when I last wrote you, so many and such stirring events have occurred. . . . It was a grand battle, and in my judgement a most decided victory, though I did not annihilate or bag the Confederate Army. This morning they retired in great haste into the mountains, leaving their dead unburied and their wounded on the field. . . . The men behaved splendidly; I really think they are becoming soldiers. They endured long marches, short rations, and stood one of the most terrific cannonadings I have ever witnessed. Baldy [Meade's horse] was shot again, and I fear will not get over it. . . . The army are in the highest spirits." — Quoted in *The Life and Letters of George Gordon Meade*, Vol. II, 125.

250 General George Gordon Meade, 1815–72, from a photograph by Gutekunst, Philadelphia

251   General Lee on Traveller, from a photograph in the
possession of the publishers

FIEBEGER'S COMMENT ON GETTYSBURG

"In his movement northward he [Lee] erred only in yielding his own judgement as to the proper movement of his cavalry to that of its commander. Had Stuart carried out Lee's suggestion to cross above Harper's Ferry, he would have reached Frederick before the Union army and the course of the campaign would have been different. Hill's movement to Gettysburg forced the battle on Lee before his army was concentrated. While it gave the Confederates a great advantage in the contest of July 1, they derived no benefit from it. . . . The battle of July 1 was badly managed by the Confederate commanders. The Confederates had the advantage both of position and numbers and should have won a decisive victory over the First and Eleventh corps. This would have been a serious blow to the Army of the Potomac. On the night of July 1, Lee erred in not carrying out his original intention of moving Ewell to the right of Hill, where Longstreet eventually deployed. He would then have been able to attack the left of the Union line with two corps instead of one, or, as Longstreet suggested, would have been able to maneuver Meade out of Gettysburg by threatening his communications. This maneuver was perfectly feasible, because the Fairfield and the Emmitsburg roads were both available for Confederate lines of communication and retreat. Ewell's corps however tied Lee's army to Gettysburg and practically compelled him to attack on the third day if he desired to prevent Meade from assuming the offensive. . . . Strategically, Gettysburg was not a good point of concentration for the Union army operating against a Confederate army concentrated on the Cashtown and Fairfield roads. The army could be easily maneuvered out of position by a Confederate movement southward. As the valleys in this vicinity run north and south such a movement would not have been difficult. Meade felt the weakness of his position and was apprehensive for his communications. Tactically, the position occupied by the Union army on the third day was very strong. . . . Meade has been criticised for not following up Pickett's repulse by a counter-attack. This criticism does not seem warranted. . . . He was also reproached for not attacking the Confederate lines near the Potomac after the retreat. . . . It is by no means certain that Meade's army would have been successful had he attacked contrary to the advice of his most experienced corps commanders. — Fiebeger, *Campaigns of the American Civil War*, 176–77.

THE SPIRIT OF THE CONFEDERATE ARMY

After Gettysburg Lee's army fell slowly back to Montpelier in Virginia where the men enjoyed a long rest. Toward its end, on September 3, the army was reviewed and in that military display showed its undauntable spirit. The scene was one of gaiety as Worsham describes it: "Gen. Lee rode to the right of the front division, which had taken its place, and, with bands playing and drums beating, the general dashed along the front of the line, followed by the large cavalcade of generals and their staffs. The men presented arms, flags were lowered,

252   From the painting *Autumn*, by Charles Hoffbauer (1875–).
© Confederate Memorial Institute, Richmond

the officers saluted with their swords, and all the pomp of war that could be shown by these old Confederates was brought into view. . . . The lines now marched forward several hundred yards, with bands playing, then left-wheeled into column of regiments, the regiment at the head guiding us to a line with the flag, where the corps marched past the stand in column of regiments. As each regiment arrived in front of Gen. Lee the men came to a shoulder arms, the flags dipped, the officers saluted, the bands played; Gen. Lee raised his hat in recognition, the ladies waved their handkerchiefs and clapped their hands and cheered us, we answering with a Confederate yell." — *One of Jackson's Foot Cavalry*, 180.

A REVIVAL IN LEE'S CAMP AFTER GETTYSBURG

"THE place selected for preaching in our camp was on a hillside, in a large wood. . . . The ground was slightly inclined; trees were cut from the adjoining woods, rolled to this spot, and arranged for seating at least two thousand people. At the lower end, a platform was raised with logs, rough boards were placed on them, and a bench was made at the far side for the seating of the preachers. In front was a pulpit or desk, made of a box. Around this platform

253   A Religious Meeting in Camp, from a sketch in the Prints Division, Library of Congress, Washington

and around the seats, stakes or poles were driven in the ground about ten or fifteen feet apart, on top of which were baskets made of iron wire, iron hoops, etc. In these baskets chunks of light wood were placed, and at night they were lighted, throwing a red glare far beyond the place of worship. The gathering, each night, of the bronzed and grizzly warriors, devoutly worshiping, was a wonderful picture in the army; and when some old familiar hymn was given out, those thousands of warriors would make hill and dell ring. In this rude place of worship thousands gathered for several weeks. The interest manifested was so great that seats were taken in the afternoon by such men as were not on duty; and when night relieved from duty those who had been drilling, etc., the men stood up in immense numbers around those who were seated . . . the converts were so numerous that they numbered not by tens and hundreds, but by thousands." — WORSHAM, 181–82.

GETTYSBURG STREET, NOVEMBER 19, 1863

MANY weeks had passed since the sleepy little village of Gettysburg had heard the crash of musketry and booming of the batteries. The tide of war had receded southward. The trampled crops of summer were maturing to a meager harvest. Those who gave their lives had long since been laid to rest — all but the rebel sharpshooter. Gardner, coming back in this quiet Indian summer for the dedication of the cemetery at Gettysburg, scrambled up to the rock fortress which he had discovered on the day after the battle. The musket, covered with rust, still leaned against the rampart of stones and the bones of the soldier were whitening in the sun. He had not been found by the burial parties. On this nineteenth of November a regiment with cadenced steps marched again along the village street. The crowd was filled with suppressed excitement as President Lincoln pronounced the following immortal Gettysburg oration, to dedicate the cemetery where lay the Blue and the Gray.

"Fourscore and seven years ago our fathers brought forth on this continent a new nation conceived in liberty and dedicated to the proposition that all men are created equal. Now we are engaged in a great civil war testing whether that nation, or any nation so conceived and so dedicated, can long endure. We are met on a great battlefield of that war. We have come to dedicate a portion of that field as a final resting-place for those who here gave their lives that that nation might live. It is altogether fitting and proper that we should do this. But, in a larger sense, we cannot dedicate, we cannot consecrate, we cannot hallow this ground. The brave men, living and dead, who struggled here have consecrated it far beyond our power to add

254   Lincoln's Address at Gettysburg, Nov. 19, 1863, from a painting by A. I. Keller in *Harper's Weekly*, Feb. 10, 1900

or detract. The world will little note nor long remember what we say here, but it can never forget what they did here. It is for us the living rather to be dedicated here to the unfinished work which they who fought here have thus far so nobly advanced. It is rather for us to be here dedicated to the great task remaining before us — that from these honored dead we take increased devotion to that cause for which they gave the last full measure of devotion — that we here highly resolve that these dead shall not have died in vain, that this nation under God shall have a new birth of freedom, and that government of the people, by the people, for the people, shall not perish from the earth."

CHAPTER V

FARRAGUT AND THE NAVY

WITHOUT the Navy and its blockade which strangled the South, the Federal Government could not have won the war. The United States Navy still had its fivefold duty to fulfill. It had to blockade three thousand miles of southern coast line; to protect sea-going commerce in and out of northern ports; to coöperate with the northern armies on every kind of navigable waters, salt and fresh; to prevent the southern navy from ever getting strong; and, finally, to do all this while engaged in the extremely hard work of multiplying its own strength seven times over before the South surrendered. The number of enlisted seamen authorized by Congress rose from seven thousand six hundred to fifty-one thousand five hundred. The number of vessels of all kinds used for any naval purpose was two hundred and sixty-four at the end of the first year; four hundred and twenty-seven at the end of the second; five hundred and eighty-eight at the end of the third; and six hundred and seventy-one at the end of the fourth.

In 1863 the Navy's task was very exacting with regard to the blockade, because many foreign vessels ran between two neutral ports and broke bulk at the second. But the Federal Government invoked the doctrine of continuous voyage, which enabled blockaders to examine cargoes on the high seas and take as contraband whatever was in excess of the normal imports needed by the second port. This American precedent was followed by the Allies blockading German and other enemy ports before the United States entered the World War.

The Confederates gallantly tried to break the blockade at several points. The southern raiders gave trouble out of all proportion to their numbers. The three most famous were the *Florida* in '63, the *Alabama* in '64, and the *Shenandoah* in '65. As the war went on, and the South became more and more enisled in a hostile sea, her only points of contact with the outside world were reduced to three: Mobile, Wilmington, and Charleston. Charleston remained till the end. But in August '64 Farragut took Mobile with a magnificently planned attack. In January, 1865, Fort Fisher (guarding Wilmington) fell before the masterly work of Admiral Porter, who commanded the largest United States fleet up to that time combined: nearly sixty fighting vessels with over six hundred guns. A sea bombardment and a land assault together won the day. This left the exhausted South with only one lone port and one lone raider: Charleston and the *Shenandoah*. Charleston fell into Federal hands on the fourth anniversary of the surrender of Fort Sumter (April 14, 1865). The *Shenandoah* committed the very last acts of war, sinking the last Federal whaling vessel in Behring Strait on June 28. On August 2 the British bark *Barracouta* told her that the Confederacy had come to its end. She then sailed seventeen thousand miles to Liverpool, where, on November 5, she surrendered to the British, who transferred her to the Government of the United States. In this upbuilding of the navy the North took full advantage of its superiority in financial and industrial power. The South could not build to meet the Federal menace on the sea.

THE CONFEDERATE NAVY

The Confederate Navy had better men than means. Mallory was a better Secretary than his "opposite number" in the Federal Cabinet, Gideon Welles. He had more administrative skill and was far in advance of Welles on the vital question of ironclads. In an official letter to the Naval Committee on May 8, 1861, less than a month after the war began, he said: "I regard the possession of an iron-armored ship as a matter of the first necessity . . . not a moment should be lost." Brooke invented the banded guns which did such excellent service, while Davidson worked hard to improve the torpedoes which Maury had invented. Mallory did all he could to further their work, as he did to further the work of everyone else connected with the southern navy. But means were everywhere deficient and the Confederate force afloat was one long emergency makeshift. The naval aspects of the Civil War displayed the difficulties encountered by a people whose life rested almost wholly upon an agricultural foundation in carrying on a war against an enemy with a long record of maritime achievements.

255 Stephen Russell Mallory, 1813–73, from a photograph in the Brady Collection

256 The *Patrick Henry*, from the *United States Official Records of the Union and Confederate Navies*, Washington, 1897

CONFEDERATE NAVAL SCHOOL SHIP

The *Patrick Henry* was a small, side-wheel, sea-going steam brigantine, converted from an Old Dominion liner by shipping ten guns. She anchored off Drewry's Bluff, seven miles below Richmond, and was expected to sink herself and block the channel if the Federal fleet tried another advance up the James, after McClellan's failure there in July, 1862. Her sixty young midshipmen, all in their teens, lived in the midst of bombardments, and the most promising were often rewarded by being sent to the batteries firing on Grant's army when he was besieging Petersburg for three hundred days, from June, 1864, to the end of March, 1865.

THE NAVAL ACADEMY PRACTICE SHIPS

During this war the United States Naval Academy was moved to Newport, Rhode Island, but the practice ships shown here were at the Boston Navy Yard in 1862, when they cruised at large, as again the following year, with the *Macedonia*, "in face of the enemy," whose active raiders were also at large. These Academy vessels did not have any sea fights. But a few midshipmen served in action elsewhere; and none better than Benjamin H. Porter, who, though only seventeen, fought his howitzers with skill and gallantry

257 Naval Academy Practice Ships at the Boston Navy Yard, from the *United States Official Records of the Union and Confederate Navies*, Washington

at Roanoke Island, and was killed at Fort Fisher among the bravest leaders in that desperate assault.

258   The *Mississippi*, from a lithograph by R. G. Skerrett, after a photo-
        graph, courtesy of the Navy Department, Washington

259   The *Colorado*, from a photograph in the possession of
        the publishers

THE UNITED STATES SHIPS *MISSISSIPPI* AND *COLORADO*

THE *Mississippi* and the *Colorado* were the typical steam frigates of the day. The old *Mississippi* was the famous ship in which Commodore Perry appeared off Tokio, when he so impressed the Japanese that they signed their first treaty with a Western power. (See Vol. II, Chapter XIII.) Admiral Dewey served aboard the *Mississippi* under Farragut at New Orleans. The *Colorado* shows the advance from paddle-wheels to screws.

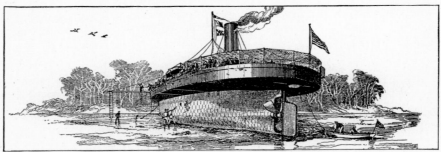

260   The Monitor *Montauk* Beached for Repairs, from *Battles and Leaders of the Civil War*, New York, 1888

SUCCESSORS OF THE ORIGINAL *MONITOR*

AFTER the battle between the *Merrimac* and the *Monitor* the naval leaders of both North and South bent their efforts to the building of ironclads. Each side tended to cling to its original type. The South with the heavy demands that the war was making on its limited foundries was unable to turn out vessels of the monitor type. The Confederates, therefore, had to content themselves with converting such ships as were available into floating batteries, protected by a heavy iron casement. A sharp iron beak on the prow made the vessel a dangerous ram. Such warships were very useful in protecting southern ports against the wooden blockading fleet. The superiority of the Federal monitors over the Confederate ironclads lay in their greater speed and mobility and in the fact that the guns in their revolving turrets could be fired in any direction.

261   The Monitor *Onondaga*, from a photograph in the United
        States Signal Corps, War Department, Washington

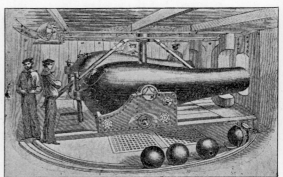

262   Interior of a turret on a sea-going monitor, from *Battles
        and Leaders of the Civil War*, New York, 1888

THE CONFEDERATE RAIDERS

THE *Florida* was early on the sea, having escaped from England in the spring of 1862 under the name of the *Oreto*. Under the enterprising Commander J. N. Moffitt she ran into and out of Mobile, giving the Federal blockaders the inward slip on September 4, 1862, and giving the outward slip to the *Cuyler*, the fastest blockader, as well as passing the flagship *Susquehanna* close aboard, on that dark and stormy night of January 16, 1863. The *Florida* raided for two full years, till rammed and overpowered by the Federal ship *Wachusett* at Bahia, a neutral port in Brazil, on October 7, 1864. The instructions

263 Destruction of the *Jacob Bell* by the *Florida*, from a drawing by G. Perkinson, in the possession of the publishers

given to the raiders "left much to discretion and more to the torch"; so that the temptation to destroy what northerners called "pirates" was too strong for Commander Collins of the *Wachusett*.

MATTHEW FONTAINE MAURY, 1806–1873

ONE of the most important naval men who threw his lot with the Confederacy was the Virginian, Matthew Fontaine Maury. When in 1861 he offered his sword to the Confederacy, he was looked up to in both Europe and America as the greatest oceanographer of his day. Maury had been a pioneer of science in an age and a nation to which the word "pioneer" connoted a covered wagon and a westward trek in search of a new home. He early turned his attention to navigation and to astronomy. By original research in materials hitherto unused he produced his *Wind and Current Chart of the North Atlantic*. The work was epoch-making and, had he done nothing more, his name would have ranked high in nautical science. The material presented was of such obviously practical value to seamen of all services that Maury received the coöperation of many navigators in his efforts to gather accurate information regarding the various oceans. In 1853 his work had achieved such international fame that a convention was called in Brussels where government experts and shipping men from all Europe flocked to help work out this extraordinary new science. Maury came home laden with honors and inspired to fresh effort. Two years later he published his greatest book and one of the most extraordinary intellectual efforts of his generation, *The Physical Geography of the Sea*. Humboldt had suggested the title.

The outbreak of the Civil War found Maury turning swiftly from scientific investigation to plans of action. Before North or South were fully aware of the immensity of the tasks which confronted them he produced a practicable program for the creation of a Confederate navy. The Government, however, ignored his recommendation until the Federal navy held the southern coast line in an unshakeable grip. Baffled here, he turned his attention to material and invented the torpedoes which gave the men of the Federal navy so many anxious moments. The Davis Government, influenced by the prejudice and opposition of the Secretary of the Confederate Navy, failed to utilize to the full the ability which Maury put at the disposal of the Confederacy. To get him out of the way the "Pathfinder of the Seas" was finally sent to England where he supervised the fitting out of the cruiser, *Georgia*, which sailed under Lieutenant William L. Maury. After the conflict was over, Maury turned his thoughts again to the work which the war had interrupted. He gave invaluable aid to Cyrus W. Field in the latter's work of laying the Atlantic cable. The great scientist spent the last years of his life as a professor at the Virginia Military Institute.

264 Matthew Fontaine Maury, from a photograph in the possession of H. P. Cook, Richmond

265   Chart of the Cruise of the *Alabama*, redrawn by Gregor Noetzel from a map in the *Century
                              Magazine*, April 1886

THE PRINCE OF CONFEDERATE RAIDERS, THE *ALABAMA*

PARTLY because she was the foremost of her type, partly because her captain was likewise foremost of his special kind, and partly because she was the only raider known to all the world, we may concentrate most attention on the *Alabama* and on Captain Semmes. A beautifully modeled thousand-ton wooden barkentine, the *Alabama* was built by the British firm of Lairds at Birkenhead in 1862. Captain Semmes, late of the United States Navy, was not only an exceptionally skillful officer in all sorts of naval work but a past master in a knowledge of all the international law which could possibly be turned to Confederate advantage. For almost two years he roved the seas, both of the Old World and the New, taking no less than sixty-six Union vessels, valued at seven million dollars, and producing great alarm and an enormous insurance rate among all kinds of Union shipping. The *Alabama's* cruising was partly done by speeding under steam, or steam and sail together. But her great spread of canvas enabled her to work vast areas entirely under sail. She ranged the seas for over two hundred degrees of longitude, from Mexican to Chinese waters. She took "Yankees" not only in the Straits of Sunda but within one day of New York. Off Brazil and the Azores she captured two lots of vessels almost as if they were two flocks of sheep. She sank a blockader off the Texan coast, evaded a Union man-of-war at the Cape of Good Hope, and kept the United States Navy guessing her most elusive presence for two destructive years. No wonder the crew of the U.S.S. *Kearsarge* were wild with hope deferred when they heard the *Alabama* was in port at Cherbourg in the north of France, and that there was a chance not only of blockading but perhaps of fighting to a finish! The map gives the record of the *Alabama's* raids, raids that seemed magnificent to southern eyes, but more or less piratical to those of the infuriated North.

265   Admiral John Americus Winslow, from
          a photograph by Brady

267   Officers on the deck of the *Kearsarge*, from a photograph in the United States
                    Signal Corps, War Department, Washington

ADMIRAL JOHN A. WINSLOW, 1811–73, CAPTAIN OF THE U.S.S. *KEARSARGE* SIGHTS THE *ALABAMA*, SUNDAY, JUNE 19, 1864

HAVING located the *Alabama* at Cherbourg and received Semmes' challenge for a duel to the death, Winslow, a splendid specimen of the United States naval officer, was conducting prayers on deck when out came the *Alabama*. Down went the book; up came the speaking trumpet. And all hands went to action quarters for the fight.

268   The Fight Between the *Kearsarge* and the *Alabama*, from the painting by J. O. Davidson in the possession of the Naval History Society, courtesy of the New York Historical Society

269   Hauling down the flag of the *Alabama*, from the painting by J. O. Davidson for *Prang's War Pictures.* © 1887

U.S.S. *KEARSARGE* AND C.S.S. *ALABAMA* "FIGHTING IN A CIRCLE" SUNDAY, JUNE 19, 1864

THE *Alabama* was not in good condition; her copper hull was foul and ragged. She had been strained by constant speeding, and her canvas was of little value in a fight. But Semmes was determined to show that she could and would fight men-of-war as well as raid merchantmen. So out she came against the trim *Kearsarge*. The *Kearsarge* had almost impenetrable concealed chain mantlets protecting her vitals. They consisted of chain cables laid against her outside and cleverly boarded over. She had a stronger hull, greater speed, fourteen more men in her more homogeneous crew, and a couple of eleven-inch pivot guns, which were far more powerful than anything on board the *Alabama*. Starboard to starboard, in a circle narrowing down from half to a quarter of a mile, the two ships fought each other hard. "Use solid shot! Our shells fall into the water," called Semmes to his executive officer, Kell. The concealed chain mantlets of the *Kearsarge*

270   Raphael Semmes, 1809–77, from a photograph in the possession of H. P. Cook, Richmond

were admirably stanch, while her superior guns quickly gained the upper hand. Strange to say, the *Alabama's* last broadside announced her own defeat by breaking out the *Kearsarge's* special Stars and Stripes run up the mizzenmast in stops on purpose to be broken out only when victory had come! Rearing like a stricken horse, the *Alabama* went down stern first, while most of her survivors were rescued by French and British boats, as well as by those of the *Kearsarge*.

THE CAREER OF SEMMES

SEMMES did not fall into the hands of his enemy. Rescued by the British *Deerhound*, he was taken to England. On February 10, 1865, back again in the Confederacy, he was made a rear-admiral and given command of the James River Squadron. Less than two months later he was handed an order from Secretary Mallory to destroy his ships; Richmond was to be evacuated. Without delay Semmes transferred his activities from the water to the land. With a commission as brigadier-general he led a marine brigade until the Confederacy had ceased to exist.

THE CONFEDERATE SHIP
SHENANDOAH, 1865

COMMISSIONED late in 1864, off Madeira, the *Shenandoah* took nine Union vessels on her way to Australia, whence she went north till she fell in with the New Bedford Whaling Fleet near Behring Strait in June, after the Confederate Government had disappeared forever. Her twenty-five captures here were therefore sheer purposeless destruction. But her captain, Waddell, never received any positive neutral war news till he spoke the British *Barracouta* five weeks later.

271   The *Shenandoah* at Liverpool, from a retouched photograph in the possession of H. P. Cook, Richmond

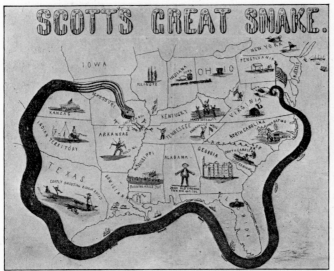

272   *Scott's Great Snake*, a satirical map of the Federal Blockade of the South, from a broadside in the possession of the Naval History Society, courtesy of the New York Historical Society

THE FEDERAL BLOCKADE,
1863–1865

THE cartoon suggests how the North got its hold upon all the southern waterways, each year making the hold tighter than before. In 1861 several points in the seacoast flank were seized and held. In 1862 New Orleans and Pensacola were secured; in 1864 Mobile; in 1865 Fort Fisher. Charleston alone remained in southern hands. But it was closely blockaded. Some Texan ports were also southern still. But they were of little use to the eastern South once the Mississippi had become a Federal river with the fall of Vicksburg and Port Hudson in July, 1863. The blockaded South suffered dire distress. The long, dull, numbing monotony of a close blockade was wearing work, wearing on machinery and hulls; still more on the human elements concerned.

But the United States Navy held firmly on, watching the long, indented coast, and watching the neutral ports from which the final dash was made.

To the end of the war the Federal navy never stopped entirely the running of the blockade. The configuration of the coast with its broad estuaries and its border of low islands made the work of preventing the Confederates' slipping out extremely difficult. New methods of evasion were devised as fast as old ones proved ineffective. The final one was the development of a special type of ship built in England and sold to private citizens of the Confederacy. These boats were long and narrow and in them everything was sacrificed to

speed. Painted gray and practically invisible beyond a distance of a few hundred yards, they made their way stealthily from Bermuda to the coast. The final dash through the blockading squadron was made at night, the roar of the breakers drowning the noise of their engines. Tremendous profits were made on these trips. Early in 1864 about two out of three of these blockade runners escaped. Before the end of the year, however, the proportion had been sharply reduced. The magnitude of the task which the Navy undertook when it began blockading the southern coast may be gauged by the fifteen hundred and four blockade runners of every size that were captured or destroyed during the conflict.

273   The *Pensacola*, from a photograph in the United States Signal Corps, War Department, Washington

CONFEDERATE VICTORY AT GALVESTON, JANUARY 1, 1863

FARRAGUT had occupied Galveston without a blow in 1862. But next New Year's Day two cotton-wadded steamers closed in on the U.S.S. *Harriet Lane*, shot down her captain and her first lieutenant, and made her next officer strike his colors. Commander Renshaw blew up the *Westfield*, the only other Federal ship, rather than surrender; and so, for a week, the blockade was broken through. But Commodore H. H. Bell then made it closer than before.

274   Attack upon a gunboat flotilla at Galveston, from *Harper's Weekly*, Jan. 31, 1863

275 Confederate Rams engaging the Federal Blockading Fleet off Charleston, from a sketch in *Harper's Weekly*, Feb. 21, 1863

INGRAHAM'S ATTACK ON THE BLOCKADERS OF CHARLESTON IN 1863

WITH great determination Ingraham's two Confederate gunboats damaged the *Quaker City*, mauled the *Keystone State*, and made the *Mercedita* strike. But presently the grim blockade was reëstablished. Charleston was a particularly difficult problem for the blockade squadron. Here was a fine harbor from which the blockade runners slipped frequently out in defiance of the close blockade. Here also the first gun of the war had been fired. The Civil War, like all wars, engendered hatred and northern hate was directed at Charleston more than any other southern community. The summer of 1863 saw a determined attack upon the city. Two able commanders were sent in 1863 to capture this cradle of secession. General Gilmore was an engineer of marked ability. Admiral Dahlgren was the Navy's greatest expert in gunnery and the inventor of the Dahlgren gun.

276 John Adolph Dahlgren, 1809–70, from a photograph by Brady, in the United States Signal Corps, War Department, Washington

GENERAL BOMBARD-MENTS OF JULY AND AUGUST, 1863

BATTERY WAGNER commanded the entrance to Charleston harbor. On July 18 the army and navy made a combined attack. The *New Ironsides*, five monitors, and a frigate threw nearly a thousand shot and shell into Battery Wagner in less than twelve hours. This terrific

277 Bombardment of Fort Wagner, from a sketch in *Harper's Weekly*, Aug. 29, 1863

bombardment however did not silence the fort. After the Navy had done its best, the troops stormed the battery with the utmost resolution, some even crossing the ditch and gaining foothold in the southern salient. But the Confederates would not be conquered. Inflicting losses much greater than they received, they drove off the assailants. The Federal troops then settled down to siege operations.

278 The Swamp Angel, from a sketch by Theodore Davison in *Harper's Weekly*, Sept. 19, 1863

In August the attack was shifted to Sumter, proudly defying the Federal forces since the surrender of Major Anderson. Batteries were placed on shore where the Federal troops had gained a foothold. From an emplacement skillfully developed in a morass the "Swamp Angel" threw cannon balls into the streets of Charleston, five miles distant. The "Swamp Angel" was a forerunner of the German "Big Bertha." From August 17 to 23 the land batteries and the fleet bombarded Sumter. The guns of the fort were unable to damage seriously the ironclad monitors while its walls crumbled under the enemy fire.

279   View of southwest angle of Fort Sumter, from a sketch in the *Atlas to Accompany the Official Records of the Union and Confederate Armies*, Washington

THE FAILURE AT SUMTER

SUMTER was finally silenced and Battery Wagner abandoned. The fleet planned to carry the great fort by storm. On September 7 Admiral Dahlgren demanded the surrender. Major Elliott replied: "Inform Admiral Dahlgren that he may have Fort Sumter when he can take and hold it." That night the Navy assaulted with a landing party and was repulsed. Charleston held out until 1865 when Sherman's conquering army attacked it from the rear.

FIGHTING AT FORT McALLISTER

SAVANNAH saw fighting in the same year that the assault was made on Charleston. The *Montauk*, one of the best of the Federal monitors, bombarded Fort McAllister on January 27, 1863. But the guns of the ship could not silence the fort. A month later the *Montauk* under Captain Worden returned to the fight with four other ships. Worden's main objective

280   The ironclad *Montauk* engaging Fort McAllister, from a sketch in *Harper's Weekly*, Feb. 21, 1863

was the *Nashville*, an important Confederate cruiser lying in the Great Ogeechee River and guarded by the fort. A line of piles prevented a dash past McAllister. Under a heavy, though somewhat wild, fire from the fort, Worden turned his guns on the *Nashville* at a range of twelve hundred yards and sank her. This exploit gave Worden almost as much satisfaction as his more famous battle with the *Merrimac*.

THE BATTLE OF WILMINGTON RIVER

ON June 17, 1863, off the mouth of the Wilmington River occurred a fight which illustrated well the respective power of the northern and southern ironclads. The *Fingal*, originally a Scotch iron ship of thirteen knots, had run the blockade out of Savannah and slipping into the Wilmington had been transformed into an ironclad ram of the most approved southern type. She was cut down and a casement was erected. She was broadened out with solid timbers bolted outside the hull until she had sides seven feet thick at the water line. Her armor plates were like those of the *Merrimac* though not made of such good metal. The wooden backing for them was only eighteen inches thick, though her designer knew the power of the fifteen-inch guns

281   Capture of the *Atlanta* by the Monitor *Weehawken*, from a sketch in *Harper's Weekly*, June 17, 1863

that she would have to face. On June 17 the *Atlanta*, as the new ram was christened, steamed down the Wilmington River under the command of Lieutenant Webb. Two monitors were awaiting her, the *Weehawken* and the *Nahant*. The *Atlanta* opened on the *Weehawken* at a mile and a half but her shooting was bad. The *Weehawken* replied at a range of three hundred yards. Her first shot pierced the casement and wounded sixteen men; her second struck the pilot house of the *Atlanta* wounding both pilots and both wheelsmen. In fifteen minutes Webb, seeing that his enemy could shoot him to pieces, hauled down his flag.

282   The gunboat *Sassacus* ramming the Confederate ram *Albemarle*, from *Harper's Weekly*, May 5, 1864

THE *ALBEMARLE* AND THE *SASSACUS*

THE *Albemarle* was probably the greatest of the Confederate ironclads. Her attempt to break the blockade from within does so much honor to the skill and heroism on both sides that it well deserves special attention. In the spring of 1864 North Carolina sought an outlet to the sea by way of Albemarle Sound; and set high hopes on the apparently impenetrable ram called after her blockaded sound. Single-handed the *Albemarle* gave battle to the Federal blockading flotilla. At first the Federal shot and shell glanced off the *Albemarle's* iron sides without doing more damage than starting some plates and rivets. As the fight developed the *Albemarle* seemed bent on doing as much destruction as the *Merrimac* had accomplished the day before she met the *Monitor*. But Commander Roe was determined to risk the complete loss of his own light-draft, paddle-wheel, double-ender gunboat *Sassacus*, if only he could put the *Albemarle* out of action. Presently he maneuvered into place at right angles to her. "All hands, lie down!" he roared, as he ordered the fires stuffed full with well-oiled waste and the throttle kept wide open. On came the charging *Sassacus*, crashing her sharp bronze beak into the *Albemarle's* side. An *Albemarle* shell burst the boiler of the *Sassacus*, scalding the engineers. But the rest of the crew fought off a gallant attempt to board; and when the vessels parted the wounded *Albemarle*, unable to face her other opponents, took refuge up-stream.

283   Lieutenant William B. Cushing, 1842–74, from a photograph in the possession of the publishers

THE DESTRUCTION OF THE *ALBEMARLE*

AFTER her duel with the *Sassacus* in Albemarle Sound in the spring, the *Albemarle* spent nearly six months up the Roanoke River in comparative safety. On the night of October 27–28, 1864, Lieutenant William B. Cushing, U.S.N., made his way up the river, in a small launch with a crew of picked men. Because of the darkness of the night Cushing was unobserved until he came close to the log boom protecting the ironclad. In the face of heavy firing he ran full speed toward the boom. His bow came to rest on the logs. In a moment with his own hand he exploded a torpedo under the overhang of the enemy ship "at the same time that the *Albemarle's* gun was fired. A shot seemed to go crashing through my boat, and a dense mass of water rushed in from the torpedo, filling the launch and completely disabling her. . . . The most of our party were captured, some drowned, and only one escaped besides myself. . . ." — W. B. CUSHING. Hiding in a swamp near the Confederate fort during the next day Cushing received confirmation through a negro of the sinking of the *Albemarle*. The following night, after capturing a skiff from a Confederate picket, he reported to his commanding officer.

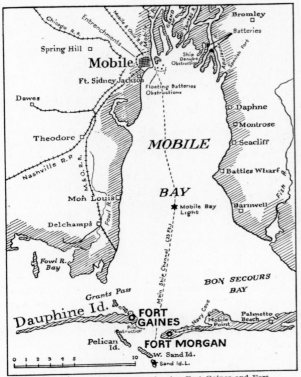

284   The Defenses of Mobile Bay, showing Fort Gaines and Fort Morgan, drawn especially for *The Pageant of America*

FARRAGUT'S THIRD DECISIVE NAVAL INROAD ON THE SOUTH, BATTLE PLAN OF MOBILE BAY, AUGUST 5, 1864

FARRAGUT'S first great naval inroad on the South was his capture of New Orleans in 1862 (see Chapter III). His second was when he helped the Federal armies to make the whole Mississippi a Union river in 1863. Now, in 1864, he was to combine with Grant's and Sherman's armies in dealing the South three fatal blows. (See map, No. 358.) While Grant was fighting Lee's army in Virginia (see Chapter VI) and Sherman was advancing against Georgia (see Chapter VII) Farragut was attacking the last great Confederate seaport in the Gulf — Mobile. The chief defenses of Mobile were Fort Morgan, a powerful work on Mobile Point, Fort Gaines on Dauphin Island, torpedoes in the channel, and in the harbor a Confederate flotilla which included the powerful ironclad ram, *Tennessee*, commanded by no less an officer than Franklin Buchanan, former Superintendent of Annapolis and commander of the *Merrimac* in the battles at Hampton Roads. These fortifications, obstructions, and ships combined to make Farragut's task unusually difficult and dangerous.

"DAMN THE TORPEDOES"

CROSSING the bar on the flood tide early in the morning Farragut closed with the enemy. The monitor, *Tecumseh*, led the fleet. The *Brooklyn* headed the line of battleships with the *Hartford*, Farragut's flagship, second. To each ship was lashed another to tow her, if necessary, out of action. The monitors formed a line on the port side of the battleships. The guns of the *Tecumseh* opened the battle for the Federals. Just as the fleet was closing with the fort and the firing was becoming intense, the *Tecumseh* was suddenly shaken by a terrific explosion and plunged almost immediately beneath the surface. A deadly torpedo had done its work so well that but a handful of the crew had an opportunity to escape. The *Brooklyn*, seeing a line of buoys ahead, halted and signaled the danger. This action nearly threw the fleet into confusion for the other ships were pushing on under full steam ahead. Farragut faced the most difficult decision of his life. At the beginning of the battle he had taken post in the *Hartford*'s port main rigging. But as the smoke obscured his view he climbed up under the maintop, where a sailor lashed him on. Tradition has it that when the warning, "'Ware torpedoes!" reached his ears he answered in the fighting spirit which had won at New

Orleans: "Damn the torpedoes!" The *Hartford* pushed into the van. Farragut knew that he was in the proper channel; he knew the Confederate torpedoes were unreliable; he knew they exploded only on special contact; and he knew that there could be no more live ones where the *Tecumseh* had gone down. Like the great captain that he was, he decided to take a reasonable risk. The torpedoes at Mobile were not self-moving torpedoes in a modern sense, but simply contact mines which frequently missed fire.

285   The Union Fleet Passing Fort Morgan Through the Torpedo Fields, from the painting *The Battle of Mobile Bay*, by J. O. Davidson for *Prang's War Pictures*.
© 1887

THE *TENNESSEE* IN ACTION

PUSHING past the *Brooklyn*, the *Hartford's* crew heard the bumping of torpedoes against the hull. But none exploded. In a few minutes the American van had passed the fort. While the guns of Fort Morgan were still trained on his flagship, Farragut saw the low, iron-covered *Tennessee* moving toward him. But Buchanan merely passed the *Hartford* plunging solid shot into her at point blank range. With a daring equal to that of his opponent the Confederate captain drove his vessel into the midst of the attacking fleet while it was passing the fort. His engines were slow; his ammuni-

286 *Farragut at the Battle of Mobile Bay*, from the painting by William H. Overend (1851–98), in the Wadsworth Atheneum, Hartford, Conn.

tion was bad, causing his guns frequently to miss fire. Yet Buchanan battered his enemy so powerfully that one Federal ship, the *Oneida*, was completely crippled and had to be towed by her consort.

287 The *Lackawanna* ramming the *Tennessee*, from a sketch by Robert Weir in *Harper's Weekly*, Oct. 22, 1864

THE *TENNESSEE* RETURNS

NEITHER the forts nor the *Tennessee* could stop Farragut. The Federal fleet made the inner harbor and formed about the *Hartford*. Then Buchanan, who had failed to stop its entrance, brought the *Tennessee* about and headed a second time toward his opponents. On this day two of the greatest sea fighters that America has produced clashed in a battle which showed each at his best. The advance of the *Tennessee* was the signal for a wild fight. This time Buchanan headed straight for the *Hartford*. Farragut, advancing to meet his adversary, avoided the jab of the *Tennessee's* sharp beak, and the two boats lying alongside plunged broadsides into each other. As the ships parted, the *Monongahela* rammed the *Tennessee* without effect because of a special armor which the Confederates had developed to meet such tactics. The *Lackawanna* tried the same maneuver with the same result. Dashing at the *Tennessee* a second time, the *Lackawanna* in the confusion rammed the *Hartford*, holing her hull within two feet of the water line.

SURRENDER OF THE *TENNESSEE*

IN spite of her solid armament the *Tennessee* was doomed. Her engines were too slow for quick maneuvering; her smokestack was shot away; and most important of all, a defect in her construction now proved a vital weakness. For some reason the steering gear of the *Tennessee* had been left exposed. When this had been shot away, the ram was quite unmanageable. Then, when he could fight no longer, Buchanan surrendered. On August 23 Fort Morgan, now at the mercy of converging fire from the Federal fleet and General Granger's army, was forced to surrender. Thus fell

288   The Surrender of the *Tennessee*, from a sketch in *Harper's Weekly*, Oct. 29, 1864

Mobile. The fall of the important Gulf port stopped permanently the blockade running at this point. More important, Farragut's victory cheered the people of the North cast down by the heavy casualties of Grant's Virginia campaign.

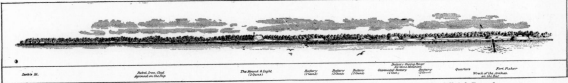

289   Confederate Defenses at the entrance to the Cape Fear River, from the *Atlas to Accompany the Official Records of the Union and Confederates Armies*, Washington

BOMBARDMENT OF FORT FISHER

FORT FISHER guarded Wilmington, the last port through which, outside of Charleston, Lee's armies could possibly get supplies. The Federal forces were determined to take it. They assembled sixty fighting vessels of which five were ironclads carrying altogether over six hundred guns. On December 23 and 25 Admiral Porter brought his ships as close as possible to the fort and subjected it to a terrific bombardment. The garrison, driven into their bomb-proof shelters, could not reply effectively. On the second day troops under General Butler were landed preparatory to an assault. Butler was no soldier. He ultimately reported the impossibility of taking the fort by assault and retired, to the rage of the fleet. Such was the end of the military career of one of the worst of the political generals.

SECOND ATTACK ON FORT FISHER

BUTLER'S army was quickly replaced with eight thousand troops under General Terry. On January 15, the fleet again bombarded the powerful fort. Two thousand seamen and marines were landed from the fleet to storm the sea face of Fort Fisher. The four hundred marines had rifles and bayonets. But the sixteen hundred sailors had only cutlasses and pistols. They were shot down by scores in the open while desperately striving to reach and climb that deadly sea face of the fort. At last they had to fall back, for flesh and blood could do no more. Terry's army was fourfold stronger than Lamb's Confederates. Well

290   Interior of Fort Fisher, from a photograph by Brady, in the L. C. Handy Collection, Washington

led and fighting with determined skill, it forced its way through every line of defense and soon compelled Fort Fisher to surrender. Just a little over a month later Charleston fell before Sherman's troops. The Confederacy was tottering to collapse.

291   The Bombardment of Fort Fisher, from a drawing by J. O. Davidson

CHAPTER VI

GRANT AND SHERMAN

IN the spring of 1864 Grant was called to the post of commander-in-chief. "My commission as lieutenant-general [the first in the United States Army since Washington's] was given to me on the 9th of March, 1864. On the following day . . . I visited General Meade, commanding the Army of the Potomac, at his headquarters at Brandy Station, north of the Rapidan. . . . Meade evidently thought that I might want to make still one more change not yet ordered. He said to me that I might want an officer who had served with me in the West, mentioning Sherman especially, to take his place. If so, he begged me not to hesitate about making the change. He urged that the work before us was of such vast importance to the whole nation that the feelings or wishes of no one person should stand in the way of selecting the right men for all positions. For himself, he would serve to the best of his ability wherever placed. I assured him that I had no thought of substituting any one for him. As to Sherman, he could not be spared from the West. This incident gave me even a more favorable opinion of Meade than did his great victory at Gettysburg the July before. . . .

"In my first interview with Mr. Lincoln alone he stated to me that he had never professed to be a military man or to know how campaigns should be conducted, and never wanted to interfere in them: but that procrastination on the part of commanders, and pressure from the people at the North and Congress, *which was always with him*, forced him into issuing his series of 'Military orders' — one, two, three, etc. He did not know but they were all wrong, and did know that some of them were. All he wanted or had ever wanted was some one who would take the responsibility and act, and call on him for all the assistance needed, pledging himself to the use of all the power of the Government in rendering such assistance. Assuring him that I would do the best I could with the means at hand and avoid as far as possible annoying him or the War Department, our first interview ended. The Secretary of War I had met once before only, but felt that I knew him better. . . . He and General Halleck both cautioned me against giving the President my plans of campaign, saying that he was so kind-hearted, so averse to refusing anything asked of him, that some friend would be sure to get from him all he knew. I should have said that in our interview the President told me he did not want to know what I proposed to do. But he submitted a plan of campaign of his own which he wanted me to hear and then do as I pleased about. He brought out a map of Virginia on which he had evidently marked every position occupied by the Federal and Confederate armies up to that time. He pointed out on the map two streams which empty into the Potomac, and suggested that the army might be moved on boats and landed between the mouths of these streams. We would then have the Potomac to bring our supplies, and the tributaries would protect our flanks while we moved out. I listened respectfully, but did not suggest that the same streams would protect Lee's flanks while he was shutting us up. I did not communicate my plans to the President, nor did I to the Secretary of War or to General Halleck. March the 26th my headquarters were, as stated, at Culpeper, and the work of preparing for an early campaign commenced." — *Personal Memoirs of U. S. Grant*, Vol. II, pp. 116–17, 122–23, Century Co.. New York, 1895.

292   General U. S. Grant, from an engraving by R. White-
church after a daguerreotype by Brady

GRANT'S OPINION OF LINCOLN AND STANTON

"THEY were the very opposite of each other in almost every particular, except that each possessed great ability. Mr. Lincoln gained influence over men by making them feel that it was a pleasure to serve him. He preferred yielding his own wish to gratify others, rather than to insist upon having his own way. It distressed him to disappoint others. In matters of public duty, however, he had what he wished, but in the least offensive way. Mr. Stanton never questioned his authority to command, unless resisted. He cared nothing for the feelings of others. In fact it seemed to be pleasanter to him to disappoint than to gratify. He felt no hesitation in assuming the functions of the Executive, or in acting without advising with him. If his act was not sustained, he would change it — if he saw the matter would be followed up until he did so. . . . Mr. Lincoln was not timid, and he was willing to trust his generals in making and executing their plans. The Secretary was very timid, and it was impossible for him to avoid interfering with the armies covering the capital when it was sought to defend it by an offensive movement against the army guarding the Confederate capital. He could see our weakness, but he could not see that the enemy was in danger. The enemy would not have been in danger if Mr. Stanton had been in the field." — *Personal Memoirs of U. S. Grant*, Vol. II, 536–37. Many another northern general shared Grant's dislike of Stanton.

293   Guard Mount at the Headquarters of the Army of the Potomac, from a photograph by Gardner, Washington

THE ZOUAVES IN THE ARMY OF THE POTOMAC

THE photograph taken during the winter before the "hammering campaign" began illustrates the perfection of drill which had been achieved by the Army of the Potomac after years of war. Guard mount is always an impressive ceremony, and the Zouaves with their uniforms of brilliant colors made the most of such occasions. In the background appear the ingenious huts which the soldiers had built for winter quarters. Such training and such ingenuity were the factors which gave the commander in chief confidence in the army he led. It was the most efficient and powerful fighting force that had appeared up to that time on the continent of North America. Equipped with every material need it seemed invincible. The genius of Lee and the southern officers and men who supported him may be measured by the fact that this magnificent weapon of war, though led by an experienced and fighting general, could not defeat on the field of battle a ragged and ill-supplied force of half its numbers. Though Grant compelled his opponent to retire from position to position he could not destroy the Confederate Army. The spirit of Lee in the Wilderness, at Cold Harbor, and at Petersburg harks back to that of Washington at Brandywine, at Germantown, and at Valley Forge.

FEDERAL COMMISSARIAT

WE have seen so often the vast difference between the superabundance of the North and the semi-starvation of the South that any emphasis on the northern commissariat in this crowning campaign would be superfluous if it were not for the fact that even Grant's critical eye found his supply and transport service practically perfect all through. The army was learning the importance of staff.

294   Commissary Department, Army of the Potomac, from a photograph by Gardner, Washington

295   Landing Supplies on the James River, 1864, from a photograph in the United States Signal Corps, War Department, Washington

FEDERAL TRANSPORT SERVICE

GRANT'S land transport train, if on a single road, would have stretched sixty-five miles. But the Federal army had the vast advantage of transport by water. The rivers were of the utmost importance in the forwarding of men and supplies to the fighting front and in the evacuation of wounded to the hospitals in Washington.

FEDERAL ARMY REPAIR SHOPS

THE Federal army had at its command practically all the necessities, and many of the amenities, of civilian life at home. The repair shops were indispensable to the advance of the wagon trains, upon which the very lives of the troops depended. Behind the fighting men labored an army of specialists.

296   Army Repair Shop, from a photograph by Gardner, Washington

FEDERAL ARMY FIELD TELEGRAPH

THE Telegraph and Signal Corps was constantly at work laying insulated wires by means of reels on muleback. Parallel lines were led rearward from each brigade till quite clear, when they were joined up at right angles, so that headquarters could instantly communicate with any unit desired.

297   United States Military Telegraph Construction Corps, from a photograph by Gardner, Washington

PONTOON BRIDGES

THE crossing of rivers was one of the main problems of Grant's army where so many parallel streams flow eastward. After much experimentation the army engineers had finally settled upon the wooden pontoon shown in the picture as the most practicable type of temporary bridge. The pontoons could be hauled from river to river and with them, as shown in the photograph, the timbers upon which the planks were laid. On reaching the bank the boats slid into the water and were towed with row boats to their proper stations. Here they were anchored. In the event of close pursuit

298   Pontoon Bridge across the Rappahannock, from a photograph by Gardner, Washington

one end of the bridge could be cut causing it to swing with the current against the bank to which the opposite end was attached. Here it could be taken up at leisure.

299   Pontoon Boat, from a photograph by Gardner, Washington

DIFFICULTIES IN RECRUITING

300   Conscription in New York, from *The Illustrated London News*, Apr. 8, 1865

"BY the spring of 1864 the people of both North and South had become weary of war. In the North the expiration of the enlistment of the three-year men of 1861 required the raising of large levies to carry on the war. Both sides had resorted to the draft to keep the ranks of their armies filled. On both sides straggling and desertion had become a problem. In the North the splendid patriotism which had been manifested in the early enlistments of the war, and which was still supreme among soldiers at the front and in the homes from which they came, was overshadowed in that sphere of money making and of business pushing which was a result of the national prosecution of the war, with its inflated currency and its steadily increasing demands for army equipment and supplies. When calls for added volunteers were made by the Government, young men who otherwise would have been ready to respond with personal service were now so busy with their money-making and their efforts to provide for the material wants of the Government that they felt they could not go themselves, but they would gladly pay to secure someone to go for them. Large bounties were offered to substitute recruits to count on the quota required by the new call; and the gift of money, rather than of service, came to be looked at for the hour as the true measure of patriotism." — H. CLAY TRUMBULL, *War Memories of an Army Chaplain*, 184, Charles Scribner's Sons, New York, 1898. The draft permitted substitution and made it possible for a man to buy exemption. Even so the passage of the draft law sent many Americans flying to Canada as suggested by these verses from a Canadian paper, under the title, *The Cowards are Coming*.

"The cowards are coming, O dear, O dear!
The cowards are coming, O dear, O dear!
    With fugitive speed,
    They are coming indeed,
And their faces are pallid with fear.

Though the exile from bondage we hail with a smile
And he's free as air on Canadian soil;
    Yet we know how to treat
    Every runaway cheat,
That shrinks from the patriot's toil, his toil."

This wretched skedaddle (I name it with pain),
Commenced in loyal, lumbering Maine:
With instinctive cunning and recreant craft,
They cleared at the 'smell' of the purgative 'draught.'

NEW YORK DRAFT RIOTS, JULY 13–16, 1863

THE substitution clause of the conscription act violated the fundamental principles of democracy by enabling the more well-to-do to buy exemption while the poorer man was compelled to serve. The law demonstrated, moreover, that the people of the North were not yet willing to compel all citizens who were needed in the emergency to fulfill their obligations to the state. When the drawing of names in New York city resulted in a list of men the great majority of whom were mechanics or laborers, class feeling appeared. Many of those conscripted, supported by many more whose names might soon be called, bitterly attacked the law on the ground of unfair discrimination. The city rang with the charge that the conflict raging south of the Potomac was "a rich man's war and a poor man's fight." Heated protests developed quickly into violence. The authorities were caught unprepared by the mobs which appeared on July 13. A reign of terror developed. On the second day the numbers of the victorious mobs were swelled by the criminal classes who sought to profit by pillaging and looting. Not until the fourth day was order completely restored.

301   Draft Riots in New York, from *Frank Leslie's Illustrated Newspaper*, Aug. 2, 1863

VII—10

302   Buying a Substitute, from a southern cartoon in the possession of the publishers

"BOUNTY JUMPING"

"THE twin evils of bounties and substitution brought into being a class of men known as 'substitute brokers,' who made it their business to secure men, 'by hook or by crook,' to enlist as substitutes, for assignment to the credit of such states as offered the largest bounties to men counting on their quota. The broker, naturally, made the best terms he could with the substitutes whom he engaged, taking as large a share of the bounty as he could secure by fair means, and sometimes by foul. It being known by these brokers that desertion from the army was comparatively easy and safe, they saw that a man could enlist as a substitute, desert and enlist again, and so on indefinitely, counting each time on the quota of the state paying the bounty, and shielding another able-bodied citizen of that state from the dreaded draft. . . . Men who were engaged by them in this branch of activity were called 'bounty-jumpers'; and they came to be recognised as among the enterprising and efficient 'patriots' of the business communities of the North. The dimensions of this evil grew at a fearful rate. It tended to the demoralization of the business community, and to the discouragement of the army. I speak of what came under my own observation, when I say that substitutes enlisted and deserted three, five, and seven times over; that in single regiments one-fourth, and again one-half, and yet again a larger proportion, of all the men assigned under the new call of the President for five hundred thousand more volunteers, deserted within a few weeks of their being started to the front." — TRUMBULL, 105–06.

THE PENALTY FOR DESERTION

WHOLESALE desertion called for drastic remedies. The situation threatened the very existence of the armies. The temper of the civilian population was the primary cause for the evil. Public opinion at home could have aided in eradicating the difficulty. In the absence of effective popular pressure the army had to deal with the situation as best it could. There seemed to be no alternative to a resort to the death penalty. Trumbull has described the extraordinary case of a man who escaped from confinement incurred for insubordination, and deserted to the enemy. After serving in the Confederate ranks for nearly two years, he deserted through the lines again expecting to be sent North. He chanced to pass through lines held by his old regiment and was recognized. . . . "The entire brigade was ordered out to witness this execution. As the command stood waiting, in three sides of a hollow square, with an open grave in the center of the fourth side, the stillness was broken by a low, soft, plaintive strain of music; which came floating on the sultry air across the plain . . . a funeral dirge from muffled drums, with the subdued notes of an accompanying band. . . . The fettered deserter was helped from the cart, just back of the open grave. The priest knelt with him in prayer; then bade him good-by and retired a little distance to kneel and continue praying in his behalf. The guard formed on the right and the left of the prisoner, and the firing party took position in front of him a dozen paces distant, as he knelt on his coffin with bandaged eyes and pinioned arms. . . . The dirge had died away. . . . 'Fire!' . . . The entire brigade marched in column by the open grave and the dead deserter. The bands struck up a lively air, as always in going from a soldier's grave, and the command returned to camp again. None who witnessed that sight could ever forget it. But it came too late in the war. . . . Desertions had already begun, and the spirit that led to them could not at once be checked." — *War Memories of an Army Chaplain*, 181–83.

303   The Firing Squad, from H. Clay Trumbull, *War Memories of an Army Chaplain*, New York, 1898

RESULTS OF THE BOUNTY AND SUBSTITUTION SYSTEM

Two cases will suffice to illustrate the results of the bounty and substitution system. One was that of a man who "had originally volunteered in a New England regiment, and he had shown himself a brave, true soldier until he was discharged for ill-health. Regaining his strength . . . he had volunteered in another regiment; but, being debauched by the prevalent sentiment in favor of 'bounty jumping' and deserting, he deserted his new command in order to join the army under an assumed name. . . . Assigned to a regiment near the one from which he had deserted, he was recognised . . . and arrested as a deserter, and was now to die for his crime under his assumed 'substitute' name. . . . But the case of the last deserter to whom I ministered was most painful of all. A boy less than sixteen years old . . . was enticed away to be sold as a substitute. He was somewhat under-witted, but simple-hearted and childlike in a peculiar degree. He said . . . that he had never passed a night away from home until the substitute broker led him off. When he found himself . . . in a camp in Virginia, he wanted to go home; . . . he started in broad daylight to go down to the landing from which he had come. He was stopped and brought back to camp. Again he started to run, making no concealment of his purpose. He was re-arrested . . . and sentenced to be shot. . . . There was no possibility of even reaching the department commander with a request for clemency in time to have it available. The sentence must be executed." — TRUMBULL, 189, 194–95.

304 A Civil War Recruiting Poster, from the original in the Division of Manuscripts, Library of Congress, Washington

LINCOLN AND ARMY DISCIPLINE

EVERY death warrant required the signature of the President. Lincoln was loath to affix his name to such papers, yet he recognized that it was an inescapable duty. Discipline in the army had to be enforced. The theory on which the death penalty was based was that only the fear of death can prevent certain men from deserting to avoid the danger of death in battle. On this theory Lincoln signed hundreds of orders. He had neither the time nor the opportunity for personal investigation of the cases that were brought to him. The details of many came to his attention through the supplication of parents. The President was peculiarly susceptible to such pleas. He believed in tempering justice with mercy. Upon one occasion he faced an angry general who charged him with destroying discipline by refusing to carry out the decisions of the courts-martial. "General," said Lincoln, "there are too many weeping widows in the United States now. For God's sake don't ask me to add to the number; for I tell you plainly I won't do it."

305 A Pardon, signed by Lincoln, for a man sentenced to death for sleeping on guard duty, from the original in the War Department, Washington

Now, therefore, be it known that I, Abraham Lincoln, President of the United States, do issue this my Proclamation, as required by said act, ordering and requiring all deserters to return to their proper posts, and I do hereby notify them that all deserters, who shall, within sixty days from the date of this proclamation, viz: on or before the tenth day of May 1865, return to service or report themselves to a Provost Marshal, shall be pardoned, on condition that they return to their regiments and companies, or to such other organizations as they may be assigned to, and serve the remainder of their original terms of enlistment, and, in addition thereto, a period equal to the time lost by desertion

306 Amnesty Proclamation, from the original
in the Department of State, Washington

A PROCLAMATION OF AMNESTY AND ITS RESULTS

IN 1864 executions for desertion increased at an appalling rate. But executions did not lessen the numbers of deserters. Trumbull says that on the contrary, it was found that execution was immediately followed by desertions in the regiment to which the condemned men had belonged. To condemn the harshness of the courts-martial is easy. The army was sometimes painted as an ogre devouring the youth of the nation. This was unfair, for the army was not responsible for the evil of desertion. The responsibility for this lay with the citizens of the North who failed to give their army adequate moral support. Military men recognized that desertion was a disease which, unless checked, might render the fighting force of the nation impotent. They used the only means at their disposal to cure the disorder. The tragedy of the situation lay in the fact that the cure was beyond the power of the army and lay in the hands of the people back home. And these folk too often were ignorant of their responsibilities or disinclined to meet their obligations. On March 11, 1865, President Lincoln issued a proclamation of amnesty for deserters. He promised that men who confessed would escape the penalty and, after completing their terms of enlistment, would receive an honorable discharge. "Hardly was the order made public, before men began to show themselves in response to it. First one came, then two, then five. While these were telling their stories and entering their names a score of others were waiting outside for their turn. Then another score, and another, came. Eighty-four men in our regiment, or one-seventh of those present for duty, confessed to being deserters. . . . They had yielded to the temptation to desert from one regiment and enlist in another, in order to 'jump a bounty.' One of them said to me, 'My old regiment is just down the road, yonder, and I've been so afraid some one would see me here. When I've been out to one of those shootings of a deserter, I've been so afraid my time would come next that I could hardly keep from taking to my heels right away.' This was the reason why an execution increased desertion. Others had been seduced and swindled by bounty-brokers, they hardly knew how." — TRUMBULL, 198–99.

THE PATRIOT NORTH

THE war entered its fourth year with profiteering and substitution threatening the very existence of the nation. Throughout the struggle the people of the North failed to recognize the citizen's first duty to the state. They had been willing to fight the war with volunteers or men who could not pay for a substitute when drafted. A Maine family represents the former class. "At the opening of the war a father and five sons from that family volunteered for army service. One son was wounded at the first Bull Run, but was soon once more at the front. After a year's service the father was mustered out for disability. One son was killed at Antietam, a second at Port Hudson, a third at Gettysburg. The son who was wounded at Bull Run received another wound at Petersburg. . . . He started across the fields on foot . . . wandered from his path in a blinding sleet storm, and finally sank down exhausted, to be frozen to death but a stone's throw from the . . . homestead whose shelter he was seeking. The fifth . . . son, a soldier in the eleventh Maine . . . had been wounded . . . in August, 1864, and was at home when his dead brother was brought in. He soon rejoined his regiment . . . and he apologized to me for being on light duty because of his wound . . . as if he wanted to have me know that he was not shirking." — TRUMBULL, 50.

307 The Spirit of the North, from a drawing
by Felix O. C. Darley, in the possession of
the publishers

308   Charge of Logan's Troops at the Battle of Resaca, May 14, 1864, from a sketch by Theodore R. Davis,
in *Harper's Weekly*, June 18, 1864

THE SPIRIT OF THE SOLDIER

"As two regiments of our brigade were endeavoring to wrest an important position from the enemy on the north bank of the James River, on a hot July day, a man of the Eleventh Maine was shot through the body, and was evidently dying. His commander, seeing him there under the broiling sun, and realizing that he had but a little while to live, called to some men to carry him to a shady place at the rear. The brave fellow, taking in the whole situation, said cheerily, 'No, no, colonel. That would take two men from the front, and every man is needed there now. I can just as well die here.' And die there he did." — TRUMBULL, 47–48.

THE BLOOD SACRIFICE

IMPOSSIBLE of overemphasis is the terrible loss of life of the war. The world had never seen such slaughter and the bloodiest year was reserved to the last. "In each of two of the greatest battles, Gettysburg and the Wilderness, the loss, of both sides together, amounted to fifty thousand killed, wounded, and missing. In both these battles the number of those who met their death in the field was larger than the death-roll of the English army during the whole of the Peninsular War, and including Quatre Bras and Waterloo. In both of them the loss of life was greater than at Gravelotte although the numbers engaged were not half so large. In the month's fighting in Virginia in 1864 the Federal army under Grant lost seventy thousand men." — LT.-COL. G. F. R. HENDERSON, *The Science of War*, 235–36, Longmans, Green & Co., New York, 1906. Such figures are mute evidence of the courage of the American soldier whether he wore the blue or the gray. They measure the price which the nation paid for its preservation.

309   Burying Confederate Dead at Fredericksburg, from a photograph in the United States Signal
Corps, War Department, Washington

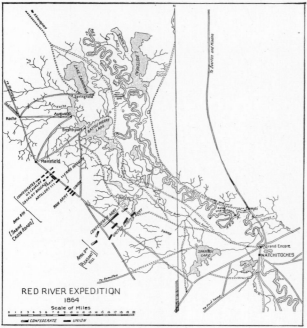

RED RIVER EXPEDITION
1864
Scale of Miles

310   Red River Campaign, redrawn from the *Atlas to Accompany the Official Records of the Union and Confederate Armies*, Washington

RED RIVER CAMPAIGN MAP, MARCH–MAY, 1864

Though the Red River expedition is beneath criticism as an operation it must be noticed here, because the mere fact that it was ever undertaken had a very bad effect on the whole Federal campaign of 1864. The expedition was planned and carried out for political ends in defiance of military means. The Confederate Southwest had already been conquered for all practical purposes by the Mississippi campaign of 1863. The forces sent were needed elsewhere in the final struggle with the still combatant portions of the eastern South. The completely ex-centric campaign up the Red River wasted lives and national resources. Banks' forty thousand veteran Federal soldiers, with Porter's invaluable fleet and all the auxiliary services needed by them both were thus withdrawn, at the very worst time, from the four naval and military forces trying to overcome the still unconquered Confederates by a combined strategic move from all four quarters of the compass — Sherman's army from the west, Grant's from the north, Butler's from the east, and what should have been a Union army to work with Farragut's fleet from the south. All the great naval and military leaders whose opinions could be given explained the mistake of trying the Red River. Even Banks himself, who commanded the army there and who was more a politician than a soldier, protested. But so insistently did the public shout "Hands off Mexico!" to France that the Government felt obliged to give the orders The Red River campaign helped to prolong the war.

311   Maj.-Gen. Richard Taylor, 1826–79, from a drawing after a photograph

312   Landing of Banks' Troops, from a contemporary sketch in the United States Signal Corps, War Department, Washington

LANDING OF GENERAL BANKS' ARMY, RED RIVER EXPEDITION

This contemporary picture gives some faint idea of the great Federal resources in men, munitions, and naval and military means of every kind, which were squandered on this expedition. Banks made his headquarters at Alexandria while assembling his army. The objective of the campaign was to gain and hold a strong position in the interior of Texas as a warning to France in Mexico. The Federal troops were handicapped from the outset by dissension between Banks and his subordinate generals, who were better trained than he was. Fortunately for the Federals, dissension also hindered the efforts of the Confederates. The able General Richard Taylor, who commanded in the field, had as his superior the Department Commander, General Kirby Smith. Had Taylor been given a free hand, Banks would doubtless have suffered more than he did.

313   Alexandria, on the Red River, from a drawing after a photograph in *Battles and Leaders of the Civil War*, New York, 1888

SABINE CROSS ROADS AND PLEASANT HILL, APRIL 8–9, 1864

In the latter part of March and early April, 1864, Banks advanced northwestward with the Red River on his right. This flank was covered by Admiral Porter's fleet, the campaign having been planned to take place during the weeks when the Red was in flood and contained enough water to carry the gunboats of the cooperating naval force. Taylor retired before Banks but, on April 8, turned on him suddenly when his army was advancing in column of march twenty miles long along the single road that led through a pine barren region. Though the van deployed quickly and fought well, it was driven back. Only the stanch resistance of General William H. Emory's division prevented a disastrous rout by an enemy whose total was only half as much as that of Banks. The fight took place at Sabine Cross Roads. The next day at Pleasant Hill the Federals had better fortune. But the losses were heavy and Banks' army had become demoralized.

314   Red River Dam, Gunboat *Lexington* passing the Rapids at Dawn, from a sketch by Rear Admiral H. Walke

RED RIVER DAM: GUNBOATS PASSING THE RAPIDS AT DAWN, MAY 9, 1864

Meanwhile the Red River, contrary to all precedent for that time of year, began to fall. Porter, apprehensive lest his craft be stranded and destroyed, hurried downstream, followed by the army. All went well until he reached the mile of rapids at Alexandria. Here the water measured a little more than three feet while the heaviest Federal vessels required seven. At this point a lieutenant-colonel from Wisconsin, one Joseph Bailey, achieved prominence. Gaining permission only with difficulty he utilized his experience as a former lumberman trained to logging on the northern rivers to build "wing dams" of logs. On May 8 some of the gunboats went through. In the early morning of May 9, the tremendous pressure of water washed out two barges used as booms. But the *Lexington* ran these rapids before the water fell too far. This sudden lowering would have stranded all remaining vessels, if Bailey, within three strenuous days, had not again dammed up the river and set the whole lot free. Then the misconceived expedition returned, having accomplished nothing, having wasted invaluable resources, and having defeated even its own political ends; for its utter failure was an encouragement to France and Mexico as well as to the still combatant portions of the South.

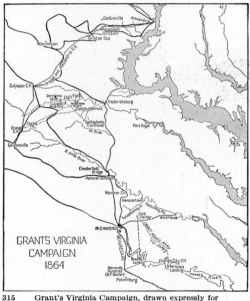

315   Grant's Virginia Campaign, drawn expressly for
                    The Pageant of America

GRANT'S PLAN FOR THE VIRGINIA OPERATIONS OF 1864

In the spring of 1864 three Federal armies threatened Virginia and Grant proposed a vast converging movement on Richmond. Sigel, commanding the Department of West Virginia, was to concentrate his troops in the upper Shenandoah and advance on Lynchburg. Butler, commanding the Department of Virginia and North Carolina, was to advance against Petersburg and Richmond from his base at Fortress Monroe. Grant himself was to take the Army of the Potomac across the Rapidan and advance on Richmond. Meade retained to the end of the war the command of this army. Grant, commander in chief of all armies, had his headquarters with Meade's force and personally directed its movements. In all three of these proposed zones of action the Federals outnumbered their adversaries by about two to one. On Grant's right wing Sigel had his concentration well under way when he was defeated on May 15 by Breckenridge and his advance temporarily checked. Butler began operations against Petersburg early in May. He failed to take Petersburg; then failed against Richmond, defended by Beauregard. Finally on May 16 the Federal general was defeated by Beauregard, compelled to retire down the Peninsula and "bottled up." On May 2 the Army of the Potomac was ordered to advance.

THE BATTLE OF THE WILDERNESS

By May 4 Grant had the greater part of the Army of the Potomac across the Rapidan somewhat west of Chancellorsville. A second time the armies of the North and South were swallowed up in that dense forest in which Chancellorsville had been fought. Lee's army lay to the west of the fords which Grant used to cross the river. Grant was therefore turning the Confederate right flank. On May 6 Lee planned to complete his concentration in the wilderness, for by that time Longstreet's corps, which had been at Gordonsville, would have reached the field. The armies were so close together, however, that they came in contact on May 5 when there was desperate but inconclusive fighting. Grant, noting correctly that Longstreet had not yet arrived, ordered a general assault on the morning of May 6. The assaults of the Federal center and right were repulsed by Confederates fighting behind breastworks they had thrown up during the night. The Federal left, under Hancock, encountered less opposition and drove the Confederates back until Longstreet's troops arrived and stopped further progress. Hancock's operations against Longstreet were less effective than they should have been because of the failure of a subordinate to carry out an order. In the engagement Longstreet was wounded by his own men and did not again take the field until the following October. On the next day, May 7, Grant moved again around Lee's right flank toward Spottsylvania Court House.

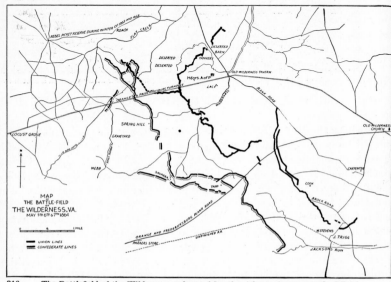

316   The Battlefield of the Wilderness, redrawn from the *Atlas to Accompany the Official
                    Records of the Union and Confederate Armies*, Washington

FIEBEGER'S COMMENT ON THE BATTLE OF THE WILDERNESS

"THIS battle was fought in a dense tangle of undergrowth, which made maneuvering almost impossible. The general officers could neither ascertain the exact position of the opposing troops nor follow the movements of their own. It was impossible for troops to keep either alignment or direction. Again and again attacking troops found that they were advancing in such a direction as to expose a flank to the concealed enemy. It was even difficult to distinguish friend from foe, as was shown by the wounding of

317   Maj.-Gen. Wadsworth fighting in the Wilderness, from a sketch by A. R. Waud in *Harper's Weekly*, June 4, 1864

Longstreet and the killing of Brigadier-General Micah Jenkins, who was with him, by Longstreet's own men. As the troops fought at short range the losses were very heavy. . . . Neither commander could claim a tactical success, but General Grant could claim a strategic success, for his army was now safely established on the south bank of the Rapidan." — *Campaigns of the American Civil War*, 261–62.

318   The Wilderness near Chancellorsville, from a photograph in the United States Signal Corps, War Department, Washington

AN INCIDENT OF THE BATTLE

ON May 4 in one of the operations of this confused fight it chanced that as the opposing lines swung back and forth across a little clearing in the woods that two men, one a Confederate and the other a Federal, became detached from their respective units and hid themselves in a gully in the field. ". . . Soon they came in view of each other, and commenced to banter one another. Then they decided that they would go into the road and have a regular fist and skull fight, the best man to have the other as his prisoner. When the two men came into the road about midway between the lines of battle, in full view of both sides around the field, one a Yankee, and the other 'a Johnny,' while both sides were firing, they surely created a commotion! This was true in our line and I suppose in the enemy's line, because both sides ceased firing! When the two men took off their coats and commenced to fight with their fists, a yell went up along each line, and men rushed to the edge of the opening for a better view! The 'Johnny' soon had the 'Yank' down, who surrendered, and both quietly rolled into the gully, where they remained until night, when 'the Johnny' brought 'the Yank' into our line. The disappearance of the two men was the signal for the resumption of firing! Such is war!" — WORSHAM, 203–04. Paradoxically a fight had, for the time being, held up a battle

SPOTTSYLVANIA COURT HOUSE

MEADE spent the morning of May 7 reconnoitering the enemy's positions and trying to determine his intentions. In the afternoon the army was on the roads for Spottsylvania Court House through country still heavily forested. Lee fell back and placed himself in front of Grant. On May 12 Grant struck him. The Federal plan of attack was frontal assaults against intrenched positions. The Confederate lines had a marked salient near the center. Federal troops attacked this on both the sides and on the nose. Lee was caught at a disadvantage because he had withdrawn his artillery from the lines during the previous night as a result

319   From the painting *Battle of Johnson's Salient*, by Allen C. Redwood, in the possession of the artist

of information, later proved incorrect, that Grant was moving around the Confederate left. He had not yet gotten the batteries back into the salient when Grant struck. The Federal formation against the nose gives an idea of the battle tactics of the Civil War and also helps to explain the reason for the huge casualty lists.

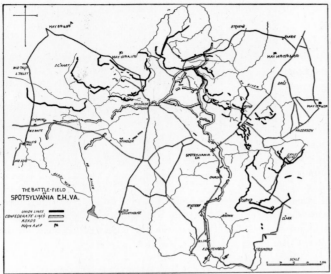

320   The Battlefield of Spottsylvania, redrawn from the *Atlas to Accompany the Official Records of the Union and Confederate Armies*, Washington

THE STRATEGY OF THE BATTLE OF SPOTTSYLVANIA

"At 4:30 A.M. on May 12, just as the fog was rising, twenty thousand men in almost a solid square assailed the front of Johnson's division from which all the guns had been removed. They swept over the parapet and captured Maj. Gen. Edward Johnson and two-thirds of his men. They also seized twenty pieces of artillery that were returning to the front." — FIEBEGER, 268–69. Once over the parapet, they became a confused mass unmanageable against the Confederate counter attack. They were saved by the Federal pressure at the angles of the salient. One of these known as "bloody angle" saw some of the fiercest fighting of the war when both sides continued until exhausted. "In making his repeated assaults on Lee's lines at Spottsylvania, Grant was no doubt influenced by his knowledge of his own numerical superiority and the desire to keep Lee on the defensive. His tactical success in capturing the greater part of Johnson's division probably compensated for his losses in these assaults. He gained a decided strategic victory when he placed his army east of Spottsylvania, from which it could move on Richmond and draw Lee still farther south. . . . Had not Lee made the mistake of ordering Ewell's artillery out of the front line on the evening of May 11, his defense would have been flawless. He was compelled, however, to remain on the defensive . . . he was unable to prevent Grant from moving around him." — FIEBEGER, 271–72.

THE DEATH OF STUART

WHILE Grant was turning Lee's flank and marching on Spottsylvania, Sheridan was making a cavalry raid toward Richmond. The rise of this young officer had been phenomenal; he was now a major-general commanding the cavalry forces of the Army of the Potomac. On May 8 Sheridan assembled three divisions of cavalry near Tabernacle Church. On the next day when his troopers headed for Richmond, his column on the road was thirteen miles long. As he pushed on toward the Confederate capital, the Government became profoundly disturbed. Six brigades only manned the defenses of Richmond, for the troops which were not with Lee's army were defending the city against Butler's attack from the south. The War Department urged Stuart to hasten to the aid of the capital. So urgent was the call that Stuart did not wait to concentrate his force but galloped toward Richmond with but two brigades. On the morning of May 11 Stuart made a stand at Yellow Tavern six miles from the city. He refused to take the more conservative course of dismounting his men and placing them behind the Richmond fortifications. He was defeated and killed, a loss to the Confederacy second only to that of Stonewall Jackson.

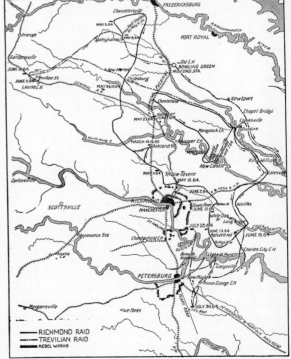

321   Sheridan's Trevilian and Richmond Raids, redrawn from the *Atlas to Accompany the Official Records of the Union and Confederate Armies*, Washington

"JEB" STUART

SHERIDAN pushed on past Richmond and on May 16 joined Butler. To this commander Sheridan turned over his wounded. Sheridan had now accomplished his mission more completely than Grant could have hoped for. The powerful Federal cavalry force was ready to assist Butler in the capture of Richmond. But Butler was defeated (see page 146) and Sheridan made his way northward back to the Army of the Potomac.

Captain W. Gordon McCabe has left a picture of the sad occasion when Lee received the news of Stuart's death. "I was sitting on my horse near to General Lee . . . when a courier galloped up with the despatch announcing that Stuart had been mortally wounded and was dying. General Lee was evidently greatly affected, and said slowly, as he folded up the despatch, 'General Stuart has been mortally wounded: a most valuable and able officer.' Then, after a moment, he added in a voice of deep feeling, 'He never brought me a piece of false information' — turned and looked away." A few days later in a general order Lee gave to the world his appreciation of Stuart. "Among the gallant soldiers who have fallen in this war, General Stuart was second to none in valour, in zeal, and in unflinching devotion to his country." — CAP-

322 General James Ewell Brown Stuart, 1833–64, from the painting by Forney in the Virginia State Library, Richmond

TAIN R. E. LEE, *Recollections and Letters of General Robert E. Lee*, 124–26, Doubleday, Page and Company, New York, 1904. On his dying bed Stuart had said to President Davis: "I am willing to die if God and my country think I have fulfilled my destiny and done my duty."

THE BATTLE OF COLD HARBOR

As the absence of Stuart at Gettysburg handicapped Lee, the absence of Sheridan on his Richmond raid proved a handicap to Grant in the operations immediately following the fight at Spottsylvania Court House. Grant moved about Lee's right flank, a maneuver promptly reported to the Confederate commander by his cavalry which were in their correct positions. Grant was not so quickly informed of his adversary's move to Hanover Junction. On May 25 and 26 the two armies were at this point facing one another in intrenched positions. Lee had forestalled Grant and the latter decided not to attack. Then Grant again moved about Lee's right and on June 2 the two armies faced each other near Cold Harbor. Both sides were well intrenched. Lee's main position was within six miles of Richmond and his right flank within three miles. Grant felt that he could gain nothing merely by crossing the Chickahominy and moving southward. He, therefore, attacked, his plan being to strike Lee's front and to attempt to turn his left flank. The assault was made at four-thirty on June 3 and was repulsed with heavy loss. At no point along the line did the Union troops win an advantage. Several hours later Grant doggedly ordered a renewal of the assault but the representations of his corps commanders caused him to rescind the order. In this engagement six thousand Federal soldiers were either killed or wounded in one hour. Cold Harbor was the most terrible shambles of the war. After the fighting was over Grant ordered his troops to entrench. Could he have penetrated the enemy center and thrown Lee's army back on the Chickahominy, Grant might have destroyed or captured the Confederate army. He failed and the war dragged on for ten more months. Cold Harbor is a blemish on the military reputation of Grant. It was a useless waste of men that impaired the morale of the army and strengthened greatly the increasing group in the North who were seeking to end the bloodshed at any cost

323   The Fight at Cold Harbor, from a sketch by William Waud in *Harper's Weekly*, June 18, 1864

324   Grant at Cold Harbor, from a photograph by Brady, in the United States Signal Corps, War Department, Washington

IN THE TRENCHES AT COLD HARBOR

"GRANT'S army remained in position in front of Lee's until the night of the 12th of June, and a more trying experience has seldom fallen to the lot of soldiers than that of the soldiers in these two armies during this time. The fire of the sharpshooters on both sides was terrible and incessant, and the country was so flat that no man dared rise during the daylight from his cramped position in the shallow trenches; by day the heat of the sun was terrific and at night the mosquitoes and insects were torture; the stench of the dead bodies of men and animals was sickening; cooking could scarcely be done at all; bathing was not thought of, and the water for drink was foul; the lines were in the midst of marshes, and malarial fever and other sickness increased with each day. On the night of the 12th Grant withdrew his army to cross the James River. . . . The main result of Grant's operations from the Rapidan to the James was to wear out Lee's army, to a greater or less degree, by the policy of 'continuous hammering'; but Grant's own army had suffered nearly three times as great a loss in men as Lee's, and it is claimed that after the desperate assault at Cold Harbor, in which the Federal loss was very great and the Confederate loss comparatively small, the morale of the Confederate soldiers was left in a better state than that of the Union soldiers. Grant's successive strategic turning movements had all failed to reach Lee's communications — to get between Lee's army and Richmond. . . . True, with each movement the Union army got nearer to Richmond; but that was not the object of the campaign. At the outset of the operations General Grant had said to General Meade, in his letter of instructions: 'Lee's army will be your objective point. Wherever Lee goes, there you will go also.' . . . Yet Grant's campaign was not a failure. His army had kept on advancing and fighting; that was much in itself. It was what the Union army had not done in Virginia under any other commander. This result was not due to a greater disparity of numbers in the two hostile armies than had existed in previous campaigns. . . . Yet, if the student looks for anything brilliant of strategy or tactics in General Grant's operations in this campaign, he will look in vain. Lee anticipated every movement the Union army made, and took prompt measures to meet it. Every battle appeared to be fought without any real plan of attack." — STEELE, 502–03.

GRANT ON COLD HARBOR

"I HAVE always regretted that the last assault at Cold Harbor was ever made. . . . At Cold Harbor no advantage whatever was gained to compensate for the heavy loss we sustained. . . . Before that, the Army of Northern Virginia seemed to have acquired a wholesome regard for the courage, endurance, and soldierly qualities generally of the Army of the Potomac. They no longer wanted to fight them 'one Confederate to five Yanks.' Indeed, they seemed to have given up any idea of gaining any advantage of their antagonist in the open field. They had come to much prefer breastworks in their front to the Army of the Potomac. This charge seemed to revive their hopes temporarily; but it was of short duration. The effect upon the Army of the Potomac was the reverse. When we reached the James River, however, all effects of the battle of Cold Harbor seemed to have disappeared." — Memoirs, 276–77.

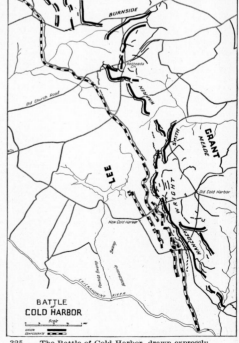

BATTLE of COLD HARBOR

325   The Battle of Cold Harbor, drawn expressly for *The Pageant of America*

THE COST OF GRANT'S ADVANCE

THERE were many wounded, for Grant's "hammering campaign" brought about some of the bloodiest fighting of the war. After the battles in the Wilderness and at Cold Harbor, casualty lists terrible in length appeared in the northern papers. Though Grant slowly advanced, the morale of the people in the North steadily declined. The peace party grew in numbers and influence. Lincoln had to assume the ultimate responsibility and his chances of

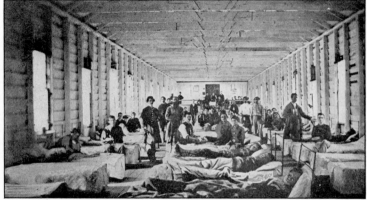

326   Wounded soldiers in hospital, from a photograph in the United States Signal Corps, War Department, Washington

being elected to succeed himself waned as Grant neared Richmond. He himself felt his election to be in doubt until after Farragut had taken Mobile and Sherman had conquered Atlanta. The year 1864 was the bloodiest one of the Civil War. After the years of terrible fighting which preceded, it was natural that there should be many persons in whose minds doubts arose as to whether the cause was worth the terrible sacrifice.

327   United States Ambulances, from a photograph in the United States Signal Corps, War Department, Washington

328   Surgeons of Harewood Hospital, Washington, D. C., from a photograph in the United States Signal Corps, War Department, Washington

AID TO THE WOUNDED

"ON the 9th of May, 1864, I received orders to go to Fredericksburg, Virginia, and to report for surgical duty to the Medical Director of the Army of the Potomac. On the same day, I was directed by another order to take charge of the battle supplies placed on board the steamers . . . and have them delivered at Fredericksburg, Virginia, for the use of the wounded. . . . In giving me these orders, the Acting Surgeon-General Barnes told me verbally, 'Doctor, our losses have been enormous, the wounded are by thousands, we don't know where they are and so far all attempts to send them supplies have failed. Take these supplies on board the steamers and get them forward at any hazard and at any loss.'" — BRINTON, 267–68.   Brinton accomplished his mission. In his race to the front he outdistanced the representatives of the Sanitary Commission which performed the work which the Y.M.C.A., the Knights of Columbus, and the Salvation Army did in the World War. He has left a somewhat caustic comment on the methods of the Sanitarians. "A favourite trick of the Sanitary Commission agents was to ride forward with a wagon or two under the protection of a military train until the lines of safety were reached; then as their own wagons were usually better horsed than those of the Medical Department, they would whip out from the line, pass the front, open their supplies (usually of lemons and canned fruit) and the next day's New York *Herald* or some such paper would announce that 'as usual the Sanitary Commission was the first on the ground to assist our wounded boys.'" — BRINTON, 270–71.

329   Pontoon bridge across the James, from a photograph by Gardner,
Washington

GRANT'S ARMY CROSSING THE JAMES, JUNE 12–13, 1864

IMMEDIATELY after Cold Harbor the siege of Petersburg was planned, with the crossing of the James as its first move. This maneuver began so secretly that, when one of Grant's own generals was explaining the new trenches he proposed to make in front of Cold Harbor, Grant astounded him by saying: "The army has already pulled out from the enemy's front, and is now on its march to the James." There it enjoyed the advantages of the vast system of water-borne transport, which kept its own strength up while it wore down the South.

MAP OF GRANT'S SIEGE OF PETERSBURG, JUNE, 1864–APRIL, 1865

IF Grant's secret start from Cold Harbor for the James on the evening of June 12 was a surprise to his own generals, it proved a puzzle to Beauregard. The actual crossing of the James, and the immense supply of shipping there, soon revealed the movement. Grant impregnably based upon the James meant the sure attrition of the South. "The Confederate cause was lost when Grant crossed the James," said the Confederate Ewell. Grant felt confidence in his own army. Yet the long resort to volunteering had killed off many of the fittest men; and, what with the various non-loyal people in the North, the substitution clause that impaired conscription, and the prevalence of bounty-jumping, many of the recruits were of inferior worth. The great superiority of numbers in Grant's favor, however, was ominous enough for the Confederates.

330   Arrival of recruits during the fight at Peebles's Farm, from a sketch by
C. H. Chapin in *Harper's Weekly*, Oct. 22, 1864

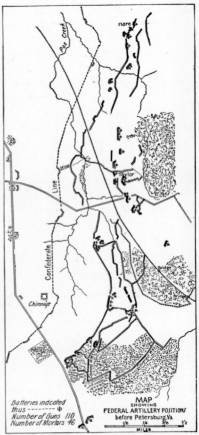

331   Federal Artillery Positions Before Petersburg, redrawn from the *Atlas to Accompany the Official Records of the Union and Confederate Armies*, Washington

NO MORE ASSAULTS

THE Army of the Potomac had, in fact, deteriorated since it had moved into the wilderness with such high hopes. Too many officers and men of the highest quality had fallen in the murderous direct assaults which the troops had been called upon to make upon intrenched positions. The recruits which were coming in from the North were untrained and of inferior quality. The Army of the Potomac failed to take Petersburg while the opportunity offered. When Grant was ready to move against the works, they were strongly held and his direct assaults were beaten back with heavy losses. Observant officers noted that in the Federal losses was a very large and quite unusual proportion of prisoners. The morale of the army was seriously affected. Lincoln's observer with the troops telegraphed: "General Grant has directed that no more assaults shall be made. He will now maneuver." So the siege of Petersburg began.

GENERAL JUBAL EARLY

LEE, given a respite from the shock of almost continuous battle, with unerring military judgment ordered a counter attack through the Shenandoah Valley. He set for the able General Early the ambitious but quite possible objective of the capture of Washington. This most adventurous Confederate had served with fine distinction all through the war. That he failed against Washington in July and was defeated by Sheridan in October does little to dim the honors he had won elsewhere, for the Federals greatly outnumbered the Confederates all over the scene of action, and he had either to take some desperate chances or give up in despair.

332   General Jubal Early, 1816–77, from a photograph in the possession of H. P. Cook, Richmond

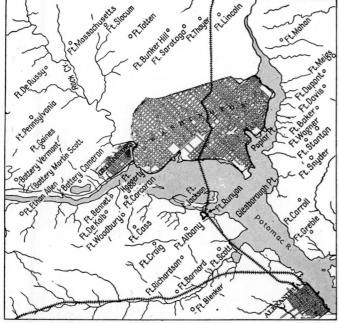

333   The Defenses of Washington, redrawn from the *Atlas to Accompany the Official Records of the Union and Confederate Armies*, Washington

EARLY'S RAID ON WASHINGTON, JULY, 1864

HUNTER, with whom Stanton interfered so much, was forced to uncover the exit from the Valley when going to his base for ammunition, which should have been sent to him at the front. Early seized the chance for a daring dash on the Federal capital. This was one of the most brilliant minor maneuvers of the war. Had it succeeded, it must have seriously embarrassed the Government at Washington and Grant in the field. The morale of the North was so shaken that Early's success might have brought an end to the war.

He swept down the Potomac with no adequate force in front of him. But Lew Wallace, though with much inferior numbers, checked him admirably at the Monocacy on the ninth. This check let so many reinforcements march into Washington that when Early reconnoitered on the twelfth he saw his chance had gone. This was the last important offensive blow of the Confederacy.

THE BURNING OF CHAMBERSBURG

AN incident of Early's invasion was the burning of Chambersburg. Years of bloody war had, by 1864, bred

an intensity of feeling that made outrages against noncombatants possible. Such an act, unnecessary from the military point of view, was the burning of Chambersburg by Early's cavalry leader. War rouses the basest passions of men. The armies were made up of soldiers of both good and bad character. Discipline could not always be perfectly maintained. The surprising feature of the Civil War is that few genuine outrages were committed by either side.

334   The Ruins of Chambersburg, from a drawing after a photograph, in *Harper's Weekly*, Aug. 6, 1864

335   Carrying Powder to the Petersburg Mine, from a sketch in *Battles and Leaders of the Civil War*, New York, 1888

MAKING THE PETERSBURG MINE, JULY, 1864

MEANWHILE at Petersburg Grant prepared a surprise for his aggressive opponent. The plan of the Petersburg mine and the method of its execution is an interesting anticipation of General Byng's famous attack at Vimy Ridge in the World War. Only on the Petersburg front in 1864–65 did typical trench warfare develop throughout the course of the Civil War. In July a regiment of Pennsylvania coal miners ran a tunnel under the Confederate works. Meade's army put four tons of powder into this mine through a gallery five hundred feet long; and six days before the explosion Grant gave Meade precise orders about the intended assault. The conduct of the actual operation fell to the corps commander, General Burnside. He blundered irreparably in assigning the task of actual assault through the crater to an inferior division led by an incompetent commander. He also failed to remove the obstacles in front of the Confederate works.

THE EXPLOSION OF THE PETERSBURG MINE, JULY 30, 1864

WITH a terrific roar and an earthquake shock the mine exploded in the early morning. A crater like a volcano's formed at once. The Confederates round it ran helter-skelter to the rear. Sixty Federal guns opened a devastating fire. And Burnside's three other divisions prepared to support the one that was making the first assault.

336   Explosion of the Petersburg Mine, from a sketch by A. R. Waud in *Harper's Weekly*, Aug. 20, 1864

337   From the painting *The Battle of the Crater*, by John A. Elder in the Westmoreland Club, Richmond

THE PETERSBURG MINE: THE BATTLE OF THE CRATER, JULY 30, 1864

LEDLIE, commanding the first division of assault, let the attack go on without him; for he was hiding safely in a bombproof in the rear. This cowardly defection spoiled the whole Federal plan. The astonished southerners rallied and hastened to the rescue. The Federals without proper leadership gave way, and the Confederates soon had the satisfaction of turning to their own advantage the crater that had been meant to work their ruin.

DUTCH GAP EXCAVATION WORK IS BEGUN, AUGUST 10, 1864

To improve communications and the transportation of Federal supplies, General Butler set General P. S. Michie to work cutting a canal one hundred and seventy-four yards long, forty-three wide at the top, twenty-seven at water level, and thirty-one deep at the northern end, the whole requiring sixty-seven thousand cubic yards of excavation. This canal saved several miles of tortuous navigation on the James within ten miles of Richmond. It was not extremely hard engineering, but it had to be done under fire; and even the steam pump had to be bomb-proofed.

338   Dutch Gap, from a photograph by Gardner, Washington

339   The Surprise at Cedar Creek, from a sketch in *Battles and Leaders of the Civil War*, New York, 1888

THE SURPRISE AT CEDAR CREEK, OCTOBER 19, 1864

AUGUST was a bad month for the Federals in arms, politics, and finance. But September brought cheering news from Sherman in his great campaign against the lower South, while October brought good news from the valley. Sheridan, finding Early's Confederates divided, swooped down and defeated one wing at Opequan Creek. Just a month later Early sought his revenge by utterly surprising the sleeping Federals at Cedar Creek. He had apparently won a decisive victory when "Sheridan's Ride" changed the tide of battle.

SHERIDAN'S RIDE, OCTOBER 19, 1864

RETURNING from Washington, Sheridan heard the roar of the Cedar Creek battle as he rode out of Winchester twenty miles north. Then an ever-increasing stream of fugitives passed him. But Sheridan unerringly picked out the stanchest, turned them back, and, setting spurs to his horse, raced for the front. There his magnetic presence changed the whole spirit of his army. It re-formed, and stood fast.

340 Belle-Grove House, Sheridan's Headquarters at Cedar Creek, from Michael V. Sheridan, *Personal Memoirs of Philip H. Sheridan*, Webster, New York, 1888

341 From a painting *Sheridan's Final Charge at Winchester*, by Thure de Thulstrup.
© 1887, *Prang's War Pictures*, L. Prang and Co., Boston

CEDAR CREEK: THE FINAL CHARGE, OCTOBER 19, 1864

"THE Confederates were astounded. They paused; found themselves attacked by those they had just defeated; and then, finding the Federals not only in superior force but with completely changed morale, they broke before the exultant charge of their now united enemy. Infantry, cavalry, and artillery — all pressed on to Federal victory. Early's broken army practically made no halt in its retreat after the battle of Cedar Creek until it reached New Market. . . . Between the date of his signal defeat and the 11th of November, the enemy's scattered forces had sufficiently reorganized to permit his again making a reconnaissance in the valley as far north as Cedar Creek, my army having meanwhile withdrawn to Kernstown, where it had been finally decided that a defensive line should be held to enable me to detach troops to General Grant and where, by reconstructing the Winchester and Potomac railroad from Stephenson's depot to Harpers Ferry, my command might be more readily supplied." — MICHAEL H. SHERIDAN, EDITOR, *Personal Memoirs of Philip Henry Sheridan*, Vol. II, 97–98, D. Appleton and Company, New York, 1904.

SHERIDAN AND THE PARTISAN TROOPS

"DURING the entire campaign I had been annoyed by guerilla bands under such partisan chiefs as Mosby, White, Gilmore, McNeil, and others, and this had considerably depleted my line-of-battle strength, necessitating as it did large escorts for my supply-trains. The most redoubtable of these leaders was Mosby. . . . I had not directed any special operations against these partisans while the campaign was active, but as Mosby's men had lately killed, within my lines, my chief quartermaster, Colonel Tolles, and Medical Inspector Ohlenschlager, I concluded to devote particular attention to these 'irregulars' during the lull that now occurred; so on the 28th of November, I directed General Merritt to march to the Loudoun Valley and

342 Maj.-Gen. Philip Sheridan, 1831–88, from a photograph in the L. C. Handy Collection, Washington

operate against Mosby, taking care to clear the country of forage and subsistence, so as to prevent the guerillas from being harbored there in the future, their destruction or capture being wellnigh impossible, on account of their intimate knowledge of the mountain region. Merritt carried out his instructions with his usual sagacity and thoroughness, sweeping widely over each side of his general line of march with flankers, who burned the grain and brought in large herds of cattle, hogs and sheep, which were issued to the troops." — *Personal Memoirs of Philip Henry Sheridan*, 99–100. Sheridan by the end of 1864 had accomplished his mission and had vastly strengthened Grant's position.

343 *Mosby Raiders Attacking Sheridan*, from a painting in the Confederate Museum, Richmond

FIEBEGER'S COMMENT ON SHERIDAN'S CAMPAIGN

"TAKEN as a whole, Sheridan's campaign in the Shenandoah Valley was one of the most brilliant operations of the war. It wholly neutralized the effects of the unsuccessful operations of his predecessors as well as the invasion of the northern States by Early. . . . Had Early known the record of his adversary in the West, he would have been less confident and more cautious." — *Campaigns of the American Civil War, 329.*

344   Bivouac in the Rifle Pits, from a sketch in *Battles and Leaders of the Civil War,* New York, 1888

TRENCH WARFARE AT PETERSBURG

FOR several months after the fiasco of the Petersburg mine the armies of Grant and Lee experienced stabilized warfare considerably like the trench fighting of the Western Front in the World War. The picture below shows an interior view of the Federal Fort Stedman, an important part of Grant's works in front of Petersburg. This work was in one of the most advanced positions occupied by the Union troops during the siege. Its parapets were within two hundred yards of the enemy trenches, and the opposing picket lines in front were scarcely seventy yards apart. The picture demonstrates the methods of the day in the construction of field fortifications. The center of the photograph shows the parapet of the work and the manner in which the earth composing it was rivetted or supported, at the base by the trunks of pines laid horizontally, then, by gabions and fascines, topped by sandbags. On the left appears the exterior of an officers' quarters and on the right an earth mound which forms the protective covering for a powder magazine. The embrasures are guarded by heavy iron gates to protect the gunners from the deadly aim of the enemy's sharpshooters. Fort Stedman was, in reality, a strong point of great defensive strength. Its plan was simpler than that approved by modern tactics based on modern weapons.

345   Sheridan's Campaigns, redrawn from the *Atlas to Accompany the Official Records of the Union and Confederate Armies,* Washington

346   View of the interior of Fort Stedman, from a photograph by Gardner, Washington

347   Chevaux-de-Frise, from a photograph in the United States Signal Corps,
                    War Department, Washington

SIEGE OF PETERS–BURG, 1864–65, CHEVAUX–DE–FRISE

THESE uncompromising defenses were only one of the many devices used for keeping an enemy at arm's length. In the days before barbed wire the chevaux-de-frise were among the best obstacles to place in advance of a fortified position. Their chief defects were the great difficulty of making them and the ease with which they could be battered to pieces by artillery.

THE SIEGE OF PETERS–BURG, 1864–65, FORT BRADY BATTERY

HEAVY long-range guns were used against Petersburg, as the

picture shows. The Civil War came about half-way between the days of smooth bores and the vastly stronger ordnance of the World War. The old smooth bores of the Revolution and "1812" could throw two hun-

dred pound shells up to three miles. But there was no chance for accuracy at such extreme range. The fourteen-inch-bore naval guns of Admiral Plunkett's United States Navy Railway Batteries in France in 1918 made good practice up to twenty miles. The Civil War guns rarely tried effective firing at much more than a mile or two; though the ones in No. 349 could hit at over five. They fired with a flat trajectory and were used to pound enemy works and to throw shells against advancing infantry. The mortar had a high trajectory and was used to drop shells into a fort or on the reverse slope of a hill. The thickness of the metal near the breach of the guns was for the purpose of absorbing a part of the energy of the exploding charge. It was also to give strength to the piece. Modern artillery uses much more

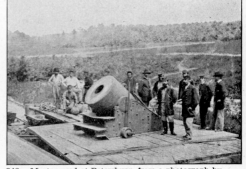

348   Mortar used at Petersburg, from a photograph by
                    Gardner, Washington

powerful explosives and has a device which allows the barrel to recoil. Though artillery played an important part in the Civil War the possibilities of the arm were much more limited than in modern times.

349   Inside of battery at Fort Brady, from a photograph in the United
       States Signal Corps, War Department, Washington

350   Bombproof rifle pit in front of Petersburg, from
                    Harper's Weekly, Nov. 5, 1864

THE SIEGE OF PETERSBURG, RAILROAD GUN

GRANT's railroad engineers were so resourceful in utilizing all means at their disposal that they made many adaptations for military purposes. One of these was the use of railway cars for rendering guns more mobile and hence of greater service. These mortars, whisked about by locomotives, did much damage to Lee's defensive works.

351   Mortar mounted on a railroad car at Petersburg, from a photograph in the United States Signal Corps, War Department, Washington

352   Federal gunboat on the Pamunkey River, from a photograph in the United States Signal Corps, War Department, Washington

FEDERAL GUNBOAT ON THE PAMUNKEY

MORE important even than the railroads were the waterways; and the waterways were still more completely under Federal control than were the railroads of Virginia. The Federal staff made full use of the waterways without which Grant's advance into Virginia must have been much more difficult.

FORT SEDGWICK, COMMONLY CALLED FORT HELL

A GLANCE at the siege map will show the reasons why this particular point acquired its special soldiers' name of Fort Hell. It was a focal point, or junction, for several lines of fire from the Petersburg defenses. The map makes clear the simple character of the Civil War trench systems. An entrenched area did not show the almost bewildering maze of communication, support, reserve and switch trenches of the World War.

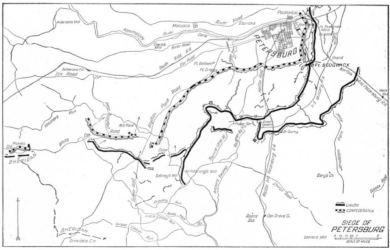

353   Siege of Petersburg, redrawn from Major Matthew F. Steele, *American Campaigns*, United States Infantry Association, 1922

354   Quarters of men in Fort Sedgwick, from a photograph by Gardner, Washington

THE SIEGE OF PETERSBURG, WINTER QUARTERS

HERE, as elsewhere, the abundance of Federal supplies ministered not only to the health, strength, and morale of Grant's army, but to its comfort as well. Nevertheless, there was a good deal of winter hardship. But no hardship on the Federal side could compare with the sufferings of the ragged, starving, worn-out Confederates.

THE INFORMAL TRUCE IN THE SIEGE OF PETERSBURG

"A MAN on one side or the other, would hold up prominently a white handkerchief, or a sheet of white paper, as a sign of a desire for a tacit or informal truce. If it were responded to by a similar sign on the opposite side, and was not at once forbidden by the officer in command, it was accepted by all as binding. . . . Often at such times the men would jump over their rifle pits, or embankments, and meet each other peacefully between the lines, swapping coffee, of which the Union soldiers had an abundance, for tobacco with which the Confederates were well supplied; exchanging newspapers, bartering 'hard tack' for corn cake, conversing pleasantly, or bantering each other with good-natured references to their local peculiarities. Sometimes two opponents would sit down for a friendly game of cards. . . . A fine sense of honor prevailed in the general recognition of the sacredness of these informal and tacit truces. Men would not fire at each other, at the close of one of these seasons, until both parties had had time to settle down to business again. If, on any occasion, an officer seemed to lack consideration for those who were on such friendly terms, his men were quite likely to feel that their 'friends the enemy' ought to be notified of the fact. 'Yanks, keep your heads under today. We've got an officer of the day on who wants us to be firing all the time; so look out.' . . . One evening at the Petersburg front, several Confederate soldiers dragged a man of our brigade into their lines, at the close

of one of these seasons of truce; and they took him as a prisoner into the presence of their commander, General Roger A. Pryor, of Virginia. . . . The Union soldier protested, and told his story. General Pryor turned to his men, and asked if this was the truth. When they admitted it was, he said quietly to our man: 'Go back, then, to your own lines'; and he added to the captors: 'Let him go back. I don't want anything of this sort in my command.''— TRUMBULL, 238–40.

355   Traffic between the lines during a truce, from a sketch in *Battles and Leaders of the Civil War*, New York, 1888

FATHER AND SON

"On one occasion, before Petersburg, a Union regiment from Maryland, serving with our brigade, was over against a Confederate regiment from the same state. During one of these tacit truces, as the men of the two brigades were together between the lines of works, a father in the Maryland Union regiment met his son, a soldier in the Maryland Confederate regiment. The meeting was a surprise to both, but it was an amicable one. Each soldier had been true to his own convictions. . . . They greeted each other affectionately, and talked together until the signal came for the ending of the truce, when they sprang apart, each to his own lines, and again they were over against each other in deadly

356   Front of a Sharpshooter's Box, in the Massachusetts Historical Society, from a photograph by Brayton, Boston

conflict. This seemed strange, but it was typical of the whole great war." — TRUMBULL, 239.

357   Attack on Fort Stedman, from a sketch in *Harper's Weekly*, April 15, 1865

CONFEDERATE ATTACK ON FORT STEDMAN, MARCH 25, 1865

WITH the approach of Sherman's Federals from the South and the wearing out of Johnston's Confederates opposing them, the whole situation became very desperate for Lee at Petersburg. He masked his plans consummately till he attacked Fort Stedman, which he hoped to hold as a shield to cover his escape southwest to where there still seemed to be some chance of holding Grant at bay. The attack succeeded for the moment. But Federal reinforcements won the position back; while the whole occurrence convinced the Federals that Lee was trying to escape. This marks the conclusion of the siege of Petersburg and the beginning of the final desperate attempt that Lee made to escape — an attempt which ended at Appomattox only fifteen days later. The war of position after many months came to an end and for a brief moment maneuver warfare began. Meanwhile in Georgia General Sherman had been carrying out a brilliant series of maneuvers which established his reputation as one of the greatest of American captains. Grant demonstrated clearly his capacity to recognize ability when he trusted Sherman with independent command. Lee at Petersburg had watched with failing heart Sherman's progress from victory to victory.

CHAPTER VII

THE ATLANTA CAMPAIGN

WHILE Grant was driving Lee's army into Richmond and Petersburg, Sherman, operating from Chattanooga, was forcing Joseph E. Johnston back upon Atlanta. The Atlanta Campaign began on the 5th of May, 1864, and ended with the evacuation of Atlanta by Hood, on the 1st of September — four months, less four days. (See map, No. 359.) "By skillful maneuvering, far more than by his assaults at Dalton, Resaca, and Kenesaw, Sherman had forced the Confederate Army back ninety-odd miles, and had captured the important city of Atlanta. During the same time Grant, in Virginia, had forced Lee back from the line of the Rapidan to the works in front of Petersburg and Richmond; but it was not until the following April that the Union Commander-in-chief succeeded in capturing these two cities. The armies of Grant and Sherman were of practically the same strength, about one hundred thousand each; those of Lee and Johnston, also were about equal to each other, numbering some sixty thousand each. But Grant, by this time, had lost upwards of sixty thousand men, while Sherman had lost not many more than twenty thousand. Grant's was a campaign of 'hammering,' while Sherman's was one of maneuvering. Both campaigns were made in difficult country; there were heavy woods in both theatres; in Georgia the topography was more broken by ridges and hills, while in Virginia the rivers, especially the James, were more difficult to cross; the incessant rains during the Georgia campaign made the roads as bad in that theatre as they were in the swamps of Virginia. . . . Several modern American and foreign writers on the subject of strategy have discussed it as a typical campaign; and they have generally found little to criticise, either in Sherman's offensive strategy or Johnston's defensive strategy. Hamley says of it with approval: 'Except in attacking the Kenesaw Mountain on the 27th of June, the character of Sherman's operations was, throughout, the same. To protect his main line from a counter-attack, he left a force intrenched across it. He then reinforced his flanking wing to a strength sufficient to cope with the whole army of the enemy, and directed it by a circuit off the main line, upon the Confederate rear. In every case the operation was successful, obliging Johnston forthwith to abandon his strongest positions, and to retreat.'" — STEELE. When Sherman moved out of Chattanooga, his army numbered just under a hundred thousand men. Assisting him were three able generals, Thomas, Schofield, and McPherson. Joseph E. Johnston, charged with the defense of Atlanta, lay at Dalton with some fifty-three thousand men in a strongly intrenched position. Johnston did not have the assistance of as able officers as his opponent. Grant had assigned Sherman a difficult mission. As he advanced into enemy country farther and farther from his base, his offensive strength inevitably declined, reducing sharply the effect of the disparity in numbers between himself and Johnston.

THE CONVERGING MOVEMENTS OF 1864

SHERMAN's campaign was not an isolated enterprise but a part of a great converging movement. When the command of all the Federal forces was placed in the hands of Grant, opportunity was given for strategy on a great scale. Grant conceived this far-reaching scheme of maneuver. He himself undertook the immediate supervision of one campaign. The others he left to trusted subordinates of his own choosing and retained only general control. Grant, as a military man, must be judged by this plan and its success as well as by his conduct of actual campaigns. In every respect the plan was sound. The history of war was not destined to reveal another such gigantic movement until Foch hurled the German armies back in 1918.

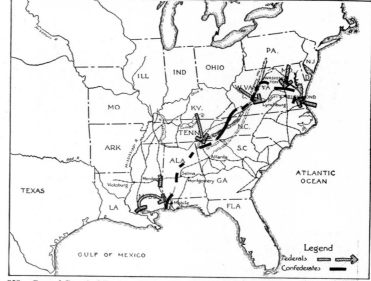

358   General Grant's Offensive of Exhaustion, from Brigadier-General C. R. Howland, *Military History of the World War*, Fort Leavenworth, General Service Schools, 1923

SHERMAN'S COMMENT ON KENESAW MOUNTAIN

"DURING the 24th and 25th of June General Schofield extended his right as far as was prudent, so as to compel the enemy on Kenesaw Mountain to thin out his own lines accordingly, with the intention to make two strong assaults at points where success would give us the greatest advantage. I had consulted Generals Thomas, McPherson, and Schofield, and we all agreed that we could not with prudence stretch out any more, and therefore there was no alternative but to attack 'fortified lines,' a thing carefully avoided up to that time. . . . The 27th of June was fixed as the day for the attempt. . . . About 9 A.M. of the day appointed, the troops moved to the assault, and all along our lines for ten miles a furious fire of artillery and musketry was kept up. At all points the enemy met us with determined courage and in great force. McPherson's attacking column fought up the face of the lesser Kenesaw, but could not reach the summit. About a mile to the right . . . Thomas's assaulting column reached the parapet, where Brigadier-General Harker was shot down mortally wounded, and Brigadier-General Daniel McCook (my old law-partner) was desperately wounded, from the effects of which he afterward died. By 11:30 the assault was in fact over, and had failed."—P. T. SHERMAN, EDITOR, *Memoirs of General William T. Sherman*, Vol. II, 60–61, D. Appleton and Company, New York, 1889.

359   Sherman's March from Chattanooga to Atlanta, redrawn from the *Atlas to Accompany the Official Records of the Union and Confederate Armies*, Washington

360   Kenesaw Mountain, from a photograph in the United States Signal Corps, War Department, Washington

361   The Army of the Cumberland Swinging about Kenesaw Mountain, from a sketch by Theodore R. Davis
in *Harper's Weekly*, Aug. 27, 1864

KENESAW MOUNTAIN AS SEEN FROM THE RANKS

"THERE was a general line of battle formed this morning and orders given to make a charge all along the lines. . . . The Eleventh and Sixteenth Iowa furnished the skirmishers for our brigade and charged the

362   General John Bell Hood, 1831–79, from a photograph in the possession of H. P. Cook, Richmond

rebels' skirmish line, but were driven back to their old line. Our side lost several in killed and wounded, and what little was gained did not pay for the loss of life. Company A of our regiment was in the charge and had one man killed; so close was he to the rebel works that our men had to raise the white flag in order to get his body. The Fifty-third Indiana made a charge on the rebel rifle pits and lost about forty men, taken as prisoners. When they made the charge, the rebels lay down in their pits, allowing them to come close up, when they rose up with their rifles drawn and said: 'Come on, boys, we won't hurt you,' and took them prisoners." — *Downing's Civil War Diary*, 201–02.

GENERAL JOHN BELL HOOD

ON July 17 Sherman began the final advance upon Atlanta. The very night that Sherman's superior numbers outflanked Johnston across the Chattahoochee, Davis, at Richmond, ordered Hood to supersede Johnston and to "fight." This was one of the gravest blunders of the Confederate president during the war. Johnston was an officer of great ability. Hood could claim nothing but mediocrity. The news of the change in command brought satisfaction to Sherman's headquarters.

THE BATTLE OF ATLANTA, JULY 22, 1864

SHERMAN was just closing in for a siege when Hood smashed in on his left; but Hood was eventually beaten, with more than twice the loss of men that Sherman suffered. There was much stern fighting on both sides and many well-planned maneuvers. But Hood's most strenuous efforts failed against Sherman's readiness to meet each emergency.

363   From the painting *Siege of Atlanta*, by Thure de Thulstrup. © 1887, *Prang's War Pictures*, L. Prang and Co., Boston

ATLANTA AND EZRA CHURCH, JULY 28, 1864

DEFEATED on the left Hood tried the right flank, but was again beaten with a heavier loss. Neither side failed in actual fighting, but the Confederates now had little chance against the superior numbers of seasoned Federals led by a veteran like Sherman.

TACTICS OF THE ATLANTA CAMPAIGN

364   Battle of Ezra's Church, from a sketch by Theodore R. Davis in *Harper's Weekly*, Aug. 27, 1864

"VERY few of the battles in which I have participated were fought as described in European textbooks, viz., in great masses, in perfect order, maneuvering by corps divisions, and brigades. We were generally in a wooded country, and, though our lines were deployed according to tactics, the men generally fought in strong skirmish-lines, taking advantage of the shape of the ground, and of every cover. We were generally the assailants, and in wooded and broken countries the 'defensive' had a positive advantage over us, for they were always ready, had cover, and always knew the ground to their immediate front; whereas we, their assailants, had to grope our way over unknown ground, and generally found a cleared field or prepared entanglements that held us for a time under a close and withering fire. Rarely did the opposing lines in compact order come into actual contact, but when, as at Peach-Tree Creek and Atlanta, the lines did become commingled, the men fought individually in every possible style, more frequently with the musket clubbed than with the bayonet, and in some instances the men clinched like wrestlers, and went to the ground together." — *Memoirs of General William T. Sherman*, Vol. II, 394.

365   The Battle of Atlanta, from an engraving after a painting by James E. Taylor in *Campfire and Battlefield*, Desmond Publishing Co., Boston, 1896

366   Fortifications before Atlanta, from a photograph in the United States Signal Corps, War Department, Washington

SHERMAN OCCUPIES ATLANTA, SEPTEMBER 2, 1864

ON the last of August a series of explosions shook Atlanta to its foundations, as Hood blew up whatever he could not carry off. The picture shows the fortifications before Atlanta. Within two days Sherman's dispatch drew Lincoln's answer, which "entitled those who had participated to the applause and thanks of the nation."

367   Battery M, Fifth United States Artillery in a captured Confederate fort at Atlanta, from a photograph in the United States Signal Corps, War Department, Washington

ATLANTA, SEPTEMBER–NOVEMBER, 1864

ATLANTA now became a Federal stronghold and the base from which Sherman's army was to make its devastating march to the sea. The capture of Atlanta meant the fall of the most important Confederate center for the manufacture of ordnance. Deficient in factories, the South suffered a staggering blow in the loss of this Georgia city. Its capture was Sherman's greatest achievement during the war. It was more, however, than the mere occupation of a place; for though he had not destroyed the army opposing him, he had so reduced its power, that he could safely divide his own army in the presence of the enemy.

ALLATOONA, OCTOBER 5, 1864

THOUGH Hood had abandoned Atlanta, he made one last effort to retake the important pass at Allatoona, thirty miles northwest. Twelve miles from Fort Allatoona stood Sherman, on Kenesaw mountain, anxiously watching. Suddenly his signal officer deciphered the flagged message that General John M. Corse was holding out. With only two thousand men Corse had beaten off double the number before Sherman's reinforcements could arrive; and the message assured Sherman that though "short a cheek bone and an ear" Corse was "able to

368   From the painting *Battle of Allatoona Pass*, by Thure de Thulstrup.   © 1887, *Prang's War Pictures*, L. Prang and Co., Boston

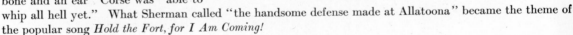

whip all hell yet." What Sherman called "the handsome defense made at Allatoona" became the theme of the popular song *Hold the Fort, for I Am Coming!*

369   General William Tecumseh Sherman, 1820–91; from a photograph by Brady, in the L. C. Handy Collection, Washington

CONFEDERATE EFFORTS TO CHECK SHERMAN

THE hard-pressed Confederates tried raiding Sherman's rear to ease the pressure on their own front. Successful at Brice's Cross Roads in June but defeated at Tupelo in July, Forrest's cavalry raided Johnsonville on the Tennessee in late October, actually taking the Federal gunboat *Undine* and a couple of transports. Forrest's raids were well seconded by those of Wheeler, another excellent southern leader of horse. But Sherman's advance was not in the least affected by them for his plan now was to establish himself on enemy ground and use enemy supplies to feed his own army. While preparing for the march he wrote to Halleck that the people of Georgia "don't know what war means but when the rich planters of the Oconee and Savannah see their fences and corn and hogs and sheep vanish before their eyes they will have something more than a mean opinion of the 'Yanks.'"

370   From the mural painting *The Mine Creek Charge*, by N. C. Wyeth, in the Missouri State Capitol, Jefferson City, Mo.

THE MINE CREEK CHARGE, OCTOBER 25, 1864

RAIDING in the rear of Sherman was not the only means by which the desperate Confederates hoped to stop his advance, regain their own foothold in the border states, and even affect the war elsewhere; they still gave battle beyond the Mississippi. Sterling Price fought Curtis stanchly round Kansas City, Westport, and Mine Creek. But his final stand near Mine Creek was swept away by a splendid charge of Federal cavalry, which broke his line, took nearly all his guns, and drove him from the field.

MAP OF HOOD'S ARMY GOING NORTH, NOVEMBER–DECEMBER, 1864

THE third Confederate attempt to stop Sherman's march through Georgia was Hood's own sortie from the closely beleaguered eastern South. Hoping to draw Sherman back, and, failing in this, to regain Tennessee, Hood marched north to Franklin. Thomas with part of Sherman's army fell back before him, the Federal force increasing as detachments which had been used to guard Sherman's communications were relieved of that duty. Hood's hope was doomed to failure, because his army was not strong enough to hold its own against the safely placed Federals, who had greater numbers and vastly superior supplies.

THE NASHVILLE CAMPAIGN

371   Operations in Tennessee and Georgia during the Nashville Campaign, redrawn from Major Matthew F. Steele, *American Campaigns*, United States Infantry Association, 1922

372   Battlefield of Franklin, Tenn., from a drawing after a photograph in *Battles and Leaders of the Civil War*, New York, 1888

THE BATTLE OF FRANKLIN, NOVEMBER 30, 1864

Hood met Thomas' advanced guard at Franklin, under General Schofield, who made a magnificent stand against the charges of an army which knew it was now or never. During that last Indian-summer day in

373   General Thomas' Council of War, from a photograph in the United States Signal Corps, War Department, Washington

Tennessee the gray lines of desperate southerners charged no less than thirteen times; charged, with the wild, high "Rebel Yell" right up to Schofield's grim blue lines; lost nearly all their front-rank leaders; fell back, re-formed, and charged again; threw in their very last reserves, and charged for death or victory once more. This final charge got home; but at a cost that left no chance of victory against the solid mass of Thomas' main army, which now had a superiority in numbers of twenty thousand. Thomas took his time, somewhat to the discomfiture of his superiors, and made thorough preparations for the final battle.

THE BATTLE OF NASHVILLE, DECEMBER 15, 1864

At Nashville the thirty-five thousand worn Confederates actually invested the fifty-five thousand Federals, till Thomas, the "Rock of Chickamauga," came out, won the best positions on the first day, and on the second struck such devastating blows that Hood's whole army, as an army, simply ceased to be. Sherman meanwhile was nearing Savannah.

374   Battle of Nashville, from a sketch by George H. Ellsbury in *Harper's Weekly*, Jan. 14, 1865

375 General Sherman and his Staff, from a photograph in the United States Signal Corps,
War Department, Washington

SHERMAN'S MARCH THROUGH GEORGIA,
NOVEMBER 15–DECEMBER 10, 1864

WHILE Hood was trying to reconquer Tennessee or draw Sherman back from Georgia, Sherman went on, instead of back, destroying all that could possibly help a southern army.

Grant approved Sherman's march to Savannah, where Fort Pulaski was a sure connection with the unconquerable sea power of the North. So Sherman marched through Georgia for twenty-five days, with sixty thousand veteran men, cutting a swath of devastation sixty miles wide. He was determined to leave no surplus products whatsoever for the fighters of the South; nor did he leave them the means of transportation, utterly destroying roads, rails and bridges on his way. His devastations aroused the bitterest resentment among all the southern people. But, though there were exceptions, as there must always be, the Federal army did not go beyond the devastation of all that could possibly be turned to military use. Up North this march was extravagantly praised, to the injury of Sherman's reputation as a great commander. For his previous campaign against Atlanta was an infinitely greater feat of arms, while his subsequent advance through the Carolinas was a much harder march in every way. Sherman's measure of the relative importance of the march to the sea, and of that from Savannah northward was "the former one, the latter ten — or the maximum." But nothing else so striking was on the central stage just then, and the much greater problems which Sherman was solving were beyond the people's comprehension.

376 Peach Tree Creek battlefield, from a photograph in the
United States Signal Corps, War Department, Washington

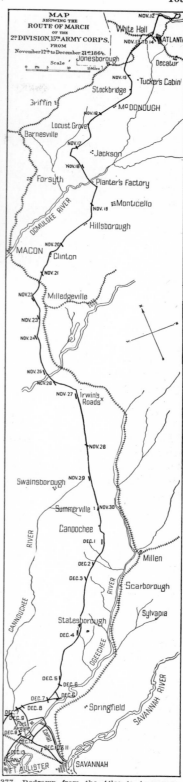

MAP
SHOWING THE
ROUTE OF MARCH
OF THE
2D DIVISION, 15TH ARMY CORPS,
FROM
November 12th to December 21st, 1864.

377 Redrawn from the *Atlas to Accompany the Official Records of the Union and Confederate Armies*, Washington

378 Sherman's Foragers on a Georgia Plantation, from a sketch by James E. Taylor in *Battles and Leaders of the Civil War*, New York, 1888

MARCHING THROUGH GEORGIA

"WE were expected to make fifteen miles a day; to corduroy the roads where necessary; to destroy such property as was designated by our corps commander, and to consume everything eatable by man or beast. . . . Our colored friends, who flocked to us in embarrassing numbers, told many stories about the fear and flight of the inhabitants at the approach of Sherman. . . . We were proud of our foragers. They constituted a picked force from each regiment, under an officer selected for the command, and were remarkable for intelligence, spirit, and daring. Before daylight, mounted on horses captured on the plantations, they were in the saddle and away, covering the country seven miles in advance. Although I have said 'in the saddle,' many a forager had nothing better than a bit of carpet and a rope halter; yet this simplicity of equipment did not abate his power of carrying off hams and sweet-potatoes in the face of the enemy. . . . When success crowned their efforts, the plantation was promptly stripped of live stock and eatables. . . . If any antiquated militia uniforms were discovered, they were promptly donned, and a comical procession escorted the valuable train of booty to the point where the brigade was expected to bivouac for the night. The regimentals of the past, even those of revolutionary times, were often conspicuous. . . . The march through Georgia has been called a grand military promenade, all novelty and excitement. But its moral effect on friend and foe was immense. It proved our ability to lay open the heart of the Confederacy, and left the question of what we might do next a matter of doubt and terror." — CAPTAIN DANIEL OAKEY, *Battles and Leaders of the Civil War*, Vol. IV, 672–74.

INCIDENTS OF THE MARCH

"MONDAY December 5/64. . . . Just before reaching this place, saw a large blaze and smoke on our right, near road, and found it was a very good dwelling house burning. Felt very indignant and grieved, but no use to make comments. But after reaching Morton's found that said dwelling house belonged to one Mr. Stubbs, — that the said Mr. Stubbs has regularly kept a pack (five or six) of 'track-hounds' and made it a business to hunt negroes with them, and also to hunt escaped Union prisoners with them; and he has a reputation of having, by means of these dogs, prevented the escape of a large number of our men who got away on one occasion from a R.R. train, got into the swamps, and were hunted down and caught. . . . Wednesday December 7/64. . . . Mrs. Elkins, at whose house we lunched today, was a regular Georgia woman. Came to gate in great fright, trying, poor woman, to hide it, — invited General (who had already dismounted) to come in, and all his officers, etc. It was quite laughable had her panic not been so real. Before long she was reassured. General sent Audenrie with her to smoke house and rescued her *clothes*, etc. which she had buried there but which soldiers were rapidly exhuming, — also saving her a quantity of provisions, etc. . . .

She knew our friend Stubbs, whose house was burned on Monday as above noted, and confirmed the account of his keeping dogs and hunting niggers with them. She spoke of hunting negroes with dogs as a customary thing, hereabouts. . . . She tells same story about all the men being *forced* to go into the army who can serve — her husband is old, or disabled, or something, — says that they were told before we came that we had been killing every body and *burning every house*." — M. A. DeWOLFE HOWE, *Marching with Sherman*, 134–35, 143, Yale University Press, New Haven, 1927.

379 Refugee Train in Georgia, from a drawing by A. R. Waud in *The Story of the Grand March*, Harper and Brothers, 1865

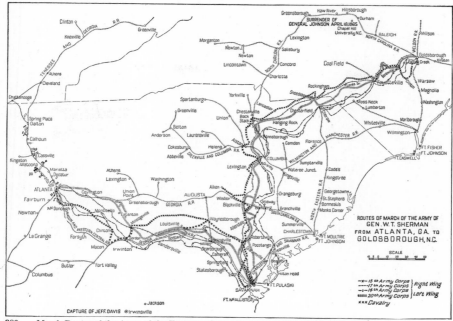

380 March Routes of the Army of the Tennessee from Atlanta to Goldsborough, redrawn from the *Atlas to Accompany the Official Records of the Union and Confederate Armies,* Washington

THE TERROR THAT RAN BEFORE SHERMAN'S ARMY

MARY BOYKIN CHESNUT, wife of Brigadier-General James Chesnut, has left a diary which reflects the feeling of South Carolinians as the invader approached. "December 14th. . . . So Fort McAllister has fallen! Good-by, Savannah! . . . December 19th, The deep waters are closing over us and we are in this house, like the outsiders at the time of the flood. We care for none of these things. We eat, drink, laugh, dance, in lightness of heart. Doctor Trezevant came to tell me the dismal news. How he piled on the agony! Desolation, mismanagement, despair. . . . The Yankees claim another victory for Thomas. Hope it may prove like most of their victories, brag and bluster. Can't say why, maybe I am benumbed, but I do not feel so intensely miserable. . . . January 7th . . . Brewster is here and stayed till midnight. Said he must see General Chesnut. . . . He described Sherman's march of destruction and desolation. 'Sherman leaves a track fifty miles wide, upon which there is no living thing to be seen.' . . . January 10th . . . if we only had our own Game Cock, Sumpter, our own Swamp Fox, Marion (see Volume VI, page 233). Marion's men or Sumpter's, or the equivalent of them, now lie under the sod, in Virginia or Tennessee. January 14th. Yesterday I broke down — gave way to abject terror under the news of Sherman's advance with no news of my husband. . . . February 16th. . . . The Martins left Columbia the Friday before I did, and Mammy,

the negro woman, who had nursed them, refused to go with them. . . . Then I met Mr. Christopher Hampton, arranging to take off his sisters. . . . He said it was time to move on. Sherman was at Orangeburg, barely a day's journey from Columbia, and had left a track as bare and blackened as a fire leaves on the prairies. So my time had come too. . . ." MARY BOYKIN CHESNUT, *A Diary from Dixie,* 339–41, 344, D. Appleton and Company, New York, 1905.

381 From the painting *Sherman's March to the Sea,* by Felix O. C. Darley

382   The Burning of Columbia, from a sketch by William Waud in *Harper's Weekly*, Apr. 8, 1865

THE BURNING OF COLUMBIA

THE burning of Columbia is an evidence of that bitterness inevitably engendered by prolonged war. Because South Carolina had initiated the secession movement many northern folk held the people of that state responsible in a peculiar sense for the agony of the Civil War. This attitude was reflected by the soldiers of Sherman's army. In the evening after the troops entered the city fires broke out and, because of the high wind that prevailed, the larger part of the town was destroyed. From the blackened ashes of Columbia has sprung a bitter controversy. Charges and countercharges fill the pages of the literature which deals with the subject. From the evidence available no certain conclusions can be drawn. The data seem to demonstrate that the burning of Columbia was the result of acts of a vengeful soldiery out of control of its officers. The destruction seems to have been contrary to the orders of the commanding general. Sherman and his generals, moreover, made strenuous efforts to check the flames. The passions engendered by the war burned so fiercely that destruction of Columbia was hailed with pleasure in many quarters in the North. But time has cooled these passions and healed the wounds of war. Sherman's attitude toward the burning was expressed in his testimony in 1873 before the British-American Claims Commission. "The burning of the private dwellings, though never designed by me, was a trifling matter compared with the manifold results that soon followed. . . . I have never shed many tears over the event, because I believe it hastened what we all fought for, the end of the war." As the march progressed northward from Columbia, the Federal soldiers became more and more demoralized. On February 20, General Howard of Sherman's column wrote sharply to his corps commanders: ". . . some of our soldiers have been committing the most outrageous robberies of watches, jewellery, etc. A case has come to my notice where a watch and several articles of jewellery were stolen by a foraging party under the eye of the commissioned officer in charge. Another, where a brute had violently assaulted a lady by striking her, and had then robbed her of a valuable gold watch. . . . I call upon you and upon all the officers and soldiers under you, who have one spark of honor or respect for the profession which they follow, to help me put down these infamous proceedings and to arrest the perpetrators." Sherman reported that in the whole march he heard of but two cases of rape.

383   Sherman's Veterans, from a photograph in the United
       States Signal Corps, War Department, Washington

THE END APPROACHES

"FEBRUARY 25th. 1865 . . . Mrs. Munroe took up my photograph book, in which I have a picture of all the Yankee generals. 'I want to see the men who are to be our masters,' said she. 'Not mine,' I answered, 'thank God, come what may. This was a free fight. We had as much right to fight to get out as they had to fight to keep us in. If they try to play the masters, anywhere upon this habitable globe will I go, never to see a Yankee, and if I die on the way so much the better. . . . February 29th. . . . Trying to brave it out. . . . But we must feed our army first — if we can do so much as that. Our captives need not starve if Lincoln would consent to exchange prisoners; but men are nothing to the United States — things to throw away. If they send our men back they strengthen our army, and so again their policy is to keep everybody and everything here in order to help starve us out. That, too, is what Sherman's destruction means — to starve us out. . . . March 5th. . . . It is also Lent now — a quite convenient custom, for we, in truth, have nothing to eat. So we fast and pray, and go dragging to church like drowned rats to be preached at. . . . 'Are the critics as violent as ever against the President?' asked I [of my husband] . . . [General Chesnut replied] 'Sometimes I think I am the only friend he has in the world. At these dinners, which they give us everywhere, I spoil the sport, for I will not sit still and hear Jeff Davis abused for things he is no more responsible for than any man at that table. Once I lost my temper and told them it sounded like arrant nonsense to me, and that Jeff Davis was a gentleman and a patriot, with more brains than the assembled company. . . . In Washington when we left, Jeff Davis ranked second to none, in intellect, and may be first, from the South, and Mrs. Davis was the friend of Mrs. Emory, Mrs. Joe Johnston, and Mrs. Montgomery Blair, and others of that circle. Now they rave that he is a nobody, and never was.' 'And she?' I asked. 'Oh, you would think to hear them that he found her yesterday in a Mississippi swamp!'" — MARY BOYKIN CHESNUT, *A Diary from Dixie*, 352–53, 357, 360. So Jefferson Davis drank the bitter cup of the defeated.

384 Sherman's March through South Carolina, from a sketch by Theodore R. Davis in *Harper's Weekly*, Mar. 4, 1865

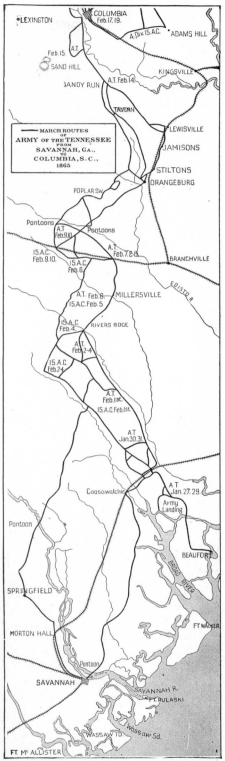

385 Routes of March of Sherman's Army from Savannah to Columbia, redrawn from the *Atlas to Accompany the Official Records of the Union and Confederate Armies*, Washington

386   Battle of Bentonsville, March 19, 1865 — Fourteenth and Twentieth Corps Engaged, from a sketch by William Waud
in *Harper's Weekly*, Apr. 15, 1865

JOHNSTON'S SURRENDER

GENERAL JOHNSTON requested an armistice on April 13 which brought to an end the major military operations of the war. On April 25 Major Hitchcock wrote from Sherman's headquarters: "Everyone is in hopes tonight that Johnston will surrender tomorrow, after all. God grant it! I cannot bear to think of this army marching any further through the country in a hostile attitude; its simple passage and subsistence, aside from the commission of any violence or outrage, would be a terrible blow to the people of the state. Johnston knows this as well as we do, and at the interviews last week expressed great anxiety to avoid the inevitable further damage that would result. It rests with him — not with us. . . . April 26th 1865. . . . The expected interview took place today, and you will know already by telegraph ere you read this that Johnston surrendered. . . . I wish you could look in at the scene here tonight at our Headquarters, — the Governor's mansion. Quite a crowd of officers have been sitting and standing all the evening on the portico in front; a fine brass band playing in the large yard in front of the house since 8 o'clock; and a little while ago, looking through the front window of the right hand parlor, from the portico, one could see Grant and Sherman sitting at the center table, both busy writing, or stopping now and then to talk earnestly with the other general officers in the room — Howard, Schofield, 'Johnny Logan,' and Meigs." — M. A. DeWOLFE, EDITOR, *Marching with Sherman*, 315–16, Yale University Press, New Haven, 1927.

387   Battle of Bentonsville, March 20, 1865 — Fifteenth Corps Engaged On the Right, from a sketch by William Waud
in *Harper's Weekly*, Apr. 15, 1865

CHAPTER VIII

THE END

THE end of this four-year war came swiftly, inevitably, within two crowded and momentous months. On the twenty-fifth of March Lee made his determined effort to use Fort Stedman as a shield to cover his escape from Grant at Petersburg. In April the last Confederate armies of the enisled, blockaded, and beleaguered South laid down their arms forever. The last act of this great tragedy is full of triumph, sorrow, and despair. With nothing to hope for abroad; with nothing to hope for at home, now that Lincoln was in far greater power after his second election; with no great seaport in Confederate hands, but close-blockaded Charleston; with no Confederate cruiser out at sea, except the *Shenandoah* in the lone Pacific; with dwindling, perishing, destroyed resources on every side; with two strong and growing Federal armies converging on the last vestige of the fighting South; with fivefold stronger Federals in the field, and fivefold more in reserve; with Confederate credit gone, and the whole Confederate light of life just on the point of flickering out: with all this ruin gathering around them, the Confederate Government appointed Lee commander in chief for the last two months of the four-year war. Lee of course at once appointed Johnston to his old position; and these two leaders, with their two heroic armies, prepared to sell their lives as dearly as they could, although these lives were now of infinitely greater value for peace than for the continuance of a hopeless war. Jefferson Davis still carried the dying Confederate Government with him; and so long as their government ordered them, so long would Lee and Johnston fight. Their armies never met; for each had an overwhelming assailant of its own.

388 From a cartoon "*With Charity to All, With Malice toward None*,"— *Abraham Lincoln*, by Thomas Nast in *The New York Illustrated Times*, Sept. 19, 1881

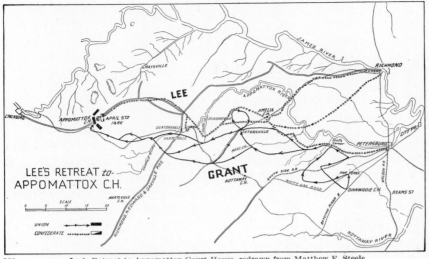

389 Lee's Retreat to Appomattox Court House, redrawn from Matthew F. Steele,
American Campaigns, United States Infantry Association, 1922

APPOMATTOX CAMPAIGN, MARCH 25– APRIL 9, 1865

INTO this short campaign of only sixteen days was crowded the rapid series of momentous events which ended with Lee's surrender. He had hoped to escape by the Richmond and Danville Railroad and then hold out either for better terms or else for orders from his Government. But Grant pursued him and Sheridan forestalled him.

FEDERAL RECAPTURE OF FORT STEDMAN, MARCH 25, 1865

CAPTURED by the Confederates before dawn, Fort Stedman was recaptured the same morning by the Federals, who thus prevented its being used to cover Lee's attempt to escape. Four days later Grant began extending his left flank from the Appomattox River to Dinwiddie

390 Sheridan at Five Forks, after a drawing by Sidney Riesenberg in *Harper's Weekly*, Oct. 26, 1912

Court House. With numbers vastly superior to Lee he was able to threaten his opponent's flank. This compelled Lee to reinforce it and the taking of troops for this purpose made his main lines dangerously thin.

391 From a drawing after the painting *With Fate against Them*, by Gilbert Gaul in
Battles and Leaders of the Civil War, New York, 1888

CONFEDERATES "WITH FATE AGAINST THEM," 1865

THE southern cause was lost. But still it called them on. Lee seems to have been determined not to surrender but to unite with Johnston, if possible, and, if no other opportunity offered, to retire to the fastnesses of the southern mountains and make what opposition he could. On April 1, he received a heavy blow when Sheridan defeated a part of the Confederate army at Five Forks. This was the beginning of the end. The next day Lee evacuated Richmond, the Confederate Government having already fled.

THE SIX HUNDRED FEDERAL
HEROES

Lee's little army fled westward toward Appomattox. Grant pursued aggressively, striving to throw his cavalry in front of the Confederate force. At Sailor's Creek the Federals took seven thousand prisoners. The day before, April 6, a Federal demolition party under Colonel Francis Washburn was sent out to destroy High Bridge over the Appomattox River. They suddenly found themselves cut off by Lee's whole force hurrying west from Sailor's Creek. At this juncture Washburn's six hundred were located by Colonel Theodore Read, whom General Ord had sent with eighty cavalry to call them back at once. What

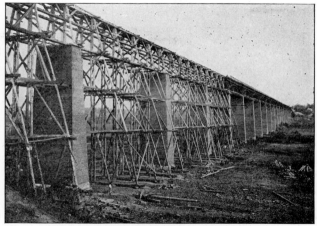

392   High Bridge Crossing the Appomattox, from a photograph
by Gardner, Washington

were Read and Washburn to do now? They had only six hundred against a good many desperate thousands, who were determined to break through all obstructions toward the west. No one, not even Sheridan and Grant, could have blamed them for surrendering, after due resistance, to this overwhelming force. The end of the war was now near, and life was, therefore, doubly sweet. But, on the other hand, there was the supreme objective of Lee's army, whose escape must be prevented by all means possible to Federal arms; and here were the means of at least delaying Lee's escape for possibly quite long enough to ensure his earlier surrounding and defeat. So, in a flash of heroic insight, Washburn and Read decided to sacrifice themselves and their six hundred for the high purpose of shortening the war elsewhere. Read led the first charge on, but soon fell mortally wounded. Then Washburn took command till he too fell. But even after this the rest fought on till the few unwounded men could fight no more.

THREE HOURS BEFORE LEE'S SURRENDER

General Pickett, three hours before the surrender, sent this letter to his wife. "Lee's surrender is imminent. It is finished. Through the suggestions of their commanding officers as many of the men as desire are permitted to cut through and join Johnston's army. The cloud of despair settled over all on the third, when the tidings came to us of the evacuation of Richmond and its partial loss by fire. The homes and families of many of my men were there, and all knew too well that with the fall of our Capital the last hope of success was over. And yet . . . these men as resolutely obeyed the orders of their commanding officers as if we had captured and burned the Federal Capital. The horrors of the march from Five Forks to Amelia Court House and thence to Sailor's Creek beggars all description. For forty-eight hours the man or officer who had a handful of parched corn in his pocket was most fortunate. We reached Sailor's Creek on the morning of the sixth,

393   Richmond in ruins, from a photograph in the United States
Signal Corps, War Department, Washington

weary, starving, despairing. Sheridan was in our front, delaying us with his cavalry (as was his custom) until the infantry should come up. . . . Ah, my beloved division! Thousands of them have gone to their eternal home, having given up their lives for the cause they knew to be just. The others, alas, heartbroken, crushed in spirit, are left to mourn its loss. . . . We have poured out our blood and suffered untold hardships and privations all in vain. And now, well, I must not forget, either, that God reigns. Life is given us for the performance of duty, and duty performed is happiness. It is finished — the sufferings, the horrors, the anguish of these last hours of struggle." — *The Heart of a Soldier*, 176–79.

General,
9th April 1865

I ask a suspension of hostilities pending the adjustment of the terms of the surrender of this army, in the interview requested in my former communication today.

Very respectfully
Your obt sevt
R E Lee

Lt Gen U S Grant
Comdg U S Army

394   Lee's letter to Grant, from the original in the Library of Congress, Washington

LEE'S LETTER TO GRANT, APRIL 9, 1865

THE famous ninth of April was the third day on which Grant and Lee exchanged communications. By now the Confederate case had grown so evidently hopeless that even the indomitable Lee was ready to surrender.

LET US HAVE PEACE, APPOMATTOX, APRIL 9, 1865

HOLDING out his hand in cordial greeting Grant said: "I met you once before, General Lee, while we were serving in Mexico, and I have always remembered your appearance." Lee shook hands with equal cordiality; and they then sat down to fix the terms for the capitulation of the Confederate forces.

395   From the painting *Lee's Surrender*, by Paul Philippoteaux. © O. R. Griffin

THE SURRENDER IN APPOMATTOX COURT HOUSE, APRIL 9, 1865

As Grant wrote out the terms his eye fell on Lee's magnificent presentation sword from old Virginia, and he immediately added a clause exempting the side-arms of the officers. When Lee read this he flushed and said: "This will have a very happy effect upon my army." Then Grant asked if he had any suggestions; whereupon Lee explained that the mounted Confederates owned their horses. So Grant, before Lee could even hint a favor, immediately added another clause, saying that all such horses could be taken home after due proof of ownership. Lee said: "This will have the best possible effect upon the men. It will be very gratifying and do much toward conciliating our people."

396   From the painting *Lee's Surrender at Appomattox*, by J. L. G. Ferris, in Independence Hall, Philadelphia

LEE RIDING AWAY FROM APPOMATTOX COURT HOUSE, APRIL 9, 1865

HAVING shaken hands most cordially with Grant, Lee bowed to the other officers and left the room. As he appeared on the steps every Federal officer in the grounds rose and saluted. Having returned their salutes he mounted Traveler and rode off slowly, holding his hat in his hand as an acknowledgment of the courteous farewell given by Grant and his generals, who remained bareheaded till Lee had ridden from their sight.

397   From the painting *Lee after the Surrender at Appomattox*, by Thure de Thulstrup

LEE'S RETURN TO HIS ARMY, APRIL 9, 1865

Now that the great ordeal, for which Lee had so proudly steeled himself, was over, and he once more was among his loved and loving comrades of this mighty war, he could no longer keep back the tears of anguish for this last farewell. As he rode slowly on past the veterans, they broke ranks to press around him, to take his hand, or even to touch his sword. The next day, April 10, General Lee issued "General Orders No. 9."

"After four years of arduous service, marked by unsurpassed courage and fortitude the 'Army of Northern Virginia' has been compelled to yield to overwhelming numbers and resources. I need not tell the brave survivors of so many hard fought battles, who have remained steadfast to the last that I have consented to this result from no distrust of them, but feeling that valor and devotion could accomplish nothing that would compensate for the loss that must have attended a continuance of the contest, I determined to avoid the useless sacrifice of those whose past services have endeared them to their countrymen. By the terms of Agreement, Officers and men can return to their homes and remain until exchanged. You will take with you the satisfaction that proceeds from the consciousness of duty faithfully performed, and I earnestly pray that a merciful God will extend to you His blessing and protection. With an unceasing admiration for your constancy and devotion to your Country and a grateful remembrance of your kind and generous consideration for myself I bid you all an affectionate farewell. R. E. LEE."

398 From the painting *General Lee's Farewell to his Troops*, by John A. Elder, in the possession of James Blair, Richmond

399   Federals sharing rations with the Confederates, from a contemporary sketch in *Battles and Leaders of the
                                              Civil War*, New York, 1888

FEDERALS SHARING THEIR RATIONS WITH CONFEDERATES, APRIL 10, 1865

FROM commander in chief to private soldier the Federal army behaved as only the noblest of conquerors behave. "The war is over," said Grant to his staff, "and the rebels are our countrymen again." And this, in kindly words or kindly deeds, said every Federal in arms, as he gladly shared his rations with the famishing Confederates.

THE CONQUERED BANNER

Furl that banner, for 'tis weary;
Round its staff 'tis drooping dreary;
　Furl it, fold it, it is best;
For there's not a man to wave it,
And there's not a sword to save it,
And there's not one left to lave it
In the blood which heroes gave it;
　And its foes now scorn and brave it, —
　　Furl it, hide it, let it rest.

Furl that banner! softly, slowly,
Treat it gently — it is holy —
　For it droops above the dead;
Touch it not, unfold it never;
Let it droop there, furled forever,
　For its people's hopes are dead.
　　　— FATHER ABRAM RYAN, "*Poet-Priest
　　　　　of the South*"

400   From the painting *Summer*, by Charles Hoffbauer.   © 1921 by the Confederate Memorial Museum, Richmond

401

From the painting *Review of the Federal Armies*, by James E. Taylor

THE SPIRIT OF LINCOLN

GRANT'S spirit of generosity came from his heart and was akin to the magnanimity of Lincoln. On March 4, a little more than a month before his assassination, the President expressed in classic phrase his own sentiments and those of the North. "On the occasion corresponding to this four years ago, all thoughts were anxiously directed to an impending civil war. All dreaded it, all sought to avert it. While the inaugural address was being delivered from this place, devoted altogether to saving the Union without war, insurgent agents were in the city seeking to destroy it without war — seeking to dissolve the Union, and divide effects, by negotiation. Both parties deprecated war, but one of them would make war rather than let the nation survive, and the other would accept war rather than let it perish, and the war came. . . . Neither party expected for the war the magnitude or the duration which it has already attained. Neither anticipated that the cause of the conflict might cease with, or even before, the conflict itself should cease. Each looked for an easier triumph, and a result less fundamental and astounding. Both read the same Bible, and pray to the same God, and each invokes His aid against the other. It may seem strange that any man should dare to ask a just God's assistance in wringing their bread from the sweat of other men's faces, but let us judge not, that we be not judged. The prayers of both could not be answered. That of neither has been answered fully. The Almighty has His own purposes. Woe unto the world because of offences for it must needs be that offences come, but woe to that man by whom the offence cometh. If we shall suppose that American slavery is one of those offences which, in the providence of God, must needs come, but which having continued through His appointed time, He now wills to remove, and that He gives both North and South this terrible war, as the woe due to those by whom the offence came, shall we discern therein any departure from those Divine attributes which the believers in a living God always ascribe to Him? Fondly do we hope, fervently do we pray, that this mighty scourge of war may speedily pass away. Yet if God wills that it continue until all the wealth piled up by the bondsman's two hundred and fifty years of unrequited toil shall be sunk, and until every drop of blood drawn with the lash shall be paid by another drawn with the sword, as was said three thousand years ago, so still it must be said, the judgments of the Lord are true and righteous altogether. With malice toward none; with charity for all; with firmness in the right as God gives us to see the right, let us strive on to finish the work we are in; to bind up the nation's wounds; to care for him who shall have borne the battle, and for his widow, and his orphan, to do all which may achieve a just and lasting peace among ourselves, and with all nations."

CHAPTER IX

THE SPANISH WAR

THRICE have the English-speaking peoples fought the Spanish Empire overseas. First, that great Elizabethan sea dog, Francis Drake, sailed around the world (1577–80) challenging Spanish claims to all the then known riches of America except those assigned to Portugal. Drake's campaign against the Spanish West Indies in 1585, and his defeat of the Spanish Armada in 1588, were the second and third blows of this first prophetic conflict. The second conflict was in 1762, when native Americans joined the other British forces that took Havana. The third conflict was the War of 1898, when the fleets and armies of the United States gave the tottering Spanish Empire its deathblow in a single short campaign.

There had been constant Cuban discontent against Spanish misrule for at least three-quarters of the nineteenth century, ever since the other Spanish-Americans had risen against Spain in the eighteen-twenties. Hopes of American intervention grew much stronger after the insurrection of 1895. Public feeling in the United States prompted the American Government to demand the recall of the "Spanish Butcher," General Weyler, in 1897. And then, just as there seemed to be some chance of compromise, the U.S.S. *Maine* was blown up in the harbor of Havana with the loss of half her crew. Exactly who was responsible for this catastrophe has never been determined. But her destruction naturally hastened the war, which was declared on April 25, 1898.

The Spanish forces, like the Spanish Empire, had been declining for many years. The Spaniards were still brave, as they abundantly proved but their army and navy were in bad condition. And in any case the national resources were not nearly enough to prolong the struggle, even if they could have been turned to warlike ends in time. Population, wealth, raw material, and manufactures, all were overwhelmingly in favor of the United States. The Spanish force in Cuba comprised nearly two hundred thousand men; but a good many were ineffective through disease, while many more were entirely occupied in fighting the Cuban insurgents. The Spanish army in the Philippines was much smaller and relatively still less effective. The Spanish navy, as shown on paper, was approximately equal to that of the United States, but for all the practical purposes of war the American was incomparably better. This alone made Spanish chances hopeless from the very first; for sea power was the prime determinant throughout.

The United States army was also better than the Spanish. Though it was composed of fine human material, the indifference of the public and the consequent neglect by Congress since the Civil War had prevented the formation of any considerable force ready for an oversea campaign. The American people ignoring the waste of lives and resources that had accompanied the use of amateur armies at the beginning of the Civil War, the public expected that, in this war with Spain, the perfect army could be raised full-grown at once from among patriotic citizens. So again there was waste — waste of lives and waste of resources. This fifteen-weeks war was fought on two widely distant fronts, one in the Philippines, the other in the Spanish West Indies. Americans were but vaguely aware of the existence of the fertile and populous Philippine archipelago off the southern coast of China, where the guns of Dewey's fleet reverberated not only across Manila Bay but from shore to shore of the United States.

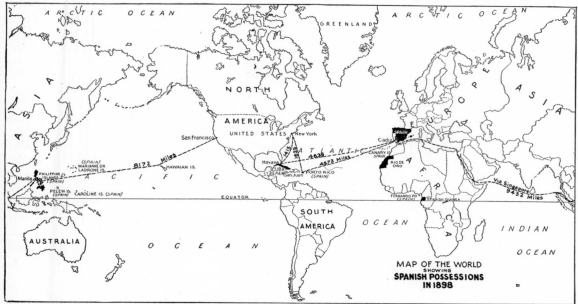

402   Map of the World showing Spanish Possessions in 1898, drawn expressly for *The Pageant of America*

THE SPANISH EMPIRE AND THE UNITED STATES, 1898

THIS shows at once that the fundamental importance of sea power was the same as it had always been throughout the centuries of rivalry between the English-speaking peoples and the Spanish Empire. The advantageous
position of the United States, as compared with that of Spain, is equally evident.

ADMIRAL ALFRED T. MAHAN, 1840–1914

MAHAN's great work, *The Influence of Sea-Power Upon History*, first published in 1888, had already begun to
influence thought in Europe and America. Public opinion on the fundamental importance of sea power before the Spanish War of 1898 offered an object lesson of the most cogent kind. Admiral (then Captain) Mahan
was a professor at the Naval War College, when Secretary of the Navy John D. Long appointed him third
member of the Naval War Board, where his colleagues were Admiral Sicard and Captain Crowninshield.

403   Rear Admiral Montgomery Sicard, courtesy of the office of Naval
       Records and Library, Navy Department, Washington

404   Rear Admiral A. S. Crowninshield, courtesy of the office of Naval
       Records and Library, Navy Department, Washington

405 The Philippine Campaign, showing the route of Dewey's fleet
from Mirs Bay to Manila Bay, redrawn from the *New York
Tribune Atlas of the Spanish-American War*, New York, 1898

MAP OF THE PHILIPPINE CAMPAIGN, MAY 1–AUGUST 13, 1898

TWENTY-FIVE years before the Spanish War Admiral
(then Commander) Dewey was in charge of the U.S.S.
Narragansett on the west coast of Mexico when news
came of the *Virginius* affair. The *Virginius* was an
American vessel filibustering along the Cuban coast. The
enraged Spanish officials had exceeded their rights when
the *Virginius* was captured in executing the captain and
some of the crew and passengers as well. War with Spain
was trembling in the balance when Dewey walked into the
Narragansett's wardroom where he found a most despond-
ent lot of officers, all gloomily supposing that their survey
work in the Pacific would cut them off from any chance
of seeing active service. "On the contrary," said the
cheerful Dewey, "we shall be very much in it. If war
with Spain is declared, the *Narragansett* will take Manila."
Dewey had studied the Philippine naval problem then,
and had kept his information always up to date.

In 1898 Dewey's squadron was not so ready as himself. This was no fault either of Dewey or of the United
States Navy, but part of the long neglect of all war
preparation. Fortunately, however, the Navy's revival
had begun and was progressing. Fortunately, too, its
political chief, Secretary John D. Long, was nearly as good
an administrator as his colleague, Secretary Alger, in charge of the Army, was bad. So all that could be done
in advance was done and, under difficult circumstances, done well. Before the declaration of war Secretary
Long sent a fast steamer from San Francisco to Honolulu, where she transferred her ammunition cargo to the
U.S.S. *Baltimore*. Even then the squadron had only sixty per cent of the ammunition for which its fighting
ships had storage room; and it was seven thousand miles from the nearest United States Navy Yard.
Moreover, event followed event so fast that foreign docks were soon closed against all belligerent vessels for
coaling and repairs. The *Baltimore* reached Hong Kong on April 22, went into dry-dock on the 23rd, and, with
the rest of the squadron, was notified to leave within twenty-four hours, on pain of internment the following
day. Dewey then took his six men-of-war into Mirs Bay, where he "tuned up" before starting for Subig in
the Philippines, where he expected to find the Spanish fleet. Not finding his enemy there, he went on to
Manila, which he approached by night, and where he found the Spaniards at daylight on the first of May.

GEORGE DEWEY, 1837–1917, ADMIRAL OF THE NAVY, 1898

IF any man ever brought the devoted expert service of a lifetime to the test
of a moment's action that man was Commodore Dewey at Manila. Dewey
had served with great distinction all through the Civil War, often under
Farragut's approving eye. He had studied naval questions ever since. And
he was born a leader of men. It was therefore entirely appropriate that he
should have been the first to strike a blow which, by its decisive results,
settled the fate of Spain in the Pacific. Perhaps more appropriate still, this
first, sudden, and most devastating blow made him the hero of the war;
for Dewey was a hero who would last. He was quite unlike the many popular
idols on whom the general public, always yearning for ready-made heroes
in time of crisis, is so very apt to squander mistaken applause. Farragut,
Dewey and Sims: these three successive chief admirals of the United States
Navy are men whose names deserve all lasting honor from the people whom
they served so well; for each was tried by the severest test of all the fires
of war — supreme command at the decisive moment; and each was found
pure gold.

406 Admiral George Dewey, from a
photograph in the possession of the
publishers

407 Maj.-Gen. Frederick Funston, 1865–1917, from a photograph. © Underwood & Underwood

THE LEADER OF THE PHILIPPINE REVOLT, AGUINALDO

THE Philippines presented their complex problems, first, to Dewey's fleet, next to Merritt's army, and finally to the Government at home. As in Cuba, so here, there was revolt against Spanish misrule. The seven million people of the Philippines, mostly Malays, had an astute leader in Aguinaldo, who, however, could not be depended on as an ally, and whose hardly half-civilized forces were afterward turned against the Americans.

408 Emilio Aguinaldo, 1869–, from a photograph. © Rau Studios, Inc., Philadelphia

GENERAL FREDERICK FUNSTON, 1865–1917

IN the pacification of the islands General Frederick Funston distinguished himself for both bravery and ability and won a place for himself among the best military leaders that America has produced. His death on the eve of America's entry into the World War prevented his almost certain selection as commander of the A. E. F.

THE FILIPINO ARMY

IF there was no Cuban army, in any proper meaning of the word, there was certainly no Filipino army; for the Cubans, on the whole, were a more advanced, if also a more mixed, people than the Philippine Malays, whose

seven millions far outnumbered the sprinkling of whites and those of mixed blood. This native revolutionary movement was to cause Americans much trouble before the island leaders were willing to accept the rule of the United States. (The subsequent campaigns against the Filipinos form no part of our subject here. They are described and pictured in another volume.)

409   Aguinaldo and his Advisers, 1899, from a photograph. © Rau Studios, Inc., Philadelphia

410 Admiral Patricio Montojo, after a sketch
from life, in *Harper's History of the War in
the Philippines*, New York, 1900

ADMIRAL MONTOJO

THE Spanish admiral, Montojo, knew he was doomed; for no naval leader with any expert knowledge at all could have expected the Spaniards to beat an equal number of Americans who were so greatly superior in training, morale, ships, guns, engines — everything. Besides, the procrastinating Spaniards had, as usual, failed to defend Subig Bay in time for Montojo to take station in this far better position than Manila.

PLAN OF THE BATTLE OF MANILA BAY, MAY 1, 1898

THE American approach to Manila by night was practically perfect in all essentials:

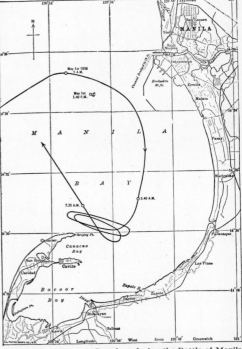

411 Track of Dewey's Squadron during the Battle of Manila Bay, from George Dewey, *Autobiography*, Charles Scribner's Sons, New York, 1912

navigation, speed, formation, and instant readiness for action. The Spanish defense, on the other hand, was bad. There were no scouting lightcraft, no torpedo boats, no effective minefields, and, stranger still, no bombardment of the American squadron till far too late. Moreover, the Spanish fleet was not found near Manila, where it would have had good support from land batteries, but in Cavite Bay, where the forts were very poor and badly gunned. Admirably led by the flagship *Olympia*, the six American warships formed a line-ahead about a mile long. When the range was five thousand yards (or less than three miles) an eight-inch gun in the *Olympia's* forward turret fired the signal shot. Instantly, and most effectively, the American broadsides crashed into their seven Spanish opponents, besides returning the fire of the two flank batteries on land. The accuracy of the American fire was far superior to that of the Spaniards.

THE BATTLE OF MANILA BAY, MAY 1, 1898

THE American battle line steamed five times past the Spaniards, port and starboard broadsides bearing in succession, and the range decreasing to almost a single mile. Attacks by two Spanish torpedo boats were easily defeated, one boat being sunk, the other so badly holed that she had to be beached. As the range shortened the Spaniards suffered more and more. Twice they made heroic attempts to charge the *Olympia*. But the instant concentration of all American batteries on the *Don Juan* and *Reina Cristina* forced these gallant vessels back. By this time the victory was won. But as the hopeless plight of the Spaniards could not be seen through the smoke, and as Dewey now received an alarming, though mistaken, report about the scarcity of ammunition, he drew off, ostensibly for breakfast. When he again closed in only the brave *Ulloa* could return his fire. Instant concentration sank her. She went down with her colors flying.

412 The Battle of Manila, from a drawing by W. A. Rogers in *Harper's Pictorial History of the War with Spain*, 1899

WRECK OF THE SPANISH FLAGSHIP

USELESSLY brave as the rest, Montojo's flagship, *Reina Cristina*, perished without doing any effective damage to Dewey's splendid line. It seems incredible, but it is true, that, while the Spanish squadron was annihilated, not one American was killed, nor was an American vessel out of action for so much as a single minute throughout that stirring day.

413   Wreck of the Spanish Flagship *Reina Cristina*, from *Harper's Pictorial History of the War with Spain*, New York, 1899

THE GERMAN SQUADRON AT MANILA, 1898

414   Principal vessels of the German Squadron in Asiatic Waters, from a drawing by H. Reuterdahl in *Harper's Pictorial History of the War with Spain*, New York, 1899

DEWEY'S victory nearly brought on an international "affair" that might conceivably have anticipated some elements of the World War. Eighteen hundred and ninety-eight was the year of the first foreshadowing German Navy Bill, as 1900 was that of the bill which definitely contemplated the issues of a world struggle. The German expansionists, having hoped to succeed the Spaniards overseas, were much chagrined by Dewey's complete success. They increased their squadron till it exceeded Dewey's. A tense situation developed in Manila Bay. For a considerable period Dewey was compelled to enforce his harbor regulations with an inferior force. The Germans, moreover, showed a disposition to flout his rules. Admiral Chichester, commanding two British ships, watched closely the developments of events. As a crisis approached, Chichester, without in any way committing his Government, intimated to the German commander that the British would support Dewey in the event of hostilities. This knowledge resolved the situation. From that point on Dewey had no trouble with the Germans. In time the American commander was reinforced.

ADMIRAL CAMARA'S ABORTIVE CRUISE, JUNE–JULY, 1898

ANOTHER menace to Dewey's squadron was Camara's fleet from Spain. By the end of June it was in the Red Sea. But when the Spaniards at home found that Watson's American fleet was preparing to visit Spain itself they forced their Government to recall Camara on July 8.

415   The Spanish Reserve Squadron on its way to Port Said, from a drawing by L. A. Shafer in *Harper's Pictorial History of the War with Spain*, New York, 1899

416   Maj.-Gen. Wesley Merritt, from a drawing by T. de Thulstrup
      in *Harper's Pictorial History of the War with Spain*, 1899

GENERAL WESLEY MERRITT, 1836–1910

ON May 19 General Merritt received orders at San Francisco to take an army to the Philippines "for the twofold purpose of completing the reduction of the Spanish power in that quarter and giving order and security to the islands while in the possession of the United States." By July 25 ten thousand troops had arrived before Manila, where the Filipino insurgents were annoying the Spanish garrison of some thirteen thousand men. No time was lost in getting the American troops into position in front of the Spanish forces. The rainy season was on and green American troops suffered from their constant wetting. They suffered also from the inefficiency of the War Department which sent most of them into this tropical country in the old blue woolen uniforms instead of the new khaki.

417   Resistance in Malate, from a drawing by Thure
      de Thulstrup in *Harper's Pictorial History of the War
      with Spain*, New York, 1899

THE SURRENDER OF MANILA,
AUGUST 13, 1898

AFTER some night work at Malate on July 31, and much hardship in the deluged trenches, the army joined in a general attack, which, by a tacit understanding, the Spaniards only resisted enough to save the honor of their flag. Besides, if they had to surrender at all, they much preferred the Americans to the vindictive Filipinos. The only hitch was the German squadron, which looked most aggressive till Chichester's British men-of-war steamed in between the Americans and Germans, playing Dewey's favorite march and again letting the Germans see that they had both fleets to reckon with. Then, with light losses, the American army closed in, while Dewey's fleet supported. By nightfall the Stars and Stripes were flying from headquarters in Manila.

418   419

Obverse and Reverse of the Dewey Medal, issued by Congress in honor of all ranks and ratings who had participated in the
Battle of Manila Bay, from a photograph of the original, courtesy of the Navy Department, Washington

CHAPTER X

THE WEST INDIAN CAMPAIGN

THE principal forces on both sides were naturally drawn to the Spanish West Indies, where this short war went through four distinct, though closely correlated and often overlapping, phases. First and fundamental, of course, was the winning of the general command of the sea, which the United States Navy achieved as soon as it had found Cervera's fleet in Santiago. The second phase was the effective blockade of Cuba, as a result of which the way was practically clear for army transports anywhere. The third phase was the American investment of Santiago both by sea and by land. This phase was marked by the only considerable naval or military actions of the war in the West Indies. The United States Army won all the outposts defending Santiago, while the United States Navy annihilated Cervera's fleet when it made its forlorn attempt to escape. The fourth phase was the attack on Porto Rico, admirably made by the United States Army, and only stopped by peace negotiations just on the eve of a clinching victory. The general result of the war, here as elsewhere, was a foregone conclusion; and the inevitable end of the Spanish Empire overseas was proclaimed on New Year's Day, 1899.

The Spanish naval work was better done than in the Philippines, but even at the best was bad. The Spaniards have always been sea slovens, however brave in battle and however good an ineffectual minority of them has been in other ways. Cervera protested that his fleet was doomed. But public opinion drove him out of Spain, and later Blanco's orders drove him out of Santiago. The United States naval work was excellent, especially considering that the little United States Navy had to be suddenly increased from under fourteen to over twenty-four thousand men, with adapted vessels in proportion.

The case of the United States Army was very different. Weak in numbers, denied all chance of practicing for modern war, without any War College for its senior officers, without any General Staff, and without a trained reserve, the little regular army of twenty-eight thousand had to be hurriedly doubled in a few weeks; while a miscellaneous mass of volunteers, two hundred thousand strong, but weak in all that makes practical soldiers, was suddenly swept together — magnificent in manhood, but hopeless in immediate effectiveness for that deadly midsummer campaign. "When war was finally declared, the War Department machinery found itself clogged with thirty years mold. The management of small detachments, which already knew pretty well how to take care of themselves, was as much as had been necessary. The shrinkage and setbacks of the army during the previous three decades were most important in the offices in Washington. There the reflection of an overconfident and militarily careless people was clearly mirrored. Humdrum methods and a tiny personnel brought little of value to an active, fighting force. What would happen were the Farmer's Bank of Smithville suddenly compelled to take over the business of the Bank of Commerce in New York City? Just what happened in our war offices at the outbreak of the war — an attempt to transform provincial methods into international facilities." — GANOE, 371. The inevitable result of lack of readiness on the part of the military establishment was unnecessary waste of money and life. In proportion to their magnitude the land operations of the war were costly indeed.

MILES AND GARCIA

420   Captain Andrew S. Rowan, from a photograph by the
United States Signal Corps, War Department, Washington

At the outbreak of the war General Nelson A. Miles was the ranking officer of the American Army. Secretary of War Alger kept him in the Adjutant-General's office at Washington. At the beginning of hostilities Lieutenant A. S. Rowan and Lieutenant H. H. Whitney had been sent to learn the condition of the Spanish military forces in Cuba and Porto Rico respectively. In the latter part of June they reported back to Miles. Rowan had reached the Cuban general, Garcia, and had brought back two of that officer's staff. Through these two Cubans Miles suggested to Garcia that he coöperate with the American forces already concentrating before Santiago. Garcia carried out the suggestions. Meanwhile the Cuban insurrectionists continued harassing the Spanish Army as they had been doing for the past three years. Their activities increased the difficulties of the Spaniards in their efforts to defend Cuba from the new American enemy. Garcia, in particular, became a menace at Santiago. The Cuban troops, however, played no decisive part in determining the outcome of the war.

421   Cuban Insurgents, from a photograph by Byron, New York

GENERAL BLANCO AND THE SPANISH ARMY, 1898

When General Weyler was removed from the Spanish command in Cuba in 1897, his place was filled by General Blanco. Of the two hundred thousand Spanish troops in Cuba not more than half were active combatants; and these were badly supplied, badly coördinated, and always distracted by sporadic outbreaks here and there. But worst of all, Blanco and his whole cause and army were entirely at the mercy of superior sea power. Whoever ruled the water, ruled the land. European observers recognized at the outset the importance of the naval aspect of the war. Many continental critics of the United States looked forward to a swift Spanish victory, because they knew very little about the new steel navy which America had brought to completion on the eve of the war. Even the British, who in contrast to the continental peoples were friendly toward the United States, doubted the naval capacity of the United States and indirectly suggested the loan of their own fleet on the *do ut des* principle. The ultimate spectacular triumph of the American Navy elevated the United States to the rank of a world power of the first importance.

422   Spanish Soldiers at Santiago, from a photograph by
Keystone View Co.. New York

ADMIRAL WILLIAM T. SAMPSON

ADMIRAL SAMPSON had been specially promoted for his professional excellence before the war; and he was again promoted for his excellence during the war. Both promotions were made for purely patriotic reasons of the highest kind, and both were amply justified. Sampson and Dewey were of the fighting breed, and quite ready to take all necessary risks. But, like Farragut, they based even their most daring risks upon a profound experience of the sea.

423 Admiral William Thomas Sampson, 1840–1902, from a photograph. © Hollinger & Co.

424 Don Pasquale de Cervera y Topete, 1839–1909, from a photograph in *Harper's Pictorial History of the War with Spain*, New York, 1899

ADMIRAL CERVERA

CERVERA was as good an admiral as it was possible to be in such a navy, but was doomed, like the less competent though equally brave Montojo, to suffer in his own person for many Spanish shortcomings. Both governments and peoples have a tendency to make a defeated commander a scapegoat even when the cause of his defeat lies in official shortcomings for which he has no responsibility.

THE COMMAND OF THE SEA AND THE HUNT FOR CERVERA

ON April 21 Admiral Sampson was appointed to command the North Atlantic station, which comprised practically all the ready United States Navy except Dewey's squadron and the new battleship *Oregon*, which, under Captain Charles Clark, made a record run of fourteen thousand miles from the North Pacific to Key West, where she arrived, completely fit for action, on May 26. Meanwhile Cervera had sailed from the Cape Verde Islands on April 29. Though quite outclassed by Sampson's fleet, and bent only on safely reaching Cuba, he became a regular landlubber's bogey all along the United States coast during his four weeks of disappearance on the high seas. He naturally wished to make San Juan, where the Spaniards had a navy yard; but Sampson was there before him. His next preference was for Havana or Cienfuegos, with their rail connections and closeness to the main Spanish Army; but American naval strategy was too threatening for this. So he ran for isolated Santiago, where he was not expected, and arrived safely on May 19.

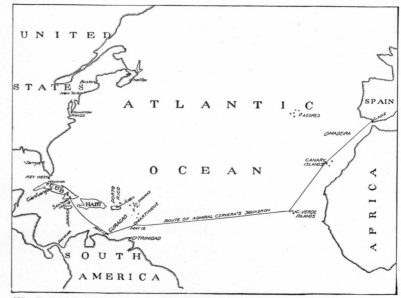

425 Route of Cervera's Squadron, from Herbert H. Sargent, *Campaign of Santiago de Cuba*, A. C. McClurg and Co., Chicago, 1907

AMERICAN NAVAL COMMANDERS

WHILE Sampson blockaded the north coast of Cuba, Schley commanded the flying squadron, which located Cervera at Santiago on May 28. Sampson then closed in and took charge of the Santiago blockade on June 1. Evans had done exceedingly well in the service already, and was to distinguish himself in action on July 3.

426   Commodore Winfield Scott Schley, 1839–1911, from a photograph by Pach Bros., New York

427   Captain Robley Dunglison Evans, 1846–1912, from a photograph by Pach Bros., New York

BLOCKING SANTIAGO, LIEUTENANT RICHMOND P. HOBSON, U.S.N.

CERVERA's decision to run into the harbor of Santiago determined the whole subsequent course of the war in the Atlantic. American naval strength was concentrated as quickly as possible before the harbor to blockade the Spanish fleet. The army was directed to coöperate with the navy and was given the mission of taking the city of Santiago. The fall of this place would make Cervera's position untenable and would force him either to surrender or to give battle on the open sea. The decisive fighting of the war, therefore, took place near Santiago. The entrance to this harbor is narrow and was commanded by land forts. Dewey's maneuver at Manila of steaming in and fighting in the bay itself could not be duplicated in the Cuban anchorage. Instead, however, the Americans determined to seal Cervera's doom by sinking a ship in the narrow harbor mouth. Lieutenant Hobson and six volunteers were chosen for the undertaking.

428   Lieutenant Richmond P. Hobson, 1870–, from a photograph by Buffham, Annapolis

429   The *Oregon*, from a painting by William F. Halsall (1841–1919) in the National Museum, Washington

430   Wreck of the U.S.S. *Merrimac*, from a photograph in the United States Signal Corps, War Department, Washington

THE *MERRIMAC* SUNK AT SANTIAGO, JUNE 3, 1898

ENTERING by night, but receiving plenty of Spanish fire, the *Merrimac* had her steering gear so badly smashed that she overran her mark, failed to turn athwart, and sank too far inside to block the exit. Cervera promptly rescued the crew and kindly reported their safety to Sampson. Hobson and his six companions at once became national heroes.

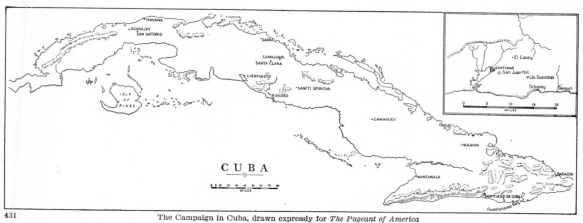

431   The Campaign in Cuba, drawn expressly for *The Pageant of America*

THE BLOCKADE OF CUBA, APRIL–AUGUST, 1898

EXCEPT for Cervera's squadron and a few wholly inadequate supplies nothing reached the Spaniards in Cuba throughout the war. The Spaniards made several futile plans, but nothing worked. Correa, the Spanish Minister of War, actually proposed sending Cervera in June from Santiago de Cuba to the Philippines, whence he could return to Cuba later on! Blanco, as commander in chief in Cuba, of course gave the only possible answer. But even he gambled desperately with the doomed squadron, when ordering Cervera to run the blockade instead of using the men at the Santiago defenses on shore. There they would have been a poor substitute for proper naval action under ordinary circumstances, but they might have helped to prolong the siege; for the American Army still had hard work from the landward side. While the Spanish fleet was crossing the Atlantic and taking its station in Santiago harbor, the cities and towns of the United States became centers of recruiting for the new volunteer army that was being raised to meet the emergency.

432 Recruiting in New York city, from a photograph in the United States Signal Corps, War Department, Washington

RECRUITING

THERE was no dearth of recruits, and of recruits who represented the American type at its best. The problem was to turn this excellent material into a well organized army overnight. Difficult at any time, this problem was made insoluble by the gross incompetence of Secretary Alger, who never grasped essentials, who prevented all real preparations under the charge of the Quartermaster-General, Commissary-General, and even Surgeon-General, and who squandered fifty million dollars on useless coast defenses when the money was needed for oversea attack.

SEA TRANSPORT

THE Spanish War brought sharply to the attention of the American people the military significance of a merchant marine. In 1898 American merchant ships on the high seas were rare. Coastwise shipping was able, however, to supply some of the necessary transport vessels, and others were hired. Securing the boats proved easier, however, than using them effectively, for the war caught the United States Government quite unprepared with plans for meeting an emergency of the character which developed. Plans made in the tension and excitement which inevitably followed the outbreak of war were too often badly conceived and improperly executed.

433 Transports at Tampa, from a photograph in the United States Signal Corps, War Department, Washington

ARMY HOSPITAL

LACK of preparation, crowned by Alger's neglect, made the army in the West Indies the easy prey of yellow fever. By mid-August the first of the twenty thousand sick men who were treated at Montauk Point began to arrive. Then, but as usual, too late, the public was horrified and indignant over the neglect which had produced such terrible results.

434 View of Hospital Camp, Montauk, Long Island, from a photograph in the United States Signal Corps, War Department, Washington

435 Maj.-Gen. Henry Ware Lawton, 1843–99, from a photograph in the United States Signal Corps, War Department, Washington

436 Maj.-Gen. William Rufus Shafter, 1835–1906, from a photograph in the United States Signal Corps, War Department, Washington

THE FIGHT FOR SANTIAGO, JUNE 20–JULY 15, 1898

THE public shouted "On to Cuba!" just as a former generation had shouted "On to Richmond!" So the flurried government ordered General Miles, the ranking officer of the United States Army, to send seventy thousand men off to Havana on May 8. But when they found they could not give him enough ammunition for a single battle, they ordered General Shafter to Mariel with a much smaller force. When, however, they found that the Navy could not possibly convoy even these fewer men they ordered twelve thousand off to Key West. But even these could not go, because Key West could not be supplied even with sufficient water. Finally, the Fifth Corps, sixteen thousand strong, under General Shafter, was hurried into thirty-two transports at Tampa, with eighty-nine war correspondents, but without any proper system of supply. On June 20 this expedition arrived off Santiago. Shafter and Wheeler would both have been "plucked in the medical" if examined for such a campaign; and both these veterans of the Civil War, were on the sick list at the crisis of San Juan Hill. Their chief subordinates, Lawton and Chaffee, were excellent leaders and distinguished themselves throughout the war. Hawkins was particularly efficient in leading his brigade at San Juan Hill.

437 Maj.-Gen. Joseph Wheeler with Colonel Leonard Wood and Lieutenant-Colonel Theodore Roosevelt, from a photograph by Underwood & Underwood, New York

438 Lt.-Col. Theodore Roosevelt, 1858–1919, from a photograph by Underwood & Underwood, New York

LIEUTENANT–COLONEL THEODORE ROOSEVELT, SECOND–IN–COMMAND, ROUGH RIDERS, 1898

THIS war was far more than three-quarters fought and won by the regular forces of the United States Army, Navy, and Marines. For one thing, it was too short for untrained, or even half-trained, units to do their manhood justice in an expert way. No one knew these truths better than the future President Roosevelt, who showed his good sense at the very start by making himself subordinate to Colonel, afterward Major-General, Leonard Wood, the future Military Governor of Cuba, because Wood had some of the expert knowledge which Roosevelt had not. Roosevelt had just resigned as Assistant Secretary of the Navy, where he had shown his appreciation of expert training. He had both humor and chivalry enough to see the penetrating double point of a certain true story of the Civil War. "Why don't you come in?" asked a lady of a soldier passing her entertainment booth at a patriotic fair, "aren't you one of our heroes?" "No, Ma'am," answered this veteran, "I'm only a regular." Congressional neglect had impaired the efficiency even of the regulars.

THE ROUGH RIDERS

THESE Rough Riders were no ordinary civilians suddenly turned into soldiers, but men of much experience in frontier work that was not bad training for a stiff campaign. Moreover, a good many had seen serious fighting before; while most, like their second-in-command, knew enough to want to learn more and learn it from the best trained regulars as well. They accompanied Shafter against Santiago.

439 Rough Riders, from a photograph by Underwood & Underwood, New York

SEIZURE OF GUANTANAMO

FORTY miles east of Santiago lies the splendid harbor of Guantanamo, now a regular United States Navy Station. In 1898 it was of great strategic importance and important to secure before investing Santiago. From this harbor General Miles made his dash on Porto Rico. Guantanamo Bay was occupied on June 7 by a landing party that met with little resistance. But the Spanish troops inland kept up a galling fire on Camp McCalla till the Marines, with some Cubans, drove them off on June 12. Guantanamo Bay, however, was too far from Santiago to be useful for a base of operations against that city. The troops were landed at Siboney and Daiquiri some miles to the west of the entrance of the bay (see map, No. 431). The operation at Guantanamo illustrates the freedom of action which control of the sea gave to the American forces.

440 Bombardment of Morro Castle, Santiago, by Admiral Sampson's Fleet, from a painting, courtesy of the Scientific American Publishing Co., New York

441   Bird's-Eye View of Santiago and surrounding country, from *Harper's Pictorial History of the War with Spain*, New York, 1899

PLAN OF THE FIGHT FOR SANTIAGO, JUNE 22–JULY 15, 1898

SANTIAGO was in itself a secondary place, but the presence of Cervera's squadron made it of primary importance to both sides. This plan shows how the United States fleet and army closed in on its defenses, for which there were no available reinforcements, except the thirty-five hundred Spaniards who passed through the inefficient Cubans in the early morning of the critical third of July.

442   United States Army Transport *Yale* at Siboney, Cuba, from a photograph in the United States Signal Corps, War Department, Washington

TRANSPORT *YALE*

THE subsidized American liners *St. Paul*, *St. Louis*, *New York*, and *Paris* were taken over by the Government at once and put to good use as transports and commerce destroyers. The *St. Louis* excelled at cutting cables. The *New York* was renamed *Harvard* by the Assistant Secretary of the Navy, Theodore Roosevelt, who, by way of intercollegiate courtesy, renamed the *Paris*, her sister ship, the *Yale*. The army had no means of landing; so Sampson's squadron did this difficult and quite dangerous work, not without some loss of life. Four days (June 22–26) were occupied in debarking fifteen thousand men at Daiquiri and Siboney.

443   United States Pack Train marching to the Front, 1898, from a photograph in the
                      United States Signal Corps, War Department, Washington

PACK TRAIN TRANSPORT

THE roads to Santiago were mere tracks, meandering through rolling country. The whole region was covered with dense tropical bushes and infested with deadly malarial mosquitoes. It took fourteen days to accumulate adequate supplies at the fighting line, only a few miles away.

444   Barbed-wire Entanglements near Santiago, from a photograph in the
              United States Signal Corps, War Department, Washington

GARCIA AT SANTIAGO

"WITH an additional force of five thousand men, General Garcia besieged the [Spanish] garrison of Santiago, taking up a strong position on the west side and in close proximity to the harbor. He had troops in the rear as well as on both sides of the garrison at Santiago before the arrival of our troops. The Cuban troops took an active and important part in that campaign, and are entitled to credit accordingly." — NELSON A. MILES, *Serving the Republic*, 280, Harper & Bros., 1911.

LAS GUASIMAS, JUNE 24, 1898

LAS GUASIMAS was a preliminary skirmish, fought while only half the American Army was ashore by about a thousand dismounted cavalry, part regulars, part Rough Riders, against nearly twice as many Spaniards. The latter were driven back on the San Juan defenses of Santiago.

445   Infantry preparing to move forward for attack on San Juan Hill, from a photograph
                      in the United States Signal Corps, War Department, Washington

THE EL CANEY WING OF THE BATTLE OF
SAN JUAN, JULY 1, 1898

THE inland Spanish left wing was at El Caney, which was strengthened by barbed wire, rifle pits, and a stone blockhouse. It was full of infantry; but there were no guns. Chaffee's splendid reconnaissance enabled Lawton to march all night so as to reach by morning the best position for attack. Lawton's seven thousand took eight hours to work forward under a galling fire to the blockhouse, which they rushed in splendid style despite the fatigues of two days and one hard night.

THE SAN JUAN WING, JULY 1, 1898

SAN JUAN HILL stood straight in front of Santiago, two miles from the bay. Here again, the tangled vegetation, bad paths, and broken country kept back the final assault for hours. Luckily the Spaniards, though little short of the Americans in number, made no serious counterstroke between San Juan and El Caney through the gap left between the two assaulting American forces. The intense heat, entangling obstructions, and biting Spanish fire could not do more than retard the American advance. The First and Ninth (negro) Cavalry and the Rough Riders worked

446   From the painting *The Advance on San Juan Hill* by C. D. Graves, in the Library of Congress, Washington

their way up Kettle Hill and sent the Spaniards flying; the Sixth and Sixteenth Infantry, led by indomitable Hawkins, pressed on and up against the biggest blockhouse; while the Tenth Infantry gallantly kept the fighting touch between these and the cavalry. But the most severely tried unit was Wikoff's brigade, consisting of the Thirteenth, Ninth, and Twenty-fourth Infantry; for during that one morning's fight the command was changed four times, each regiment's colonel holding it in turn after the brigadier was killed.

447   Fort on San Juan Hill, from a photograph in the United States Signal Corps, War Department, Washington

448   San Juan Hill and the fort, from a photograph in the United States Signal Corps, War Department, Washington

CERVERA'S SORTIE FROM SANTIAGO, JULY 3, 1898

449   Morro Castle, from a photograph by Keystone View Co., New York

THE American victory of San Juan convinced the Spaniards that Santiago must soon fall. The arrival of the thirty-five hundred Spanish reinforcements enabled Cervera to withdraw all seamen from shore duty; and the result of a conference between the Spanish Governor, General Blanco, and the senior German naval officer at Havana was a cast-iron order to attempt immediate escape at any risk. Despairing of maneuvering under the incessant searchlights, Cervera came out by day. Within an hour his fate was sealed; and in another two his last and swiftest vessel (*Colón*) was run to death. Sampson reported the annihilation of every Spanish ship, with a total American loss of only one killed, a few wounded, and no ship badly damaged.

450   Wreck of the Spanish cruiser *Oquendo*, from a photograph in the United States Signal Corps, War Department, Washington

SAMPSON AND SCHLEY

FOLLOWING the defeat of Cervera an unfortunate controversy arose regarding the credit for the victory over the Spanish fleet. When Cervera ran for the open sea, Sampson chanced to be at Siboney on official business. Admiral Schley, the senior officer present, was in actual command of the American ships during the engagement. Both officers proved themselves worthy of the responsibilities placed upon them. Sampson had admirably disposed his warships and Schley, in the words of General Miles, "with great skill and valor met, fought, pursued, and destroyed the Spanish fleet."

451   Capron's Battery in action, July 10, 1898, from a photograph in the United States Signal Corps, War Department, Washington

452   Infantry Intrenchments at the Siege of Santiago, from a photograph in the United States Signal Corps, War Department, Washington

SURRENDER OF SANTIAGO, JULY 17, 1898

ON July 11 General Miles arrived before Santiago. Two days later Miles and Shafter met the Spanish general, Toral, in command of the city. Miles proposed liberal terms which included the transportation home of the Spanish army by the United States. On July 14 Toral, speaking for General Blanco, accepted. On the same day Miles directed Shafter to take measures to check the ravages of yellow fever which was menacing the army. On July 17 the fighting in Cuba ended when the troops of General Toral laid down their arms.

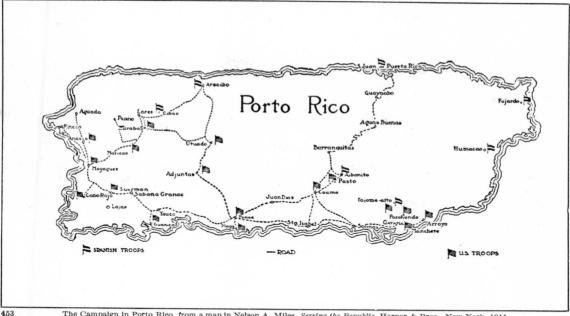

453   The Campaign in Porto Rico, from a map in Nelson A. Miles, *Serving the Republic*, Harper & Bros., New York, 1911

MILES IN PORTO RICO, JULY 25–AUGUST 13, 1898

"I WAS anxious to proceed as quickly as possible to the island of Porto Rico, and so cabled the authorities at Washington. After some delay authority was granted, and I started from Guantanamo on July 21st, with 3,415 infantry and artillery, together with two companies of engineers and one company of the Signal Corps, on nine transports. . . . I decided to go direct to Guanica. . . . The landing of marines, sailors, and our troops immediately commenced, and after a short skirmish the Spanish troops were driven from the place. . . . In this movement, as in subsequent ones, I was ably and cordially assisted by the Navy, which rendered valuable aid in disembarking the troops and supplies from the transports. . . ." — MILES, 296–99.

GENERAL NELSON A. MILES, 1839–1925

PORTO RICO gave Miles little chance for a great campaign. But all he did there he did well. His admirable plan was to march four columns on San Juan, where he would join forces with the fleet. On July 28, 1898, at Ponce, Miles issued a proclamation to the people of Porto Rico. ". . . The chief object of the American military forces will be to overthrow the armed authority of Spain and to give to the people of your beautiful island the largest measure of liberty consistent with this military occupation. We have not come to make war upon the people of a country that for centuries has been oppressed, but, on the contrary, to bring protection, not only to yourselves but to your property, to promote your prosperity and bestow upon you the immunities and blessings of the liberal institutions of our government. It is not our purpose to interfere with any existing laws and customs that are wholesome and beneficial to your people, so long as they conform to the rules of military administration of law and justice. This is not a war of devastation, but one to give to all within the control of its military and naval forces the advantages and blessings of enlightened civilization." The capture of Porto Rico was quickly effected.

454   Maj.-Gen. Nelson A. Miles, from a photograph in the United States Signal Corps, War Department, Washington

455   Unloading horses from lighters during the United States occupation of Porto Rico, from a photograph in the United States Signal
Corps, War Department, Washington

THE MILITARY ACHIEVEMENT

"At the time the protocol was signed our troops were engaged in actual fighting in Porto Rico and the Philippine Islands, twelve thousand five hundred miles apart, under similar conditions. At the same time preparations were in progress for a demonstration on the Spanish coast and the islands of Spain in the Mediterranean as well as in the Atlantic, and hostilities would have been opened there had not the terms of peace been agreed upon. The achievements of our army, notwithstanding the embarrassments of its limited equipment and transportation and the scandal of its corrupt food supply, were successful to a marked and unprecedented degree. . . . The sons of the North, South, East and West . . . had exhibited patriotism, heroism, and fortitude to the highest degree. . . . The Spanish War was unique in many respects. The campaign had been aggressive from start to finish. Not a single reverse or disaster had occurred. Not a single soldier, gun, color, nor an inch of ground was captured by the enemy, which is unusual in the history of wars." — Miles, 304.

456   Artillery Shelling the Blockhouse at Coamo, Porto Rico, from a photograph in the United States Signal Corps, War Department, Washington

CUBA

At last, after four hundred years of Spanish rule, the hoisting of the Stars and Stripes over the Palace at Havana proclaimed a change of government. For a few years following, Cuba was governed by General Leonard Wood, during which time great progress was made in the establishment of law and order, in sanitation, and in the checking and control of that scourge of the tropics, yellow fever. In 1902 the military government turned Cuba over to a government chosen by its own people. The pledge of the nation, given at the time of the declaration of war on Spain, had been redeemed.

457   American troops entering Havana, from a photograph in the United States Signal Corps, War Department, Washington

CHAPTER XI

THE BOXER EXPEDITION

IN the summer of 1900 news flashed over the world that an organization of Chinese known as Boxers had suddenly fallen upon foreigners living in and near Pekin. Many of the whites had been killed and the remainder were being besieged in the legation quarter of the Chinese capital. The explosion in China was the result of steady aggressions against China by the nations of Europe. In 1900 the Celestial Empire seemed on the verge of disintegration. Cartoonists pictured the great nations of the world watching, like vultures, awaiting the moment when they could share the carcass of the dismembered state. The Boxers were patriots who sought to check the aggressions of the foreigners and preserve China for the Chinese. Their rallying cry, "Kill the foreign devils," brought unwonted terror to the white communities that dwelt in China. The besieging of the legation quarter riveted on Pekin the attention of the civilized world. Days lengthened into weeks with no news from Pekin save that the Boxers were still at the legation gates but had not yet entered. The legation guard, standing at bay, seemed able to keep out the Chinese. The question on the lips of everyone was; how long will the food supply hold out? Not a moment could be lost in sending aid to the endangered Europeans and Americans. All the Governments whose nationals were involved hurried expeditionary forces to China. Within a short time troops wearing several different uniforms were debarking on the Chinese coast.

John Hay, McKinley's urbane Secretary of State, had watched for some time the developments in China with growing apprehension. America wanted no slice of China yet the United States could not sit idly by and see the Flowery Kingdom partitioned among the powers of Europe. Americans desired to trade in China. They feared that in the areas in which different powers were dominant restrictions on trade would appear. The United States proposed the policy of the "Open Door." Up to the Boxer uprising in 1900 Secretary Hay was meeting with success in his diplomatic efforts to secure the Open Door. This catastrophe threatened not only the lives of the besieged foreigners but the integrity of China itself. Impotent China lay at the mercy of the world. The bloody massacre of the Boxers had aroused the western nations to anger. The stage was set for the entrance of China by a military force and its dismemberment as indemnity to the great powers for the injuries they had sustained. The Government of the United States was bound to send troops to aid in the task of rescuing its endangered citizens in Pekin. America sent with the utmost dispatch a considerable force with orders to coöperate in the joint expedition against Pekin. By virtue of the participation of those soldiers in the military operations America was represented at the peace table when the emergency ended. Chaffee's khaki-clad battalions were in fact fighting for the Open Door as well as speeding to the rescue of their endangered fellow countrymen.

458   Fortifications at Taku, China, from a photograph in the United States Signal Corps,
                              War Department, Washington

THE CAPTURE OF TAKU AND TIEN-TSIN, JUNE–JULY, 1900

ON June 16 orders were sent to General MacArthur at Manila to rush a regiment to Taku, from which place the move against Pekin would begin. Nineteen days after he received his instructions Colonel Liscum and his regiment, the Ninth Infantry, debarked at Taku. This feat, enhanced by the fact that Liscum was delayed by a typhoon, was evidence of the training and efficiency of the Regular Army. On June 17 Taku had fallen before the batteries of the warships of European powers. On July 13 an allied army composed of British, French, and Japanese besides the Americans moved against Tientsin. A wall surrounded the city and the defenders fought bitterly. The Americans advanced on a front which afforded very little cover. For fifteen hours they fought, suffering heavy losses. Then Tientsin fell to become the base for the operations against Pekin. The pleasure of the American troops at the victory was marred by their mourning for their efficient leader, Liscum.

GENERAL ADNA R. CHAFFEE, 1842–1914, AND STAFF

FROM the day, twenty-six years before, when he led a charge of the Sixth Cavalry against the Comanches and Kiowas near the Red River, Chaffee had been a marked man in the United States Army. His fine work in the recent Spanish War naturally increased his service reputation. And so it was with great expectations that he was sent to China, where his little force would be the comrade in arms of picked troops from all the European powers. Chaffee was hastening across the Pacific when Tientsin fell.

459   Maj.-Gen. Adna R. Chaffee and his Staff at headquarters, China Relief Expedition, Pekin, China,
                   from a photograph in the United States Signal Corps, War Department, Washington

THE MARCH FROM TIENTSIN TO PEKIN, AUGUST 4–13, 1900

THE Boxers resisted stubbornly along the banks of the Pei-Ho during the first few days of August. There were fights at Pei-Ts'ang and Yang Tsun, the latter a quite severe engagement. The days were hot. Though the Chinese retreated they did not cease fighting. Chinese soldiers, hidden in villages or along roadsides, kept up a desultory fire at the troops advancing toward the capital of the Flowery Kingdom. The Chinese, however, were notoriously poor soldiers. They had neither the armament, the discipline, nor the leadership of western troops. They had fallen upon the foreigners in their midst without realizing their own military impotence. The advance continued within twelve miles of Pekin. The allies agreed to spend the 13th in reconnaissance; but the Russians, who had been slowest on the march, now attacked the Tung-pien-men gate of Pekin in order to steal first honors for themselves. Though they did force an entrance, they fell into confusion and were glad of help next day. The Russian breach of etiquette quite naturally offended their allies.

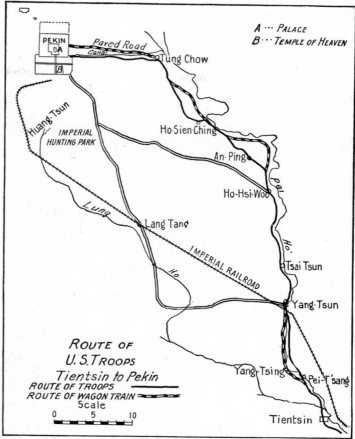

ROUTE OF U.S. TROOPS Tientsin to Pekin
ROUTE OF TROOPS ————
ROUTE OF WAGON TRAIN ≈≈≈
Scale
0   5   10

460   March Route of United States troops from Tientsin to Pekin, August 4–13, 1900, drawn expressly for *The Pageant of America*

MOVING ON PEKIN

ON the forenoon of August 14 General Chaffee's battalions came in sight of the ancient walls of Pekin. At eleven A.M. two companies of the Fourteenth Infantry scaled the wall and planted their regimental flag on its battlements. With the aid of the soldiers on the ground these companies drove off the defenders from the corner of the wall as far as the east gate into the Chinese city where, later in the day, the British entered without opposition.

461   The desperate dash of American Marines along the wall of Pekin, from a drawing by Gordon Grant in *Leslie's Illustrated Weekly*, Sept. 15, 1900.

462   On Top of Gate of the Tartar Wall, where Captain Reilly, Fifth Field Artillery, was killed, from
a photograph in the United States Signal Corps, War Department, Washington

UNITED STATES ARTILLERY SWEEPING THE TARTAR WALL OF PEKIN, AUGUST 14–15, 1900

RILEY's battery swept the Boxers off the wall to the west of the Tung-pien-men gate, while the Fourteenth drove them southward to the Sha-Huo gate. This, with the concurrent entry of the main British forces, and the united advance of all the allies, relieved the besieged legations.

GENERAL CHAFFEE ENTERING PEKIN

AT three P.M. American soldiers arrived opposite the legations. The siege of the Boxers had been raised. The endangered foreigners were saved. The emotion of the beleaguered whites when they realized that they had at last been rescued may be inferred from the message of the American minister to Chaffee: "The patriotic purpose with which you hurried more than half around the world, the heroic courage displayed, and the tremendous sacrifices made in your victorious march from Tien-tsin to Pekin deserve a more fervent expression of our sincere appreciation than can ever be given. . . . We deeply deplore the loss of the splendid heroes who died that we might live. . . ."

463   General Chaffee entering Pekin, from a photograph in the United
States Signal Corps, War Department, Washington

464   Battery "F," Fifth United States Field Artillery, at the Third Gate to the Forbidden City,
from a photograph in the United States Signal Corps, War Department, Washington

THE FALL OF THE FORBIDDEN CITY

ARMED forces of the enemy still held the Forbidden City, from the walls of which they delivered a sniping fire. On August 15 Chaffee joined in the move to crush all resistance. In the fighting of that day Reilly's battery distinguished itself and Reilly himself was killed while standing beside Chaffee watching the effect of the fire of his guns. To one of Reilly's platoon commanders, Lieutenant Summerall, went the credit of battering the opening through which the infantry entered the Forbidden City.

WITHIN THE FORBIDDEN CITY

On August 28 the Allied armies entered the Forbidden City. "I opposed the performance," reported Chaffee, "as one based on curiosity merely and not one of military or political necessity, but was over-ruled. The city of Pekin has been sacked; looted from corner to corner in the most disgraceful manner imaginable; such is my opinion. I had no idea that civilized armies would resort to such proceedings. It is a race for spoil. I have kept my own command fairly clean, thank God, but with all my efforts

465   Fourteenth United States Infantry in the Palace Grounds, Pekin, from a photograph in the United States Signal Corps, War Department, Washington

it is not spotless. . . . It requires but one example of the sort I have witnessed to convince one that every nation's hand is against the Chinese Empire — innocent and guilty. The United States alone, of all the powers, may not wish to see the Chinese Empire destroyed, but she will not be able to stay the march of events." The friendliest relations between any two of the Allied forces were those between the Americans and British. When the evacuation began, the British sent their Indian Pipers to show the Americans special honor by playing them out of Pekin.   A small American detachment has remained at Tientsin to the present.

CHAFFEE AND COUNT VON WALDERSEE

The Germans under Count von Waldersee had arrived too late to participate in the Pekin fighting. The character of Chaffee is displayed in a letter which he wrote to the Count when the Americans learned that the Germans were removing from the Chinese observatory some ancient Chinese astronomical instruments: "I have the honor to inform Your Excellency that my government would vehemently denounce any officer of its service who might enter upon spoliation of this sort, and it will sincerely regret to learn that any nation with which it co-operated to relieve the besieged Legations in Pekin authorizes or permits its troops to in-

466   Indian Pipers Playing Americans out of Pekin, from a drawing by Sydney Adamson in *Leslie's Illustrated Weekly*, August 17, 1901

jure or remove any instruments or other parts of the observatory. . . ." Chaffee was later promoted to the rank of Lieutenant-General.   Vice-President Roosevelt in his letter of congratulation expressed the popular attitude toward the American commander: "We are all your debtors for what you have done in China — for everything, from the way you fought, to the way you have done justice, and the stand you have taken on matters generally, including your letter to Waldersee."   Soon after the close of the World War a defeated Germany returned to China the stolen astronomical instruments.

467   United States Cavalry at the Great Wall of China, from a photograph by Captain C. F. O'Keefe, in the United States Signal Corps, War Department, Washington

CHAPTER XII

AMERICA ENTERS THE WORLD WAR

IN July 1914 Americans, as was their wont, were busy with the prosecution of their own domestic affairs. In particular they were interested in a business reaction that was threatening to become a depression. There were some Republicans, moreover, who did not look upon the dark possibilities as an unmixed evil. Depression would embarrass their ancient enemies, the Democrats, who had so unceremoniously thrown them out of power less than two years before. Suddenly without warning, at least so far as that mythical personage, the average American, was concerned, the murder of an archduke and his wife at Serajevo brought Europe to the verge of war. The eyes of Americans were riveted on the Old World; in bewilderment they watched the swift developments of the latter days of July. They thought of that intricate and powerful web of business interests which bound together the industrial nations of Europe. They remembered the cultural ties and those which spring from friendly intercourse of neighbors. They could not believe a war between the most highly civilized nations of the world within the realm of twentieth-century possibility. To the very last they read the pronouncements of the Foreign Offices and the news of mobilizations with the conviction that it was largely a game of bluff that would soon blow over and be forgotten. Yet war came. Day after day Americans read the incredible news of the German invasion of Belgium, of the collapse of the forts at Liége, Namur, and Maubeuge, of the drive toward Paris, of the consternation in the French capital. Not until the time when Joffre stopped the invader at the Marne did the average American adjust himself to the fact of war in Europe. But another surprise awaited him. He saw the swift movements of maneuver warfare slow down on what he had learned to call the Western Front. Then he vaguely began to realize that men were fighting in trenches. The war was as strange in its conduct as in its origin. But, by the spring of 1915 he had become accustomed to think in terms of trenches; he read eagerly accounts of life and fighting in them. By this time he was thoroughly adjusted to the fact of conflict.

In fact he caught a glimpse close at hand of an interesting by-product of the war. The average American heard rumors of the arrival in America of English, French, and Russian commissions and of gigantic deals with American manufacturers. Then he saw in the industrial section of the United States fine, modern factory buildings going up as fast as the builders could rivet the girders. Cities small and large began to boom. Industrial America was busy, feverishly busy, producing munitions for the Allies. No Germans came, for the sea lanes were closed to them. But while America was echoing with the builder's hammer and the clatter of new machines, the people of the United States watched with unflagging interest the thrusts and counterthrusts of the titanic struggle in the Old World.

Long since they had begun to discuss with animation the causes which had brought it about. Intelligent Americans struggled through the mass of ephemeral and, for the most part, propagandist literature that purported to explain the reasons for the tragedy. Amid the babble of tongues which arose two groups of disputants quickly appeared, those who favored the Allies and those who sympathized with the Central Powers. The latter were likely to be of German or Austrian descent. There were also many bewildered people who, for a time, followed literally the warning of the President to be neutral in thought as well as in deed. But more and more Americans found it impossible to hold their sympathies in leash. The average American took the side of the Allies. His sense of what is honorable and decent had been outraged by the unprovoked attack upon Belgium. Instinctively he sympathized with Belgium and with France, who appeared the underdogs, and whose people were fighting desperately to drive the invader from their very doorsteps. He had had a tendency to look upon France as an artistic but effete nation until the Marne suddenly revolutionized his ideas. Then he discovered suddenly a new and unsuspected France and admiration took the place of doubt. He admired also the spirit of those thousands of British young men who rallied as volunteers to the colors. Then he read accounts of sinkings by submarines, a weapon which one American had invented and another perfected. To his surprise the German submarine commanders left noncombatant crews to drown or to starve in open boats. His mind was prepared to receive and believe strange and terrible tales of German atrocities in Belgium. When the average American discoursed with animation in his club or lodge on these or kindred subjects, he was more than likely to find in the circle about him one or more who disagreed with his point of view. With enthusiasm equal to his own for the Allies the supporter of the Central Powers pointed to the patriotism and *élan* with which the German people had marched off to war. The adversary countered the criticism of the attack on Belgium and of the tactics of the German submarines with tales of the horrors of starvation which followed in the wake of the deadly British blockade. But the pro-German, though he pressed it hard, rarely won his point with his audience; from first to last he remained in a minority. After the sinking of the *Lusitania* on May 7, 1915, he was on the defensive. On the day when the news of the *Lusitania* covered the front pages of the newspapers, the minds of Americans could not comprehend how civilized human beings could lie in ambush and, in cold blood, bring about such suffering and sorrow. Impatiently they brushed aside the explanations of the apologists. Impatiently many of them followed the long-drawn-out correspondence between their President and the Imperial German Government. Then Germany, upon the insistence of the Government of the United States, stopped the ruthless sinkings of the submarines, and the average American felt, with a sense of pride, that his nation had struck a blow for humanity. But in his heart rankled a phrase coined by his President which described him as "too proud to fight."

Yet he did not want to fight. The war was Europe's war; America had no part in its making. In 1916 the Americans, now quite familiar with the general characteristics of trench warfare, watched, sick at heart, one of the most terrible aspects of the struggle. The German Crown Prince was trying to take Verdun. The resultant suffering and slaughter was beyond the power of the mind to grasp. Breathlessly Americans waited day after day. With clenched fists they repeated the words from across the sea, "They shall not pass." They did not pass, but France had been bled white. England also had suffered appalling losses. Russia had failed to hold the gains her armies once had made. Rumania and Serbia had collapsed. The German arms were in the ascendant. What of America? What of the average American? Then it was that the American people entered the Garden of Gethsemane. They were torn between a passionate desire to remain aloof from the European shambles and an equally passionate desire to aid in bringing down what they had come to look upon as a bloody military colossus that had raised its head in the Old World and, if victorious, might be expected to turn upon the New. They berated the President for his slowness to develop the defenses of the nation, yet they reëlected him because he had kept them out of war. As the year 1916 drew to a close the people of the United States were distracted as they had not been since those terrible early months of 1861.

468   Alan Seeger, from a drawing in red chalk by John Elliott
      (1858–1925), in the National Gallery of Art, Washington

469   Paul Pavelka, from a drawing in red chalk by John Elliott,
      in the National Gallery of Art, Washington

AMERICANS IN FRANCE BEFORE 1917

BEFORE America entered the war, from all parts of the United States came young men whose imaginations had been stirred by the conflict in the Old World and who were drawn irresistibly into the vortex of that terrible struggle. They blazed a trail which their countrymen were later to follow and they set standards of heroism and efficiency which were not surpassed by the American hosts who came after them. They fought in the armies of Canada, Great Britain and France. Just as America was entering the war a Frenchman, Paul Louis Hervier, wrote a history, *American Volunteers In the Ranks of the Allies.* "The Americans who offered their services to France," said he, "after the outbreak of the war in 1914 were recruited without solicitation in all classes of society: millionaires, writers, lawyers, engineers, former soldiers and sailors, boxers, butchers, explorers, and especially university students. . . . American volunteers, who wished, in August, 1914, to join their French brothers in defending the ideal represented by the word 'Liberty,' almost all entered the Foreign Legion. One of them, Paul Rockwell, grievously wounded in Champagne, sent to a New York editor this response, which is sweet to our hearts: 'In the Foreign Legion about two hundred Americans are serving or have served. The bitterest regret of my life is that so few Americans have come to aid France.' . . . Men will long continue to speak of the services to the French Army by the American Escadrille; they will long recount the exploits of Norman Prince, who died for France on Oct. 15, 1916; of Victor Chapman, who died for France in June, 1916, of Kiffin Rockwell, who died for France on September 23, 1916; of Dennis Dowd, the skilled pilot, who died in an airplane accident at the Buc airdrome in the beginning of August 1916; of William Thaw, the Pittsburgh millionaire; of Elliott Christopher Cowdin; of Lufbery, of Bert Hall, of Paul Pavelka, James R. MacConnell, and all the rest. . . . Let us glance at the golden book of American volunteers. We shall find there the names of Edward Mandell Stone, a graduate of Harvard, the first American volunteer killed; of Henry W. Farnsworth, killed in Champagne; of the poet, Alan Seeger, an idealist, dead for France; of John Earle Fiske, a former American soldier, killed June 16, 1915; of Russell A. Kelly, killed the same day; of Nelson Larson, a former American sailor, killed on the anniversary day of American independence, 1916; of Frank Clair of Columbus, dead of wounds; of René Phelizot of Chicago, a daring hunter of big game, killed at Craouelle in February, 1915; of Harman Edwin Hall of Chicago, killed June 16, 1916, &c. We shall not forget their acts of devotion. . . . At the end of January, 1917, seventy citations in official orders had been merited and bestowed upon these brave men [American volunteers]."

470   Bert Hall, from a drawing in red chalk by John Elliott,
      in the National Gallery of Art, Washington

"THE PLATTSBURG IDEA"

As the contestants in Europe swayed back and forth in the titanic struggle, more and more Americans began to turn their attention to their own inadequately defended shores. Shaking off that indifference toward military matters which they had inherited from their forefathers, they began to consider the problem of a defense policy. General Leonard Wood was a conspicuous figure in a group of pioneers leading the way. To his influence and activity was due to a large extent the establishment in 1915 of a training camp for business men at Plattsburg Barracks, New York. This was not the first citizens' camp. In 1913 camps under the direction of the army were established for college students at Gettysburg, Pennsylvania, and Monterey, California. In 1914 similar camps were held elsewhere. By 1915 serious tension had developed between the United States and Germany. War loomed on the eastern horizon. The men who tramped the roads about Plattsburg in the summer of 1915 mostly realized this. They were far-sighted citizens, striving by their activities to hasten the military preparation of the nation against that day when the United States should be pitted against the powerful and experienced German army. They had the satis-

471   Maj.-Gen. Leonard Wood, 1860–1927, from a photograph by Harris & Ewing, Washington

faction of seeing in the following year their Government take important forward steps in the creation of an adequate army and navy. Many of these original Plattsburg men returned to the great camp of the following year which was held under the provisions of the National Defense Act of 1916.

LACK OF MILITARY POLICY

To that great Secretary of War, Lindley M. Garrison, belongs the distinction of bringing the work of General Emory Upton to fruition. Upton had exposed with completeness and candor the lack of military policy which had characterized the American people from the beginning of their national history. Garrison, with equal candor, in 1915, on the eve of the war with Germany, laid before the people of the United States the trifling size of the mobile army of the United States, the shortage of officers, and the lack of equipment and ammunition. At the time the Army of the United States possessed some twenty-one airplanes, six hundred and thirty-four modern guns six inches or less in caliber, two days' fire of ammunition, and a thousand machine guns, for the most part of the obsolete Gatling and Colt models. Spurred by the activities of Garrison and by a popular demand for preparedness that arose after the sinking of the *Lusitania*, Congress in the winter of 1915–16 gave serious attention to the problem of defense. In the battle between alternate plans which developed Garrison resigned. He had fought hard for the scheme which, from the service point of view, was the best. When the President ceased to support him and accepted a plan, less efficient but more in harmony with the military traditions of the American people, Garrison felt that his usefulness had ended.

472   Maj.-Gen. Emory Upton, 1839–81, from a photograph in the United States Military Academy, West Point

473   United States Troops on the Mexican border, from a photograph in the United
States Signal Corps, War Department, Washington

THE NATIONAL DE–FENSE ACT OF 1916

THE act as finally passed, after the resignation of Garrison had stirred the country, contained most of the provisions of his plan. "The regular army was to consist of sixty-five regiments of infantry, twenty-five of cavalry and twenty-one of field artillery, an equivalent of ninety-three companies of coast artillery, eight aero squadrons, seven regiments of engineers, and the corresponding staff of officers. This organization gave the country a peace force of one hundred and seventy-five thousand men as fighting units. The army of the United States was to include the regular army, the volunteer army, the officers' reserve corps, the enlisted reserve corps and the National Guard (while in the service of the United States). The mobile troops of the regular army were to be organized into divisions and brigades on a tactical basis. . . . An officers' reserve corps was provided for by giving commissions to civilians proven to be qualified by examination. An enlisted corps was to be built up by soldiers furloughed to the reserve, the enlistment of the regular soldier being three years with the colors and four years with the reserve. Vocational training of the soldier was provided for, and by federalizing about four hundred and twenty-five thousand National Guard could be had under the law. The medical corps was to consist of medical corps proper, medical reserve corps, dental corps, veterinary corps and nurse corps. . . . The President, when authorized by Congress to use the land forces, could draft the National Guard and the National Guard Reserve into the service of the United States. . . . Altogether legislation allowed the army a maximum war strength of two hundred and eighty-seven thousand, eight hundred and forty-six men." — WILLIAM A. GANOE, *History of the United States Army*, 457–58, D. Appleton and Company, New York, 1924.

THE MEXICAN BORDER

AN important factor in bringing about the new military policy was the experience on the Mexican border immediately preceding the passage of the Act of 1916. The border patrol and the Pershing Punitive Expedition brought into the open the defects of the American military system. This experience was not only of value to army men in the formulation of new plans but was a demonstration which convinced many a reluctant congressman of the need for a thoroughgoing revision of the military policy of the United States.

474   Maj.-Gen. John J. Pershing and his staff on the Mexican border, from a photograph
in the United States Signal Corps, War Department, Washington

475   Maj.-Gen. John J. Pershing reviewing the troops at Dublan, Aug. 21, 1916, from a photograph in the United
States Signal Corps, War Department, Washington

THE NAVAL PROGRAM OF 1916

476   Josephus Daniels, 1865–, from a photograph in the United States Signal Corps, War Department, Washington

In July, 1915, on the very day that President Wilson dispatched his third *Lusitania* note to the Imperial German Government (see Vol. IX, p. 298), he called upon the Secretary of the Navy, Josephus Daniels, to authorize the experts of his department to prepare a comprehensive plan for the expansion of the Navy. On October 19, 1915, a five year program was laid before the President. It involved the construction of ten dreadnaughts, six battle cruisers, ten scout cruisers, fifty destroyers, fifteen fleet submarines, eighty-five coast submarines, and various other ships. This program without important modification was adopted by Congress. The most significant variation was the reduction of the five year building period to three.

U–53 AT NEWPORT, RHODE ISLAND, IN THE FALL OF 1916

WHILE the United States was preparing to strengthen the national defenses, a significant visitor appeared in American waters. U–53 (Unterseeboot No. 53) was a very historic submarine, and the one, above all others, which the United States Navy would have done anything to "get." Her commander was, after von Weddingen, the most famous of all enemy submarine commanders. "Old Hans is out again" the Americans and British in the convoy room would say whenever Hans Rose and his "sub" revealed their dangerous presence by their well known traits. To his credit be it said that Rose showed himself one of the most humane of all submarine commanders. He would sometimes wait to see all the lifeboats filled, would give them food, and sometimes even a tow until the avenging destroyers appeared on the horizon. When, as we shall later see, he sank the United States destroyer *Jacob Jones*, he sent out a wireless S.O.S. on behalf of the survivors of her crew. But he and his U–53 were not very welcome visitors to Newport in the fall of 1916, when Americans were aroused at the practices of the German submarines. The U–53 torpedoed half-a-dozen merchantmen off Nantucket, possibly as a gentle hint of what German submarines could do along the American seaboard in case of war. She was afterward dangerously depth-charged by American destroyers. She was somewhere out of the way when the submarines surrendered to the Allied fleet after the Armistice.

477   The German Submarine U–53 at Newport, R. I., from a photograph. © Waleman, Norfolk, Va.

478 Walter Hines Page, 1855–1918, from a photograph by Harris & Ewing, Washington

DISCOVERY OF A GERMAN PLOT AGAINST THE UNITED STATES IN JANUARY, 1917

IN January, 1917, Zimmerman, of the German Foreign Office in Berlin, sent Eckhardt, the German Minister to Mexico, the following secret message by three different routes so as to insure certain delivery. But Sir William Hall, Chief of British Naval Intelligence, had learned the German secret code. He caught the wireless on its way to Sayville, decoded it for Lord Balfour, then head of the British Foreign Office, who revealed it to Ambassador Page, who secretly transmitted it to President Wilson. "We intend to begin on the first of February unrestricted submarine warfare. We shall endeavor in spite of this to keep the United States of America neutral. In the event of this not succeeding, we make Mexico a proposal of alliance on the following basis: make war together, make peace together, generous financial support and an understanding on our part that Mexico is to reconquer the lost territory in Texas, New Mexico, and Arizona. The settlement in detail is left to you. You will inform the President [that is, President Carranza of Mexico] of the above most secretly as soon as the outbreak of war with the United States of America is certain and add the suggestion that he should, of his own initiative, invite Japan to immediate adherence and at the same time mediate between Japan and ourselves. Please call the President's attention to the fact that the ruthless employment of our submarines now offers the prospect of compelling England in a few months to make peace."

SUBMARINE BLOCKADE

ON January 31, 1917, the German Government handed to the American ambassador a note which said that Germany "must abandon the limitations which it has hitherto imposed upon itself in the employment of its fighting weapons at sea," defining the forbidden zones around the Allied coasts, permitting only one United States steamer to enter only one British port, Falmouth, each week, provided that this carefully obeyed all German regulations, and announcing that all other sea traffic was to be stopped "by all weapons" from the very next day. Speed was essential to Germany; for, as the German Chancellor explained, "the blockade must succeed within a limited number of weeks, within which America cannot effectively participate in the operations." When American "extras" carried the news of this portentous decision, it became clear to all thinking citizens that war was at hand. From that day until November 11, 1918, the shadow of the World War darkened the fields and cities of the United States.

479 German Submarine Zone of Feb. 1, 1917, redrawn from Shipley Thomas, *History of the A. E. F.*, George H. Doran Company, New York, 1920

480   The Sinking of the *Illinois*, from a photograph, courtesy of the Navy Department, Washington

481   The *Illinois* disappears from view, from a photograph, courtesy of the Navy Department, Washington

AMERICAN OIL–TANKER *ILLINOIS* SUNK MARCH 18, 1917

PRESIDENT WILSON announced that the Government of the United States would await an overt act before taking measures against the Germans. On March 2, a German submarine sank without warning the American steamer *Algonquin*. On March 18, 1917, a submarine suddenly appeared and, without warning, began shelling the *Illinois*, then in the English Channel under the Stars and Stripes. The two photographs now in the United States Navy Department at Washington were taken on board the submarine, presumably as evidence of the sinking. The first, with the submarine deck in the left lower corner, shows the stricken *Illinois* settling down by the stern. The second shows her going straight to her death. Two other American boats were sunk by the Germans on the same day.

482   From a cartoon *Herod's Nightmare*, by Louis Raemaekers in *Raemaekers War Cartoons*, The Century Co., New York, 1917

THE SIGNIFICANCE OF THE SUBMARINE WARFARE

THE ruthless submarine campaign which began in February, 1917, was the final act which convinced the great majority of the American people that the Imperial German Government was waging war in an unnecessarily inhuman and barbarous manner. Americans in the spring of 1917 believed that Germany was a nation gone mad, that its government, which had violated the neutrality of Belgium, would stop at nothing to achieve that world domination which it sought, and that the hands of its fighting men were red with the blood of innocent noncombatants slain in Belgium, in northern France, and on the sea. The American people were aroused as seldom before in their history when the German methods were brought home to them by the sinking of American ships. The demand for war was unmistakable. Americans were about to embark upon a crusade to rid the world of what they were convinced was an international criminal, whose success in Europe would be a deadly menace to the security and well being of the United States. The fighting blood of the people was roused.

483   Woodrow Wilson, from a gravure after a charcoal
drawing. © Harris & Ewing, Washington

PRESIDENT WILSON'S WAR MESSAGE

ON the evening of April 2, 1917, the two houses of Congress of the United States, in extra session, sat in the hall of the House of Representatives. The tension was so great as to be painful. At eight-thirty the President entered, mounted the desk, and addressed them. "I have called the Congress into extraordinary session because there are serious, very serious, choices of policy to be made, and made immediately, which it was neither right nor constitutionally permissible that I assume the responsibility of making." Amid a dead silence the speaker went on to recount the declaration of the German submarine blockade, the sinking of American ships, accompanied by the ruthless destruction of life. "It is a war against all nations. American ships have been sunk, American lives taken, in ways which it has stirred us very deeply to learn of, but the ships and people of other neutral and friendly nations have been sunk and overwhelmed in the waters in the same way. . . . The challenge is to all mankind. . . . There is one choice we cannot make, we are incapable of making; we will not choose the path of submission and suffer the most sacred rights of our nation and our people to be ignored and violated. The wrongs against which we now array ourselves are no common wrongs; they cut to the very roots of human life. With a profound sense of the solemn and even tragical character of the step I am taking and of the grave responsibilities which it involves, but in unhesitating obedience to what I deem my constitutional duty, I advise that the Congress declare the recent course of the Imperial German Government to be in fact nothing less than war against the Government and people of the United States; that it formally accept the status of belligerent which has thus been thrust upon it; and that it take immediate steps not only to put the country in a more thorough state of defense, but also to exert all its power and employ all its resources to bring the Government of the German Empire to terms and end the war. . . . We are, let me say it again, the sincere friends of the German people, and shall desire nothing so much as the early reëstablishment of intimate relations of mutual advantage between us, however hard it may be for them for the time being to believe that this is spoken from our hearts. We have borne with their present Government through all these bitter months because of that friendship, exercising a patience and forbearance which would otherwise have been impossible. . . . But the right is more precious than peace, and we shall fight for the things which we have always carried nearest our hearts — for democracy, for the right of those who submit to authority to have a voice in their own Governments, for the rights and liberties of small nations, for a universal dominion of right by such a concert of free peoples as shall bring peace and safety to all nations and make the world itself at last free."

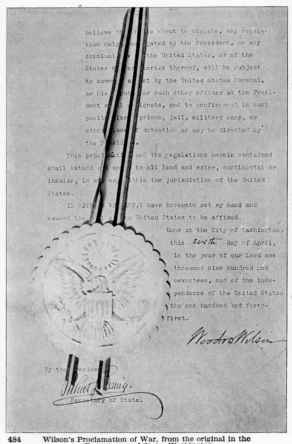

484   Wilson's Proclamation of War, from the original in the
Department of State, Washington

REACTION OF ALLIES

THE entrance of America into the war was peculiarly dramatic because in that same spring of 1917 revolution was taking Russia out of the war. England and France looked forward to the transfer of large bodies of German troops from the Eastern to the Western Front. At the same time Germany planned to paralyze the British effort by a submarine blockade which would isolate that island kingdom from the world. Such was the background against which the Allies saw America take up the sword. On April 20 England formally celebrated "American Day." "It was not for nothing," wrote Hall Caine, "that the flags of Great Britain and America hung side by side under the chancel arch [of St. Paul's Cathedral] on Friday morning. At one moment the sun shot through the windows of the dome and lit them up with heavenly radiance. Was it only the exaltation of the moment that made us think invisible powers were giving us a sign that in the union of the nations which those emblems stood for lay the surest hope of the day when men will beat their swords into plowshares and know war no more? The United States of Great Britain and America! God grant the union celebrated in our old sanctuary may never be dissolved until that great day has dawned." From France came words of equal feeling. "The cry of children and of women," said Paul Deschanel, President of the French Chamber of Deputies, "from the depths of the abyss into which they have been hurled by an abominable crime, has echoed to the ends of the earth. The ashes of Washington and Lincoln have stirred; their mighty souls inspire America."

PRESIDENT WILSON

ON March 25, twelve days before the actual declaration of war, April 6, the virtual mobilization of the American army had begun. On that day President Wilson issued orders calling out the National Guard in nine eastern states and the District of Columbia for the purpose of forestalling any outbreak by enemy agents upon the expected declaration of a state of war. On the next day units from eighteen western states were called to the colors. By April 12 sixty thousand National Guardsmen were under arms doing police service in cities, guarding important railroad bridges,

FRANCE AROUSED BY OUR DECISION
Members of Both Chambers Cheer for America — Many Cities Adopt Resolutions.
POINCARE CABLES WILSON
Deputies Suggest Offering Us the Port of Brest as a Naval Base.

PARIS, April 5.—This was America's day in France. Extraordinary scenes of enthusiasm over the United States's entry into the war were witnessed in both houses of Parliament, while municipal councils met in cities throughout the Republic and adopted resolutions acclaiming the United States.

In Paris the American flag was seen everywhere. The appearance of the Stars and Stripes in different parts of the city multiplied rapidly as the day advanced, and soon the available supply was exhausted. Such was the demand for newspapers that the evening editions giving the vote of the United States Senate on the war resolution were quickly exhausted. The crowded subway cars were more animated than at any time since the war began, while knots of soldiers and civilians in front of all cafes and at all street corners discussed the great event with manifest satisfaction

485 From the *New York Times*, Apr. 5, 1917

and serving in every capacity that would make them useful in preventing riots or destruction of property. No important disorder, however, accompanied the transition to war. The Council of National Defense and its advisory Commission, both of which had been created by the National Defense Act of 1916, went promptly and seriously to work. The council consisted of the Secretaries of War, Navy, Interior, Agriculture, Commerce, Labor, and the Advisory Commission of seven men drawn from civil life, and put in charge, one of munitions, another of transportation, another of food, clothing, and supplies in general, another of labor, another of raw materials, minerals and metals, another of engineering, another of medicine, surgery, and sanitation. Behind them was the President. He had been slow to take the lead in securing for the nation an adequate army and navy; but, once the decision had been made, he bent every energy toward the bringing of the conflict to a successful termination at the earliest possible moment. Yet, even the President scarcely realized the desperate plight of the Allies or the immensity of the task which lay ahead.

486 Woodrow Wilson, 1856–1924, from the painting by Edmund C. Tarbell (1862–), in the possession of the Municipal Art Commission, New York

487   Balfour's Mission (Balfour seated in front row, seventh from left),
          from a photograph by Harris & Ewing, Washington

ORGANIZING COÖPERATION WITH THE ALLIES

FOURTEEN days after the American declaration of war a British mission of diplomats and army and navy officers headed by Arthur J. Balfour arrived in the United States. Four days later, April 24, a similar French mission headed by M. Viviani and containing Marshal Joffre proceeded from Hampton Roads to Washington on the President's yacht, the *Mayflower*. Later on Italian and other missions arrived. The coming of the British and French missions was an event of the greatest importance. Up to that time American statesmen, adjusting themselves to the fact of war, had been thinking of American participation in the conflict in terms of lending money and building ships. In the first days after the declaration the idea of an American army in France was not taken seriously into consideration. Then Balfour, Joffre, and Viviani with complete candor explained to the American leaders the desperate straits of the Allies. Americans had hoped that the great drive on the Western Front led by General Nivelle would go far toward ending the war. The commissions made clear that the drive had failed. They pointed out that with Russia leaving the battle front there could be no hope of a decision before 1918. They pointed out that the morale of the French and British soldiers had suffered serious impairment. With the presentation of the depressing situation they rested their case.

THE PLAN OF THE AMERICAN GOVERNMENT

IN coöperation with the Allied missions the Americans worked out the general outlines of the plan which their nation should follow in carrying on the war. They declined to assume the obligations of an alliance with any of the warring powers but they pledged complete coöperation and guaranteed that they would continue until the war had been brought to a successful conclusion. They would participate in the conflict first, and immediately, with money; second with food; third with assistance in the war upon the submarine; fourth by organizing and sending to France a large force to take part in the campaign of 1918; and fifth by sending, at once, a small expeditionary force overseas to give the soldiers and populations of the Allied countries renewed heart. On April 24, Congress passed the War Finance Act which authorized the Secretary of the Treasury to raise seven billions of dollars to meet the cost of the conflict and which authorized the loan of three billions of the amount to the Allied Governments. On the following day a treasury warrant for two hundred million dollars was handed to the British ambassador. The total amount ultimately loaned, according to the figures of August 15, 1920, which included some deductions on account of payments, was, in round numbers, nine billion-seven hundred and eleven million dollars. The immediacy and the magnitude of this financial assistance was of vital importance in winning the war because, in the spring of 1917, France and England were rapidly approaching the limit of their financial strength. Most of this money which the United States loaned the Allies was expended in America in the purchase of munitions and supplies. As soon as the financial transactions were out of the way the Washington Government turned its attention to the other parts of its war program.

Sixty-fifth Congress of the United States of America;

At the First Session,

Begun and held at the City of Washington on Monday, the second day of April, one thousand nine hundred and seventeen.

AN ACT

To authorize an issue of bonds to meet expenditures for the national security and defense, and, for the purpose of assisting in the prosecution of the war, to extend credit to foreign governments, and for other purposes.

Be it enacted by the Senate and House of Representatives of the United States of America in Congress assembled, That the Secretary of the Treasury, with the approval of the President, is hereby authorized to borrow, from time to time, on the credit of the United States for the purposes of this Act, and to meet expenditures authorized for the national security and defense and other public purposes authorized by law not exceeding in the aggregate $5,000,000,000, exclusive of the sums authorized by section four of this Act, and to issue therefor bonds of the United States.

The bonds herein authorized shall be in such form and subject to such terms and conditions of issue, conversion, redemption, maturities, payment, and rate and time of payment of interest, not exceeding three and one-half per centum per annum, as the Secretary of the Treasury may prescribe. The principal and interest thereof shall be payable in United States gold coin of the present standard of value and shall be exempt, both as to principal and interest, from all taxation, except estate or inheritance taxes, imposed by authority of the United States, or its possessions, or by any State or local taxing authority; but such bonds shall not bear the circulation privilege.

The bonds herein authorized shall first be offered at not less than par as a popular loan, under such regulations prescribed by the Secretary of the Treasury as will give all citizens of the United States an equal opportunity to participate therein; and any portion of the bonds so offered and not subscribed for may be

488   War Finance Act, from the original in the Department of State, Washington

FOOD

BEFORE the arrival of the missions from abroad the Council for National Defense had created, on April 11, a Committee on Food Supply and Prices with Herbert Hoover as chairman. On May 20 President Wilson appointed Hoover Food Commissioner. Urged by a strong appeal from the Allied missions the Food Commissioner undertook two missions: first, to stimulate food production by every possible means, and, second, to prevent the hoarding of food and to secure its proper and effective distribution. He issued a call to the country. "The deep obligation is upon us to feed the armies and the peoples associated with us in this struggle. The diversion of forty million of their men to war or war work; the additional millions of women drafted to the places of their husbands and brothers; the toll of the submarine, have all conspired to so reduce production that their harvests this Autumn will fall five hundred million bushels of grain below their normal production. Therefore, whereas we exported before the war but eighty million bushels of wheat per annum, this year, by one means or another, we must find for them two hundred and twenty-five million bushels, and this in the face of a short crop. . . . There is no royal road to food conservation. It can be accomplished only through sincere and daily coöperation in the twenty million kitchens and the twenty million dinner tables in the United States." The response of the nation to this appeal and the self denial which was practiced until the very end of the war

KEEP *it* COMING

"We must not only feed our Soldiers at the front but the millions of women & children behind our lines"
Gen. John J. Pershing

WASTE NOTHING

UNITED STATES FOOD ADMINISTRATION

489 From a Food Control poster *Keep it Coming*, by George Illian (1894–)

is one of the finest and most amazing episodes in the annals of the American people. The British later frankly acknowledged that, although a shortage of ships and railway congestion in the United States caused the shipment of food to fall much below the schedule, the supplies which Hoover did send saved the desperate situation in the winter of 1917–18. In the autumn of 1918 Hoover called attention to the great accomplishment of American food production and conservation in aiding to maintain the health and strength of the Allied peoples while at the same time supporting the American troops. "Our contributions to this end could not have been accomplished without effort and sacrifice, and it is a matter of further satisfaction, that it has been accomplished voluntarily and individually. It is difficult to distinguish between various sections of our people — the homes, public eating places, food trades, urban or agricultural populations — in assessing credit for these results, but no one will deny the dominant part of the American woman."

490 Herbert Hoover, 1874–, from a painting by Edmund C. Tarbell (1862–), in the National Museum of Art, Washington

491 General Pershing welcomed by General Foch in Paris, from a photograph in the United States Signal Corps, War Department, Washington

THE SENDING OF PERSHING

On June 9, 1917, General Pershing together with a staff of fifty-three officers, aided by one hundred and forty-six enlisted men, arrived in London where he went immediately into consultation with the British military authorities. Four days later he reached Paris. He had been chosen primarily because of the ability he had demonstrated in his leadership of the Punitive Expedition into Mexico in 1916 and because of the manner in which he obeyed both the letter and the spirit of his instructions under most trying circumstances. The British and the French, observing his military bearing, his mastery of himself, and his complete confidence, felt instinctively that the leader of the American hosts that were to follow was fitted to bear the tremendous responsibility that had been placed upon him. The Allied peoples greeted the tiny American contingent with tremendous enthusiasm. There was a wistful as well as generous quality in the ceremony at the tomb of the great Napoleon. Here, for a moment, the commander in chief of the American forces bore the sword of the military genius of the early nineteenth century, an honor hitherto accorded to no man. Behind this act of the French was the hope that the Americans would help to bring the victories of Napoleon again to French soil.

AT THE TOMB OF LAFAYETTE

On June 26, thirteen days behind Pershing, the First Division arrived at Paris. On July 4 a battalion of the 16th Infantry paraded in Paris. With the commander in chief they went to the tomb of that French nobleman who played so conspicuous a part in the American Revolution. Here, it was reported, Pershing pronounced those words which electrified the French nation: "Lafayette, we are here!"

492 General Pershing in Paris with General Joffre, President Poincaré and M. Briand, July 4, 1917, from a photograph in the United States Signal Corps, War Department, Washington

MOBILIZATION AT SEA

Long before the scene at Lafayette's tomb the American navy was in the fray. The joint resolution of the Senate and House of Representatives declaring a state of war became effective at eighteen minutes after one on the afternoon of April 6. At five minutes past four Secretary Daniels signed an order for the mobilization of the navy. A few minutes later from the office of Admiral William S. Benson, Chief of Naval Operations, a hundred code messages flashed by wire and wireless. There were approximately three hundred and sixty-one vessels completed and fit for service, including twelve first-line battleships, twenty-five second-line battleships, nine armored cruisers, twenty-four other cruisers, together with a large number of smaller auxiliary craft. The order called out those retired officers who had been registered in the Department as fit for duty. It also included the more than eight thousand five hundred members of the naval militia, a considerable number of Naval Reserves, and the men in the Coast Guard Service. Before darkness fell on that sixth of April the machinery was in motion to put the navy on a war footing.

493 Admiral William Shepherd Benson, 1855–, from a photograph in the United States Signal Corps, War Department, Washington

494 A United States Navy recruiting poster, drawn by James Montgomery Flagg

495 A United States Navy recruiting poster, drawn by Charles Dana Gibson

496 A United States Navy recruiting poster, drawn by Milton Bancroft

NAVAL RECRUITING

WHEN the mobilization order left the office of the Secretary of the Navy, thirty-five thousand men were needed to bring the naval establishment to its full authorized strength of eighty-seven thousand. For the past few weeks recruiting had been carried on with exceptional energy but the net increase had been some twenty-five men per day. Almost immediately after the declaration of war the recruiting campaign began. Bill boards, store windows, and countless vehicles on the streets carried the posters which told the nation of the Navy's need for men. The response was immediate. By April 17 recruits were coming in at the rate of nearly a thousand per day. Young men with and without sea experience crowded the recruiting offices to sign up before it was too late. The posters and the crowds of men who were joining the Navy were the first concrete evidences that the war was on. In many a family circle laughter gave way to serious discussion, as a brother reached his decision to go off to war.

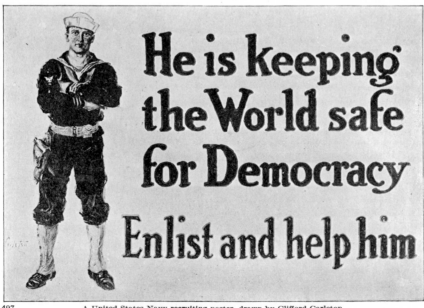

497 A United States Navy recruiting poster, drawn by Clifford Carleton

498   A United States Marine Corps recruiting poster, drawn by Joseph C. Leyendecker, from a photograph in the United States Signal Corps, War Department, Washington

THE NAVY NEEDS YOU!

THE Navy did need well-educated men; for naval service now-a-days is full of complex and very sudden problems for which quick and well trained heads are quite as essential as good stout hearts. The number of specialists aboard a big super-dreadnaught battleship, and the variety of specialties concerned, are a revelation to the landsman whose only acquaintance with the navy is confined to a general view of decks and hulls. Not a quarter of all the men belong to the purely seaman class,

499   A United States Marine Corps recruiting poster, drawn by Sidney H. Riesenberg, from a photograph in the United States Signal Corps, War Deparment, Washington

that is, to the class which in the old days comprised far more than three-quarters of the crew and did all-round duty from stem to stern and keel to truck. What with torpedo and gunnery ratings, mechanics, airmen, wireless operators, electricians, shipwrights, the force in the engine rooms, and the considerable number engaged in auxiliary services, such as the clerical and medical staffs, not to mention the Marines, the whole crew forms a self-contained world of its own.

THE SHIPPING BOARD

SHIPS of commerce as well as ships of war were needed to combat the menace of the submarine. In 1916 the Shipping Board had been created primarily for the development of the South American trade. With the outbreak of hostilities it became virtually a war board and was clothed with extraordinary powers. One of the first acts of the United States was to take over the German shipping which had for so many months been interned in American ports. This, together with that taken later from Austria, added some seven hundred and twenty thousand gross tons to the American merchant marine. Ten days after the declaration of war the Shipping Board created the United States Shipping Board Emergency Fleet Corporation, capitalized at first at fifty million dollars. The mission of this organization was to buy, build, equip, lease, charter, maintain, and operate merchant vessels. Major-General Goethals, the builder of the Panama Canal, was made manager but soon resigned because of a dispute over the relative merits of steel and wooden ships. By October 1, 1918, the Emergency Fleet Corporation had constructed three hundred and eighty-four steel

ships and two hundred and eighty-nine wooden ships aggregating together a little more than two million tons. In addition by requisitioning all ships over twenty-five hundred tons under construction in American yards the Corporation secured an additional three million tons. So was built the bridge across the Atlantic which made possible that transfer of American food, munitions, and men without which the war could not have been won.

500   Shipbuilding at Redwood City, Cal., from a photograph in the United States Signal Corps, War Department, Washington

501   United States Warships throwing out smoke screen to protect troop ships, from a photograph in the United States Signal Corps, War Department, Washington

THE SUBMARINE CAMPAIGN OF 1917

In the year 1917 the highest German hopes were fixed upon the water, not the land. By land the Germans, Turks, Bulgarians, and Austrians were holding their own or more. The famous Berlin-Byzantium-Bagdad line seemed safe. The Southern Slavs in Serbia and Montenegro had been completely overrun. Gigantic Russia was entering the penumbra of total eclipse. And Italy was being prepared for her collapse at Caporetto. Thus Germany was free for a death-grapple with the Allied armies on the Western Front, where she planned massing all the best troops who could now be spared elsewhere. This massing, however, would take the whole year, during which the Allies could strengthen their lines and perhaps be helped by Americans. So, for three most cogent reasons, Germany decided to strike first by sea; and strike to kill. The submarine campaign was designed to sink enough tonnage to ruin both the morale and the oversea resources of the Italians, the French, and the British. Secondly, this appalling loss of their oversea supplies would weaken the Allied armies so much that the greatly reinforced Germans would certainly win on the Western Front. Thirdly, and clinchingly, if enough vessels could only be sunk, the American armies would never reach Europe at all.

THE TOLL OF THE SUBMARINE

During that momentous April nearly nine hundred thousand tons of Allied and neutral shipping were sunk, Germany exulted; for, while the Allied and neutral shipyards of 1917 were building less than three million tons, the April sinking had reached a yearly rate of more than ten million tons. It was already clear that a net loss of twenty thousand tons a day could not go on much longer without weakening the Allied peoples, making their armies a conquerable force, and cutting them off from American help. Moreover, Germany hoped and believed that she could increase her rate of sinking as the days grew longer.

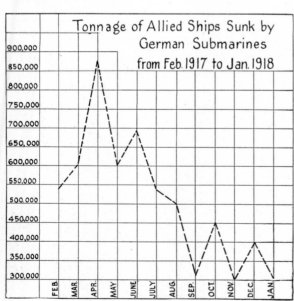

Tonnage of Allied Ships Sunk by German Submarines from Feb. 1917 to Jan. 1918

502   Drawn expressly for *The Pageant of America*

Tonnage at all costs, and especially tonnage bound for England or France was the desperate need of the hour. The German submarine commanders avoided the Allied fleets, not from cowardice but simply because, to gain their ends, they had to sink the greatest amount of tonnage in the shortest possible time; and unarmed merchant vessels were the easiest to sink. If this entailed loss of life, against all the accepted rules of war — well, how could submarines save so many lives; and how could Germany blockade her enemies except with submarines? For choice, the Germans would rather not have murdered. But, they argued, how could they win the war except by "ruthless" sinking? They even sank hospital ships, not to outrage humanity, but partly because hospital ships were tonnage, and mostly to force the Allied navies to escort these vessels with so many feared destroyers as to leave other vessels unprotected and therefore easier to sink.

503   German U-boat 111, from a photograph in the possession
of the publishers

THE GERMAN U–BOATS

At the time of the American declaration of war Germany was exultant. She was building at the rate of one hundred and fifty-six U-Boats a year. She had suffered enemy-proved losses of only fifty-four U-Boats since the war began. And she was now sinking Allied and neutral tonnage at nearly a million tons a month. Her Kaiser said: "I expect this weapon to break our enemy's war will." Karl Helfferich, one of his cabinet ministers, said: "We have considered, we have dared. Certain of the results, we shall not allow it to be taken from us by anybody or anything." The few captured U-Boat officers said very much the same when questioned in London. "Yes, you have got *us*. But that makes no difference. We can build a dozen U-Boats for every one you take or sink. Anyway the war will be over in a few months from now." U-Boats were attacking tonnage everywhere, and they were helped by mine-layers, of which there were seventy. Fear chilled the hearts of those officials in the Allied Governments who knew the facts at first hand. Fear also gripped the Allied peoples, particularly of England and France, as they read the communiques which the Governments published. Events moved swiftly to a crisis. Breathlessly men awaited the outcome. Would England be able to conquer the submarine? The greatest test of English sea power in modern times had come.

GERMAN TORPEDOES

Invisible, stealthy, and sly, the German submarines had it very much their own way in April, 1917, when their attack on unprotected tonnage had risen to its height. The sorely harassed British could not spare nearly enough destroyers, the submarines' worst enemies, to patrol the immense area open to attack. First, they had to keep over a hundred destroyers always ready with the Grand Fleet, for the side without enough de-

stroyers in a great pitched battle was bound to suffer the loss of many battleships and cruisers; and if the Grand Fleet were defeated, the Allies were bound to lose the war, because the German surface craft would reinforce the submarines and sweep Allied and neutral tonnage from the sea. Besides, the British had to make the English Channel absolutely safe in order to keep the Western Front supplied. And they did make the channel crossings safe — so safe that twenty million persons were ferried over without the loss of a single man, though the Germans were particularly anxious to break into the charmed circle of that destroyer screen. Then Gibraltar and the Mediterranean claimed many other British destroyers. There were not enough destroyers to go round; and the sea lanes into the British Isles were therefore very open to the attack.

504   Men on a United States transport watching an encounter with a submarine, from a photograph, courtesy of the Navy Department, Washington

505 United States Destroyer *Parker* at sea, from a photograph, courtesy of the Navy Department, Washington

AN AMERICAN DESTROYER

SUBMARINES had their weak points. They were "tender," easily sunk by well-placed shell fire, certain to be fatally cut by ramming, and apt to get out of gear from various causes. They were slow; making only eight knots submerged (with the electric motors, which had to be used on account of air exhaustion) and under fifteen on the surface. Their deadly torpedoes were few and very expensive, which made the use of gunfire or bombs preferable. But gunfire attracted attention, while bombs required a boarding party, which took too much time. The torpedo is really an automotive submarine, exploding when its war-head hits. But hitting a fast moving target is no easy matter. Your own and your target's course, speed, and range have all to be exactly worked out before you release the torpedo; and then, if you miscalculate, or your target slows down, speeds up, or changes direction, you will miss. Again, your torpedo can only be fired from bow or stern, not from the side; for the submarine is very narrow. This means careful maneuvering. Furthermore, your exact position is revealed at the moment of release, for the torpedo's propeller and its compressed air propulsion cause a surface wake nearly five feet wide and very distinct. When a destroyer got close enough the submarine had little chance. First, the destroyer drew only ten feet, so that the torpedo, set fifteen feet deep to escape wave-deflecting, passed underneath. Next, the destroyer had torpedoes of far greater range and easily fired from the side. Then, the destroyer's guns outranged the submarine's. Finally, the destroyer was incomparably handier and more than twice as fast. Nevertheless, the vast area concerned, the immense amount of comparatively helpless tonnage, the vital needs of the Allies, the submarines' invisibility, and the courage, skill, and "ruthlessness" with which they were handled, all combined to make the necessity for American destroyers very urgent indeed.

THE DEPTH–CHARGE

THE general public, patriotic, excited, and quite ignorant of what really could be done at sea, clamored for some invention which would "kill" the submarine. The British experts examined no less than forty thousand inventions, but the deadly depth-charge alone answered the imperative requirements. This terrific weapon looked like the domestic ash can. But it contained the volcanic explosive known as TNT; and its firing apparatus was so set as to go off by the simple pressure of the water at any required depth.

506   Automatic release for depth mines on the destroyer *McCall*, from a photograph, courtesy of the Navy Department, Washington

507 Admiral William S. Sims, from the painting by Irving
     R. Wiles (1862–), in the National Museum of Art, Wash-
     ington

ADMIRAL WILLIAM S. SIMS, 1858–, UNITED STATES NAVAL COMMANDER IN CHIEF

ADMIRAL SIMS was a marked man long before the World War. He had been United States Naval Attaché in France and Russia, Naval Aide of the President of the United States, the great gunnery expert of the United States Navy, admiral commanding the Destroyer Flotillas of the Atlantic Fleet, President of the United States Navy War College, and the foresighted prophet who, in 1910, when commanding the United States battleship *Minnesota* in European waters, reported to his admiral that the World War would begin within four years.

Toward the end of March, 1917, the Navy Department ordered Sims and his aide, Commander Babcock, to board the American steamer *New York* secretly in civilian clothes, and under the names of Richardson and Davidson; for, though the most urgent reasons of state required an American admiral in London immediately, the United States was still neutral in spite of German provocation. On approaching Liverpool the *New York* was holed by a German mine, and the passengers had to be taken off by another steamer. On reaching London the truths of that appalling April were calmly laid before Sims by his old British friend, Admiral Jellicoe, then First Sea Lord of the Admiralty and virtually the commander in chief of the whole British Navy. Sims, ready as ever, sent a secret message to the United States Navy Department on the 14th. It contained such statements as these: — "The recent operations and rapidity of construction constitute the real crisis of the war. . . . Supplies and communications of forces on all fronts are threatened and control of the sea actually imperilled. . . . Hospital ships will continue to be sunk, this in order to draw destroyers away. . . . To defeat submarine campaign immediate active co-operation absolutely necessary. . . . Maximum number of destroyers to be sent. . . ." On the 27th Sims conferred with Ambassador Page, who immediately sent a still more urgent secret message to President Wilson and Secretary Daniels. "There is reason for the greatest alarm about the issue of the war . . . a million tons every month till the shorter days . . . by that time the sea will be about clear of shipping. . . . Whatever help the United States may render in the future, our help is now more seriously needed in this submarine area. . . . I cannot refrain from most strongly recommending the immediate sending over of every destroyer and all other craft that can be of anti-submarine use. . . . There is no time to be lost."

COMMANDER JOHN V. BABCOCK, U.S.N.

"FROM April to August, 1917, the American navy had a very small staff organization in Europe. During these extremely critical four months the only American naval representatives in London, beside the regular Naval Attaché and his aides were my personal aide, Commander J. V. Babcock, and myself; and our only office in those early days was a small room in the American Embassy. For a considerable part of the time we had no stenographers and no clerical assistance of our own. . . . Commander Babock had a small typewriter, which he was able to work with two fingers, and on this he laboriously pounded out the reports which informed the Navy Department of the seriousness of the Submarine situation." — SIMS, 240–41.

508   Commander John V. Babcock, from a photograph,
       courtesy of the Navy Department, Washington

ADMIRAL JELLICOE, 1859–, HEAD OF THE BRITISH NAVY IN 1917

ADMIRAL JELLICOE and Admiral Sims had service records not unlike each other. Both were experts in naval gunnery, both were tireless in their efforts to keep themselves and their commands ready for all emergencies, both saw the World War coming, and both these old friends agreed completely on the policy which had to be pursued. Jellicoe had long been a marked man in the British navy; and during this war had been commander in chief of the Grand Fleet, until, a few months before Sims arrived, he had been raised to the position of First Sea Lord of the Admiralty: that is, chief admiral to the First Lord, who is the cabinet minister concerned.

509 Admiral John Rushworth Jellicoe, from a photograph by International Newsreel, New York

UNITED STATES NAVY DEPARTMENT, WASHINGTON, D. C.

FROM this headquarters building of the whole United States Navy went forth the following Secret Order, on the very same day that Sims' own first report was sent from London. It was literally an epoch-making order.

510 State, War and Navy Building, Washington, from a photograph by Underwood & Underwood, New York

Having gone "fifty miles due East of Cape Cod" Commander Taussig opened these carefully sealed orders and read (in part) as follows: — 1. The British Admiralty have requested coöperation of American destroyers near the coasts of Great Britain and France. 2. Your mission is to assist naval operations of Entente Powers in every way possible. 3. Proceed to Queenstown, Ireland. Report to Senior British naval officer present, and thereafter coöperate fully with the British navy. 4. Base facilities will be provided by British Admiralty. 5. Communicate orders and operations to Admiral Sims at London and be guided by such instructions as he may give you. Make no reports of arrival to Navy Department direct. — JOSEPHUS DANIELS.

This statesmanlike document sounded the keynote which was predominant all through the war. "Two captains sink the ship"; and two independent fleets might well lose the war. It was necessary that the American and British navies should work together as one single force.

THE FIRST AMERICAN DESTROYERS

ON April 24, 1917, the six destroyers of the Eighth Destroyer Division, Atlantic Fleet, steamed out of Boston, led by the *Wadsworth*. Ten tempestuous days ended in brilliant sunshine. The British minesweepers had cleared the sea lane which the Germans had just sown thick with mines, in the track of the Americans. And the two friendly navies met as brothers in arms.

511 The first United States destroyers to arrive at Queenstown, from the painting by B. Poole, courtesy of the Navy Department, Washington

512   Commander Joseph K. Taussig, from a photograph
by Harris & Ewing, Washington

COMMANDER JOSEPH K. TAUSSIG

WHEN Midshipman Taussig was wounded during the Boxer Expedition of 1900 he became fast friends with Captain Jellicoe, the British Chief-of-Staff, who lay, very badly wounded, in the next cot. Taussig never thought for a moment that the then Chief-of-Staff, who was now at the head of the greatest of naval forces in the greatest of naval wars, would ever remember the very junior young American in that little cot in China more than sixteen years before. But Jellicoe did remember; and sent by hand the following note of personal greeting to Taussig and his whole command.

"My dear Taussig:

I still retain very pleasant and vivid recollections of our association in China, and I am indeed delighted that you should have been selected for the command of the first force which is coming to fight for freedom, humanity, and civilization. . . . There is no navy in the world which can possibly give us more valuable assistance. . . . I must offer you and all your officers and men the warmest welcome possible in the name of the British nation and the British Admiralty, and add every possible good wish from myself. . . ." The voyage across the Atlantic had been utilized to put the ships in readiness for the work which lay ahead. They were met by an excited and enthusiastic British crowd at the water front. The coming of the American ships was the first tangible expression of the military power that America was to bring to bear against the common enemy. Their advent gave new life to the hard-pressed British.

ADMIRAL SIR LEWIS BAYLY

ADMIRAL BAYLY is of especial interest to Americans as he was for eighteen strenuous months the commander in chief of the united American and British naval forces which fought the German submarines along that most critical area which covered the approaches to the English Channel. He belonged to the finest type of British seadog and had a splendid record of forty years' service. Keen, expert, and exacting the very last profitable ounce from everybody under his command, he inspired more awe than affection from his juniors at first sight; yet he was full of sympathy and insight. His short, but cordial, note of welcome, asking the six American commanders to dinner, ended with the characteristic postscript "Dine in undress, no speeches." His first question, after shaking hands, was "When will you be ready to go to sea?" Taussig immediately answered "Now, Sir, just as soon as we finish refuelling." Bayly then gave them four days from the hour of arrival. His advice was much to the point. "Beware of ramming periscopes, which are often lures for floating bombs, and therefore should be shelled." Then he gave three imperative orders; first, always destroy the sub-

513   Admiral Sir Lewis Bayly with Secretary Daniels, from a
photograph by International Newsreel, New York

marine, if possible; secondly, protect Allied and neutral shipping; last of all, save lives. This was a grim philosophy made necessary by the urgency of destroying the death-dealing submarine.

CAPTAIN E. R. G. R. EVANS, BRITISH LIAISON OFFICER WITH AMERICANS

THE appointment of Captain Evans as the connecting link with the British navy was intended as the best compliment that could be paid to the Americans in that particular way; for Evans had had a very distinguished career, both as an Antarctic explorer and in the Great World War. Just before Taussig's arrival Evans had fought and beaten six German destroyers with his own British three. The name of Evans' flagship, the *Broke*, was reminiscent of one of the greatest frigate duels of the War of 1812 in which the *Shannon*, commanded by Broke, defeated the *Chesapeake*, commanded by Lawrence. The *Broke* in a peculiar sense emphasized the fact that former enemies were now comrades in arms.

514   Captain E. R. G. R. Evans, 1883–, from a photograph in his book, *Keeping the Seas*, Low, Marston & Co., London, 1919

CAPTAIN J. R. P. PRINGLE, U.S.N.

CAPTAIN PRINGLE was Chief-of-Staff at Queenstown, where he was specially recommended by Admiral Bayly for his "tact, energy, and ability," and where, after Admiral Sims' short stay there was over, he was the American senior naval officer. American destroyers kept arriving from May till July, when there were thirty-four, a number that remained fairly constant till November.

515   Captain Joel R. P. Pringle (right),·and Admiral Wemyss of the British Navy, from a photograph, courtesy of the Navy Department, Washington

COMMANDER DAVID C. HANRAHAN, U.S.N.

COMMANDER HANRAHAN was the senior American destroyer commander at Queenstown all through the summer of 1917. Later on he commanded the American mystery ship *Santee*. Still later he commanded the daring group of American aviators who so vigorously bombed the German submarine bases on or near the Belgian coast, where his colleague was Major A. A. Cunningham of the United States Marines.

516   Commander David C. Hanrahan, from a photograph, courtesy of the Navy Department, Washington

517   Submarine at periscope depth in Bantry Bay, from a photograph, courtesy of the Navy Department, Washington

COMMANDER ROGER WILLIAMS, U.S.N.

ONE day Admiral Bayly ordered Commander Williams to cross the Irish Sea and bring back a certain ship in safety. Bayly knew that the steering gear of Williams' destroyer, *Duncan*, was badly damaged. But neither man said a word. Williams calmly, and with consummate skill, backed out of Queenstown harbor, five miles long, backed on until there was sea room for a "damaged" turn, then sped away and back again, bringing the wanted ship to port in time. From that moment Williams was one of Bayly's most highly cherished comrades.

ADMIRAL SIMS AS COMMANDER IN CHIEF AT QUEENSTOWN IN JUNE, 1917

THIS was the first time in history that any British naval forces had ever been commanded by a foreigner. Admiral Bayly "hauled down" while he went away for a short leave of absence. Admiral Sims, on the cordial invitation of the British Admiralty, thereupon "hauled up." This significant change of flags showed friend and foe alike how perfectly united were the two great English-speaking peoples and their respective navies. The original idea of this exchange of flags is said to have emanated from King George, who was a first-rate naval officer before his duties as Prince of Wales and sovereign called him away from the service that he loved.

518   Admiral Sims with British and American Staff Officers at the raising of the Admiral's Flag at Queenstown, from a photograph, courtesy of the Imperial War Museum, London

519   The British Grand Fleet, from a photograph by International Newsreel, New York

THE BRITISH GRAND FLEET

FAR from the landsman's ken, silent, sufficient, and grimly determined, the Grand Fleet stood incessantly on guard against the German High Seas Fleet, which, if once triumphant, would, with the German submarines, have swept all neutral and Allied shipping to its doom in one extinguishing campaign. The Grand Fleet was the hub of the World-War wheel; for sea power was never more essential, and without that mighty central force the armies and air service, as well as all subsidiary naval forces, simply could not work. The one great drawback was that at least one hundred destroyers had to be kept as the Grand Fleet's screen against the equal number always with the German High Seas Fleet.

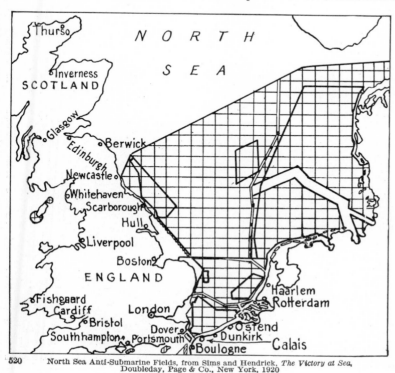

520   North Sea Anti-Submarine Fields, from Sims and Hendrick, *The Victory at Sea,* Doubleday, Page & Co., New York, 1920

NORTH SEA ANTI– SUBMARINE MINEFIELDS

IT sometimes took ten German surface craft to get one submarine quite safely through the minefields planted by the Allies. But the submarines did get through, and round the north of Scotland to the south and west of Ireland, where the American destroyers did their best against them. The large area, entailing many gaps, and the often very clever German work, combined to nullify many a well-laid mine.

A TYPICAL SITUATION WITH
FOUR DAYS PLOTTINGS

521   Admiralty chart of Submarine Movements, from Sims and Hendrick, *The Victory at Sea*,
Doubleday, Page & Co., New York, 1920

GERMAN SUBMARINE MOVEMENTS

THIS typical Admiralty track-chart shows the carefully plotted movements of four successive days. As the war went on the British naval secret service far surpassed the German. The German submarines, moreover, were extremely talkative; and though they talked in code the British learned to decode their messages. Wireless communication lent a new and strange excitement to this life-and-death game of blindman's buff at sea.

522   Depth-charge exploding, from a photograph, courtesy of the Navy
Department, Washington

A DEPTH–CHARGE CIRCLE

ONCE a submarine was well located a speedy destroyer could cut a circle of deadly depth-charges all around it soon enough to "wing it" if not put it out of action altogether. Two destroyers working around one well located submarine would ensure a "kill." The spot of oil that appeared upon the surface of the sea was mute evidence of the effectiveness of the crashing explosives under water.

523 Depth-charge dropped by United States destroyer in submarine area, from a photograph in the United States Signal Corps, War Department, Washington

THE FIRST GERMAN SUBMARINE CAPTURED BY AMERICANS

ONE gloomy autumn day "O Q 20" put out of Queenstown. "O Q 20" consisted of eight American destroyers, led by the *Nicholson*, Commander Frank Berrien, and assigned to the duty of escorting a big convoy through the danger zone. Suddenly close to the *Fanning*, for one exciting moment, glittered a tiny "finger" periscope, of the emergency kind only used at short ranges. The big British merchant vessel *Welshman* was just about to be

524   The U-58, captured by the U.S.S. *Fanning* and U.S.S. *Nicholson*, from a photograph, courtesy of the Navy Department, Washington

torpedoed when down flashed the periscope and down went the submarine; for her commander had sighted the *Fanning*. Lieutenant Walter S. Henry, the *Fanning's* deck officer, turned at full speed, located the submarine with exactitude, and depth-charged her. Meanwhile the *Nicholson* came down full-tilt and completed the depth-charging circle all round the doomed Germans. For a time nothing happened, and exultation was giving way to the normal disappointment when up came the submarine. So the destroyers began a quick shelling. Then another surprise was sprung upon them, as the conning tower opened and out came commander and crew, each crying "Kamerad!" as he emerged. The surrender accepted, two Germans at once went below and opened the sea-cocks. Then all the Germans swam for the *Fanning*, where the Americans treated them well. Kapitän Amberger saluted Lieutenant A. S. Carpender. Though the hull of the U-58 had apparently remained quite intact, the navigating gear had been jammed by the depth-charges. Amberger therefore had to choose between certain death by suffocation, or an immediate rise to the surface.

THE LONDON FLAGSHIP

THE one and only coign of vantage from which the American naval commander in chief could control the forces under his command and correlate their multifarious activities with those of the Allies was not the quarterdeck of a man-of-war but London. For centuries London had been the greatest shipping center of the world, and much more so in control and interests than in mere amount of tonnage. There stood the original Lloyd's, the head and center of all marine insurance. There stood the British Admiralty, directing the greatest of all national navies. It is one of the finest aspects of the American war effort as a whole that the American forces by sea and land and air were so admirably worked into the general Allied effort, with a complete self-sacrifice of all natural, and quite legitimate, pride in distinctively separate efforts of their own. The Allies had been carrying on the war for three years already. The crisis had to be faced at once and by whatever means were readiest. Beginning with the merest handful of assistants, Admiral Sims went on increasing his headquarters staff in London until, at the time of the Armistice, it was directing nearly four hundred vessels and eighty thousand men, whose work had all sorts of connections from London to Washington, from Queenstown to Corfu, and from Murmansk in the north of Russia right down to the Azores.

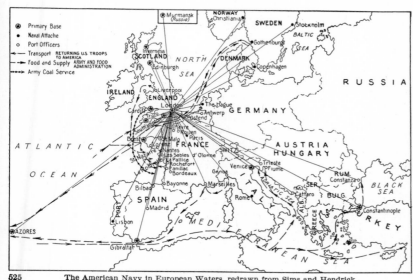

525   The American Navy in European Waters, redrawn from Sims and Hendrick, *The Victory at Sea*, Doubleday, Page & Co., New York, 1920

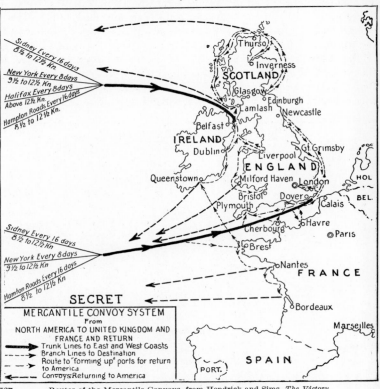

Routes of the Convoys, from Sims and Hendrick, *The Victory at Sea*, Doubleday, Page & Co., New York, 1920

CONVOY WORLD–ROUTES

THE convoy system was the greatest factor in solving the desperate problem of the submarine campaign. Until the spring of 1917 Allied and neutral shipping had either not been attacked, or had taken individual chances, or had been occasionally escorted, or else had been imperfectly defended by destroyers on patrol. Under the convoy system merchantmen in fairly close formation could be so surrounded by destroyers that, to reach the merchantmen, the submarines were obliged to approach formed lines of their deadliest enemies, who would immediately attack. In a word, the convoy system had over the patrol system all the advantages which a close and sharp-sighted attack has over a scattered defense. Admiral Sims was a vigorous advocate of the convoy system. So were the British naval chiefs. But the merchant skippers, unused to mass formations, were almost a unit against it, until the "ruthless" campaign forced some supreme effort to be made at once. In May, 1917, the first regular convoy went, quite immune, from Gibraltar to England. Within three months the convoy system was established over all the nearer routes. Before the close of 1917 the whole world's shipping was convoyed as shown upon this chart. In very distant waters no escort at all was needed. In medium-distant waters, including the United States coast, surface men-of-war would form the escort against a possible surface raider. Inside the danger zones destroyers faced the submarines.

CONVOY ROUTES TO THE BRITISH ISLES

THIS chart shows how the convoy system worked within the zone of greatest danger. As unarmed, or imperfectly armed, merchant craft approached great ports, like Liverpool or Brest, they naturally tended to crowd together and become like a flock of sheep at the mercy of the sea wolves. But the convoy system kept the flocks comparatively safe within the circle of the destroyer escort, which, with gunfire, torpedoes, depth-charges, and ramming fought off submarines.

Routes of the Mercantile Convoys, from Hendrick and Sims, *The Victory at Sea*, Doubleday, Page & Co., New York, 1920

528   Convoy as seen from the air, from a photograph, courtesy of the Navy Department, Washington

CONVOY AS SEEN FROM THE AIR IN 1918

THIS convoy, as seen from the air in 1918, gives a good idea of how well the merchantmen, with their urgently needed supplies, were shepherded through the danger zones by escorting destroyers ever ready to attack the lurking submarines. The submarines were now forced either to risk attack at close quarters or give up in despair.

529   Convoy of American vessels, from a photograph in the United States Signal Corps, War Department, Washington

VICE–ADMIRAL SIR ALEXANDER DUFF

ADMIRAL DUFF was the British head of the convoy system, from whose London office in the Admiralty ten thousand vessels were routed across the Seven Seas. One entire side of his immense head office was occupied by an enormous chart on which were shown the daily doings of every ship between the New World and the Old, as well as the last reported position of every German submarine.

530 Captain Byron A. Long, from a photograph
by Harris & Ewing, Washington

CAPTAIN BYRON A. LONG, U.S.N.

WHEN in 1918 the greatest troop movement in the history of the world was undertaken, the methods which had hitherto been employed in routing merchant shipping were now applied to the problem of transporting soldiers. Captain Long was the chief American convoy officer, a man who did his complex task in such a manner that Admiral Sims "eliminated the whole subject from my anxieties."

531 Rear-Admiral Henry B. Wilson, 1861–, from a
photograph by Harris & Ewing, Washington

REAR-ADMIRAL HENRY B. WILSON, U.S.N.

"GIBRALTAR was the 'gateway' for more traffic than any other port in the world. It was estimated that more than one quarter of all the convoys which reached the entente nations passed through these straits. . . . In July, 1917, the British Government requested the coöperation of the American Navy . . . at Gibraltar; and on August 6 the U.S.S. *Sacramento* reached that port, followed about a week afterward by the *Birmingham* flying the flag of Rear-Admiral Henry B. Wilson." — HENDRICK AND SIMS, *Victory at Sea*, Doubleday, Page & Co., New York, 1920.

532 Rear-Admiral Albert P. Niblack, 1859–, from
a photograph by Harris & Ewing, Washington

REAR-ADMIRAL ALBERT P. NIBLACK, U.S.N.

ADMIRAL NIBLACK succeeded Wilson at Gibraltar, where he supervised the American part of the convoy system through the rest of the war. The American force which was finally assembled at Gibraltar consisted of some forty-one ships, including yachts, scout cruisers, gunboats, coast-guard cutters, and some old destroyers. There was a personnel which averaged more than four thousand enlisted men. During the period of Niblack's service the Americans and British at Gibraltar escorted more than five hundred convoys. The number shows the importance of the Gibraltar station.

533 Smoke screen laid down by British destroyers to protect American vessels, from a photograph, courtesy
of the Navy Department, Washington

534   American Subchasers in the Mediterranean, from a photograph, courtesy of the Navy Department, Washington

SUBCHASERS

SUBCHASERS were the final touch to the submarine campaign. They were small, handy, and built quickly in great numbers to chase and "spot" the elusive submarines with the help of their most efficient hydrophones and quick direction plotting. Three together would pick up the sound of a prowling submarine, find (with their hydrophone direction-pointers) where the three direction lines met at a single point, and then would hold this "fix" until the hunting destroyers would come up and destroy the submarine with a depth-charge or force it to surrender.

SUBCHASER DEPTH–CHARGING

THIS picture, taken just off Land's End, at the southwest corner of England, shows how rapidly the active little subchasers developed aggressive powers of their own. They could not equal the far larger and far better armed destroyers. But, when it is remembered that this shows the surface effect of a charge of the terrific TNT, fired off at a depth of a hundred and fifty feet, the anxiety with which the German submarine commanders viewed such an addition to their foes can be readily understood.

The highest efficiency of the general convoy system, and of the subchasers too, was not reached during the central storm and stress of the submarine campaign of 1917. But practically all the improvements effected in 1918 were at least forecast in 1917. Admiral Sims and his assistants were always in the forefront of both promise and performance.

535   Depth-charge dropped by United States subchaser, from a photograph,
courtesy of the Navy Department, Washington

CHAPTER XIII

THE SPIRIT OF THE ARMY

"HAVING entered the World War, the United States did so whole-heartedly. There has been no other instance when all the military, naval, and civilian resources of a country were so promptly and completely mobilized and thrown into a conflict. The country had almost unlimited resources and yet was totally unprepared, as it always has been on the eve of war. The immediate necessity at the time we declared war was, therefore, to develop our military strength with the utmost rapidity. We ought never to forget that between us and our enemy stood our gallant Allies who for nearly three years had withstood the blows of the most formidable military machine the world has ever seen. But still another year was to pass before our intensive effort could be felt and our soldiers become a factor on the Western Front and aid our friends on the firing line. The strength of a country for war is not gauged by the resources of that country unless these are developed, and our worn Allies must have found the days infinitely long while waiting for our help." — MAJ.-GEN. HUNTER LIGGETT, *Commanding an American Army*, 10–11, Houghton Mifflin Company, Boston, 1925.

For a whole generation, ever since the eighteen-eighties, the sadly neglected United States Army had been effecting its own renaissance. Though stinted in men and means, and though mostly ignored by Congress and the nation, the army worked its own way up to higher use. Its best officers practically made themselves into a post-graduate school of war, which linked education and self-education close together, from cadet to commander in chief. Then came the Staff and War Colleges, which brought together many future leaders. Meanwhile a few far-seeing statesmen did what they could to further this renaissance. Elihu Root, when Secretary of War, took special interest in the education of the staff. Roosevelt, when President, chose both the future commanders in chief — Sims and Pershing — for special naval and military advancement of the most significant kind. Lieutenant Sims was made the navy's chief gunnery expert; while Captain Pershing was unprecedentedly promoted to Brigadier-General direct. At last, when the Great War came, the whole nation turned to its army. And well did the army answer to the nation's call. It formed the nucleus round which a much greater number grew into those efficient units which were the first to take the field. It supplied those instructors who trained hundreds of times their own numbers into fitness for later service at the front. And out of its carefully selected leaders — leaders who till then had never led anything larger than a few odd thousands against comparatively ineffective Spaniards, Filipinos, Mexicans, or Chinese — there suddenly grew up a body of commanders and staff officers who led two million victorious Americans against the German hosts in France.

THE PROBLEM OF RAISING AN ARMY

On April 1, 1917, the strength of the Regular Army stood at five thousand, seven hundred and ninety-one officers and one hundred and twenty-one thousand, seven hundred and ninety-seven enlisted men; while at the same time the National Guard numbered seven thousand, six hundred and twelve officers and one hundred and seventy-four thousand and eight men. The armies engaged in the World War were numbered in millions. The prompt expansion of the armed forces of the United States was the most vital of the many questions confronting the American people in the months of April and May, 1917. On the day following President Wilson's war message Colonel Roosevelt volunteered to recruit a division for early service in France. The mere public mention of the plan brought requests from thousands of Americans to be included in the organization. The Roosevelt offer was ultimately declined. At the moment the War Department was wrestling with the provisions of what was to be the Administration's plan for army expansion. While popular interest in the Roosevelt scheme was at its height, Americans read one day in their newspapers that Congress had begun the consideration of a draft law. To thousands of men and women the country over this news brought for the first time a realization of the seriousness of the step which their government had taken when it had declared war upon Germany.

NONUNION LABOR
Walking Delegate from U. S. War Department (to Col. Roosevelt): "Hold up here! You're not a member of the Life-Savers' union."

DARLING in New York Tribune

536   From a cartoon *Nonunion Labor*, by J. N. Darling in the *New York Daily Tribune*, May 19, 1917

Sixty-fifth Congress of the United States of America;

At the First Session,

Begun and held at the City of Washington on Monday, the second day of April, one thousand nine hundred and seventeen.

AN ACT

To authorize the President to increase temporarily the Military Establishment of the United States.

Be it enacted by the Senate and House of Representatives of the United States of America in Congress assembled, That in view of the existing emergency, which demands the raising of troops in addition to those now available, the President be, and he is hereby, authorized—

First. Immediately to raise, organize, officer, and equip all or such number of increments of the Regular Army provided by the national defense Act approved June third, nineteen hundred and sixteen, or such parts thereof as he may deem necessary; to raise all organizations of the Regular Army, including those added by such increments, to the maximum enlisted strength authorized by law. Vacancies in the Regular Army created or caused by the addition of increments as herein authorized which can not be filled by promotion may be filled by temporary appointment for the period of the emergency or until replaced by permanent appointments or by provisional appointments made under the provisions of section twenty-three of the national defense Act, approved June third, nineteen hundred and sixteen, and hereafter provisional appointments under said section may be terminated whenever it is determined, in the manner prescribed by the President, that the officer has not the suitability and fitness requisite for permanent appointment.

Second. To draft into the military service of the United States, organize, and officer, in accordance with the provisions of section one hundred and eleven

537   Selective Service Act, from the original in the Department of State, Washington

THE SELECTIVE SERVICE ACT

On May 18, 1917, the most momentous single piece of legislation in the military annals of the United States became a part of the law of the land. The Selective Service Act provided that the President might raise the Regular Army to its authorized war strength of two hundred and eighty-seven thousand men by voluntary enlistment, that he might take into the service of the United States the National Guard and the National Guard Reserve, that he might raise by selective draft an additional force of five hundred thousand men, and at a later time another force of five hundred thousand, and that he might recruit four volunteer divisions at his discretion. The Draft Act was a complete surprise to the enemy, who had estimated that the American Government would follow its traditional policy of calling for volunteers and would, as a consequence, be slow in the creation of an army capable of affecting the outcome of the war. The Allies took heart as they read the welcome news of May 18. The President by proclamation fixed June 5 as the day for enrolling the men of draft age.

538 Munition factory workers capping 14-inch shells, from a photograph in the United States Signal Corps, War Department, Washington

539 Training soldiers at Camp McClellan, Ala., from a photograph in the United States Signal Corps, War Department, Washington

JUNE 5, 1917

THE reasons which induced Congress to resort immediately to the draft were simple and conclusive. The state offered equal opportunities to all of its citizens; it asked them, therefore, to share equally the responsibilities of the emergency which had arisen. Team work on a nation-wide scale was necessary for the effective prosecution of the war, and, as a consequence, the President must be in a position to say that some men should fight and that others should remain in the factories, the shipyards, and on the farms that made possible the maintaining of armies in contact with the enemy. Universal compulsory service did not come as a surprise to thinking Americans. For months the conviction had been growing among them that only in this way could the ideal of democracy be achieved and justice and equality obtained for all members of a vast community. "The whole nation must be a team," said the President in his proclamation calling upon those subject to registration to enroll, "in which each man shall play the part for which he is best fitted. To this end, Congress has provided that the nation shall be organized for war by selection; that each man shall be classified for service in the place to which it shall best serve the general good to call him. The significance of this cannot be overstated. It is a new thing in our history and a landmark in our progress. It is a new manner of accepting and vitalizing our duty to give ourselves with thoughtful devotion to the common purpose of us all. It is in no sense a conscription of unwilling; it is, rather, selection from a nation which has volunteered in mass."

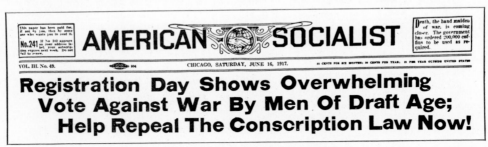

540   From the *American Socialist*, June 16, 1917

OPPOSITION TO ENROLLMENT

THE unanimity of the nation in support of the war was emphasized by the smallness of the group which opposed registration. But this was a vociferous and at times an aggressive minority. "Every man," said a pamphlet issued from the headquarters of the Socialist party, "who is determined to uphold the dearest rights of personal liberty, every man who refuses to become a victim of the war declared by the Government to protect the millions loaned the Allies by the capitalists of this country should refuse to register for conscription." "If this is a popular war, why conscription?" Out of Kansas came an envelope printed by a Socialist paper from the back of which flamed a violent appeal. "Let those who want great victories go to the firing line and get them. . . . They say, war is Hell, then let those who want Hell go to Hell." But the campaign was without avail. On June 5 more than nine million five hundred thousand young men presented themselves to the draft boards of their local communities and placed their names on the rolls from which the National Army was to be selected.

THE FIRST OFFICERS' TRAINING CAMP

THREE days before the President signed the Selective Service Act some forty thousand civilians reported at sixteen camps scattered throughout the country. They found in the rough barracks being rushed to completion roofs for their heads and but little else. Sanitary arrangements in many cases were those used for the camp of an army in the field. They stepped from civilian life abruptly into the primitive conditions and the necessary improvisations of war. It was an experience which stood them in good stead when they faced the problems of the A. E. F. in France. To receive them was a

541   Soldiers Pitching Tents at the Plattsburg Officers' Training Camp, from a photograph by International Newsreel, New York

handful of regular officers, mostly captains, with a few majors and other field officers. The scarcity of instructors can be accounted for by the vast demands which the war had suddenly placed upon the limited personnel of the Regular Army. In the average case the instructor received from one hundred and fifty to one hundred and seventy-five candidates who had immediately to be clothed, fed and equipped. The captain, moreover, had neither lieutenants nor the indispensable noncommissioned officers to assist him. He was forced to fall back on reserve officers who had been ordered to camp to "assist in instruction" and incidentally to undergo a test as to their own fitness for the commissions which they held. Many of these were men who before the war had expressed their desire for more adequate national preparedness by taking examinations and enrolling in the reserve corps provided for by the act of 1916. Their lot at the First Officers' Camps was a hard one for most of them had but the slightest military experience. There was some doubt, in view of the orders they had received, as to whether they were officers or candidates. They held in fact an unhappy and anomalous position between the two. At the end of the camp many were promoted while some were demoted.

THE OFFICER CANDIDATES

THE candidates who came in May, 1917, to the training camps whose shacks still echoed to the sound of the carpenters' hammers were volunteers selected from among many applicants and representing in very truth the pick of the nation. For the most part they were college men, recent graduates, together with some who looked forward to receiving their degrees in the following June. Many were above the draft age. Successful business and professional men stood in ranks side by side with youngsters whose careers were yet to be made.

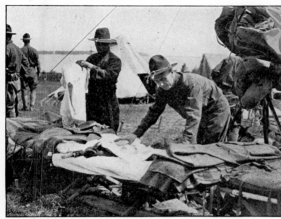

The regular army instructors had never in their lives faced such companies. Many an inconspicuous rear-rank candidate clad in ill-fitting quartermaster khaki possessed high intellectual capacity. The task of the instructor was to discover it. He must discover also whether intelligence was joined with personality for leadership, for either without the other would be valueless. He was given three short and crowded months in which to estimate his one hundred and fifty men. He made many mistakes but they were errors due to judgment rather than to improper influence. The influence of politics, wealth, and social position had been left outside the gates. Only the inherent qualities and abilities of the candidates counted in the long hard grind of those spring and summer days.

542   Officer candidates at the Plattsburg Officers' Training Camp, from a photograph by International Newsreel, New York

543   From a drawing *On the Mat*, by J. R. Barrett in *The Pick*, published at the Third Officers' Training Camp, Camp Devens, Mass.

544   From a drawing *Rumors is Rumors*, by J. R. Barrett in *The Pick*, published at the Third Officers' Training Camp, Camp Devens

THE TENSION OF THE CAMPS

HARDLY had the camps begun when the officer candidates became aware of the fact that elimination had commenced.   The few obviously unfit were quickly plucked from the ranks and permitted to return to their homes.   An atmosphere of indescribable apprehension developed which persisted until the day on which the commissions were announced.   A similar atmosphere pervaded all the officers' training camps that followed the pioneer attempts.   Deep was the anguish of the men who were told to drop out of ranks and report to the orderly room.   As they packed their belongings, donned their civilian attire, and made their way to the nearest railway station, they considered themselves disgraced for life.   Rare indeed was the candidate who was not convinced that he would be the next to go.   Of the songs sung by the men tramping under full pack along the dusty roads which led toward Plattsburg none expressed more fully the tension and the candidate's ability to poke fun at it than the parody sung to the popular tune, *Don't Take Me Home*.

> Don't send me home, please don't send me home.
> Tell me, where did I make that break?
> Oh, oh, oh, oh, have a little pity.
> I'm a poor candidate, in search of war I roam,
> I'll do anything you want me to, but don't
> Send me home.

The same sentiments were later reflected in a song of the Third Officers' Training Camp **at** Camp Devens, sung to the tune, *Good-Morning, Mr. Zip-Zip-Zip*.

> Good morning, Mr. Candidate,
> With your chances just as slim as mine!
> Good morning, Mr. Candidate,
> You're surely looking fine.
> Route step marches and close order drill,
> If the Captain don't get you the Lieutenant will;
> Good morning, Mr. Candidate,
> With your chances just as slim as,
> Your chances just as slim as,
> Your chances just as slim as mine!

THE WORK OF THE OFFICER CAMPS

The work was hard. First call blew at five-thirty and taps did not sound until ten. Most of the intervening period was taken up with drills, marches, conferences, lectures, or study. The manual of arms, close and extended order drill, range practice, musketry, minor tactics with Sergeant Hill's approved solutions, instruction in guard duty, company administration, the manual of the court martial, and the technique and handling of the various arms were some of the things which filled the candidate's day. In the old army before the war the regular had had relatively little experience with schools after his West Point days and even less with instruction. Moreover much of the technique and many of the weapons of the

545 Artillery Instruction at Camp Taylor, Ky., from a photograph in the United States Signal Corps, War Department, Washington

trench warfare which had developed on the Western Front were unfamiliar to him. With little guidance from their superiors the captain-instructors at the training camps did the best they could with the training schedule which had been provided for them. And all the time they had to be observing their men, trying to pick out from among them the ones who should be majors, captains, first and second lieutenants. As for the candidate, the most important officer in the army from his point of view was the captain. He occasionally saw a major; he heard vaguely at times about a colonel. His point of view and the spirit of banter which the grind and the worries of camp could not destroy were summed up in that song which echoed through the pines on the margin of Lake Champlain in the summer of 1917, sung to the air, *I Want To Be Back Home in Dixie.*

> I want to be, I want to be, I want to be at least a Colonel,
> Majors handing me salutes, and a boy to black my boots.
> I want to be, I want to be at least a Colonel,
> C-O-L-O-N-E-L
> Sit behind a desk and give the Captains Hell!
> I want to be, I want to be, I want to be a Colonel *now!*

THE SPIRIT OF THE CAMPS

Hard physical drill, mental labor, and an unremitting nervous strain told on the men as the weeks passed. There were candidates who attempted suicide. But there was little complaint and less loafing. The men were determined to master the different branches in which they were being instructed. The Sunday holiday would be utilized for further practice with the semaphore or wig wag, or for fixing in the mind the complicated maneuvers of battalion drill. What a boon it would have been for these candidates if this drill had been discontinued before instead of after the camp! Out of the First Officers' Training Camps came the war words of a popular song expressing perfectly the spirit of the men who were to be the junior officers of the National Army.

> There's a long, long trail before us,
> Into No-Man's land in France,
> Where the shrapnel shells are bursting,
> And we must advance.
>
> There'll be lots of drill and hiking,
> Before our dreams all come true
> But some day we'll show the Germans,
> How the Yankees come through.

546 Graduating Exercises of the Second Officers' Training Camp, Fort Meyer, Va., from a photograph in the United States Signal Corps, War Department, Washington

547   Dug-out at Officers' Training Camp, Fort Sheridan, Ill., from a photograph in the
United States Signal Corps, War Department, Washington

THE SECOND OFFICERS' TRAINING CAMPS

ON August 15 the first camps came to an end and the men were commissioned. Three days later the second camps began. The instructors of these were mostly men who had received their commissions on August 15. The regular army captains were sent, many of them, to duty in the cantonments where the National Army was about to be mobilized. The instruction of the second camps profited by the experience in the first. The character of the candidates and spirit of the camps, however, were practically identical with those of the first. This spirit was summed up in entries in an anonymous diary kept at Fort Sheridan in November 1917.

"*Tues.*, 27th. — No more 'walk my post in a military manner,' keeping horses from committing nuisance. 'Reposing special trust and confidence in my patriotism, valor, fidelity and abilities' W. Wilson, Esq., has this day appointed me 1st Lieut., Field Artillery, of his army. He's an optimist.

Wed., 28th. — Savings of a lifetime to the profiteers. Riding boots, whipcord breeches, calling cards, sterling silver identification tag, Sam Browne belt and other essentials of what a commission calls 'grade and position.' Wonder if officers have to buy their own coffins.

Thur., 29th. — Getting used to being saluted. Losing the Uncle Tom feeling of 'candidate.' Occupied with size, shape and position of shoulder bars. Feel like a Knight of Pythias." — *Wine, Women and War*, 3, Anonymous, Copyrighted 1926, J. H. Sears & Co., Incorporated, New York.

The greatest army song sung at the training camps and throughout the war was *The Field Artillery Song*, written by Colonel (then Lieutenant) Edmund L. Gruber while in the Philippines in 1908. Four verses and the chorus of this song are given below.

Over hill, over dale, we have hit the dusty trail,
And those caissons go rolling along.
"Countermarch!   Right about!" hear those wagon
    soldiers shout,
While those caissons go rolling along.

CHORUS
For it's Hi-yi-yee! In the field artillery,
Let us call off our numbers loud and strong.
    (*Spoken*)   Call off!
And where'er we go, everybody shall know
That those caissons are rolling along.
    (*Spoken*)   Keep 'em rolling!
That those caissons are rolling along.

With the cavalry, boot to boot, we will join in the pursuit,
And those caissons go rolling along,
Action front, at a trot; volley fire with shell and shot,
While those caissons go rolling along.

Should the foe penetrate, every gunner lies in wait,
And those caissons go rolling along.
Fire at will, lay 'em low, never stop for any foe,
While those caissons go rolling along.

But if fate me should call, and in action I should fall,
Keep those caissons a-rolling along.
Then in peace I'll abide when I take my final ride
On a caisson that's rolling along.

548   The Newly Commissioned Officer, from a drawing by
J. R. Barrett in *The Pick*, published by the Third Officers'
Training Camp, Camp Devens, Mass.

THE OFFICERS OF THE NATIONAL GUARD

THE graduates of the First and Second Officers' Training Camps were not the only men who passed from civilian life to the responsibilities of an army officer. For years before the outbreak of the World War many a National Guard officer had been in the service. Since the passage of the Defense Act of 1916 which provided for the federalization of the Guard, he had stood ready to answer the call to the colors if an emergency arose. Many of these men had seen service in 1916 on the Mexican border.

549 Officers of the 69th Regiment, New York National Guard. From left to right: Major Michael Lynch, Captain Felix McSherry, Captain Bernard F. Cummings, Captain E. M. Dillon, Chaplain Francis P. Duffy and Captain B. J. Glynn

While the candidates at the First Officers' Training Camps were struggling to master the elements of their new profession, many National Guard officers were ordered to the Army War College at Washington for a course of instruction. In the summer of 1917 they went into camp with their units enlarged to war strength as a result of the enlistment of volunteers. In the World War the National Guard rendered service unsurpassed. Until August, 1918, the military forces of the United States were divided into three parts, the Regular Army, the National Guard, and the National Army. The insignia of the first was U. S., of the second U. S. N. G., and of the third U. S. N. A. As the fighting developed and units were depleted in battle, replacement officers and men blurred the distinction between the different parts of the army. For this reason and for the sentimental value of the change the designation of the three parts was dropped and all soldiers, becoming members of the one Army of the United States, wore the U. S. on their collars.

550 General View of Camp Lewis, Washington, from a photograph in the United States Signal Corps, War Department, Washington

THE WAR SPIRIT IN THE WEST

GENERAL LIGGETT'S experience on the Pacific coast presents a picture of a typical response of the American people to the demands of the war. In April, 1917, he was recalled from duty in the Philippines to take command of the Western Department. "My work in the Western Department in the spring of 1917 included the selection of Training Areas and camp sites, and the establishment of Training Camps to develop officers. . . . Each Camp had to be large enough to accommodate one Division of war strength, comprising approximately twenty-seven thousand men, and the Camp had to be located near ground sufficiently extensive and varied in terrain for the training of these large numbers. The people of Pierce County, Washington, donated to the Government ninety thousand acres of ground suited in every way for the mobilization and training of troops. This Training Area, known as American Lake Camp, was large enough for two Divisions. A second fine Training Area, for one Division, was selected at Linda Vista, near San Diego, California. Here, too, the patriotic citizens of the vicinity were of great assistance. This was, as respects climate, probably the very best Camp in the United States, as men could be trained there every day of the year. A third Camp and Training Area was obtained at Palo Alto, near San Francisco, available for one Division. About fifty thousand acres were included in this Area, leased without charge, to the Government for one year." — HUNTER LIGGETT, *Commanding an American Army*, 11–13, Houghton Mifflin Company, Boston, 1925.

551 Ninety-first Division in training at Camp Lewis, Washington, from a photograph in the United States Signal Corps, War Department, Washington

552   National Guard in training at Fort Sill, Okla., from a photograph in the United States Signal Corps, War Department, Washington

GENERAL SCOTT, CHIEF OF STAFF

At the outbreak of the war Major-General Hugh L. Scott, a real soldier, was Chief of Staff at Washington. "He had made his reputation among the Indians and the Moros. He was . . . perhaps the greatest expert on sign languages, a man who could go among wild men in any part of the world, make himself known to them and come away their friend. He was not suited, however, by training, experience, or temperament to sit behind a desk and direct the destiny of . . . the War Department, in time of war. He was succeeded in September, 1917, by General Tasker H. Bliss and the latter in turn by General Peyton C. March. . . ." Maj.-Gen. Johnson Hagood, *The Services of Supply*, 25, Houghton Mifflin Company, Boston, 1927.

AMERICAN SYSTEM OF ORGANIZATION

On August 7 the War Department announced a new system of organization of American troops for the World War. The ratio of artillery to infantry was greatly increased and the machine gun arm was also materially enlarged. The new division consisted in part of two brigades of infantry of two regiments each and one brigade of artillery of three regiments. In addition to the machine gun companies in the infantry regiments a division machine gun battalion of four companies was organized. The order specified sixteen divisions of the National Army to be organized and numbered from seventy-six to ninety-one, both inclusive. It provided that

THE REGULAR ARMY AND THE NATIONAL GUARD

From the outbreak of war until nearly the middle of August voluntary enlistment filled up the ranks of the Regular Army and the National Guard. By August 9 these two branches of the service numbered together some six hundred and fifty thousand men. This was to be the nucleus of that great army which America was planning to put into action on the Western Front. Americans gained an inkling of the size of this force on September 7 when Secretary Baker announced that on January 1, 1918, the United States Army would have a strength of two million thirty thousand men. Such a force had never before been dreamed of in the western hemisphere. It was evidence that America intended to put forth the full strength of the nation.

553   Maj.-Gen. Hugh L. Scott, 1853–, from a photograph by Harris & Ewing, Washington

the sixteen divisions of the National Guard then organized should be reorganized to conform to the new plan as soon as practicable after their arrival in the training camps. The Regular Army, the National Guard, and the National Army were all to conform to the same plan. The scheme that the War Department provided called for a period of sixteen weeks of intensive training for all divisions of the National Guard and National Army, at the end of which time the divisions would proceed to France as soon as transportation was available. The training in America was basic training and had to do primarily with the individual, though there was some instruction in the handling of the smaller tactical units.

554   Troops on a practice march at Camp McClellan, Ala., from a photograph in the United States Signal Corps, War Department, Washington

THE DRAFT IN OPERATION

ON July 20, 1917, a huge glass bowl stood in a large room in the Senate Office Building. In it were ten thousand five hundred capsules of black celluloid each containing a slip of paper on which was written a number. Beside the bowl stood the Secretary of War with a bandage across his eyes. On that day in every city, town, and rural hamlet throughout the nation an interested and anxious group watched a bulletin board. The Secretary of

555   Blackboard in the Senate Office Building showing record of numbers drawn in the draft July 20, 1917, from a photograph, courtesy of the War Department, Washington

War drew from the bowl a capsule and handed it to the announcer. A moment later "Number 258" was telegraphed to the remotest corner of the country and appeared on countless bulletin boards. That number showed in red ink on the registration cards of four thousand five hundred and fifty-seven men, for that was the number of registration districts. For sixteen hours and a half the drawing continued without interruption. At the end of that time one million three hundred and seventy-four thousand young men had been drafted into the National Army. The nation had never before witnessed such a spectacle.

AWAITING THE NATIONAL ARMY

ON August 15, 1917, some thirty thousand Americans were graduated from the First Officers' Training Camps and became Reserve Officers in the military establishment of the United States. The plan had been to have each camp furnish the junior officers for a division. So far as possible each training company provided the officers for a regiment. The senior officers were men from the Regular Army. In late August the Regulars and the Reserve Officers arrived at the cantonments designated for the National Army. They saw about them great empty wooden cities, silent save for the pounding of hammers and the whine of saws. Here and there gangs of workmen hurried to bring the camps to completion. In a few days those quiet streets would be throbbing with life as the draft contingents came in and the creation of the National Army began. The day which had so long been looked forward to and which had been so many times discussed at training camp was at hand.

556   Camp prepared for the Draft Army, from a photograph in the United-States Signal Corps, War Department, Washington

It was a tense moment. What would the draft be like? Would the citizens of the United States accept that discipline without which no army can be effective? What would the young officer, the freshness of whose shoulder bars displayed their newness, do in the event of insubordination or mutiny? These and a thousand questions like them flashed through the minds of lieutenants and captains as they waited in nervous expectation the arrival of the men who were to comprise their platoons and companies.

THE MOBILIZATION OF THE NATIONAL ARMY

557 President Wilson leading the parade of drafted men in Washington, from a photograph in possession of Underwood & Underwood, New York. © G. V. Buck.

SEPTEMBER 5 was the date set when the first thirty per cent of the first quota should report at the cantonments. The nation from end to end stirred with excitement. On September 3 the President issued a message of welcome to the men who had been called to the colors and who were so soon to don the uniform of the United States.

"To the Soldiers of the National Army: You are undertaking a great duty. The heart of the whole country is with you. Everything that you do will be watched with the deepest interest and the deepest solicitude, not only by those who are near and dear to you, but by the whole nation besides. For this great war draws us all together, makes us all comrades and brothers, as all true Americans felt themselves to be when we first made good our national independence. The eyes of all the world will be upon you, because you are in some special sense the soldiers of freedom. . . ." Two days later groups of men from every community gathered at the railroad stations and boarded the special trains that bore them to the cantonments.

THE DEPARTURE OF THE SELECTED MEN

"THE time set for entrainment was generally made by the local board an occasion of formality and ceremony, and in most communities it took on the marks of a public festivity. The men were assembled at the office of the local board, which was sometimes the courtroom of the county-seat, or a large hall, a public school, or a municipal building. When the contingent was a large one, it was drawn up in ranks in the street or public square. A photographer officiated to preserve for the participants' families a pictured memento of the occasion. The chairman made an address, reminding them of the significance of the occasion, and calling attention to the various regulations to be observed in their progress from home to camp. Usually other short addresses were made, sometimes by the mayor of the town or by other notables. At the station sometimes the whole of the town would be found assembled to cheer the parting moments of 'the boys.' For the town felt that these men represented its own honor and patriotism; it looked proudly upon its own contribution to the national defense; and it was keenly desirous to make them feel that they represented the honor of the town, the county, and the state in the new service to which they were called." — *Second Report of the Provost-Marshal General*, 237. Weeping mingled with the cheers and the music of the bands as the trains bearing the soldiers-to-be drew out of the familiar yards. So the war came home to the people of the United States.

558   Location of the training camps in the United States, drawn expressly for *The Pageant of America*

THE ARRIVAL AT CAMP

"On a certain day in September last the inhabitants of the small town of Ayer, Massachusetts, located thirty-six miles northwest of Boston, were treated to a strange sight. Before the dingy, old-fashioned railway station stopped train after train, coming from every state in New England and from counties in Northern New York. From these trains burst a veritable flood of young men, carrying suitcases, valises, bundles wrapped in newspapers, and even ancient carpet-bags; many brought nothing. In that motley throng were men of means, clerks, mechanics, day laborers, operatives from factory towns, lumberjacks, and backwoodsmen from the Maine forests and from the Adirondacks. . . . Out of the trains they poured, forming themselves into groups, and at once becoming part of a great straggling procession making its way down the curving road, through the little village, and out into the rolling country beyond to that stretch of land seven miles long by two miles wide that

559 Drafted men being mustered into the army, from a photograph in the United States Signal Corps, War Department, Washington

constitutes Camp Devens. Forward they went with awkward, uncertain steps, for the average civilian is not taught how to walk. Chins were thrust out, shoulders were uneven, hands otherwise unoccupied were thrust into pockets. . . . Two weeks after that first detachment arrived at Camp Devens a young reserve officer who had been ordered there from Plattsburg wrote home: 'We are all of us astonished and delighted at the spirit shown by the first increment of men. . . . The men show no apathy, and are not indignant at being drafted. They don't like the word "draft," and the term "conscription" seems furthest from their thought. They feel, and rightly, that they are members of a National Army of their own creation, and are behaving as such.'" — Henry Rood in *The Century Magazine*, February, 1918.

560 Qualification record for drafted men, from a photograph in the United States Signal Corps, War Department, Washington

THE NEW SOLDIER

"Self-conscious at first in their uniforms, the men of the National Army came to be proud of them. It took about a fortnight for the transition. Then came inquiries at the regimental exchange for needles, thread, and eradicators. One began to see men going off on Saturday, on pass, sprucing up before they left barracks. One wondered at their thoughts as they passed among the civilians in nearby cities and towns. One saw them occasionally moving through the streets, heads erect, with swinging carriage, unconsciously walking the one hundred and twenty steps to the minute prescribed by drill regulations — now become a habit. Some of them were more careful of their deportment in uniform than in the days of civilian clothing. A spirit of pride of uniform was developing in the National Army. It affected the conduct of the wearer. There was a dignity to it that got under the skin." — Captain E. L. Fox in the *Forum*, January, 1918

561 The first days of training, from a photograph in the United States Signal Corps, War Department, Washington

562   Bayonet practice, from a photograph in the United States
Signal Corps, War Department, Washington

THE SPIRIT OF THE NATIONAL ARMY CAMPS

CHRISTOPHER MORLEY writing to the *New York Times* under the date of October 24, 1917, has given the impression which Camp Dix made on the mind of a visitor. "Here is taking place something so marvelous, so portentous for our nation, so vast a democratic experiment, that one watches it with a tingle of consecration. . . . A visit to one of the cantonments is unforgettable. The greatness of this superb effort to raise an army that will be truly national — drawn from every rank of the nation, every man playing the part for which he is best fitted — floods the heart with fire and pride. These molten pools of manhood have been poured into the crucible. The dross is being purged, the hardening metal tempered and welded. The finished weapon will be terrible in edge and onset. I think it will be the finest army the world has ever seen, because it is a true cross section of a nation . . . throughout all ranks the spirit is the same. These men are out to do a big job, in no sense of heroics or swank, but soberly, advisedly, with intent to see it through. . . . Men who a month ago had no conception of citizenship, no pride of country, and even only a smattering of English, now show a fine and mettlesome temper that is perfectly astounding."

THE MOOD OF THE AMERICAN SOLDIERS

"IT is a stoical determination to see the thing through. They have entered this war after reading of it for three years. They know its horrors. In this they are unlike the men of any nation whom circumstances rushed into war, as into an unknown adventure. Our men know this war; they followed it in the press since its outbreak. They are going in, dogged and grim; theirs is a solid courage — which is the most sublime." — CAPTAIN E. L. FOX, in the *Forum*, January, 1918.

563   Life in camp, from a photograph in the United States Signal
Corps, War Department, Washington

A MILITARY TYPE

THERE were American soldiers, however, who passed through their training in a state of bewilderment. No one has surpassed Lieutenant Edward Streeter's letters of "Bill" to "Dere Mable" in the depiction of this American warrior. "Were still up at the artillery range shootin. I dont know what at. Our guns is pointed right at some woods. Weve been shootin at those woods now for a week and haven't hit them yet. Theres a fello stands behind the guns and yells things all day like it was a poker game. 'Up five, up ten.' . . . I heard a lot of talk when I first came up about a gun park. I thought it would be a nice place to go Sundays and have some fun. I asked the Captain if there was a lake where a fello could get a canoo and have a little paddle. He said no but they had a fine collecshun of animals. . . . One day I asked the sargent where it was while we were unhitchin. He said we were in it then. It isnt nothin but a big field without a blade of grass or a tree and just the guns in the middle. I told him if he thought this was a park he ought to see Weewillo Park home. . . . They got a drill over here called the standin gun drill. The names misleadin. . . . They make you get up and sit on the gun. Before you can get comfortable they make you git down again. It looks like they just didnt know what they did want you to do." There were many "Bills" in the army.

564   From a drawing *You Walk a Post but there aint no Post*, by Bill Breck in Edward Streeter, *Dere Mable.* © 1918, Frederick A. Stokes & Company, New York

SINGING

THE singing that had characterized the First and Second Officers' Training Camps became general throughout the service. Songs of the old regulars were taken up by the new citizen army.

> The Infantry, the Infantry with the mud behind their ears,
> The Infantry, the Infantry with the mud behind their ears,
> The Artillery and the Cavalry and the nasty Engineers,
> Oh, they never could lick the Infantry in a hundred thousand years.

A part of the army was the Marine Corps vastly expanded by enlistments. The Marines were used as land troops in the same way as other units of the army. Behind the corps was a long history of active service in many parts of the world. Aggressiveness, efficiency, and devotion to duty were part of the Marine tradition. As the recruits came in the "old timers" passed on to the newcomers the attitude and slang of the famous corps. Not many weeks passed before the company streets in the cantonments where the Marine rookies were being trained rang with the old song of that corps which expresses so well the spirit and traditions of these amphibious soldiers.

> From the halls of Montezuma
> To the shores of Tripoli,
> We fight our country's battles
> On the land as on the sea.
> First to fight for right and freedom
> And to keep our honor clean
> We are proud to claim the title
> Of United States Marine.
>
> Here's a health to you and to our corps
> Which we are proud to serve
> In many a strife we've fought for life
> And have never lost our nerve.
> If the Army and the Navy
> Ever look on Heaven's scenes
> They will find the streets are guarded by
> The United States Marines.

565 The Spirit of the Army, from a photograph in the United States Signal Corps, War Department, Washington

SONGS OF THE NEW ARMY

BEFORE the newly formed National Army had been a month in its cantonments crowds of soldiers whose training was only just beginning were bellowing a new song that had made its appearance.

Some of the songs, already sung in the Officers' Training Camps, were taken over from the British, of which the best was *Pack Up Your Troubles In Your Old Kit Bag*. Meanwhile the country was being flooded with songs from the popular writers of the day. After a process of selection certain of these were accepted by the army and the people as well.

> Good-bye, Maw! Good-bye, Paw!
> Good-bye, Mule, with yer old Hee-haw!
> I may not know what this war's about,
> But you bet, by gosh, I'll soon find out;
> And, O my sweetheart, don't you fear,
> I'll bring you a King fer a souvenir:
> I'll bring you a Turk and a Kaiser, too.
> An' that's about all one feller can do!

Those that stood the test were among the best war songs that America ever had. They did not have the spontaneity of the songs of the First and Second Officers' Training Camps nor the ballad origin of that later classic of the battlefield, *Parlez-vous*, but the very fact of their selection made them, in reality, expressions of the sentiments of the American people. *Over There, Smiles, Oh, How I Hate To Get Up In The Morning, Good Morning, Mr. Zip-Zip-Zip*, and *The Long, Long Trail* have become a part of the permanent heritage of the nation. There can be no denying that *The Old Gray Mare* helped materially to win the war. One of the variations to the words that went with this tune that was being sung in American camps before the end of 1917 bears the earmarks of soldier origin.

> Our Uncle Sammy, He's got the Infantry;
> He's got the Cavalry;
> He's got Artillery.
> And now, by gosh, we'll all go to Germany,
> God help Kaiser Bill.

566 From the original in the New York Public Library

VII—17

THE 304TH INFANTRY

567 Gun drill at Camp Devens, from a photograph by Underwood & Underwood, New York

THE close relationship between the First Officers' Training Camps and the National Army was nowhere better shown than in the 304th Infantry at Camp Devens. This regiment was largely officered by men from the Fourth Company, New England, of the first camp at Plattsburg. Naturally the regiment inherited the *ésprit* of the candidate company, a factor of immense impor-

568 Men singing in the Knights of Columbus Hall, Camp Devens, from a photograph by Underwood & Underwood, New York

tance in getting the training of the recruits promptly and effectively under way. At the very outset officers of the regiment knew each other and already had had many experiences in common. They undertook their work with the regiment in the same spirit of wishing to make their outfit excel which had marked their candidate days at Plattsburg. The connection between the regiment and the original candidate company was made complete by the transforming of the company song into the regimental song. Through its long training period in the United States and to that sad day in France when it was broken up to be used as replacements the company streets of the 304th Infantry rang again and again with the strains of the song which had first been heard on the shores of Lake Champlain.

> Way up in Plattsburg, right near the northern border.
> They sent us off in May,
> There for three months to stay,
> So we could all become lieutenants.
> Then when they put us all in comp'nies
> We made New England Four.
> It's the finest little company
> That ever did Squads Right and ran into a tree.
> New England, you've got to hand it to us —
> Good old Company Four!

SOME PECULIARITIES OF THE WORLD WAR

THE World War is unique not only because of its magnitude and the number of men engaged but because of the peculiar conditions which developed on the Western Front. The war was fought by highly developed industrial nations whose nationals had a long inventive experience behind them. Behind the fighting lines scientists and practical mechanics were working feverishly to develop new devices of destruction or of defense against destructive weapons. The Germans surprised their foes with a gas attack and later developed the flame thrower. The British invented the tank. Each side sought to outdo the other in aviation. The technique of the use of wireless and the telephone in signal communications was mastered. The influence of industrial development was clearly marked in the ever more and more complex equipment of the troops.

569 Training in Trench Warfare at Fort Sill, Okla., from a photograph in the United States Signal Corps, War Department, Washington

But, if the war was fought with new devices which were the product of an industrial age, it also saw the revival of obsolescent weapons and practices. The stabilized warfare which developed on the Western Front caused the putting into practice on a gigantic scale the methods of siege warfare of the eighteenth century. The soldiers of the twentieth century had to familiarize themselves with trenches of all kinds, with parapets, parados, gabions, and fascines. The armies of France and Britain were in very truth besieging a fortress extending from the Swiss border to the sea. The almost forgotten hand grenade, that weapon of the eighteenth-century grenadiers, was snatched from obscurity and used with telling effect particularly by the French. In the World War the old and the new appeared side by side until the war assumed a complexity beyond that of any conflict hitherto known to man.

SCHOOLS

THE complexity of the war made the problem of developing raw recruits into trained soldiers a formidable one. The army had become in a very real sense an aggregation of specialists. The machine gunner must know the peculiarities and the tactical use of his piece. The same was true of the artilleryman. Specialization even entered the infantry, long considered the one unspecialized branch. The infantry regiment of the World War had its one-pounder and its trench mortar platoons, its signal communications platoon, and its intelligence section. The rifle companies had their automatic riflemen and their riflemen equipped with rifle grenade throwers. An army

570 Instruction in the use of a scissors instrument at Camp Taylor, Ky., from a photograph in the United States Signal Corps, War Department, Washington

numbering millions of men required the swift creation of millions of specialists. The school was the only possible solution of the problem. Every division of the Regular Army, the National Guard, and the National Army had under way from the very outset of its training an almost bewildering number of schools. Some were for officers, some for noncommissioned officers, and some for selected privates. At these the students received for one, two, or more weeks intensive and exclusive instruction in gas defense, the use of the bayonet,

571 A Scotch sergeant showing American troops how to charge over the top of a trench, from a photograph in the United States Signal Corps, War Department, Washington

grenade throwing, signal communications, cooking, and a multitude of other subjects. Sometimes the purpose of the school was merely the training of the students who attended the course. More often the students were expected to return to their regiments and become, in their turn, instructors. There were schools, like the School of Fire at Fort Sill, which drew artillery officers from all divisions. From the beginning to the end of the war the school system was the corner stone upon which rested the whole structure of army training. Without it an efficient A. E. F. could never have come into being.

FOREIGN OFFICERS

THE school system made possible the rapid transfer of knowledge from the fighting front to the more than two millions of men under arms in the United States. The British and French commanders selected officers for instruction duty with the troops in America. These men brought to the soldiers of the New World their first-hand knowledge of the fighting methods in use on the Western Front and they sought to carry with them across the Atlantic something of the spirit of the troops who for years now had been fighting the enemy. They taught American baseball players the technique of throwing the hand grenade. They brought with them that manual of the bayonet which the British had developed and which made them such formidable fighters with that terrible weapon. They explained the different methods for utilizing machine gun fire in offense and defense. They thrilled the Americans with vivid and technical accounts of certain important operations concerning which their hearers had only the knowledge to be derived from the newspapers. The foreign officer worked almost exclusively through the school. Through the selected students who passed under his instruction he made his influence felt throughout the army.

572 French officer giving instruction in use of hand grenades, from a photograph in the United States Signal Corps, War Department, Washington

573   Infantry on the march, from a photograph in the United States Signal Corps, War Department, Washington

THE WORK OF THE CAMPS

THE men of the National Guard and National Army had little time for sentiment. The cantonments were hives of activity. With a rapidity almost past belief the junior officers of the National Guard and the reserve officers recently graduated from the First and Second Officers' Training Camps, working under the direction of their more experienced seniors, turned into soldiers the raw material brought in by enlistments and the Selective Service Act. The training fields echoed to the sharp commands and the "hun, two, three, four" of close-order drill. Whistle and arm signals betokened the practice of open-order formations. Day after day the rifle and artillery ranges heard the crack of the Enfield rifle or the bark of the three-inch gun as company and battery were put through their range practice. There was constant physical drill to keep the men in the best condition.

574   Bayonet drill, from a photograph in the United States Signal Corps, War Department, Washington

575   Artillery training at Camp Kearney, Cal., from a photograph in the United States Signal Corps, War Department, Washington

576 Barbed wire entanglements at a training camp, from a photograph in the United States Signal Corps, War Department, Washington

577 Trench construction at a training camp, from a photograph in the United States Signal Corps, War Department, Washington

TRENCHES IN AMERICA

MUCH time was spent in the cantonments in teaching the technique of trench warfare. Elaborate trench systems were constructed with dugouts for P. C.'s (command posts) and telephone communication. Into these companies were put under simulated war conditions. They learned the methods of the defense of such field fortifications. They practiced "going over the top." They received instruction in "mopping up" conquered enemy trenches. The trench is primarily an instrument of defensive warfare. The Americans were being trained for offensive fight but they must understand fully the defensive arrangements of the enemy if they were to conquer him. And, from time to time, they, too, must resort to defensive measures. A thorough knowledge of trench warfare was essential to success.

578 Soldiers charging through gas while in training at Fort Lewis, Washington, from a photograph in the United States Signal Corps, War Department, Washington

579 American soldiers learning to adjust gas masks under the direction of French instructors, from a photograph in the United States Signal Corps, War Department, Washington

GAS WARFARE

THE American soldier received as part of his training instruction in gas warfare. He was taught the use of that hated piece of equipment, the gas mask. He was sent through a "gas house" filled with chlorine or an area saturated with gas in order that he might have a real experience of this new weapon of war. He did not enjoy it. In general he looked upon gas and the gas mask as among the most diabolical inventions of man.

580   American troops learning to make a night attack, from a photograph in the United States
Signal Corps, War Department, Washington

AMERICAN HAND GRENADE

THE picture shows the fragmented exterior of an American hand grenade with the lever which fired it. The object was, of course, to explode it among the enemy with the greatest effect at just the right time and distance. It was, therefore, so fragmented by indentations that each fragment would fly off from the common center. The apparatus on the top allowed the fuse to be set for the number of seconds required.

NIGHT ATTACK PRACTICE

THE experience of the armies on the Western Front had taught the importance of night fighting. Patrols were sent out under cover of darkness to reconnoiter the enemy lines or to cut his wire. Trench raids were usually night time enterprises. General offensives were frequently launched just before dawn. As a consequence the War Department emphasized the importance of training in the darkness.

581   Hand grenade, from a photograph in the United States Signal Corps, War Department, Washington

THE UNITED STATES ARMY RIFLE, 1917

IN 1908 the Springfield magazine rifle completely superseded the Krag, which it far surpassed in

582   Inspecting a British Enfield rifle, from a photograph in the United States
Signal Corps, War Department, Washington

speed, hitting force, and accuracy. But as there was no sufficient reserve, or even plant for manufacturing what the World War needed, the A. E. F. had to depend largely on Allied resources in this as in many other munitions of war. The British Enfield rifle was the weapon of the American infantryman during the conflict.

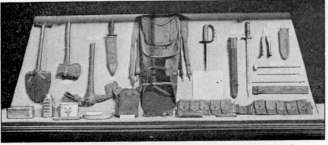

583   A. E. F. Equipment, from a photograph in the United States Signal
Corps, War Department, Washington

SOME A. E. F. EQUIPMENT

No single man ever carried all this equipment but a glance at this display will give some idea of what weapons were used in trench warfare. The soldier in the trenches not only had to shoot, cut, stab, and bludgeon enemies, but he also had to dig, chop, pick, cut, slash and camouflage the churned and tormented ground itself, with all its wire entanglements and other defenses.

THE COMPLETE DOUGHBOY

THIS fully trained and fully equipped American infantry veteran was sketched by Captain Harry Townsend in France as a good specimen of the typical doughboy.

LEWIS MACHINE GUN SHOULDER SHOOTING

THE picture shows a machine gunner of the Thirty-first Division at Camp Wheeler, Georgia, firing his weapon from the shoulder. The ordinary position was prone. The Lewis gun was a light weapon in the same class with the famous French Chauchaut. General Johnson Hagood's comment is pertinent, "The Lewis gun, invented by an American army officer, was good enough for the British. Next to the French seventy-five, it was perhaps the greatest weapon of the war. But it did not suit us. We wanted something better. We got it — too late to be of importance in the conflict."

584 The Complete Doughboy, from a sketch by Captain Harry Townsend, in the United States Signal Corps, War Department, Washington

585 Lewis Machine Gun in operation at Camp Wheeler, Georgia, from a photograph in the United States Signal Corps, War Department, Washington

586 Browning water-cooled machine gun, from a photograph in the United States Signal Corps, War Department, Washington

BROWNING MACHINE GUN

THE Browning machine gun was undoubtedly the best weapon of its kind developed during the war. It is a water-cooled gun capable of sustaining fire for a considerable period of time. Extra barrels are provided to take the place of those that become too hot. It is portable, relatively simple of mechanism, and capable of withstanding the rough usage of service conditions. The difficulty with the Browning, however, was that so much time was used up in developing it that the war was over before it could be of significance. Since the war the United States Army has perfected a machine gun of greater caliber and almost double the range of the Browning. It is a weapon vastly more formidable than any of the World War machine guns.

587   Machine gunners of the Twenty-ninth Division at Camp McClellan, from a photograph in the United States Signal Corps,
War Department, Washington

MACHINE GUNNERS

THE finished product into which the recruits were turned during the winter of 1917–18 was an efficient fighting force. The picture shows machine gunners equipped with Lewis guns. These men were fresh, vigorous, alert. They had inherited that individual initiative which has characterized the American fighter from the beginning.

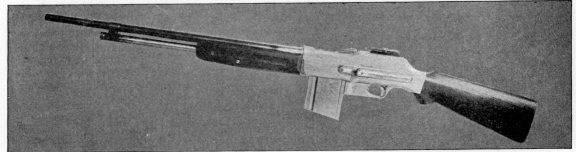

588   "Light Browning" Automatic Rifle, from a photograph in the United States Signal Corps, War Department, Washington

"LIGHT BROWNING" RIFLE

THIS air-cooled, light-weight, automatic rifle was authorized for the army early in 1918. It weighed only fifteen pounds, and could be fired from hip or shoulder in twenty-round bursts, or else by single shots. To facilitate ammunition supply it took the same cartridge as the Springfield. In the World War these guns were usually fired from the hip. Since the war this practice has been given up as less effective and the guns are fired from the shoulder in bursts of two or three shots.

589   Drill with dummy guns at Camp Lewis, Washington, from a photograph
in the United States Signal Corps, War Department, Washington

DRILL WITH DUMMY GUNS

EMBRYO artillerymen, as at Camp Lewis in the illustration, were compelled to begin with dummy wooden guns because there were not enough of the real ones even at the very end of 1917.

UNITED STATES THREE–INCHERS AND FRENCH SEVENTY–FIVES

THE American three-inch field gun was never used in France, because the war was over before this gun was ready. The photograph shows the famous French "Seventy-five," so called from its seventy-five millimeter bore. This was the gun which the A. E. F. had to use because its own could not be made in time.

590   French Seventy-fives, from a photograph by International Newsreel, New York

SEVENTY–NINTH INFANTRY BRIGADE SUPPLY TRAIN

To bring supplies on time to the points where they were needed was a complex task.   The picture shows a Brigade Supply Train learning its work in California during the spring of 1918.

591   Supply train of the 79th Infantry Brigade at Del Mar, California, from a photograph in the United States Signal Corps, War Department, Washington

592   Rolling kitchen in France, from a photograph in the United States Signal Corps, War Department, Washington

ROLLING KITCHEN

ON September 12, 1918, when the Americans began their drive against the salient of St. Mihiel, this United States rolling kitchen followed the advance of the victorious troops. Twelve miles from breakfast to lunch, twenty altogether before the evening meal, was the record of that day, when no doughboy failed to get his "chow."

593   Training in use of Signal Corps equipment, from a photograph in the United States Signal Corps, War Department, Washington

SIGNAL CORPS TRAINING AT CAMP McCLELLAN, FEBRUARY, 1918

THE Signal Corps was responsible for every means of signal communication known to military men, from "wig-wagging" to telephone and wireless. These chapters have shown already what an immense amount of original evidence for the American part of the World War is to be found in the official photographs taken by the Signal Corps.

594   Student aviator assembling a Lewis gun blindfolded, from a photograph in the United States Signal Corps, War Department, Washington

STUDENT AVIATOR BEING TESTED IN ADAPTABILITY

ONE of many hundreds of prospective aviators is this blindfolded student at the School of Military Aeronautics, University of California, who is being given only seventy seconds to "assemble" an aircraft machine gun.

THE MEDICAL SERVICE

To many members of the National Guard or National Army drill is not the most vivid recollection of the cantonment phase of their army experience. Their minds run back to those endless weeks of quarantine when no one could go on pass and when the company to which they happened to belong was held under the strictest discipline as virtual prisoners merely because one member had contracted the mumps or the measles. The regimental surgeons and their assisting "medicos" were the tyrants of the quarantine and they were heartless enough to extend it when new cases of disease broke out in the company during the original quarantine period. These medical officers were determined that, so far as it lay within their power, the soldiers of the United States during their period of training should keep well. These same officers had given every man who came to the regiment as a recruit a searching physical examination and had sent home many whom the local medical boards had passed. Every morning one or more of these officers listened to and prescribed for the ailments of those men who answered to sick call. Their inspections of the personnel and quarters of the various units in the regiment were never ending. They gave the innoculations to prevent typhoid and paratyphoid and vaccinated against small pox. Their activities were of basic importance to the defense of the nation. The prevalence of disease which had marked previous wars of the American people did not prevail until that dread plague, known as the "flu," invaded the United States and attacked citizens and soldiers alike. In this dread time the medical service was taxed to the utmost at home and abroad.

The spirit of the men under these restraints is reflected by a song of the Fourth Company of the Third Officers' Training Camp at Camp Devens sung to the tune, *Three Crows:*

> One, two, three, four —
> The Fourth is on its toes.
> They say we've got the measles
> And they've got us here for keeps.
> We're under Doctor's orders
> And we won't get out for weeks.
> But we can drill the best and march the best
> And laugh at all our woes,
> And it's one, two, three, four —
> The Fourth is on its toes.

In every cantonment a base hospital cared for cases too serious to be handled by the regimental surgeons with the resources at their disposal. In these hospitals labored that splendid corps of volunteer nurses.

595   Spraying soldiers' throats at Camp Wheeler, Ga., from a photograph in the United States Signal Corps, War Department, Washington

596 Field ambulance drill at Camp Hancock, from a photograph in the United States Signal Corps,
War Department, Washington

FIELD AMBULANCE DRILL AT CAMP HANCOCK

BETWEEN the battlefield and nearest hospital the Field Ambulance plied its beneficent trade in sick and wounded men. But its own personnel required much careful training before its work could be a really efficient aid to armies at the front. So practice, practice, practice was the order of the day at every training station in the land. Physicians who volunteered for duty were for the most part put through medical officers' schools in which they were taught how to cope with the peculiar problems which confront the medical corps. Particularly those men who were to be attached to regiments must be soldiers as well as doctors. They had to learn the hated army "paper work," morning reports, rotation requisitions, and a hundred other things unfamiliar to civilian life. Cut No. 597 shows stretcher practice under the conditions of trench warfare. Many a man had to be lifted out of the trenches when one false move might mean death. Therefore trench stretcher drill was most assiduously taught.

597 Drill in lifting wounded from the trenches, from a photograph in the United States Signal Corps, War Department, Washington

GENERAL WILLIAM C. GORGAS

CIVILIANS are apt to forget how much the efficiency of the fighting services owes to the devoted work of their non-combatant branches, to good commissaries and others in the supply departments, or to good army doctors. General William C. Gorgas "cleaned up" Cuba, killed yellow fever all over the Panama Canal Zone, and made an admirable Surgeon-General of the United States Army during the World War.

598 Maj.-Gen. William C. Gorgas, 1854–1920, from a photograph in the United States Signal Corps, War Department, Washington

599   Artillery training at Camp Taylor, Kentucky, from a photograph in the United States Signal Corps,
War Department, Washington

THE THIRD OFFICERS' TRAINING CAMP

AFTER the conclusion of the Second Officers' Training Camp the War Department changed the methods of recruiting officer candidates. In the division cantonments throughout the country officers' training camps were instituted and their students drawn from the enlisted personnel of the local division. These camps were highly efficient, profiting as they did by the experience of their predecessors. Their candidates were almost universally men of high caliber. They had the great advantage over the candidates of the first and second camps of being soldiers before undertaking their officer training. They had been privates. They knew how the enlisted man felt and what were his joys and sorrows. They had the *élan* of men who had lifted themselves by their own efforts, from privates to corporals, from corporals to sergeants, and from sergeants to the officers' school. The spirit of these men on graduation was the spirit of the American army at its best. "We are an experiment — we of the Third Officers' Training Camp. And we know it. We have been an experiment since that fateful day last summer when the War Department determined to see what the National Army could do in the way of providing its own officers out of its own ranks. We are still an experiment, and we will be until each one of us is set down upon the soil of Europe. . . . We have been disciplined, drilled, trained; we have been taught the fundamentals of what the word soldier means; we hope that we have developed, in so far as our individual limitations have permitted, the essential qualities which make men fit for leadership. Beyond that we cannot go, yet. But whatever transpires, however we are used, whatever duty is given each one of us to do, we stand firm in the belief that the United States can at least expect of us what she does expect. The rest is up to us." — *The Pick* (publication of the Third Officers' Training Camp at Camp Devens), **7.**

600   Training in signalling at Camp Taylor, Kentucky, from a photograph in the United States Signal Corps,
War Department, Washington

THE BREAKDOWN OF THE WAR DEPARTMENT

WHILE training was progressing apace in the cantonments, all was not well with the War Department. General Johnson Hagood, Chief of Staff of the S.O.S., has made a sharp analysis of the conditions which brought about some of the most outstanding American failures of the war. "The fourteen years, 1903 to 1917, during which the General Staff had been in existence had not been spent in making plans for war . . . but in squabbling over the control of the routine peace-time administration and supply and in attempts to put the blame for unpreparedness upon Congress. . . . But our unpreparedness did not come from lack of money, lack of soldiers, or lack of supplies. It came from lack of brains, or perhaps it would be fairer to say, lack of genius. For example, if between 1914 and 1917 anyone had had the brains — or the genius — to decide that if we did get into the war, we should use the designs of the British or French guns being manufactured in this country, instead of trying to invent some new design of our own, we should not have spent a billion dollars on artillery without firing a hostile shot. . . . And if between 1914 and 1917 anyone had had the brains — or the genius — to decide that if we got into the war, we should use airplanes of British or French design instead of trying to invent new ones of our own, we should not have spent another billion dollars without getting a single combat plane to the front.

601　Colonel Arthur L. Wagner, 1853–1905, from the portrait in the United States Military Academy, West Point

And why between 1914 and 1917 did we not have the brains — or the genius — to send someone to Europe to find out something about war cantonment construction instead of spending millions upon millions erecting ridiculous little villages, with concrete streets and sidewalks, with the most modern and expensive plumbing and everything else, regardless of cost or time, and then have the war close down on us before the job was finished? . . . If with five times as much motor transportation as all the rest of the world combined, we had only sent some of it to France instead of trying to standardize design and manufacture! . . . Pages could be written about what the General Staff should have been doing and was not doing between 1903 and 1917, especially after the conflagration started and we saw it coming our way . . . the whole General Staff and War Department organization, generally, fell like a house of cards and a new organization had to be created during the process of the war. . . . As I was on duty in the War Department for seven of the fourteen years of misspent energy, it might be asked why, seeing these things, I did not do something to correct them. The answer is that I did not see them or, seeing them, did not understand. Hindsight is better than foresight, and I, like all the rest, did not have the brains — or the genius — to see preparedness in its true light." — *The Services of Supply*, 23–27. Wagner was one of the severest critics of the War Department, seeking always greater efficiency of the military organization.

602　French Renault Tanks used by American troops, from a photograph in the United States Signal Corps, War Department, Washington

603 General Tasker H. Bliss, 1853–, from a photograph by the
United States Signal Corps, War Department, Washington

CHANGING PERSONNEL IN THE WAR DEPARTMENT

AFTER General Scott was relieved as Chief of the General Staff General Tasker H. Bliss occupied that post. General Bliss reached the age of retirement on December 31, 1917, but the President decided that he should retain his position with Major-General Biddle as Assistant Chief. During most of 1917 Major-General H. G. Sharpe was Quartermaster-General, Major-General E. M. Weaver was Chief of Artillery, Major-General W. Crozier was Chief of Ordnance, and the Judge-Advocate-General who was also Provost-Marshal-General in charge of the draft was Major-General E. H. Crowder. On December 18 some important changes were made. Major-General George W. Goethals was recalled to duty and appointed Acting-Quartermaster-General in place of Sharpe. Weaver was relieved by Brigadier-General Barette while Brigadier-General Charles Wheeler assumed the duties of Crozier. These changes did not, however, complete the reorganization of the War Department. That task had, in fact, only begun.

THE ATTACK UPON THE WAR DEPARTMENT

DURING the autumn of 1917 rumblings of discontent at the inefficiency of the War Department were heard.

Finally on January 19, 1918, the storm broke when Senator Chamberlain, a Democrat from Oregon, publicly criticized the war preparations of the National Government in a speech at New York city and charged that the War Department had "fallen down." President Wilson rallied to the support of Secretary Baker and issued a stinging reply. But the senator returned to the attack and the Senate Committee on Military Affairs began

a series of hearings on the subject. On January 28 Secretary Baker himself appeared before the committee. He defended his department vigorously and explained many apparent failures. He emphasized in particular the care of the soldiers. "We have got those young men in camp, and they are surrounded, from the day they left home until the day they come back to it, if in God's providence they can come back, with more agencies for their protection and comfort and health and happiness, physical, spiritual, and mental, than any army that ever went out on a field." He called attention to the fine work of branches like the Medical Corps, the Signal Corps, and the Engineering Department and added "when it is all told, Mr. Chairman, it will be a story which I am sure your committee will be glad to report to the Senate of the United States as being a tremendous response to a tremendous responsibility, and when you have [completed] this investigation I know that the American people will feel, as I think they have a right to feel, that we are in this war to win it; that we are in it to hit, and hit hard; that we are in it to coördinate our strength with that of our associates; that the problem is not one of individual star playing, but of team play . . . that more has been done, perhaps, than the country expected — more than the wisest in the country thought possible to do."

604 Newton D. Baker, 1871–, from a photograph in the United
States Signal Corps, War Department, Washington

GENERAL PEYTON C. MARCH, 1864–

On February 6 was announced the appointment of Major-General Peyton C. March as Acting Chief of the General Staff. At the time of his appointment he was Chief of Artillery under Pershing in France. He replaced General Tasker H. Bliss, who, while nominally Acting Chief of the General Staff, was actually in France serving as the American military representative on the Inter-Allied War Council. Two estimates of March by brother officers will suggest the quality of the man whom Baker put in charge of the War Department. "General March had been through the Russo-Japanese War as an observer. He had gone with Pershing's expedition to France and knew our conditions there. He was a practical man who knew the War Department thoroughly, having served there both as a General Staff officer and as an Adjutant General. He was keen, cold-blooded, and quick on the trigger. He turned the War Department upside down and organized it on a working basis." — Hagood, 25. "Our staff and supply officers," wrote General Bullard of conditions in France in the fall of 1917, "had from necessity to answer calls with promises: 'We expect to'; 'We are going to'; 'We will when —'; but rarely, oh so rarely, could they say: 'Yes, here it is'; 'Granted, go ahead.' And this continued so long and so wearily, with one result, failure, that I for one soon

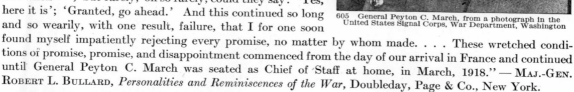

605   General Peyton C. March, from a photograph in the United States Signal Corps, War Department, Washington

found myself impatiently rejecting every promise, no matter by whom made. . . . These wretched conditions of promise, promise, and disappointment commenced from the day of our arrival in France and continued until General Peyton C. March was seated as Chief of Staff at home, in March, 1918." — Maj.-Gen. Robert L. Bullard, *Personalities and Reminiscences of the War*, Doubleday, Page & Co., New York.

606   Edward R. Stettinius, 1865–, from a photograph by Harris & Ewing, Washington

THE REORGANIZATION OF THE WAR DEPARTMENT

Four days after the announcement of the appointment of General March a thoroughgoing reorganization of the War Department was outlined in an order issued by Secretary Baker. "The planning of the army program in its entirety," the order said, "the constant development thereof in its larger aspects, and the relation of this program to the General Staff and the entire army will be the duty of the Chief of Staff and the War Council." The Chief of Staff was to be the immediate adviser of the Secretary on all matters relating to the military establishment. Five divisions of the General Staff were organized as follows: an Executive Division under an Executive Assistant to the Chief of Staff, a War Plans Division under a Director, a Purchase and Supply Division under a Director, a Storage and Traffic Division under a Director, and an Army Operations Division under a Director. The Senate committee had criticized particularly the army purchasing system as supervised by the Council of National Defense. So the new order set forth the scope of the Purchase and Supply Division in great detail. More than two weeks before the order was issued Edward R. Stettinius, of J. P. Morgan and Company, had been appointed Surveyor-General of all army purchases.

607　　American women sewing for the soldiers, from a photograph in the United States Signal Corps, War Department, Washington

THE WORK OF THE WOMEN

WHILE the War Department was being revamped to meet the needs of the crisis the women of America were meeting the emergency with a spirit equal to their brothers. The well-nigh forgotten art of knitting was suddenly revived and millions of needles clicked incessantly producing socks, sweaters, mufflers and helmets to be distributed to the soldiers. The most approved methods for "turning heels" entered into the discussions of the sewing circles. Other groups of women specialized on the making of bandages. A call for nurses went forth and was answered by volunteering akin in spirit to that of the men.

608　　A group of girls making surgical dressings, from a photograph in the United States Signal Corps, War Department, Washington

WOMEN IN INDUSTRY

THE war drained the industries and offices of America of necessary men. Women stepped in to take the place of the workers who had gone. An idle woman was looked upon as a "slacker." The spirit of service which permeated the army found its counterpart in the communities from which the soldier came. The war gave to the American woman her greatest opportunity. Taboos and prejudices which had come down from antiquity and which were being weakened by the economic developments of the late nineteenth and early twentieth centuries were suddenly swept away. In a trice women achieved economic equality, quickly followed by political equality. But this victory in 1917 and 1918 was incidental. In these years American women were mobilized to win the war. Other considerations were forgotten as they gave their thought and energies to the accomplishment of their mission.

609　Woman munitions worker at the Frankfort Arsenal, from a photograph in the United States Signal Corps, War Department, Washington

THE ROAD TO FRANCE

BEFORE the end of 1917 a considerable force had gone to France. As the months of January and February, 1918, saw the northern cantonments held in the grip of winter, division after division quietly embarked for duty overseas. The American people were stirred as they had not been since the Civil War as they bade good-bye to the boys home for the last time on pass or as they lined the streets of their great cities and watched the divisions of which they were so proud put on their last parades before entraining for the transports.

"GOOD–BYE, SOLDIER BOYS!"

THE spirit and thinking of war-time America bidding farewell to the boys trained for war and embarking for service overseas is nowhere shown more clearly than in an editorial in the Oakland (California) *Enquirer* when Oakland's first contribution marched away. "The lads that go now . . . go to bleed and do and die in a war that is fought under water, on the surface, and in the air above. They go to face the clouds of poisonous gas and the barrage of fire. They go in the face of all these, to give

610 The Seventy-seventh Division leaves New York, from the painting by Clifford Carleton

blow for blow, to pit American wits, initiative and courage against these qualities in the servants of imperial ambition. . . . They go, God's own avengers of the unspeakable suffering of the people of Belgium, Northern France, Poland, Serbia, Rumania and Armenia. As they march, unseen in the clear air above them are the spirits of the American mothers and babies that perished in the roaring sea, murdered in the *Lusitania*. They go to cleanse the earth of the men who began by violating treaties and have progressed by violating the common promptings of humanity which have been held sacred even by the red Indians of America and the black tribes of Africa.

611 Watching their soldiers march away, from a photograph by Underwood & Underwood, New York

"They are the armed guards of American honor, of the covenants of Almighty God. On this great mission we send them with every blessing, with every ascription of honor. They go to prove that this great Republic is great not only in material things, in its proud cities, its far-flung fields, and its laden orchards and purpling vineyards, but great in the ineffable things of the spirit, in the courage of its people and in its purpose to fling high and far the banners of the best civilization created by man. Goodbye, boys, acquit yourselves like men!"

CHAPTER XIV

ORGANIZATION AND SUPPLY OF THE A. E. F.

THE problem of organizing an American army in France large enough to play an effective part in the war was vastly different from that which confronted either the French or the British military leaders. The former were fighting on their own soil and had at hand a military organization built up many years before the outbreak of the conflict. The British army lay just across the English channel from the home base. The A. E. F. was three thousand miles from its base and dependent for men and supplies on water transportation that was subject to the unremitting menace of the submarine. The War Department in Washington could not direct the organization and supply of the A. E. F. in the detail which was possible from the war offices of Paris and London. The War Department retained control over the troops training in the United States and over the forwarding of men and supplies to France but it controlled the A. E. F. chiefly through its supervision of the commander in chief of the American forces abroad.

One of the first problems which General Pershing confronted was, therefore, the creation of a General Headquarters which was located in the little village of Chaumont. In this should be centered the staff departments without which it would be impossible for the army to function. A corollary to the general problem of building up a G. H. Q. was the creation of an organization for the receiving, storage, and transportation of supplies from America. Before making his initial decisions regarding both these problems General Pershing and the small staff which he took with him made a survey of the solutions of British and French for similar problems. Pershing selected those methods and arrangements of the Allies which seemed best suited to American needs. He did not hesitate to depart from European practice where he thought such departure would be for the best interest of the American cause. From the point of view of the American army Pershing's work was that of a pioneer. The staff organization which he developed in France was new to the American service. The exigencies of the war were such that it was never perfected. At best it was a hasty improvisation. This should not have been true for the basic principles and organization should have been worked out in time of peace. The fact that Pershing had to perform such fundamental labor in the face of the enemy is the measure of American unpreparedness for war. The A. E. F. has sometimes been criticized for confusion and what seemed sometimes almost like imbecility in its use of certain men. The phrase, "the army way of doing things," took on an implication of inefficiency. The fundamental reasons for the confusion were the lack of preparation in time of peace for the emergency and the demands of war in that critical spring and summer of 1918 when the conflict was almost lost. In months when American soldiers were flooding into France at a prodigious rate and when anxiety daily increased as Von Hindenburg developed his mighty drive, the wonder is not that there was confusion in the A. E. F., but that there was so little of it. Since the conclusion of hostilities this pioneer work of Pershing and his associates has been used as the basis for perfecting the staff organization of the Army of the United States.

PERSHING'S MISSION

PARAGRAPH five of the President's instructions to General (then Major-General) Pershing dated May 26, 1917, reads as follows: "In military operations against the Imperial German Government, you are directed to coöperate with the forces of the other countries employed against that enemy; but in so doing the underlying idea must be kept in view that the forces of the United States are a separate and distinct component of the combined forces, the identity of which must be preserved. This fundamental rule is subject to such minor exceptions in particular circumstances as your judgment may approve. The decision as to when your command, or any of its parts, is ready for action is confided to you, and you will exercise full discretion in determining the manner of coöperation. But until the forces of the United States are in your judgment sufficiently strong to warrant coöperation as an independent command, it is understood that you will coöperate as a component of whatever army you may be assigned to by the French Government." Pershing was destined to meet many difficult problems in complying with this order.

613   General Pershing, from the painting by Douglas Volk in the National Museum, Washington

ARMY ARTILLERY

612   Army Artillery, from a chart *General Organization Project*, Approved, July 11, 1917, in General Pershing's *Final Report*

GENERAL PERSHING

IN February, 1918, General (then Colonel) Johnson Hagood jotted down his impressions of the man whom President Wilson had chosen to lead the American army in the World War. "I have never in my life been so impressed with anyone as I was with General Pershing last night. He talked in a quiet, familiar way, speaking of the biggest projects of the war in the same simple language and as if he were discussing the minor routine of an army post and at the same time indicating his absolute mastery of the whole situation. I said I hoped I would have a chance for an active command at the front and would not have to spend the entire war in the L.O.C. [Line of Communications, later S.O.S.]. He replied that everyone should be proud to participate in this greatest conflict in the history of the world, no matter in what capacity; that when the war broke out he had hoped of course to be in it, but that he never dreamed that he would be Commander-in-Chief; that he probably would not continue so, but that he was willing to continue in any capacity; and that if he had his real desire, he would command a regiment, as this was the highest command in close touch with soldiers." — *The Services of Supply*, 136.

614   United States troops in London, from a photograph in the United
States Signal Corps, War Department, Washington

THE GREAT DECISION

WHEN Pershing arrived in France, General Nivelle's drive had failed and General Petain had taken his place. Marshal Haig was making an effort to secure the submarine bases at Ostend and Zeebrugge which was destined to achieve only a partial success. The Allied plan, in fact, called for a strategic defensive on the Western Front awaiting the arrival of the American forces. For some time England and France had been organizing and training their forces on the theory that they would be used in trench warfare or "war of position" as it had come to be called. As already noted, the British were emphasizing the bayonet and the French the hand grenade. Both they and their enemy were also exploiting the machine gun. The advantage of the war of position was that it conserved man power, a vital necessity for nations that had already suffered appalling losses. The weakness of the plan was that it made a decisive victory practically impossible and offered scant hope for anything but a negotiated peace. Pershing estimated that the United States was the only nation with sufficient man power, fresh and vigorous, to break the will of the enemy. This could only be done by driving him out of his trenches. The American commander understood that the machine gun, that unsurpassed weapon of defense, would make the accomplishment of this purpose exceedingly costly. He decided, however, that America had no alternative but to pay the price. He, therefore, ordered that the training of American troops should be founded on the theory that they would be used in offensive maneuver warfare and that the American infantry should look to the rifle and bayonet as the chief weapons with which to defeat the enemy. On July 6, 1917, he cabled Washington "Plans should contemplate sending over at least one million men by next May."

A BASIC ORDER

IN October, 1917, the commander in chief published his decision in a general order that ranks as one of the most important of the war. "1 . . . (b) All instruction must contemplate the assumption of a vigorous offensive. This purpose will be emphasized in every phase of training until it becomes a settled habit of thought. (c) The general principles governing combat remain unchanged in their essence. This war has developed special phases of training, but the fundamental ideas enunciated in our Drill Regulations and other service manuals remain the guide for both officers and soldiers and constitute the standard by which their efficiency is to be measured, except as modified in detail by instructions from these headquarters. (d) The rifle and bayonet are the principal weapons of the infantry soldier. He will be trained to a high degree of skill as a marksman, both on the target range and in field firing. An aggressive spirit must be developed until the soldier feels himself, as a bayonet fighter, invincible in battle. (e) All officers and soldiers should realize that at no time in our history has discipline been so important; therefore discipline of the highest order must be exacted at all times. The standards of the American army will be those of West Point. The rigid attention, upright bearing, attention to detail, uncomplaining obedience to instructions required of the Cadet will be required of every officer and soldier of our Armies in France."

615   French instructors of American troops, from a photograph in the United States Signal
Corps, War Department, Washington

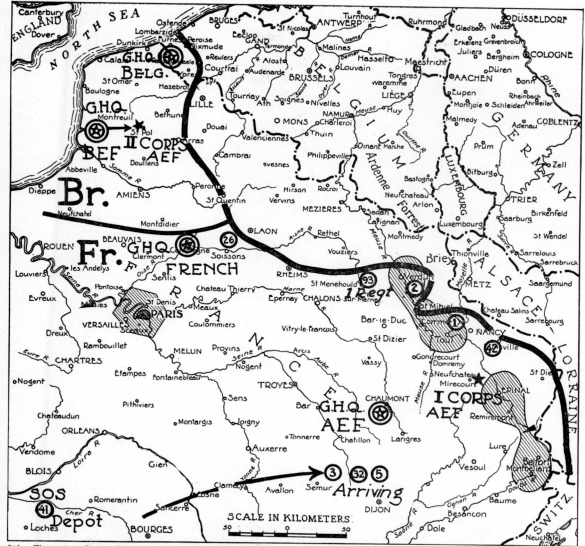

616   The western theater of operations, March 20, 1918, from Brig.-Gen. C. R. Howland, *Military History of the World War*, General Service Schools Press, Fort Leavenworth, Kansas, 1923. Figures in circles indicate locations of American Divisions

SELECTION OF AN AMERICAN FRONT

HAVING decided upon a general plan Pershing turned his attention to the problem of determining in consultation with the French and British the zone of action for the army which he led. He was guided by his mission and by certain peculiarities of the Western Front. Because his mission was an aggressive one he must choose a front from which he could deliver a decisive blow against the Germans. His choice was limited by the fact that the most effective place for the British to fight was at the northern end of the Allied line where they were near their bases on the Channel. The French, moreover, were bound to fight in front of Paris. Considerations of strategy as well as expediency pointed to the front from Verdun to the Swiss border as the logical line from which to deliver the American effort. This was, in fact, the most sensitive German area on the Western Front. A successful penetration in the direction of Metz would secure the Briey iron mines, vital to the Germans for the manufacture of munitions, would threaten the Saar coal mines, and, if pushed far enough, would cut the German line of communications south to the Ardenne forest and compel the retirement of the German armies from France. The supply of an American army operating in the Lorraine region would, moreover, interfere least with the supply arrangements of the Allied armies. The event proved that the choice of the front on which the American troops should operate was wisely made.

617   Chaumont, from a drawing by Captain J. André Smith, in the United States Signal
                            Corps, War Department, Washington

PERSHING AT CHAUMONT, SEPTEMBER 3, 1917

ON September 3, 1917, General Pershing established G.H.Q. at Chaumont, a small and relatively inaccessible village off the main routes of travel. Perhaps this is the reason why the French were not using it and why Pershing found it vacant. Here he established the organization which represented his solution of the staff problem of the army. As finally organized the General Staff at G.H.Q. consisted of an Administrative Section, usually called G1; an Intelligence Section, G2; an Operations Section, G3; a Supply Section, G4; and a Training Section, G5. The abbreviations were a useful and time-saving feature of the plan. The staffs of the corps and divisions had divisions corresponding to those of the General Staff save that G4 was merged with G1 and G5 with G3. The organization and the nomenclature were new to the American army in which the development of the staff had lagged far behind that in European armies. The soundness of Pershing's work may be judged by comparing it with the staff organization of the United States Army in the second quarter of the twentieth century. In this army the staff is divided into four instead of five groups; G1, Personnel; G2, Intelligence; G3, Plans and Training; and G4, Supply. In the World War this staff organization extended only as far as the division; since the war it has been extended to include the battalion. A staff officer is an assistant to the commander and aids him in making his decisions.

618   General Headquarters at Chaumont, from a drawing by Captain J. André Smith, in the
                            United States Signal Corps, War Department, Washington

AN IMPRESSION OF CHAUMONT, JULY, 1918

"G.H.Q. a shock. Expected to see Gen. Pershing like Napoleon at Friedland, on white charger, spy glass under arm, surrounded by gold laced officers in swords and high boots. Found instead group huge stone barracks, around court, with million typewriters clicking at once. Reminded me of Sears Roebuck. More field clerks and stenogs than soldiers, though slight concession to fitness of things in sentries, band and retreat with bugles." — *Wine, Women and War*, 159, Anonymous.

THE LINE OF COMMUNICATIONS

AFTER the selection of a probable front the next most pressing problem was the arranging of a system of supply for the combatant troops who would occupy the lines in the Lorraine region. On July 11 General Pershing had cabled to Washington a plan of organization for combat troops from the brigade through the army corps and the army. This was the basis for the War Department reorganization order noted on page 246. Less than a month later, August 5, the commander in chief forwarded his solution for the problem of supply. Behind the Zone of Operations was the Line of Communications, later known as the Services of Supply, or S.O.S. This was divided into six Base Sections, an Intermediate Section, and an Advance Section. The Base Sections were the areas in which men and supplies were received from the United States. The southern Atlantic ports of France, particularly St. Nazaire and Bordeaux, were selected for the receipt of supplies, forwarding of which from these cities would cause the least dislocation of the railway service behind the French lines. The whole French coast, however, had to be organized in order to provide for the vast inflow of troops and materials which the emergency of 1918 made necessary. The Intermediate Section

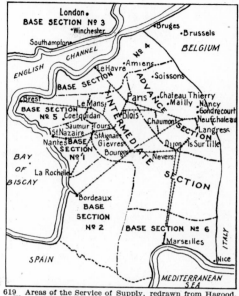

619   Areas of the Service of Supply, redrawn from Hagood, *The Services of Supply*, Houghton Mifflin Company, Boston, 1927

contained the main storage depots. These were far enough in the rear of the Zone of Operations for safety and near enough to be easily accessible. The Advance Section in the immediate rear of the Zone of Operations contained the billeting and training areas of the earlier arriving divisions. Within it supplies were distributed directly to combat troops whether in training or on the line. The original order provided for the distribution of reserve supplies; forty-five days' supplies in the Base Sections, thirty in the Intermediate, and fifteen in the Advance Section.

AMERICAN DIVISIONS IN FRANCE IN 1917

EARLY in the morning of June 26, 1917, a crowd of silent French people at St. Nazaire watched an American convoy come up the harbor and move to the docks. To these French men and women the memory of the defeat of their army two months before along the Chemin des Dames was still vivid. They were depressed; they did not, at first, sense the significance of the arrival of the Americans. The troops were organized in France into the First Division and were moved by rail to the Gondrecourt Area for training. In September the first elements of the Twenty-sixth Division, made up of the New England National Guard, set foot in France and proceeded to their training area, about Neufchateau. In September also the arrival of Marine and Regular Army regiments made possible the organization of the Second Division with one brigade, the Third, of infantry soldiers and the other, the Fourth, of Marines. In October and November the Forty-second or Rainbow Division made up of National Guard units from almost every state assembled in the Valcoulers Area. In December the Forty-first Division, made up of the National Guard of the Northwestern states, was ordered to St. Aignan and transformed into the First Depot Division. Its function was to train and equip replacements. By January 1, 1918, General Pershing had in France one depot division and four combat divisions. On that day the German drive of 1918 was scarcely eleven weeks off.

620   Disembarkation of the Fifth Marines at a French port, from a photograph in the United States Signal Corps, War Department, Washington

621   Maj.-Gen. Francis J. Kernan, 1859–, from a
photograph in the United States Signal Corps, War
Department, Washington

THE INADEQUACY OF THE LINE
OF COMMUNICATIONS

IN late autumn, 1917, Major-General Francis J. Kernan was appointed commanding General of the L.O.C. when the headquarters of the organization were at Paris. On December 2 Colonel Johnson Hagood reported to Kernan as Chief of Staff. On January 15 the headquarters of the L.O.C. were moved to Tours where they remained throughout the war. The Hôtel Métropole was the first building used for offices. "I began at once to look for more space," wrote Hagood, "but this was resisted by G.H.Q. I estimated that we needed two hundred and fifty thousand square feet, or fifteen times what we had, but even this estimate was too small, as we eventually occupied more than a million square feet of office space in the city of Tours, which is the equivalent of a sixteen-story building a quarter of a mile long." — *The Services of Supply*, 118. But in the very month in which the move was made the faultiness of the arrangements for the L.O.C. was becoming apparent. The chief weakness was the complete mutual independence of the officers in charge of supply and those in charge of transportation. By the end of January a reorganization was imperative. The supply service was failing in the mission assigned to it by General Orders No. 73 organizing the Line of Communications. "The function of the L. of C. is to relieve the combatant field forces from every consideration except that of defeating the enemy."

THE BIRTH OF THE S.O.S.

ON February 8, 1918, General Pershing appointed a board "to consider the desirability of any changes in the present organization of the Headquarters A. E. F." Colonel Hagood was senior officer and with him were associated Colonel A. D. Andrews, Lieutenant-Colonel F. R. McCoy, Lieutenant-Colonel R. C. Davis, and Major S. P. Wetherill. As a result of their work a new plan of organization was devised which provided for that "single and direct line of responsibility for all matters of supply" which was vital to efficiency. The new scheme also relieved "the Commander-in-Chief from the immediate direction of the administration of supply and placed direct and complete responsibility therefor upon some other competent authority." In March "was launched the great S.O.S., christened by General Pershing, himself, the 'Services of Supply,' but usually called at Tours the 'Service of Supply' or simply the 'S.O.S.' The organization thus created remained in effect without material change until the Armistice. . . . The command changed from Kernan to Harbord on July 29th . . . but all the principal staff officers and the general method of doing business remained the same, subject, of course, to a tremendous expansion and to a very rapid and healthy growth to keep pace with the steady increase in the number of arriving troops." — HAGOOD, 157.

622   Headquarters of the S.O.S. at Tours, from a photograph in the United States Signal Corps,
War Department, Washington

THE FLOW OF SUPPLIES

THE diagram illustrates the flow of supplies from their original source to the combat troops. It should be noted that the S.O.S. headquarters at Tours controlled the flow as far as the advance depots. The direct line from the base depots to the advance depots was an emergency precaution of fundamental importance. The liaison between Headquarters S.O.S. and G.H.Q. was maintained by direct telephone wires and by a special train, known as the "Atterbury Special," which ran each day between Tours and Chaumont. The Assistant Chief of Staff for Supply (G4) at G.H.Q. at Chaumont controlled the flow from the advance depots to the troops. He directed it by means of orders to the regulating officers in charge of the regulating stations. This was the line of responsibility and control which was established by the Hagood Board.

THE WORK OF THE S.O.S.

THE tremendous task which confronted the S.O.S. is made clear in Hagood's account. "On March 1, 1918, we had two hundred and thirty-three thousand troops in France. The rate of arrival during the preceding sixty days had been about one thousand per day. Under the programme of two million men in France by January, 1919, this rate of arrival would have to be increased to five thousand per day. . . . On March 1st we were discharging about seven thousand tons of cargo per day. . . . British experience indicated that forty pounds of freight of all kinds per man per day was necessary to keep their army going. But the Americans were attempting to do a great deal more than the British. We were planning to build railroads with American rails and cross-ties and to operate them with American locomotives and cars. We were planning to dredge harbors and build docks. . . . No artillery brigade had yet fired fourteen million dollars' worth of ammunition in ninety days. It did not seem likely, therefore, that the American Army could make out with less than the British allowance of forty pounds per man per day. Two million men in France meant forty thousand tons every twenty-four hours. It seemed impossible to increase our rate of discharge sixfold, so we determined upon the arbitrary figure of twenty-five thousand tons per day and determined to find a way to get this much unloaded." — HAGOOD, 158–59. The problems of the S.O.S. give an idea of the magnitude of the American effort.

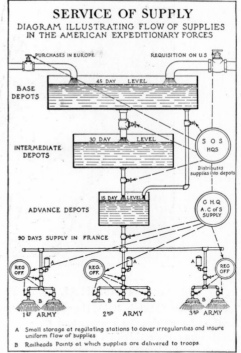

SERVICE OF SUPPLY
DIAGRAM ILLUSTRATING FLOW OF SUPPLIES IN THE AMERICAN EXPEDITIONARY FORCES

A Small storage at regulating stations to cover irregularities and insure uniform flow of supplies
B Railheads Points at which supplies are delivered to troops

623   From Bond and Crouch, *Tactics*, New Military Library, Annapolis, 1923

624   Unloading War Material at St. Nazaire, from a drawing in the United States Signal Corps, War Department, Washington

625   American-built docks in France, from a photograph in the United States Signal Corps,
War Department, Washington

PRINCIPAL CONSTRUCTION PROJECTS OF THE S.O.S.

"At this time (March, 1918) the principal ports turned over to us by the French were Saint-Nazaire, Bordeaux, Nantes, La Pallice, Le Havre, and Brest. . . . At Bordeaux we were planning two construction projects — the Bassens project, which included ten new berths four hundred and ten feet each in length and to be served by four tracks, together with electric Gantry cranes, and all other most modern American apparatus; and the Saint-Sulpice project, which was a general storage depot similar to the one described below for Montoir, but about half its size. The Montoir project (near Saint-Nazaire) included eight berths for ships, four million square feet of covered storage space, and two hundred and sixty-one miles of siding and storage tracks. At Giévres was planned the Intermediate Depot, with four million four hundred and ninety-two thousand square feet of covered storage space, two hundred and forty-three miles of trackage, storage for four million gallons of gasoline and oil, and a refrigerating plant with a capacity of five thousand two hundred tons. At Is-sur-Tille was to be the principal advance depot, with a capacity of two million square feet of covered storage space and ninety-six miles of trackage." — Hagood, *The Services of Supply*, 160–62. The projects were not all completed; but the construction which was carried out is one of the most amazing aspects of American participation in the war. Had the war continued into 1919, as all experts confidently predicted, the above projects would have been needed to supply the proposed American army.

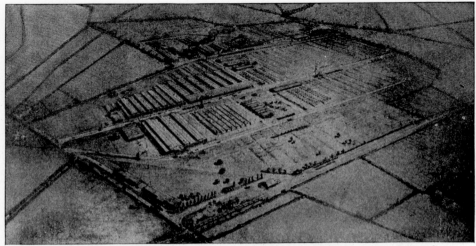

626   Aeroplane view of the Motor Transport Corps, Reconstruction Park, Ceucy-la-Tour, from a photograph
in the Engineer Department, United States Army

627   American Motor Transport, from a photograph in the United States Signal Corps,
War Department, Washington

THE SHORTAGE OF MOTOR TRANSPORT

"THROUGH no fault of those in France, I believe that in motor transportation the United States has less to be proud of than any other activity with which the S.O.S. was concerned. With more trucks, automobiles, chauffeurs, and auto mechanics in the United States than in all the rest of the world put together, the A.E.F. had to go through the war with less than fifty per cent of the vehicles and thirty per cent of the personnel prescribed in the . . . organization tables. With the streets of Washington jammed with army and civilian cars, the Thirty-third Division on the British front did not have a single car that could be trusted to go twenty miles without a breakdown. (Statement made to me by the Division commander, July 27, 1918.) In the effort to get standard designs we failed to send over available vehicles and spare parts and the Sixty-sixth Field Artillery Brigade had to manufacture its own spark plugs out of gas pipes, copper wire and chewing gum. . . . On Armistice Day we had in France only seven thousand six hundred and four motor cars, five thousand five hundred and sixteen ambulances, thirteen thousand nine hundred and twenty-eight motor-cycles . . . twenty-four thousand and fifty-five cargo trucks, four thousand one hundred and ninety-seven ammunition trucks, and some four thousand seven hundred other trucks . . . less than half of what was needed." — HAGOOD, 343–44.

628   Cleaning up the fields behind the lines, from a drawing by Captain Harry Townsend,
in the United States Signal Corps, War Department, Washington

SALVAGE

A FEATURE of the S.O.S. new to the Army of the United States was the Salvage Service. The function of this branch was the collection and rehabilitation of partly worn and unserviceable equipment. In February, 1919, the total personnel of the service exceeded eleven thousand. One of the outstanding accomplishments of the service was the clothing and equipping of some forty-seven thousand German prisoners at a saving to the Government of nearly three million dollars. The total value of saving to the Government by salvage in the A.E.F. from January 1, 1918, to March 31, 1919, was more than one hundred and eleven million dollars.

629 Brig.-Gen. Merritte W. Ireland, 1867–, from a
photograph by Harris & Ewing, Washington

THE MEDICAL DEPARTMENT

"Owing to the shortage of material and labor it became evident in the early part of the game that there would not be available sufficient bed space in regularly organized hospitals to care for the American sick and wounded. The Chief Surgeon was therefore compelled to go out into the cities and secure hotels and other large buildings and even private residences in which to establish hospitals. This separation of activities

630 A dressing station near Bois de Belleau, from
a drawing by Captain Wallace Morgan, in the
United States Signal Corps, War Department

greatly increased the difficulties of the shortage in personnel. Medical officers could not attend as many patients if they were scattered about and many places did not have proper sanitary or other conveniences for rapid work. In October the Chief Surgeon feared that the number of wounded on the American front would be greater than he could properly care for. This would have been the case if the Americans had done more fighting. Even as it was, from the 10th of September to the 11th of November the admissions were considerably greater than normal capacity. On the 23d of October the number of patients exceeded normal capacity by twenty thousand. The Chief Surgeon, however, was prepared to handle what he called crisis capacity by excessive crowding. Never was the crisis capacity approached, on the whole, but there were many times when the particular hospitals were overcrowded. . . . At all times the personnel available was only half of that estimated as necessary to look after the sick under the assumption that all beds were occupied. There were about one hundred and forty-five thousand patients in the base hospitals the day the Armistice was signed. However, I have already said I thought our soldiers were better fed, better clothed, and better shod than any other soldiers in Europe. I am absolutely certain that they had better medical attention." — Hagood, 345–46.

631   A first-aid station close to the front, from a drawing by Captain J. André Smith, in the United States
Signal Corps, War Department, Washington

THE EVACUATION OF THE WOUNDED

THE diagram represents an approved and generalized solution of the problem of the evacuation of the wounded. It shows the system used in the World War though, of course, special conditions made changes necessary. Wounded who were able to walk were directed to the battalion aid station the location of which was always announced in orders. Those who were too badly hurt to move were picked up by members of the collecting company of the regimental or divisional medical unit and were carried back.

A MAGNIFICENT ACHIEVEMENT

JOHN W. WRIGHT, author of the *Organization of the S.O.S.*, has summed up the achievements of that great service. "Previous to the World War, the greatest oversea expedition in the annals of the world, that is, in point of numbers, was the British South African War. As I recollect, they did not have over three hundred thousand men. We sent across the sea two millions of men and fed and clothed them, maintained them, on a scale hitherto not seen in any military force. Owing to the limited shipping, submarine risk — something new in war — it was found necessary and desirable to procure approximately half our supplies in Europe, so the S.O.S. was not only a great distributing agency but also a procuring agency — a War Department. It should also be remembered that this army was supplied in a war where there was the greatest expenditure of material ever known. . . . During the war there was not a failure in this system of supply. Practically everything we accomplished in the S.O.S. was unprecedented. We constructed more temporary shelter than any other army in history ever constructed. The rate of troop arrivals in France during the last three months was phenomenal; yet they were cared for, provided with food and shelter, and transported promptly to their assigned destinations, training areas, which were found ready to receive them. Our hospitalization was on a scale never before even contemplated. [Two hundred and twenty-five miles of barracks; one hundred and twenty-seven miles of hospital wards. The project called for twice this amount.]" — Quoted in HAGOOD, 335–36. Service in the S.O.S. was marked by hard work and no glory.

632 Diagram illustrating the system of evacuation of the Medical Department, from Bond and Crouch, *Tactics*, New Military Library, Annapolis, 1923

633 American stores arriving at Brest, from a drawing by Captain J. Duncan, in the United States Signal Corps, War Department, Washington

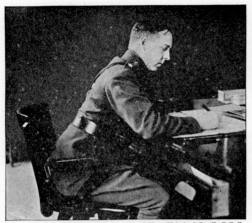

634   Maj.-Gen. Johnson Hagood, 1873–, Chief of Staff, S.O.S.,
from a photograph in the United States Signal Corps, War
Department, Washington

THE MEN OF THE S.O.S.

IT is a characteristic of combat troops to look with some condescension upon the men who supply them. This tendency was increased in the World War by the practice of sending officers who failed in the fighting to the S.O.S. to see if they could be made use of there. Hagood makes a spirited reply to the insinuations that the men of the S.O.S. were of second-rate ability. "They were the best America had, and words can say no more. Dawes, Atterbury, John J. Carty, Henry P. Davison, Franklin D'Olier, Willard Straight, and William S. Thayer were not looking around for scrubs to help them out. Ireland, Rogers, Hart, Williams, Patrick, Taylor, Jadwin, Hull, and Fries were not made major-generals and since the war placed at the heads of their respective services in the War Department because they did not make good in France. Meriwether Walker was not sent back to organize and command the Motor Transport Corps and after the war made Governor of the Panama Canal Zone because he was lacking in fighting qualities. Nor was Harbord 'canned' when he came back to Tours! On the contrary, in testifying before a Congressional committee, General Pershing pronounced him his best general. . . . It is true that the S.O.S. was frequently 'combed' for combat officers. But it was 'combed' not to find officers for combat duty, but for officers who could be spared for combat duty. . . . It is true that we had about two thousand officers that had been sent back from the front (about six per cent of our total). Some of those who came back in September and October were demoted generals, but these men were only extras. They filled in gaps in the ranks but no one of them performed any big part in the organization. And finally we must remember that a great many men who came back to the S.O.S. after being relieved from duty at the front had been condemned unjustly. 'War is Hell,' and when troops did not reach their objective or were accused of not doing so, commanders were relieved first and investigated afterwards! In one case a colonel who had been relieved and sent back to report to me was afterwards returned to his regiment, given a D.S.C. and the brigade commander was relieved for having relieved him — all based on the same incident." — HAGOOD, 337–39.

BILLETS IN FRANCE

THERE was little tenting on the old camp ground in France. Tents were conspicuous and could be easily seen by enemy aviators. Their presence would not only invite aerial attack but give valuable information to the enemy. France, moreover, is a densely cultivated area and could not spare the ground necessary for the camps of the millions of men fighting on French soil. The country is dotted with villages where the houses and barns of the peasants are huddled together in a small space. Such villages made excellent billets and the French people were accustomed to the billeting of soldiers. So the American army was brought into intimate contact with the French people. The soldier who had never been outside the confines of his own state found himself living beside a strange people and watched with interest their daily life.

635   Bomb-proof billets, from a sketch by Captain Wallace Morgan, in the United States Signal
Corps, War Department, Washington

THE SPIRIT OF THE TROOPS

THERE was also considerable friction. The Americans were broadened by the contact. It had, however, its bad features. Americans were no exception to the generalization that war brings out the best and the worst in men. As in the Civil War so in the World War there was much vice among the fighting forces.

636 The morning wash-up, from a sketch made at Neufmaison, France, by Captain Wallace Morgan, in the United States Signal Corps, War Department, Washington

It is only fair to add that there was considerable vice among these men before ever they entered the army. In France the spirit of the troops was even better than that found in the cantonments in America. They were nearer to the enemy, nearer to the great test. They carried with them that spirit of banter, of poking fun at their troubles and at one another which had originally manifested itself at the First Officers' Training Camps. Nothing shows more clearly the attitude of the American soldier in France than that song, for the most part unprintable, which grew up about the billets.

Farmer, have you a daughter fair?
  Parlez-vous?
Farmer, have you a daughter fair?
  Parlez-vous?
Farmer, have you a daughter fair
Who could wash a soldier's underwear?
  Hinky-dinky, parlez-vous?

Mademoiselle from Armentieres,
  Parlez-vous?
Mademoiselle from Armentieres,
  Parlez-vous?
Mademoiselle from Armentieres
Never heard of underwear,
  Hinky-dinky, parlez-vous?

Mademoiselle from gay Paree
  Parlez-vous?
Mademoiselle from gay Paree
  Parlez-vous?
Mademoiselle from gay Paree
An S O S for a B V D
  Hinky-dinky, parlez-vous?

A PRIVATE'S IDEA OF A BILLET

SERGEANT SETH T. BAILEY in *Henry's Pal to Henry* first printed in the *Stars and Stripes*, the newspaper of the A. E. F., has depicted with as much accuracy as humor the reaction to many of the situations which confronted him in France of "The Poor old Buck Private of the A. E. F.," to whom the letters are dedicated.

"On the wall was printed billet 56 — 35 men. . . . Well Henry I went to sleep on the [barn] floor. It was kind of dark in there and I couldn't see just where I was sleeping. About 2 P.x. an old cow came in and laid down long side of me. She'd been out to a lawn party maybe I guess and was kind of late about making camp. But I didn't mind her coming late if she'd left her could she kept chewing on. It made me hungry to listen to her Henry. When I woke up about this a.m. Henry there was one of them long haired goats that they milk

637 An Embarrassing Moment, from Seth Bailey, *Henry's Pal to Henry*, courtesy of W. B. Gumbart

laying on the foot of my bed. There was another guy sleeping opposite to me from where the cow slept and long side of him was a fat old coshone which's Frensh for hog Henry. After breakfast I went down to get some sleep and a little while ago the owner of the place come in and starts making false motions at me like as if he's going to start an offensive or something and throw me out on my ear. Pretty soon I made out that he's going to unload a cartfull of hay into the loft and that if I don't get out the horse will walk all over my stummick. So I rolled up my blankets and here I am out here back of the henhouse or duckhouse or something writing to you. This is some war Henry. Good bye Henry.

S.T.B."

638   Headquarters of the Knights of Columbus at Dravegny in the interior of a sixteenth-century church, from a photograph in the United States Signal Corps, War Department, Washington

SERVICE ORGANIZATIONS

WITH the soldiers in the cantonments in the United States, in the billets in France, and at the front were the service organizations. The Salvation Army, the Knights of Columbus, the Y. M. C. A. and the Y. M. H. A. each played a useful rôle. One of their chief functions was to establish places where the soldiers could assemble for good times of one sort or another. They provided movies and other entertainment. The "huts" of these organizations were in reality clubhouses where the soldiers could find reading matter and facilities for letter writing. The best of the workers were very efficient at discovering the needs of the men with whom they were thrown and in serving them. These organizations aided the chaplains in ministering to the religious needs of the soldiers. Without them the army would have been poor indeed.

639   Salvation Army girls serving doughnuts and coffee to the soldiers, from a photograph in the United States Signal Corps, War Department, Washington

640   Y. M. C. A. canteen in the shed of an old monastery, Rangeval, France, from a photograph in the United States Signal Corps, War Department, Washington

THE TRAINING PROGRAM FOR THE A. E. F.

At the same time that the S.O.S. was being built up and perfected the training of the combat divisions arriving from the United States was being carried forward.

"Division Training areas. (1) Based on the assumption that divisions would arrive from the United States with their basic training completed, a three months' training program was prescribed for them in France, as follows: First month: Instruction of small units from battalion down. Second month: Battalions in quiet sectors on the front. Third month: Field practice in open warfare tactics by divisions

641   Students at the First Corps School, Gondrecourt, from a photograph in the United States Signal Corps, War Department, Washington

including artillery. (2) Division training areas were selected and divisions assigned to them in rear of the Lorraine front, where General Pershing was later to strike the American blow. (3) During the first two months, the division artillery units were to train in special localities such as Valdahon, Coetquidan, Meucon, Souge, where the instruction was carried on in conjunction with French artillery. In the third month, the artillery was to be assembled with its own division and its training was to be carried out in coöperation with the division infantry, in field practice.

"With the assistance of Marshal Haig and General Petain, who placed officers and men at his disposal for use as instructors, and by using experienced American officers, General Pershing started a system of schools. . . . A General Staff College was organized in November, 1917, at the great French school center at Langres. This college graduated five hundred and thirty-seven officers. At the same place, Langres, a Line school, which graduated four hundred and eighty-eight officers, was organized. . . . At corps centers of instruction for units of all arms and for noncommissioned officers, twelve thousand eight hundred and ninety-one officers and twenty-one thousand three hundred and thirty noncommissioned officers were graduated. . . . From the Candidates' Schools, where carefully selected enlisted men sought to win commissions, eleven thousand men were graduated and commissioned. . . . Special Service Schools were organized for each arm where, in well coördinated curriculums, the doctrine of tactics and technique for the particular arm was taught. . . .

642   Brig.-Gen. Alfred W. Bjornstad (on the left), 1874–, from a photograph in the United States Signal Corps, War Department, Washington

In addition, American officers were sent to Allied technical schools with a view of preparing American experts in the technique and tactics of new weapons. Upon return those officers were used as instructors in similar American schools or in their organizations." — Brig.-Gen. C. R. Howland, *Military History of the World War*, 216–17, General Service Schools Press, Fort Leavenworth, Kansas, 1923. General A. W. Bjornstad on November 28, 1917, became the first head of the General Staff College. Before the combat officer was tested in action, his position frequently depended on his school record.

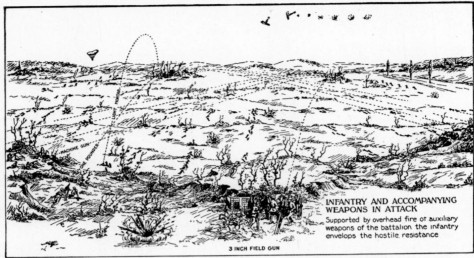

INFANTRY AND ACCOMPANYING WEAPONS IN ATTACK

Supported by overhead fire of auxiliary weapons of the battalion the infantry envelops the hostile resistance

3 INCH FIELD GUN

643   From Bond and Crouch, *Tactics*, New Military Library, Annapolis, Md., 1923

THE WEAPONS OF THE INFANTRY

In the schools of the A. E. F. the spirit of the offensive was instilled into all the students who came. The picture depicts the infantry weapons and the manner of their use in an attack. The men are shown going forward by rushes. They lie prone and engage in a fire fight with rifles with the enemy until they gain fire superiority. Then they rush forward a little way and again lie prone and take up the fire fight. These advancing infantry men are supported by one pounders, light or trench mortars and machine guns. The one pounder with its flat trajectory is shown firing at a definitely located machine gun nest. It is also effective against enemy tanks. The light mortar with its high trajectory is shown dropping shells in a woods where the enemy is known to be concentrated and where he has some machine gun nests which have not been definitely located. The mortars are also useful in laying down fire on the reverse slope of a hill. The machine guns are located on a small hill and are supporting the advancing infantry by what is called "direct overhead fire." When the assaulting infantry has progressed to a point where the bullets from their own machine guns would fall among them, these guns will cease firing, will be carried forward to another hill, and will open up again with direct overhead fire. This is called "advancing by bounds." The one pounders and trench mortars execute the same maneuver. Pieces of light artillery were sometimes used close to the infantry in the World War. Its position is farther to the rear where it supports the advance by overhead fire. In the distance may be seen airplanes and an enemy observation balloon. The picture illustrates the need for training specialists even in an infantry regiment. All the weapons shown vary somewhat in purpose and in use. Picture Number 643 and those that immediately follow it should be compared with the diagrams in Volume VI, chapter VII, to see the difference which a little more than a century has made in fighting methods.

644   American Machine Gunners in action, from a wax sculpture group by Dwight Franklin, New York

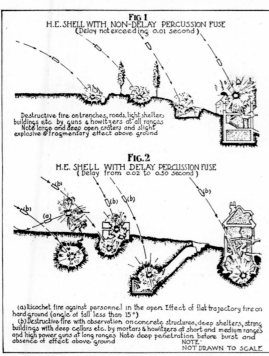

FIG 1
H.E. SHELL WITH NON-DELAY PERCUSSION FUSE
(Delay not exceeding 0.01 second)

Destructive fire on trenches, roads, light shelters
buildings etc. by guns & howitzers at all ranges
Note large and deep open craters and slight
explosive & fragmentary effect above ground

FIG.2
H.E. SHELL WITH DELAY PERCUSSION FUSE
(Delay from 0.02 to 0.50 second)

(a) Ricochet fire against personnel in the open Effect of flat trajectory fire on
hard ground (angle of fall less than 15°)
(b) Destructive fire with observation on concrete structures, deep shelters, strong
buildings with deep cellars etc. by mortars & howitzers at short and medium ranges
and high power guns at long ranges Note deep penetration before burst and
absence of effect above ground
NOTE:
NOT DRAWN TO SCALE

645   From Bond and Crouch, *Tactics*, New Military
Library, Annapolis, 1923

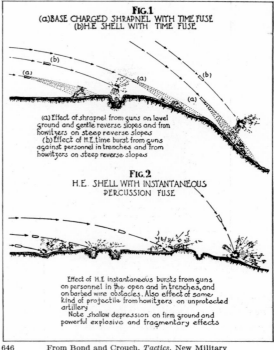

FIG.1
(a) BASE CHARGED SHRAPNEL WITH TIME FUSE
(b) H.E. SHELL WITH TIME FUSE

(a) Effect of shrapnel from guns on level
ground and gentle reverse slopes and from
howitzers on steep reverse slopes
(b) Effect of H.E. time burst from guns
against personnel in trenches and from
howitzers on steep reverse slopes

FIG.2
H.E. SHELL WITH INSTANTANEOUS
PERCUSSION FUSE

Effect of H.E. instantaneous bursts from guns
on personnel in the open and in trenches, and
on barbed wire obstacles. Also effect of same
kind of projectile from howitzers on unprotected
artillery
Note shallow depression on firm ground and
powerful explosive and fragmentary effects

646   From Bond and Crouch, *Tactics*, New Military
Library, Annapolis, 1923

ARTILLERY FIRE

ARTILLERY is a weapon used to destroy the personnel of the enemy, his artillery, his lines of communication, and his defensive works. The high explosive (H.E.) shell is particularly effective against trench systems and buildings. When equipped with delay percussion fuse it will penetrate to some distance below the surface destroying trenches, dugouts, and buildings. With the instantaneous fuse it is particularly effective in tearing away the enemy's barbed wire entanglements. Shrapnel explodes above the surface and is intended either to destroy enemy soldiers or to keep them under cover where they cannot fire on the attackers. The illustration shows its use on the reverse slope of a hill. The high explosive shells were of particular importance in the artillery preparation which almost invariably preceded an assault. At the end of one of these preparations the trench system of the enemy would be seriously impaired, if not destroyed.

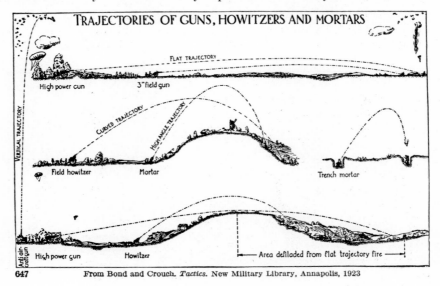

TRAJECTORIES OF GUNS, HOWITZERS AND MORTARS

FLAT TRAJECTORY

High power gun   3" field gun

VERTICAL TRAJECTORY

CURVED TRAJECTORY

HIGH ANGLE TRAJECTORY

Field howitzer   Mortar   Trench mortar

Anti aircraft gun

High power gun   Howitzer   Area defiladed from flat trajectory fire

647   From Bond and Crouch. *Tactics*. New Military Library, Annapolis, 1923

ASSAULT ECHELON
ADVANCING TO THE ATTACK
through zone of artillery fire
Line of squad columns: each
squad preceded by two scouts

648   From Bond and Crouch, *Tactics*, New Military Library, Annapolis, 1923

AN ASSAULT ON AN ORGANIZED POSITION

AN organized position is one which the enemy has developed for defense by digging trenches and building obstacles. Picture No. 650 represents a mode of attack that was normal to the Americans in advancing against the Germans. Two platoons appear. The forward one is deployed as skirmishers in two waves; the one in rear is advancing in squad columns. These infantrymen are being supported by their own one pounders, trench mortars, and machine guns and also by an artillery barrage that creeps or rolls forward at a predetermined rate equal to that of their

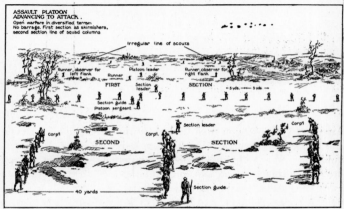

649   From Bond and Crouch, *Tactics*, New Military Library, Annapolis, 1923

advance. The purpose of their scattered formation is to reduce as much as possible their losses resulting from enemy machine gun and artillery fire. Picture No. 649 shows the two sections of a single platoon advancing after the enemy has been driven out of his trenches and is fighting in the open. Note the line of scouts, and the observers to right and left to keep contact with adjoining units and to avoid surprise. This is a typical formation of the warfare of maneuver the preparation for which was the objective of American training.

ATTACK OF AN
ORGANIZED POSITION
WITH ROLLING BARRAGE
Two waves of skirmishers, with cleaners
up (in line or small columns) Support
echelon of companies in lines of squad columns

650   From Bond and Crouch, *Tactics*, New Military Library, Annapolis, 1923

THE USE OF TANKS

THE Allies developed in the tank a most effective weapon of assault. Picture No. 652 shows a platoon of tanks advancing one hundred yards in front of the infantry against the enemy trenches. The tank is particularly useful in overrunning the enemy's wire and in destroying his machine gun nests. Picture No. 651 shows the assaulting infantry about to close with the enemy in a bayonet fight. When the

ATTACK OF AN ORGANIZED POSITION.
Assault waves entering the position. Support echelon advancing in line of small columns

651   From Bond and Crouch, *Tactics*, New Military Library, Annapolis, 1923

defenders were heavily armed with machine guns, as were the Germans, such an attack as the one pictured was bound to be very costly. The pictures depict admirably the instruction received by the American divisions in their training areas. Trained in such methods of attack and in shooting and the use of the bayonet and filled with the spirit of the offensive these troops were indeed formidable adversaries. In the summer and autumn of 1918 their training was put to the test on the field of battle.

TANKS AND INFANTRY ADVANCING IN AN ATTACK OF POSITION.

652   From Bond and Crouch, *Tactics*, New Military Library, Annapolis, 1923

THE FIRST AMERICANS TO ENTER THE FRONT LINE

HAVING completed its very intensive course of preliminary training, the First Division of United States regulars entered the front line on the night of October 20, 1917. French and American battalions alternated all along the line; and French generals still held command. The American artillery began its experience in the same way, supporting its own infantry by alternate batteries with the French. Battery C, 6th Field Artillery, First Division, fired the first shot on October 23. The gun that fired this shot is now among the trophies at West Point. It is interesting to note that more than six months had elapsed between the declaration of war and the firing of the first shot against the enemy by an American military force. In the same space of time in 1914 France had stopped the drive on Paris, and, with the aid of the British, had stabilized the Western Front. Going into the lines in a quiet sector was, in fact, a continuation of the training period in which the troops were prepared for the decisive fighting to come.

653 Americans Enter the Battle Line, from Shipley Thomas, *History of the A. E. F.*, George H. Doran Company, 1920

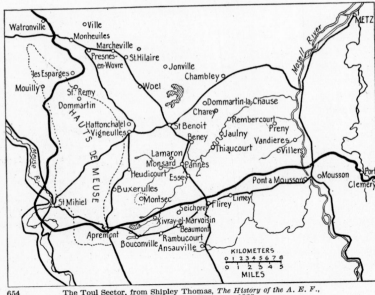

654   The Toul Sector, from Shipley Thomas, *The History of the A. E. F.*,
George H. Doran Company, 1920

THE TOUL SECTOR, FLANKING ST. MIHIEL

On January 15, 1918, the First Brigade of the First Division took over from the French the first part of the Toul Sector, flanking St. Mihiel from the south. The front lines ran through an oozy valley so that the trenches were almost awash with clammy mud. Nor were either they, nor yet the support lines, pleasant places otherwise; for, a mile behind the German front, Mont Sec rose menacingly up four hundred and fifty-seven feet above the valley. A perfect observation point and an eminence from which artillery could harrass the country for miles around.

BRIGADIER–GENERAL GEORGE B. DUNCAN, 1861–

General Duncan commanded the First Brigade of the First Division when it took over part of the first sector allotted to the A. E. F. at Toul on January 15, 1918. The Americans were jubilant over coming at last to grips with the enemy. Duncan afterward ably commanded the Seventy-seventh (New York) Division.

655 Maj.-Gen. Charles P. Summerall, from a photograph in the United States Signal Corps, War Department, Washington

656 Brig-Gen. George B. Duncan, from a photograph in the United States Signal Corps, War Department, Washington

MAJOR–GENERAL CHARLES P. SUMMERALL, 1867–

General Summerall commanded the First Field Artillery Brigade when it fired the first American shot of the war. He was a very keen gunner. He won deserved promotion to the command of the First Division, with further promotion to command a corps. He was an excellent all-round soldier and one of the best American generals produced by the war. Like most men who succeed in high command, he had devoted his whole life to military work and had distinguished himself in the Philippines.

NOVEMBER, 1917

NOVEMBER, 1917, is one of the most memorable months of the war. Within its thirty days came the disastrous Italian defeat at Caporetto, the establishment of the Bolshevist régime in Russia, the British victory in Palestine and British and French gains on the Western Front, the appointment of Clemenceau as French premier, the first American troops in the trenches and the decision to form a Supreme Allied Council of War. The plan for the organization of a Supreme War Council was the direct result of the Italian defeat and was drawn up and signed at Rapollo, Italy, on November 7. According to its terms the Council was to meet at Versailles and was to consist of the Prime Minister and one member of the Government of each of the powers fighting on the Western Front. There was also to be a military representative from each of the nations. General Tasker H. Bliss was appointed American representative.

PERSHING FACES LLOYD GEORGE

IN December the whole American plan of coöperation with the Allies was called into question by the Governments of France and Great Britain, deeply apprehensive of the future because of the collapse

657   General Tasker H. Bliss, from a photograph in the United States Signal Corps, War Department, Washington

of Russia and the defeat of Italy. They wanted American men as replacements rather than as organized armies. As early as May 5, 1917, a month after the American declaration of war, the British Mission to the United States had requested the immediate sending of five hundred thousand untrained men to England where they would be trained and used in the British armies when needed. In December the British Prime Minister urged Colonel House to secure the consent of his Government to a proposition to replace one company in each British battalion with an American company or, if not this, to replace one battalion in each British regiment with an American battalion. The implication with regard to the American senior officers was patent to all. On January 29, 1918, General Pershing and General Bliss had a conference with Lloyd George and his supreme military chiefs at Versailles. The British Prime Minister urged that the existing situation required the immediate placing of American soldiers in British units. Pershing's reply gives the measure of the man. He called attention to the fact that the submergence of Americans in the British army would antagonize the American people and might easily cause such severe criticism of the President as to paralyze the American war effort. He suggested that compliance with the request would raise the question as to whether the United States was in the war to fight for Great Britain. He pointed out that the request reflected on the competence of American military officers. And he reminded the British that they had not amalgamated with the French in the early years of the war nor had they absorbed the Canadian forces. Pershing stood stubbornly by Wilson's order to keep the American army as much as possible an independent fighting force.

658   David Lloyd George, 1863–, from the painting by Douglas Volk in the National Museum, Washington

659   Georges Clemenceau, 1841–, from a photograph
       by Underwood & Underwood, New York

BEARDING THE TIGER

THE French through their original mission to the United States had suggested the possibility of America being a reservoir for French replacements. At about the time Lloyd George was conferring with Colonel House, General Petain approached Pershing with the request that one American regiment be incorporated in each French division. His argument was the changed situation which resulted from events in Russia and Italy. Pershing called to his attention the differences in language, in military methods, and in national characteristics between the soldiers of the two armies. Under such circumstances complete coöperation in battle would be difficult if not impossible. The French Government, unwilling to accept Pershing's negative, went over his head to Washington. When Secretary Baker informed the commander of the A.E.F. of this fact, Pershing addressed the following letter to Clemenceau, the President of the Supreme War Council. "May I suggest to you, my dear Mr. President, the inexpediency of communicating such matters to Washington by cable? These questions must be settled here eventually on their merits, through friendly conference between General Petain and myself, and cables of this sort are likely, I fear, to convey the impression in Washington of serious disagreement between us which is not the case." Captain B. H. Liddell Hart of the British army has expressed the opinion that this "rebuke from a mere soldier to the chief of an allied state, especially when that chief was Clemenceau, deserves to go on record as one of the boldest acts of the war."

THE ATTACK ON PERSHING'S THEORY OF TRAINING

PERSHING's decision to train for maneuver warfare was as sharply assailed as that to build up an independent American fighting force. Captain Shipley Thomas of the First Division has portrayed the attitude not only of the French and British but of the junior American officers. "Officers returning from the British schools [in the winter of 1917–18] were full of the new British plan of defense, the policy of 'let them come on' [which was to prove so costly to the British in the spring drive] — the great British machine-gun defense in trench warfare. The French were also practicing the niceties of trench warfare, and the plan of the 'yielding defense' was put forth in mid-winter, and at once, throughout the French sectors, work was begun on second and third lines of defense with belts of barbed wire ten miles behind the front. Meanwhile, in the sleet and bitter cold, through snow, and over the frozen hills of Lorraine, during that awful winter, the Americans were practicing open warfare. Each evening the junior officers would gather in one room, each bringing with him his precious small armload of wood, and while they vainly tried to get warm, they would pour out their troubles which almost amounted to mutiny. They talked — as junior officers always do, in a cocksure way . . . of Gen-

erals who 'had learned nothing since Custer and apparently couldn't learn' . . . of Generals who taught open warfare and attack, 'when any fool could see that it was the Germans, and not us, who were going to attack.'" — SHIPLEY THOMAS, *The History of the A.E.F.*, 55–56, George H. Doran Company, 1920.

660   Troops advancing in open formation, from a photograph in the United States Signal
       Corps, War Department, Washington

PERSHING'S ESTIMATE OF THE SITUATION

On December 2, 1917, General Pershing cabled to the War Department: "The Allies are very weak and we must come to their relief this year, 1918. The year after may be too late. It is very doubtful if they can hold on until 1919 unless we give them a lot of support this year. It is therefore strongly recommended that a complete readjustment of transportation be made and that the needs of the War Department . . . be regarded as immediate. . . . It is of the utmost importance to the Allied cause that we move swiftly. The minimum number of troops we should plan to have in France by the end of June, 1918, is four army corps of twenty-four divisions in addition to troops for service of the rear." In January Pershing organized the First Corps with headquarters at Neufchateau, under General Liggett. In February he organized the Second Corps to supervise the training of six American divisions which the British in January had undertaken to transport across the Atlantic without interfering in any way with Pershing's schedule of priority. These were to be trained with the British and coöperate with them. In March the German drive began.

661   Maj.-Gen. Hunter Liggett, 1857–, from a photograph in the United States Signal Corps, War Department, Washington

THE ATTITUDE OF A SOLDIER IN FRANCE TOWARD THE ENEMY

The American soldiers had come to France after many busy months of training during which time they had been almost completely absorbed in the life of the cantonment where they happened to be stationed. Their attention was centered upon learning how to do the job that lay ahead of them. For this reason the overwrought emotions of civilian America did not manifest themselves so sharply among the soldiers. In the States he had had some difficulty in hating his adversary-to-be; in France he found it harder still. He still talked of the "Huns" but more often of "Heinie" or "Fritz." This, however, implied neither admiration nor fondness for the men who were vigorously throwing bullets and shells in the direction of the Americans. Instead of hating the German the dominant emotion of the doughboy was to go in and "clean him up" in much the same spirit in which unsavory messes are always cleaned up. One officer has left a striking reaction to the hate talk which drifted from the United States to the American billets in France. "Pitiable spectacle of some of our best clergy trying to write foot-note to words of Christ anent forgiveness of enemies. Church cutting sorry figure in this business. Incredible puerility of 'Jesus never knowing Germans.' Don't seem to grasp utter sterility of hate. God knows I shan't love word 'German' after this. But that's weakness. Pray the Ruler of things that children be spared it. Damned be he who tries to carry venom that has rotted entrails of this generation into as-yet sweet lives of the next." — *Wine, Women and War*, 95.

662   American soldier's equipment, from a photograph in the United States Signal Corps, War Department, Washington

CHAPTER XV

THE CRISIS OF 1918

THRICE did the mighty German war machine dash all its available forces against the Western Front. The first drive was against Paris in 1914 and was stopped at the first battle of the Marne. The second was made in 1916 against the steadfast salient of Verdun, which the French held safe, though with enormous loss. The third began on March 21, 1918. All winter the leaders of Britain and France awaited the drive of 1918 with deep apprehension. They knew that great bodies of German troops were being transferred from the Eastern to the Western Front. To fight off this invading host they had armies that were experienced, but tired after three years of fighting. They had also the aid of the American troops, but these were untested in battle, and their constant training in open warfare made French and British alike doubt their usefulness in the great struggle which impended. Though the shadow of coming events lay deep over London and Paris, the Governments of England and France could not bring themselves to take the one step which would give them more security than any other single development. They were fighting the war in accordance with what military men call the principle of coöperation. The forces of each nation had a supreme commander. A maximum of coöperation was insured by the useful device of the Supreme War Council. But, as the event demonstrated, the difference between the Council and unity of command was nothing less than the difference between defeat and success. Before the March drive began, however, the rock on which the plan for unity of command foundered was mutual fear. If a Frenchman were chosen, the British feared that he would instinctively give the defense of Paris precedence over that of the Channel ports and hence jeopardize the integrity of England. If the supreme commander were a British officer, the French feared that he would prefer in the moment of extreme crisis the defense of the Channel ports to that of Paris. So each Government retained control of its army. But each recognized that the weakest point in the Allied line on the Western Front was the point of junction of the forces. To strengthen this as much as was possible under the plan of coöperation the commanders in chief of the two armies were ordered to maintain reserves to protect this junction point. So the Allied commanders waited, knowing the blow would come; but not knowing exactly where it would fall. Their plan was a strategical and tactical defensive until the building up of an American army in France should give them superiority. Not without significance was the fact that General Pershing soon after his arrival in France had urged, in accordance with sound military principles, the establishment of unity of command.

663   Camouflaged artillery supporting the First Division, from a photograph in the
United States Signal Corps, War Department, Washington

VON HINDEN-BURG'S PLAN

VON HINDENBURG estimated that the weakest point in the Allied line was the junction of the French and British. He estimated that the weakest unit was the British Fifth Army under Gough, the right of which was in contact with the French left. The weakness of the Fifth Army was due to the fact that it defended a wider sector than any other army. He planned, therefore, to deliver his main

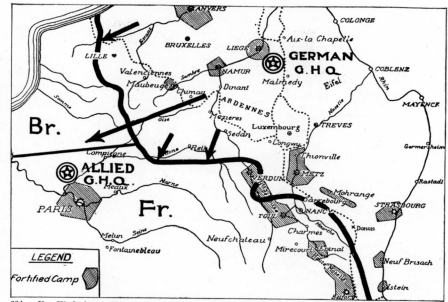

664   Von Hindenburg's Plan, 1918, First Phase, from Brig.-Gen. C. R. Howland, *Military History of the World War*, General Service Schools Press, Fort Leavenworth, Kansas, 1923

blow against the Fifth Army. At the same time he ordered diversions to be made on the Lys and from the Aisne. The latter would make the French apprehensive for the safety of Paris and would tend to keep French reserves away from the point where the main blow would fall. The fears of the French were to be increased by aerial bombing and long-range shelling of the French capital. He planned to break through between the two armies, capture Amiens, thus cutting the railroad connecting the British and the French, and envelop both flanks of the British Army while the Crown Princes of Germany and Bavaria were holding the French Army in their assault from the Aisne.

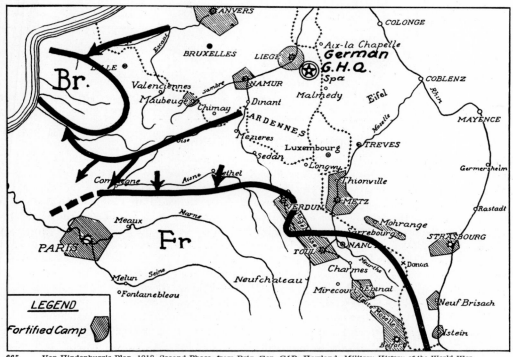

665   Von Hindenburg's Plan, 1918, Second Phase, from Brig.-Gen. C. R. Howland, *Military History of the World War*, General Service Schools Press, Fort Leavenworth, Kansas, 1923

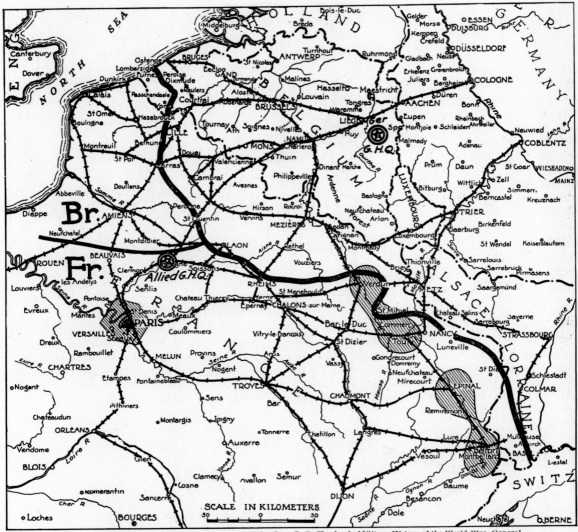

666   Railroad Map of the Western Front, 1918, from Brig.-Gen. C. R. Howland, *Military History of the World War*, General
Service Schools Press, Fort Leavenworth, Kansas, 1923

THE MARCH 21 OFFENSIVE

THE German artillery preparation began at 4:30 A.M. March 21, and the infantry assault started at 9:45 A.M.
Leading it were Von Huttier, victor of Riga, Von Marwitz, victor of the Cambrai counter-offensive, and Von
Below, victor of Caporetto. By March 24 the British Fifth Army was nearly routed. On this day General
Petain sent the French Third Army to the British area, and, on Marshal Haig's request, General Humbert,
its commander, took over the defense south of the Somme. Already the weakness of the principle of coöpera-
tion in dealing with the situation had appeared. Haig's first objective was the defense of his communications
with the Channel ports; contact with the French was secondary. At the same time the defense of Paris was
the primary purpose of Petain and maintaining contact with the British a secondary consideration. On
March 26 a conference of the Allies at Doullens named General Foch supreme commander on the Western
Front. He immediately issued the famous order: "Hold — hold at all costs — every man where he is."
The appointment was made in the very nick of time. Foch took prompt measures to stop the German main
blow. On the night of March 27–28, however, Von Hindenburg achieved the break which he sought. An
eight-mile gap opened north of Montdidier; nothing stood between the Germans and the vital railroad center
at Amiens. But no force went through the gap that night. The next day the opportunity had passed, for
Foch had closed the break. On March 31 the German drive was stopped.

PERSHING AND FOCH

ON March 27 Pershing turned over to Foch at the latter's headquarters at Bombon the supreme direction of the American Army. "I have come to tell you that the American people would consider it an honor for our troops to be engaged in the present battle. I ask you for this in their name and in my own. Infantry, artillery, aviation — all that we have is yours. Use it as you wish. More will come in numbers equal to requirements." The emergency which had arisen postponed the building up of an independent American Army. Pershing estimated that, for the time being, American soldiers would be of most use in fighting as part of Allied armies. The Second, Twenty-sixth and Forty-second Divisions promptly took over quiet sectors.

667   Ferdinand Foch, 1851–, from the painting by Edmund C. Tarbell in the National Museum of Art, Washington

668   Field-Marshal Sir Douglas Haig, 1861–1928, from the painting by John C. Johansen, N.A., in the National Museum of Art, Washington

BATTERING THE BRITISH ARMY

THE German General Headquarters were surprised and deeply disappointed at the failure of the March 21 drive to achieve decisive results. Von Hindenburg decided to continue the assault on the British. On April 4 he struck again with great violence toward Amiens but was stopped by reserves that Foch had concentrated in front of that vital position. Five days later the German commander struck the British left along the Lys, drove his adversary back beyond Mount Kemmel, but did not succeed in making a penetration. The Lys offensive lasted until April 25. On that day Von Hindenburg, believing that the fight along the Lys had drawn off the British reserves, struck a third time toward Amiens. Light tanks preceded the assault which was covered by a dense fog. But British heavy tanks stopped them and British counter-attacks threw back the enemy. Yet the Germans remained within artillery range of Amiens. The fighting was desperate and the losses on both sides appalling. The Germans made a supreme effort to win a decision and failed. So ended, for the time being, the assault on the British Army. Foch had rushed large French reserves to the assistance of Haig. Unity of command had saved the Allied cause.

669 American troops landing from a transport in France, from a sketch by Captain J. Duncan, in the United States Signal Corps, War Department, Washington

REQUEST FOR AMERICAN TROOPS

THE morale of the Allies suffered in spite of the fact that the first German drives of 1918 had been checked. Von Hindenburg still retained the offensive and he had inflicted heavy losses upon his enemies. Under the circumstances the Allied Governments on March 27 renewed their requests for American troops who would, in reality, serve as replacements to fill up shattered British and French units. They asked that infantry and machine gunners be sent immediately. Pershing agreed to this as a temporary measure but, when he discovered that the Allies expected to absorb permanently the American replacements they received he cabled Washington that the priority of infantry and machine gun units should be limited to four divisions, plus forty-five thousand five hundred replacements, future priority to be determined later. Just after the Germans had been stopped for the third time in front of Amiens the Supreme War Council met at Abbeville on May 1 and 2. The whole question of the amalgamation of the Americans with the French and British was reopened. Pershing was convinced that such amalgamation was unsound. As a result the so-called Abbeville Agreement opened with the following sentence: "It is the opinion of the Supreme War Council that, in order to carry the war to a successful conclusion, an Amercian Army should be formed as early as possible under its own commander and under its own flag." The agreement further provided, in the words of Pershing's *Report*, that "British shipping was to transport ten American Divisions to the British Army area, where they were to be trained and equipped, and additional shipping was to be provided for as many divisions as possible for use elsewhere." British shipping in vast amounts was deflected from other duties and sent to the United States to carry troops. During the months of May and June half a million troops embarked from the United States. This rate was continued and even bettered until the Armistice. When the sending of troops abroad was halted on November 11, two million and forty-five thousand soldiers together with thirty thousand Marines had embarked from the United States for France.

THE SEICHEPREY RAID, APRIL 20, 1918

GERMAN morale suffered somewhat as a result of the failure to break through the opposing lines in March. The assaulting troops had suffered devastating losses, for the British machine guns had been many and had been well served. Time was running against the Germans for they knew that American troops were being rushed to France by every available ship. The German command felt that it would be desirable for the purposes of morale to create the impression that the Americans could not fight. The result was the Seicheprey raid. Waiting until just after a relief had taken place at Seicheprey, the Germans put down a box barrage which encircled the village on all sides save that toward the front. Under protection of this barrage the enemy captured almost the entire garrison of the forward position, some one hundred and seventy-nine men with twenty-four machine guns. The Germans remained in the captured position for twelve hours before they were driven out by a counter-attack in which the French aided the Americans. From the radio station at Berlin details of the affair were broadcast over the world and German airplanes dropped pictures of the raid in neutral countries. The Twenty-sixth Division was the one that suffered the reverse

670 A tank surprises a machine gun nest, from a drawing by Captain Harry Townsend, in the United States Signal Corps, War Department, Washington

CANTIGNY, MAY 28, 1918

GERMAN success in the Seicheprey raid was entirely due to the fact that a mere handful of Americans not fully trained had been caught unaware by veterans. But it rankled in the minds of the A. E. F., and the First Division welcomed its first chance of hitting back. The First came north from Toul staffed to perfection; for its twenty-eight thousand men, seventeen hundred animals, and one thousand vehicles crossed crowded French lines of communication, running from east to west, without a single hitch. Pershing then addressed all the officers, telling them they would now have their chance of showing how trained Americans could fight. For one whole month, however, the First had to endure terrific shell fire from masked batteries which knew each inch of the range. Then, with perfect secrecy, the staff planned taking and

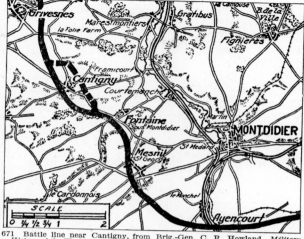

671 Battle line near Cantigny, from Brig.-Gen. C. R. Howland, *Military History of the World War*, General Service Schools Press, Fort Leavenworth, Kansas, 1923

holding Cantigny, the German stronghold just in front and at the very tip of the salient threatening the direct line south from Amiens to Paris. Except for ten French tanks and a platoon of French flame-throwers, it was to be an All-American ordeal, and under the searching eyes of British, French, and Germans.

672 American troops advancing under cover of French tanks at Cantigny, from a photograph in the United States Signal Corps, War Department, Washington

THE ADVANCE ON CANTIGNY, MAY 28, 1918

THE day before the attack the suspicious Germans raided the whole front line, which they also cut off from supports by a drenching of fifteen thousand deadly gas shells. But they got only one prisoner and he knew nothing. That night the whole rear was silently astir with men supplying the front. At 5:45 A.M. the sudden American intense barrage tore Cantigny to shreds. At 6:45 the barrage as suddenly changed into a rolling barrage that advanced one hundred meters every two minutes for a period of six minutes, thereafter one hundred meters every four minutes. The advance was further protected by heavy destruction and interdiction fire on the German rear areas. Then the infantry, tanks, and flame-throwers advanced. The first Americans began their first advance against their first objective.

CANTIGNY, MAY 28, 1918

PERFECTLY led by its own barrage, and keeping close touch with its ten French tanks, Colonel Ely's Twenty-eighth Infantry killed, captured, or disabled every German in eighty-eight minutes. Then the Twenty-eighth, admirably supported by the First Battalion of the Eighteenth, one company of the First Engineers and the Division Artillery, dug in, and beat off the bitterest counter-attacks. Next morning the last and most determined counter-attack was rolled back in confusion. Then it was that these first of all fire-tested Americans stood victorious before both friend and foe. Cantigny was significant of the soundness of the training that had been in progress for more than a year and of the fighting qualities of the American troops. It forecast the work in the Argonne of the next autumn. General Bullard wrote: "The moral effects to flow from this proof of the reliability of the American soldier in battle far outweigh the direct military importance of the action itself."

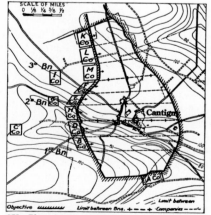

673 Plan of infantry operation against Cantigny, from Brig.-Gen. C. R. Howland, *Military History of the World War*, General Service Schools Press, Fort Leavenworth, Kansas, 1923

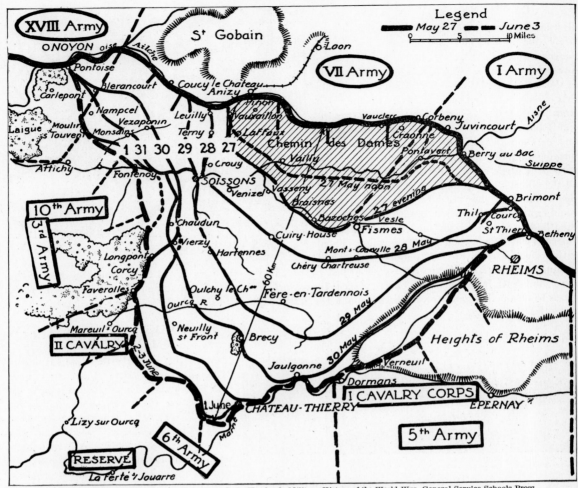

674   Building the Marne Salient, from Brig.-Gen. C. R. Howland, *Military History of the World War*, General Service Schools Press,
Fort Leavenworth, Kansas, 1923

THE CLIMAX OF THE GERMAN DRIVE OF 1918

By June, 1918, the great German drive was only partly successful. Von Hindenburg had struck first at the junction of the British and French armies. He had gained much ground but had failed to break the line. He had also failed to penetrate between the British and the Belgians on the Lys. He had believed that these two terrific blows would shatter the British line, and in this he was disappointed. His original plan called for the destruction of the British forces before launching a major offensive against the French. The Crown Prince had made the necessary preparations for this second assault. It would take considerable time to prepare for another offensive against the British, and the Germans seem to have feared that, if they paused, they would lose the offensive and give Foch an opportunity to strike back at some of their vulnerable salients. Von Hindenburg, therefore, decided to deliver the blow against the French, meanwhile preparing for a final assault against the British. "His [Hindenburg's] plan of maneuver against the French was to deliver a blow, in the general direction of Soissons-Fismes, that would threaten Paris; to cut the Paris-Epernay railroad; and then, under the protection of the interruption in the French line of communications, to thrust a powerful penetrating blow through the vicinity of Epernay-Chalons, and exploit the penetration against the inner flanks of the two dislocated wings of the French forces." — HOWLAND, 275. Forty-two German divisions and four thousand pieces of artillery were secretly assembled for the attack which was launched on May 27 at 4 A.M. For four days the French went back while the Germans crossed the Aisne, the Vesle, the main road to Paris, and appeared on the banks of the Marne. May 31 was one of the tensest days of the war.

AMERICAN ASSISTANCE

BRITISH, French, and Americans realized that the supreme crisis was at hand and that the Germans might then and there win the war before a sufficient American army had been brought to France. On May 30, Pershing placed the Second Division under General Bundy and the Third Division under General Dickman at the disposal of the French commander in the threatened area, General d'Espérey. The Third Division was quickly ordered to help hold the line of the Marne. While the division was being brought up the division motorized machine gun battalion was sent ahead. On May 31 at 4 P.M. they went into action at Chateau Thierry amid the cheers of the French.

675   Street barricade at Chateau Thierry, from a drawing by W. J. Aylward, in the United States Signal Corps, War Department, Washington

AMERICAN MACHINE GUN NESTS IN CHATEAU THIERRY

HERE, in these houses, the American machine gunners held off the Germans, who sought to cross the Marne at Chateau Thierry just where the French had destroyed this bridge. The battle is best told in the words of the general order of the French General Duchesne, commanding the Sixth Army. Commending the Seventh Machine Gun Battalion, he said that they "prevented the enemy from crossing the Marne. In the course of violent combats, particularly on May 31 and June 1, this bat-

676   Buildings at Chateau Thierry occupied by American machine gunners of the Third Division, July 21, 1918, from a photograph in the United States Signal Corps, War Department, Washington

talion disputed the northern suburbs of Chateau-Thierry foot by foot, inflicted severe losses on the enemy, and covered itself with glory by its bravery and ability." On June 1 the Germans, prevented from crossing the Marne at Chateau Thierry, crossed it a few miles to the east at Jaulgonne. Their immediate objective was the cutting of the French communications between Paris and Epernay. The Fifth Brigade under General Sladen and the Sixth Brigade under General Crawford after a long, forced march went into action beside the tired French. In a desperate fight the French and Americans gained fire superiority and forced the enemy to recross the Marne.

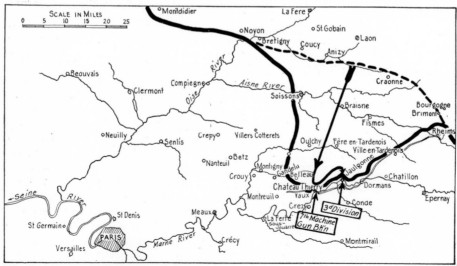

677   Third American Division prevents German crossing of the Marne, from Brig.-Gen. C. R. Howland, *Military History of the World War*, General Service Schools Press, Fort Leavenworth, Kansas, 1923

678   The Field of Mars, from a drawing by Captain J. André Smith, in the
        United States Signal Corps, War Department, Washington

THE FIELD OF MARS

TANKS, trenches, aircraft, barbed wire, poison gas, rifles, bayonets, hand grenades, bludgeons, daggers, liquid fire, a perfect tornado of bursting shells, and incessant streams of machine-gun bullets; these were what made the Field of Mars so deadly in the great World War. Into this inferno, where the French and British had suffered so long and had fought so heroically, the Americans had finally plunged. With joy the weary veterans of Europe saw the fresh and vigorous soldiers from across the Atlantic advancing under fire beside them. The Americans fought hard and effectively and their very presence heightened the morale of their comrades in arms, and in this crisis morale was of vast importance.

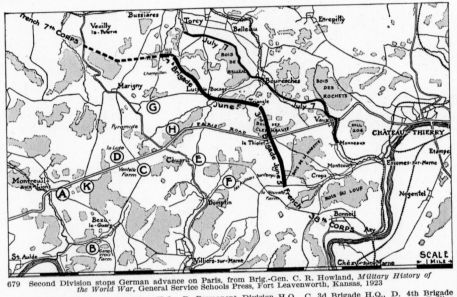

679   Second Division stops German advance on Paris, from Brig.-Gen. C. R. Howland, *Military History of
        the World War*, General Service Schools Press, Fort Leavenworth, Kansas, 1923

LEGEND: A. Temporary Division H.Q., B. Permanent Division H.Q., C. 3d Brigade H.Q., D. 4th Brigade
H.Q., E. 23d Infantry H.Q., F. 9th Infantry H.Q., G. 5th Marines H.Q., H. 6th Marines H.Q., K. Rolling
kitchens.

THE SECOND DIVISION ASTRIDE THE PARIS ROAD

WHILE the Third Division was operating on the Marne, the Second, hurrying northward to relieve the First, was suddenly deflected to meet an emergency as desperate as that at Chateau Thierry. The Germans in great force were advancing along the Paris road. For days they had been coming on and the exhausted French had been falling back before them. On June 1 General Bundy was sent into action to take up a position between the French Seventh and Thirty-eighth Corps. He was ordered to hold the line from La Nouvette Farm through the Bois des Clermebauts to Hill 142. The French Twenty-first Corps, which had opposed the Germans here, was worn out after five days of desperate fighting. The French had no infantry reserve. If ever the Americans were needed, it was here on the Paris road north of the Marne. The story is told that soon after the French fell back past Bundy on June 4 leaving the Second Division in the front line an American captain from a good observation point discovered great masses of German infantry on the road some distance in advance of the American front. Swiftly the word was carried to division head-quarters. A few moments later the American artillery laid obliterating fire on the enemy columns. On June 4 the Americans, unaided except by French artillery, beat back the German attacks. On June 5 they took over the sector. The drive toward Paris had been stopped.

FORTIFYING BELLEAU WOOD

THE American position on July 5 as shown on Map No. 679 was unfavorable for defense. The American troops were much in the open and had no woods behind them. They were, moreover, on the lower part of a hill slope. The German main line was above them and just forward of the crest of the hill. The Germans had the advantage of woods, particularly the Belleau Wood. In a little valley in the rear of the German front line lay the villages of Belleau, Bouresches, and Vaux. The German command hastened forward two of the best German divisions to oppose the Americans astride the Paris road. They were anxious to push the Second Division out of the

680 On the edge of Belleau Wood, from a drawing by Captain J. André Smith, courtesy the United States Signal Corps, War Department, Washington

way in preparation for a further advance along this road. They were also aware that the record of the First Division at Cantigny, the Third at Chateau Thierry, and the Second on the Paris highway had raised the prestige of the American troops to a point where it was affecting favorably the morale of the Allies and was depressing that of the soldiers of the Fatherland. The Germans, therefore, decided to attack, starting from Belleau Wood and Bouresches. Before proceeding to offensive action, however, they prepared the region thoroughly for defense. Every existing weapon that could be used was utilized to make Belleau Wood impregnable. Machine gun nests were so placed in Belleau Wood that the victors over one nest would find themselves at once under fire from supporting nests. Before the Germans could launch their attack, however, the American attack had begun.

To the Fourth Brigade, made up of Marines and commanded by General Harbord, was given the mission of taking Bouresches and Belleau Wood. On June 6 Harbord's men moved out behind a rolling barrage and penetrated Belleau Wood. Here the Marines struggled for days against veteran infantry fighting desperately. It was a machine gun and bayonet fight. In hand to hand personal encounter the Americans pushed back their adversaries concealed in the dense undergrowth. The casualties were appalling. Harbord was always with his men, visiting the various units, inspecting their dispositions, and encouraging them. On June 15 the Seventh Infantry from the Third Division relieved the Third Brigade and for six days held the line. It fought almost continuously and made a little progress. Then Harbord's men came back and finished

681 Maj.-Gen. James G. Harbord, 1866–, from a photograph in the United States Signal Corps, War Department, Washington

the job. On June 26 the Germans were entirely out of Belleau Wood. General Duchesne, the commander of the French Sixth Army with which the Second Division was coöperating, commended the Americans in a general order: "Thrown into the thick of the battle in a sector violently attacked by the enemy the brigade broke up a powerful German attack at a very important point of the position and afterwards carried out a series of attacks. Thanks to the bravery, fighting spirit and tenacity of the men, who stoically bore fatigue and losses, thanks also to the activity of the officers, as also to the personal influence of its commander, General J. Harbord, the efforts of the Fourth Brigade were entirely successful. Acting in close coöperation, the two regiments and machine gun battalion of the brigade advanced from fifteen hundred to two thousand yards on a two and one half mile front, after twelve days of incessant fighting [from June 2 to 13, 1918], over very difficult ground, capturing a large quantity of material and five hundred prisoners, inflicting heavy losses on the enemy, and carrying two very important positions, the village of Bouresches and the fortified Belleau Wood."

682   Village Square of Bouresches, from a drawing by Captain J. André Smith, in the United States Signal
Corps, War Department, Washington

THE CAPTURE OF VAUX

On July 1 General Lewis with the Third Brigade had his turn. About noon of that day, after several hours of artillery preparation, he moved out following a barrage that rolled forward one hundred meters every three minutes for twenty-four minutes. When night fell the village of Vaux and the Wood of La Roche were in his possession and he had repulsed the German counter-attack. He had also captured five hundred prisoners and many machine guns. It was a brilliant achievement. The French on his right failed to take Hill 204, which dominated Vaux and commanded Chateau Thierry. Despite this Lewis held what he had won.

683   The village of Vaux, from a drawing by Captain J. André Smith, in the United States Signal Corps,
War Department, Washington

KAMERAD!

No finer compliment has ever come to the Second Division than the comments published by the enemy to warn the German soldiers of the quality of the Americans. "The Second American Division must be considered a very good one and may even perhaps be reckoned as a storm troop. The different attacks on Belleau Woods were carried out with bravery and dash. The moral effect of our own gun fire cannot seriously impede the advance of the American Infantry. The Americans' nerves are not yet worn out. The qualities of the men individually may be described as remarkable. They are physically well set up, their attitude is good, and they range in age from eighteen to twenty-eight years. They lack at present only training and experience to make formidable adversaries. The men are in fine spirits and are filled with a naïve assurance; the words of a prisoner are characteristic: '*We kill or we get killed.*'" — Quoted in HOWLAND, 281.

684 From a drawing *Kamerad!* by Captain Harvey Dunn, in the United States Signal Corps, War Department, Washington

THE SIGNIFICANCE

THE significance of the capture of Belleau Wood, Bouresches, and Vaux during those bloody days of June becomes clearer when viewed in the light of the following memorandum. "General Foch has presented to us a statement of the utmost gravity . . . as there is no possibility of the British and French increasing the numbers of their divisions. . . there is great danger of the war being lost unless the numerical inferiority of the Allies can be remedied as rapidly as possible by the advent of American troops. . . . [signed] D. Lloyd George, Clemenceau, Orlando. Versailles Conference, June 12, 1918." At a time when the French and British were stunned, they beheld the Second Division, fighting against the very nose of the enemy's salient, not only stop the assault but push the adversary back two kilometers on an eight-kilometer front, capturing in the enterprise more than sixteen hundred prisoners. Clemenceau announced a great victory to the French people who faced the future with renewed hope.

685 Hill 204, from a drawing by Captain J. André Smith, in the United States Signal Corps, War Department, Washington

THE NAVAL FLANK OF THE WESTERN FRONT GUARDED BY GRAND FLEET

MEANWHILE it should be remembered that the Western Front did not stop short at the coast. It went right north to Scapa Flow, beyond the tip of Scotland, where the powerful British Grand Fleet had now been joined by Admiral Rodman's United States battleships *New York*, *Wyoming*, *Florida*, *Delaware*, *Arkansas*, and *Texas*. The combined fleets of Britain and America kept the German navy from turning the flank that rested on the coast. History has no parallel for the colossal organization and the coöperation of men and units, separated from one another by great distances, such as the World War called into being.

686   The German fleet at Kiel, from a photograph in the possession of the publishers

687 German plan for the Second Battle of the Marne, from Brig.-Gen. C. R. Howland, *Military History of the World War*, General Service Schools Press, Fort Leavenworth, Kansas, 1923

THE GERMAN DILEMMA

THE chief result of the powerful drive of the Crown Prince had been the creation of a great salient near the apex of which was Chateau Thierry. Within this Marne salient were some forty German divisions. The salient was unstable because this great body of troops was dependent for supplies upon a single railroad line from Laon to Soissons. Having failed to include another railroad in the salient by the taking of Compiegne, Von Hindenburg decided to launch a great offensive toward Chalons, southeast of Rheims. The success of this maneuver would put adequate railroad facilities in the hands of the Germans. But Von Hindenburg planned to do more. He estimated that the success of the operation would force the evacuation of Verdun. In fact he planned nothing less than the breaking of the French line and the folding of the eastern segment back on Switzerland and the western segment on Paris. He concentrated eighty-five divisions on the front just east and west of Rheims, which gave him a preponderance of fifteen divisions over the French and Americans in that particular sector. Von Hindenburg was making his supreme and, as it turned out, his final bid for victory. Had he won this second battle of the Marne, Germany must have been the victor in the war before the Americans could have brought sufficient troops to France to turn the balance in favor of the Allies. Picture No. 688 shows the bridge at Chateau Thierry which had been destroyed by the French.

NO MAN'S LAND

No maps can show the horrors of that ghastly stretch of tortured ground which lay between the Germans and Allies, and which, though shifting with the fortunes of each retirement or advance, was always the same accursed No Man's Land. To the outward eye, indeed, the whole of a modern battlefield may sometimes seem one vast, appalling No Man's Land, from one end to another; for there are many occasions on which hundreds of thousands of men may be fighting each other without a single one in sight. Hidden in dugouts, or even when firing from trenches, they are invisible to every groundsman's eye at any distance. Only the airmen, like hawks, see those whose heads and hands furtively appear when serving guns and rifles.

688 Rebuilding the bridge at Chateau Thierry, from a drawing by Captain J. André Smith, in the United States Signal Corps, War Department, Washington

689   From a drawing *No Man's Land*, by Captain Harvey Dunn, in the United States Signal Corps, War Department, Washington

690   Snipers in a shell hole, from a drawing by Captain Harry Townsend, in the United States Signal
Corps, War Department, Washington

AMERICAN SNIPERS

ALONG the lines the snipers on both sides continued their deadly work day after day. These men were dead shots and were seeking to wear down the enemy strength. They played an important part in the conflict. They were active along the Marne in the tense days which preceded the final German assault.

691 Outpost duty in the Vosges Mountains, from a photograph in the United States Signal Corps, War Department,
Washington

THE SECOND BATTLE OF THE MARNE, PHASE EAST OF RHEIMS

THE Second Battle of the Marne did not surprise Marshal Foch. On July 13 he estimated that his enemy would strike on the fifteenth, which proved to be a correct conclusion. Von Hindenburg, however, had taken extreme precautions to keep his concentrations secret, all troop movements being made under cover of darkness. The success of the French staff work is evidenced by an order issued by General Gouraud to the French and American soldiers of the Fourth Army, which occupied the Champagne region just east of Rheims. "We may be attacked at any moment. You all know that a defensive battle was never engaged in under more favorable circumstances. We are awake and on our guard. We are powerfully reinforced in Infantry and Artillery. You are fighting on a terrain that you have transformed by your work and your persever-ance into a redoubtable fortress. This invincible fortress and all its passages are well guarded. The bombardment will be terrific. You will stand it without weakness. The assault will be ferocious, in a cloud of smoke, dust, and gas. But your positions and your armament are formidable. In your breasts beat the strong hearts of free men. None shall look to the rear, none shall yield a step. Each shall have but one thought: to kill — to kill a plenty — until they have had their fill. Therefore, your General says to you: you will break this assault, and it will be a happy day. Gouraud."

692   Second Battle of the Marne, Phase east
of Rheims, from Brig.-Gen. C. R. Howland,
Military History of the World War, General
Service Schools Press, Fort Leavenworth,
Kansas, 1923

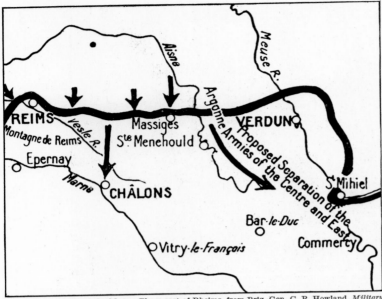

693 Second Battle of the Marne, Phase east of Rheims, from Brig.-Gen. C. R. Howland, *Military History of the World War*, General Service Schools Press, Fort Leavenworth, Kansas, 1923

THE FIGHTING EAST OF RHEIMS

BREAK it they did, but largely because of the brilliance of the commanding general himself. Expecting an attack on the morning of the fifteenth Gouraud executed a raid early in the evening of the fourteenth. He learned that the Germans were massed in great force ready to strike, that their artillery attack would begin at midnight, and their infantry move forward at 4:30 in the morning. Immediately Gouraud ordered his own artillery to commence firing. The guns opened at 10:45 P.M. and, taking the Germans completely by surprise as they stood in the darkness in massed formation, inflicted terrific losses upon them. At midnight the enemy opened such a barrage as even France had never seen. For fifteen miles back from the front the ground was illuminated; even Paris saw the light. Then the German infantry rushed forward. The enemy artillery and infantry concentrated their tremendous effort upon the first battle position. But Gouraud was too clever for them; he had purposely withdrawn from this position leaving it occupied only with outposts. The German blow was, therefore, in the air. In a newly developed intermediate battle position the French and Americans, using artillery, machine gun, and rifle fire, fought off the assaulting host and destroyed thousands of men. The intermediate position was never carried. The attack east of Rheims had failed. In this decisive battle the following American units participated: the Forty-second Division under General Menoher, the Three Hundred and Sixty-ninth, Three Hundred and Seventy-first and Three Hundred and Seventy-second regiments of infantry operating with French divisions, and a part of the Thirtieth Brigade of the Coast Artillery Corps. The following is a French estimate of the Forty-second Division: "It had the honor of rivaling its French comrades in courage and daring. Its men went under fire as if to a football game, in shirt sleeves rolled up over sinewy biceps. In one trench where they worked with our chausseurs one could count 60 bodies in less than 750 feet. Oh! the Germans who have seen them at work can't any longer doubt that they are here, or even as our soldiers say, 'quite a bit here.'" The details of this battle and the quotations are taken from HOWLAND, 287–97. On July 16 Gouraud congratulated the French Army: "It is a great day for France. I count on you to do the same every time he dares to attack you, and from my heart as a soldier, I thank you."

694   From a wax sculpture group, *Over the Top*, by Dwight Franklin, courtesy of the artist

THE SECOND BATTLE OF THE MARNE, THE PHASE WEST OF RHEIMS

SIMULTANEOUS with the attack east of Rheims was the assault across the Marne. Here in a vital sector just east of Chateau Thierry stood the Third Division. General Dickman had organized its position in such a way as to prevent the enemy crossing the Marne or, in the event that he got over, to drive him back by counterattack. Infantry and machine gun outposts lined the river bank. The outpost line of resistance was the Aqueduct Line, while the reserve line was known as the Wood Line. The French commander, General Degoutte, drenched the enemy lines with gas at 8 P.M. on July 14. At 11:30 he began his general counter preparation fire. At midnight the Germans opened with five hundred batteries. Then they assaulted. Against the Third Division they sent the Tenth Division and parts of the Thirty-sixth Division and of

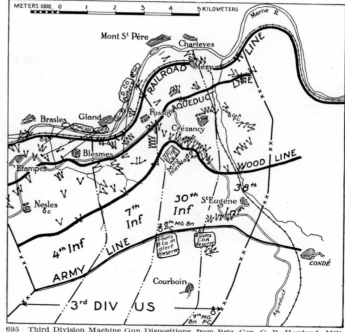

695   Third Division Machine Gun Dispositions, from Brig.-Gen. C. R. Howland, *Military History of the World War*, General Service Schools Press, Fort Leavenworth, Kansas, 1923

the Tenth Landwehr Division. Under cover of fog and a smoke screen they began crossing the Marne. The rifles, machine guns and hand grenades of the American outposts on the river bank inflicted a heavy loss and sank many boats seeking to cross the stream. But they could not stop the overwhelming onrush. The Germans made the bank and rushed forward to the Railroad Line. The map shows the location of machine guns and the sectors of the various regiments.

THE VICTORY OF THE THIRD DIVISION

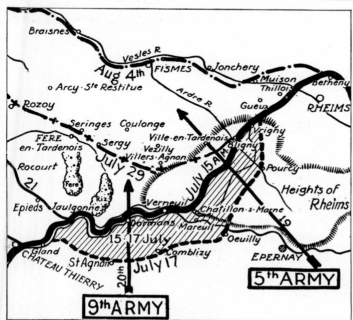

696   Second Battle of the Marne, from Brig.-Gen. C. R. Howland, *Military History of the World War*, General Service Schools Press, Fort Leavenworth, Kansas, 1923

THE resistance of the Americans had slowed up the German onslaught. Then General Dickman prepared to counterattack. Informing the commander of the French Corps of his intention, he was told to wait. He refused. After the terrific fighting was ended, General Dickman reported: "Although the rush of the German troops overwhelmed some of our first-line positions, causing the infantry and machine gun companies to suffer, in some cases, a fifty-per-cent loss, no German soldier crossed the road, Fossoy-Crezancy, except as a prisoner of war, and by noon of the following day [July 16] there were no Germans in the foreground of the Third Division sector except the dead." The map shows the line at which the French stopped the Germans. The Third Division which threw the enemy back across the river stood opposite Gland.

697   The railroad embankment at Mèzy, from a drawing by Captain J. André Smith, in the United States Signal Corps, War Department, Washington

THE RAILROAD AT MÈZY

THE official description of the sketch made soon after the battle is as follows: "A battlefield at Mèzy, looking east along the railroad track, with hill 231 in the distance; at the foot of the hill and to the right are the roofs of the village of Moulins, while to the left of the track a line of trees marks the mouth of the Surmelin River. The foreground shows the scene of the heaviest fighting in this sector, the railroad embankment at this point being the German objective and our line of defense. The graves along the edge of the track are American graves."

THE WORK OF THE 38TH INFANTRY

THE Thirty-eighth Infantry occupied the right flank of the Third Division, its left somewhere near the crosses in the foreground of Cut No. 697. The Germans advanced from the right. They faced a terrific and well led assault. "On this occasion," said Pershing in his *Final Report*, "a single regiment of the Third Division wrote one of the most brilliant pages in our military annals. It prevented the crossing at certain points on its front, while on either flank the Germans who had gained a footing pressed forward. Our men, firing in three directions, met the German attacks with counter-attacks at critical points and succeeded in throwing two German divisions into complete confusion, capturing six hundred prisoners." Colonel McAlexander commanded. Number 699 shows a view of the battlefield from the junction of the French left with the right of the Thirty-eighth. The German positions were on the right, the Americans on the left, and the assault from right to left. Along the railroad in the foreground was organized the Railroad Line or outpost line of resistance (see map, No. 695).

698   Brig.-Gen. Ulysses Grant McAlexander, from a photograph in the United States Signal Corps, War Department, Washington

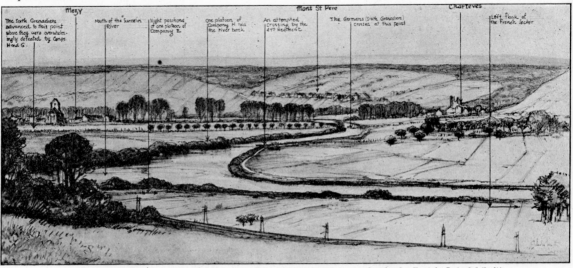

699   A view of the Valley of the Marne in the sector of the 38th Regiment, from a drawing by Captain J. André Smith, in the United States Signal Corps, War Department, Washington

700 Between shells at Chateau Thierry, from a drawing by Captain George Harding in the United States Signal Corps, War Department, Washington

THE QUALITY OF THE 38TH INFANTRY

LIEUTENANT LOVEJOY of the Thirty-eighth Infantry has left a record of the fighting of the terrible July 15. "Day was just breaking; and through the mist, fog and smoke one could see the boats and rafts loaded to the gunwales with enemy infantrymen and machine gunners set out for the southern bank. That was about 3:30 o'clock. Yet not one crossed that day in the center of the sector, in front of Company H or on the right in front of Company E. Men of the Thirty-eighth, who had escaped the hours of shelling, met every attempt with rifle and automatic-weapon fire. Scores of those boats were shattered and sunk or else disabled and sent drifting harmlessly down the river. Hundreds of Huns jumped into the water and were drowned. Those who reached our side by swimming were either killed or captured. Soldiers wounded in the early morning remained at their automatic rifles or in their rifle pits unflinchingly until killed. One man of Company G was later found lifeless with his rifle and pistol empty, and in front of him a heap of twelve dead Germans. Another private's body was found surrounded by five of the enemy, all killed by a bayonet; but his own rifle was clutched in his hands, ready for more work when he was stopped by a bullet from a machine gun. At this time Company G was really the pivotal point of the attack, because in front of this company the Germans had erected a pontoon bridge, over which swarmed a host of machine gunners. By means of a second pontoon bridge, the enemy was enabled to direct a flanking fire on the left. But Company G, under Captain Wooldridge, made heroic counter-attacks, in the course of which it took more than four hundred prisoners, in spite of overwhelming odds." — Quoted in SHIPLEY THOMAS, 118–19.

701 General Joseph T. Dickman, from a photograph in the United States Signal Corps, War Department, Washington

GENERAL JOSEPH T. DICKMAN, 1857–

FROM the time he first organized it at Camp Greene, Charlotte, North Carolina, down to August 31, 1918, when he became a corps commander, General Dickman led the Third (or "Marne") Division, led it through its long intensive training, led it through its heroic stand against the German rush of mid-July, and through the victorious counter-stroke as well.

702 General Erich Ludendorff, 1865–, from a photograph by International Newsreel, New York

VON HINDENBURG'S PLANS

VON HINDENBURG listened to the reports of the German offensive at the Second Battle of the Marne with some dismay. He quickly found that his troops east of Rheims were "bleeding to death" without accomplishing any useful purpose. He ordered them to halt and consolidate the small gains they had won. On July 17 he found himself stopped west of Rheims. Though his divisions had made a considerable advance south of the Marne, they had not accomplished the fall of Rheims. They had not broken through the French

703 Field Marshal Paul Von Hindenburg, 1847–, from a photograph by International Newsreel, New York

army. The Marne salient was as unstable as ever. The failure to capture Rheims had left its means of supply inadequate. Von Hindenburg estimated, however, that he was still master of the situation for he believed that Foch had thrown all his reserves into the line to stop the drive. The German commander, therefore, contemplated making preparations for a further assault south of the Marne. This would mean giving up the offensive for a time. The German troops knew that the final objectives had not been taken but their morale was good for they expected the decisive blow that would end the war to follow speedily. When the lines ceased to advance the Germans busied themselves reaping the French wheat fields to secure a slight addition to that food supply which was running so dangerously low in the Fatherland. Meanwhile, Von Hindenburg with his wonted aggressiveness planned to make even his failures serve his ends. He sent General Ludendorff north to manage and expedite the great drive in Flanders which was to shatter the British army. The Second Marne would become, therefore, a diversion to distract attention from this vital blow to come in August.

FOCH'S PLANS

FOR once Von Hindenburg had badly misjudged his opponents. Both Marshal Foch and General Pershing stand out as having played determining parts in the events which wrecked the plans of the German commander. Many months before the German drive of 1918 Pershing, as has already been noted, had aroused adverse comment on the part of both French and British commanders by his policy of training the American army in offensive open warfare rather than concentrating his entire attention on defensive trench warfare. He had sought to fill the American fighting units with the offensive spirit. When the Second and Third Divisions had stopped the German advance in the region of Chateau Thierry about June 1 Pershing at once saw the weakness of the Marne salient and advised General Foch to make an immediate

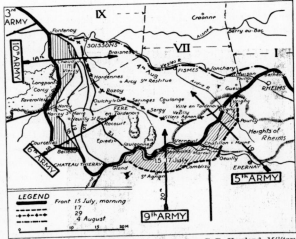

704 Second battle of the Marne, from Brig.-Gen. C. R. Howland, *Military History of the World War*, General Service Schools Press, Fort Leavenworth, Kansas, 1923

counter-attack on the western side of the salient toward Soissons. On June 23 and again on July 10 he urged the French commander to concentrate the best American divisions under American command and hurl them against the salient. Foch welcomed Pershing's recommendation. On July 7 he reached the decision that the counter-offensive would be in the direction of Soissons and ordered plans prepared for the maneuver. These were completed nine days later. Then the French commander waited for a favorable moment. By July 13 Foch was convinced that the Second Marne would open on July 15. He then fixed July 18 as the date of the counter-offensive and set aside twenty-eight divisions for the task. He felt sure that his defensive dispositions were sound and that he would be able to defeat Von Hindenburg's drive across the Marne. The map shows the armies that were to coöperate in the counter-offensive, the Tenth Army to be the chief assaulting force.

THE COUNTER–OFFEN–SIVE OF JULY 18

THE plans for the counter-offensive were developed in absolute secrecy. Contrary to the usual custom the important orders were all given verbally. As a result Foch concentrated in the wooded country west of the salient a force much stronger than that which held the German lines in its immediate front. The Tenth Army under General Mangin consisted of five army corps including the

705 German position on a sunken road used as a trench, captured by French and American troops, from a photograph in the United States Signal Corps, War Department, Washington

Twentieth which was four-fifths American, being made up of the First and Second Divisions and a Moroccan division. The Twentieth Corps was selected to be the spearhead of the attack. General Summerall commanded the First and General Harbord the Second with General Bullard in administrative charge of both. The Americans were tense with excitement. They sensed the terrible ordeal which lay ahead. But they hoped that this movement would be the beginning of the end. On July 18 at 4:15 A.M. the Twentieth Corps assaulted behind a rolling barrage. There had been no artillery preparation. Foch had the satisfaction of achieving a complete strategical and tactical surprise. The French and Americans had complete control of the air. The infantry, preceded by light tanks, swept across the German lines and advanced in the direction of Soissons. Picture No. 705 shows a sunken road far in the rear of the German front lines from which the enemy was driven on the second day of the counter-offensive. The abandoned caisson on the left is evidence of the haste of the German retreat.

THE ACCOMPLISHMENTS OF THE FIRST AND SECOND DIVISIONS

THE First and Second Divisions advanced with a splendid *élan*. The offensive spirit which Pershing had sought to inculcate was manifesting itself. Moreover they had swept the Germans out of the trenches and were meeting them in the open fully prepared for such combat by the months of training of the immediate past. Seldom has the correctness of the foresight of a commander been more fully demonstrated. Practically from the day when the Soissons offensive began, criticisms of Pershing's policy in teaching open warfare ceased. At the end of the second day the Second Division was relieved at the request of General Harbord. It had advanced more than eight miles against stubborn resistance, had captured three thousand prisoners and sixty-six field guns, and had sustained three thousand seven hundred and eighty-eight casualties including one hundred and fifty-four officers. The First Division advanced three days and spent two in consolidating its new position. In these five days of terrific fighting it had captured three thousand eight hundred prisoners and seventy guns from the seven German divisions used against it. It suffered very heavy losses, seven thousand casualties with one thousand killed. Sixty per cent of the infantry officers were casualties and seventy-three per cent of the infantry field officers. These two divisions were the real spearhead of the thrust toward Soissons.

706 Artillery of the First Division placing a gun in a new position during the advance, July 17, 1918, from a photograph in the United States Signal Corps, War Department, Washington

707 American troops entering a village during the advance of
July 18, 1918, from a drawing by Captain George Harding, in the
United States Signal Corps, War Department, Washington

A SOLDIER'S THOUGHTS

"DURING the third day before Soissons there was a tiny knoll that, they told me, was taken and retaken six times, at the end remaining in our lines. Toward night-fall there was a lull in the storm; one could go forward with comparative safety. Just at dusk I came to the slope leading up to that knoll. And everywhere I looked the trampled wheat was dotted by recumbent figures. There was one field, two or three acres, on which it seemed you could not have stood ten feet from some one of those figures. They might have been wearied troops that had thrown themselves down to sleep. They slept indeed, the sleep no earthly reveille could disturb. I wish you could have seen that silent company under the summer twilight. It was not gruesome then, and it was not all tragedy. There lay the best of America, not dead nor sleeping, but alive so long as we will it to live. For America, if it is anything lasting, means what they showed — free, unswerving loyalty to an ideal. Who shall say that they who died there lacked vision of that ideal, even though on their unschooled tongues it could never have become articulate? They paid to the uttermost for their faith. And an even greater thing was found a little beyond — the thin line of the survivors; too weary for words, for four days and nights sleepless, without food save the crusts they had gleaned from the packs of enemy dead, souls lacerated by their ordeal. They had just been told that the expected relief was not at hand, that in the morning they were to leapfrog the first wave and go over again; most of them, they knew it, to join their comrades in sleep. And not a quiver, not a doubt, not a fear, not a regret. They were ready. While that spirit endures, America shall live." — HENRY RUSSELL MILLER, *The First Division*, v–vii, 1920.

RESULTS OF THE SURPRISE OFFENSIVE

BRIG.-GEN. C. R. HOWLAND has summed up the results of the offensive to the southwest of Soissons. "The accomplishments of the First and Second American Divisions in the American Third Corps are most impressive. . . . Aside from the French Twentieth corps [see page 311], the Tenth Army made practically no advance. The result of that blow was that Von Hindenburg, abandoning all other plans, gathered reserves wherever he could get them and sent them to stop the offensive southwest of Soissons. From the high ground captured, the railroad net near Soissons was interdicted by artillery and, as a result, trains carrying troops and material were compelled to unload near Laon from which place troops were sent forward by forced marching. Von Hindenburg decided to evacuate the Marne salient. It is an outstanding fact of the World War that the American First and Second Divisions of the American Third Corps by their magnificent dash and power in open warfare before Soissons turned the tide of the World War against Germany." — *Military History of the World War*, 342–43. In awarding the Grand Cross of the Legion of Honor to General Pershing on August 6, 1918, the French representative said: " . . . you arrived on the battlefield at the decisive hour. . . ." The German Chancellor, Count von Hertling, later remarked: "At the beginning of July, 1918, I was convinced, I confess, that before the first of September our adversaries would send us peace proposals. . . . We expected grave events in Paris for the end of July. That was on the fifteenth. On the eighteenth, even the most optimistic among us understood that all was lost. The history of the world was played out in three days."

708   Morning on the Marne, from a drawing by Captain Harvey Dunn, in the
United States Signal Corps. War Department, Washington

CHAPTER XVI

FIGHTERS OF THE SEA AND AIR

THE United States Naval Headquarters Staff in London grew from the two officers who arrived there in April, 1917, to the two hundred officers and one thousand others who were working there the day of the Armistice, in November, 1918. The United States Naval Force in active operation grew from the six destroyers which arrived at Queenstown in May, 1917, to the seven hundred and eighty-three regular vessels of the United States Navy which were in full commission at the Armistice. But this does not by any means show the whole of the United States naval work. Not counting the Marines, there were eighty thousand three hundred and twenty-seven men of all ranks and ratings on April 6, 1917, the day the United States went to war. On Armistice Day there were five hundred and thirty-five thousand one hundred and ninety-eight. Nor is this all. No less than five hundred and seventy-nine large non-naval vessels came under United States naval control. Of smaller vessels there were eight hundred and forty; while of the smallest kind there were as many more. On the other hand, this great general increase must not mislead us into thinking that the regular fighting vessels were, or could have been, increased in the same way during this nineteen-month war. The regular United States Navy fighting tonnage began with one million four hundred and forty-four thousand nine hundred and forty-seven and ended with one million eight hundred thousand one hundred and eighty-one, an increase of not much more than a quarter. Nor was the most highly skilled part of the fighting personnel increased so much or so fast as the miscellaneous total. But, all things considered, quantity and quality alike were excellent, both in growth and in fruition.

With all the four great headquarters in constant touch — Washington, London, Paris and Rome — but with London, in a general sense, as the world headquarters, the Allies and Americans watched the Austro-Germans everywhere, but especially in the North Sea, the Atlantic and the Mediterranean. The United States Navy had battleships, cruisers, destroyers, chasers, mine-layers, submarines, supply ships, auxiliaries, and aircraft, all hard at work, from the home ports to the front. There were battleships with the Grand Fleet at Scapa Flow and battleships in Bantry Bay; cruisers, destroyers, and chasers on convoy protection; with submarines, supply ships, auxiliaries, and aircraft, each doing appropriate work. Moreover, there were mine-layers creating a barrage over the whole North Sea; and a very powerful United States Naval Railroad Battery in France. Meanwhile the German navy lay in protected waters, except for the submarines, virtually idle. The enthusiasm and aggressive spirit withered and decayed through inactivity. "Hence" the weapon which failed to strike when it ought to have struck turned against our Fatherland and helped to bring about our defeat." — *Memoirs of the Crown Prince*, 80.

709   Admiral Hugh Rodman, 1859–, from a photograph by Harris & Ewing, Washington

710   The American Fleet joining the British at Scapa Flow, from the painting by
Francis Gribble, in the Navy Department, Washington

ADMIRAL HUGH RODMAN, U.S.N.

ADMIRAL RODMAN ably commanded the United States battleships that formed the Sixth Battle Squadron of the British Grand Fleet, which, as we have seen already, was the hub of the wheel of the war. If this Grand Fleet had been defeated, so as to let the German High Seas Fleet sweep in triumph over the surface of the sea, while the unchecked German submarines attacked from below, then all the Allied and neutral tonnage in the world would have been just so much easy prey, the inevitable loss of which would have starved the Allied armies to death, while equally pre-venting the arrival of the A. E. F.

THE TWO GREAT ENGLISH–SPEAKING NAVIES FORMING ONE GRAND FLEET

DECEMBER 7, 1917, was a day of great significance in both British and American history. On that day Admiral Rodman's United States battleships gathered at Scapa Flow became the Sixth Battle Squadron, and therefore an inseparable part of the body, soul, and spirit of the one Grand Fleet in which the two great English-speaking peoples joined forces. *New York* leading, on they came, *Wyoming, Florida, Delaware, Texas,* and *Arkansas,* in stately, faultless line-ahead, cheered to the echo by thousands of British tars.

ADMIRAL LORD BEATTY

ADMIRAL LORD BEATTY, the British commander in chief, Grand Fleet, had married an American and, like Lord Jellicoe, was a firm friend of the United States in general and the United States Navy in particular. He had greatly distinguished himself early in the war at the Battle of the Bight and again at Jutland in 1916. In the latter engagement he commanded the Battle Cruiser Fleet, which brought on the action.

711   Admiral Lord Beatty, 1871–, from a portrait
by Cecilia Beaux, in the National Museum,
Washington

THE GERMAN SUBMARINE NEST IN BELGIUM

CAREFULLY screened at Bruges, with alternative exits at Zeebrugge and Ostend, the German submarine nest in Belgium gave endless trouble till the splendid Northern Bombing Group of the United States naval airmen, under Captain David C. Hanrahan, seriously injured the enemy. The British destroyed Zeebrugge by a heroic naval landing attack on April 23, 1918.

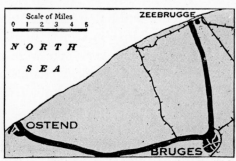

712   The Submarine Nest, from Sims and Hendrick,
The Victory at Sea, Doubleday, Page & Co., New York,
1920

THE PROJECT FOR A NORTH SEA MINE BARRAGE

IN 1917 when the "ruthless" submarine campaign threatened the vital supply lines of the British Isles, there was much popular discussion in both England and the United States of a possible North Sea mine barrage. Some naval officers favored the scheme but those charged with high command were practically unanimous in rejecting the proposal. Their reasons were simple and conclusive. The mines in use up to this point in the war were of the contact variety which must actually be touched in order to explode. To make a barrier against

713   Mine-laying, courtesy of the Navy Department, Washington

under-sea craft such mines would have to be planted at varying depths down to two hundred and fifty feet. Four hundred thousand mines would be required to lay a barrage of any strategical value. The manufacture of such a number of mines would be a colossal task. It could be accomplished, however, but laying them was quite beyond the realm of possibility. A large number of specially equipped mine-layers would be required and these would have to be guarded by destroyers. This last was the clinching argument. The destroyers, protecting convoys and the battle fleet and carrying on an unremitting offensive against the submarine, could not be spared. To have detached the number required for the defense of a mine-laying fleet would have jeopardized the defense against the U-boat and might have lost the war.

714   Mines being taken aboard a mine-layer, from a photograph in the United States Signal Corps, War Department, Washington

THE NEW MINE

IN the summer of 1917 the Bureau of Ordnance of the United States Navy under the direction of Commander S. P. Fullinwider was working hard in coöperation with Ralph C. Browne, an electrical engineer of Salem, Massachusetts, to perfect a new type of mine. By August, 1917, the Bureau was satisfied that it had solved the problem. A little later orders were given for the immediate manufacture of one hundred thousand of the new mine. The distinguishing characteristic of the new device was a long "antenna" or copper cable, supported by a small metal buoy, which extended from the mine upward to within a few feet of the surface. A metal vessel, touching this wire at any point, would set up an electric current which would explode the charge of TNT. One of the new mines could do the work of four of the old. This invention coupled with the fact that by the end of 1917 the submarine had ceased to be a vital menace made practicable the laying of a mine barrage.

FROM THE FACTORY TO THE NORTH SEA

"IF we wish a complete picture of our operation, we must call to mind first the hundreds of factories in all parts of our country, working day and night, making the numerous parts of these instruments of destruction and their attendant mechanisms; then hundreds of freight cars carrying them to the assembling plant at Norfolk, Virginia; then another small army of workmen at this point mixing their pasty explosive, heating it to a boiling point, and

715   A train load of mines *en route* to a quay, courtesy of the Navy Department, Washington

pouring the concoction into the spherical steel cases; then other groups of men moving the partially prepared mines to the docks and loading them on the cargo ships; then these ships quietly putting to sea, and, after a voyage of ten days or two weeks, as quietly slipping into the Scottish towns of Fort William and Kyle; then trains of freight cars and canal boats taking the cargoes across Scotland to Inverness and Invergordon, where the mines were completed and placed in the immense storehouses at the bases and loaded on the mine-layers as the necessity arose." — SIMS AND HENDRICK, 298.

CAPTAIN REGINALD R. BELKNAP

To Captain Belknap fell the main rôle in the great task of laying the American section of the barrage. Sims has said of him: "An organizer of rare ability, this officer deserves well of the nation for the conspicuous part which he played in the development of the North Sea Mine Barrage from start to finish." During the summer and early autumn of 1918 the American boats laid fifty-six thousand five hundred and seventy-one "eggs" as the sailors called them, and the British thirteen thousand five hundred and forty-six.

716 Captain Reginald A. Belknap, from a photograph in the Navy Department, Washington

717 Depth-charge dropped by a United States Subchaser, from a photograph in the Navy Department, Washington

RESULTS OF THE BARRAGE

"Just what the North Sea barrage accomplished, in the actual destruction of submarines, will never be definitely known. We have information that four certainly were destroyed, and in all probability six and possibly eight; yet these results doubtless measure only a small part of the German losses. In the majority of cases the Germans had little or no evidence of sunken submarines. . . . But the disconcerting thing about the North Sea barrage, from the viewpoint of the Germans, was that it could do its work so secretly that no one, friend or enemy, would necessarily know a thing about it. . . . The German records disclosed anywhere from forty to fifty submarines sunk which did not appear in the records of the Allies; how these were destroyed not a soul knows or ever will know. They simply left their German ports and were never heard of again. That many of them fell victims to mines, and some of them to the mines of our barrage, is an entirely justifiable assumption. . . . The results other than the sinking of submarines were exceedingly important in bringing the war to an end. It was the failure of the submarine campaign which defeated the German hopes and forced their surrender; and in this defeat the barrage was an important element. That submarines frequently crossed it is true . . . but its influence in breaking down the German morale must have been great." — Sims and Hendrick, 306–07.

The four placarded affairs shown in picture No. 718 are marking buoys ready to be dropped overboard. Smoke making apparatus, depth-charges, and a touring spar are also within the camera's vision. The *Baltimore's* own mine field was laid between Ireland and Scotland; and laid so well that two German submarines which tried to pass it were both blown up. Thereafter it was avoided.

Admiral Rodgers commanded the United States battleships *Nevada*, *Oklahoma*, and *Utah*, which were stationed at Berehaven, in Bantry Bay, on the southwest coast of Ireland, in case any German surface raiders should get to sea and run amuck there.

718 The stern of the *Baltimore* as a mine-layer, from the *World's Work*, August 1919

719 Admiral Thomas S. Rodgers, 1858–, boarding the *Mayflower*, from a photograph, courtesy of the Navy Department, Washington

SUBCHASERS IN THE MEDITERRANEAN

ONE of the most active of the American chaser flotillas was based on Corfu with the primary mission of fighting German and Austrian submarines in and near the Adriatic Sea. These boats, thirty-six in number and little more than large sized motor launches, made their way six thousand miles from New London to Greece under Captain Nelson, a genial and unusually competent officer. Within a day or two after reporting at Corfu they began work in a barrage at the Strait of Otranto. The water here was forty miles wide and some three thousand six hundred feet deep so that nets like those

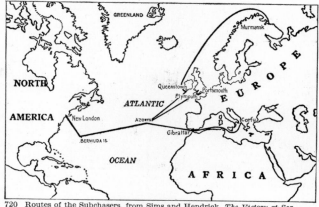

720 Routes of the Subchasers, from Sims and Hendrick, *The Victory at Sea*, Doubleday, Page & Co., New York, 1920

in the English Channel were useless. The barrage in this case was a miscellaneous lot of vessels: trawlers, drifters, motor launches, and kite balloon sloops all protected against enemy surface ships by a line of British destroyers. All the boats were equipped with the American listening device. After Nelson's flotilla arrived in July, 1918, it became practically impossible for a submarine to pass under the barrage even in stormy weather. Two weeks after their arrival their active little boats had caused a mutiny in the Austrian submarine force and no more Austrian subs attempted to make the Mediterranean.

721 Subchasers in foreign waters, from a photograph, courtesy of the Navy Department, Washington

NELSON AT DURAZZO

IN September, 1918, the British and Italians planned to shell the Austrian port of Durazzo whence supplies had been shipped to Bulgaria. Nelson was asked for twelve chasers to screen the bombarding squadrons. While the warships were destroying the water front of the Austrian seaport, Nelson's boats sank two submarines that came out to do battle with the invaders. Sims' comment on the affair follows: "Not a man in the whole American force was injured; in a brief time the excitement was all over, and the great ships, screened again by the wasps of chasers, started back to Brindisi. The impression made upon our Allies was well expressed in the congratulatory message sent to me in London by Commodore Kelley, who commanded the British cruisers in this action. 'Their conduct,' he said, 'was beyond praise. They all returned safely without casualties. They thoroughly enjoyed themselves.'" — SIMS AND HENDRICK, 238.

"SUB" AGAINST "SUB"

AT the outbreak of the war the belief was general that submarines could not be effective against boats of their own kind. The experience of the conflict proved quite the contrary. The Allied submarines had the great advantage over their enemies of not having to fear surface craft. There were cases, however, of destroyers failing to detect the signals arranged to identify the friendly under-sea boats causing them to dive for safety in the same manner as the enemy. In 1918 the sea area was blocked off in rectangles or "billets" in each of which there was a submarine patrol. In all, the British subs accounted for twenty

722 Submarines at Bantry Bay, Ireland, courtesy of the Navy Department, Washington

enemy U-boats which was a higher percentage of sinkings than any of the surface craft attained. The Americans had seven submarines based on Berehaven, Ireland, whose "billets" were located in the approaches to the Irish Sea. They were not fortunate enough, however, to send down an enemy.

723 The Deck of the *Santee* after being torpedoed, from *The World's Work*, January 1920, courtesy of Doubleday, Doran & Co., New York

THE UNITED STATES NAVY MYSTERY SHIP, *SANTEE*

THE British Navy developed the mystery ship. In appearance such a boat was a tramp, a harmless merchantman. The hold was packed to prevent sinking in case of a hit by a torpedo and guns were skillfully concealed. A carefully drilled "panic party" simulated abandoning the ship after an attack by a submarine. The purpose was to decoy the enemy vessel in close so that the concealed guns could sink her. These Q-ships as they were called destroyed twelve submarines. The Americans naturally wanted to participate in this form of warfare. The British admiralty turned over a vessel which was named the *Santee*. When Sims called for volunteers, he found himself embarrassed by the number of those who desired to go. As the event proved the *Santee* had little luck. Sailing from Queenstown to Bantry Bay late in December, 1917, she was struck by a torpedo. She did not sink because her hull was so well packed with wood. The panic party got off but no submarine appeared. After a time the *Santee* was towed back to port. Admiral Sims has emphasized that the "most important accomplishment of the mystery ships was not the actual sinking of submarines, but their profound influence on the tactics of the U-boats. It was manifest in the beginning that the first information reaching Germany concerning the mystery ships would greatly diminish the chances of sinking submarines by this means, for it would cause all submarines to be wary of all mercantile craft. They were therefore obliged to abandon the easy, safe, and cheap methods of sinking ships by bombs or gun fire, and were consequently forced to incur the danger of attacking with the scarce and expensive torpedo." — SIMS AND HENDRICK, 197. Mystery ships were used by the British with more success than fell to the lot of the *Santee* while under American command.

724   American convoy following a zig-zag path, courtesy of the Navy Department, Washington

NAVAL RESULTS OF THE GERMAN DRIVE OF 1918

THE success of the German drive in March and April, 1918, brought the Allied cause perilously near to disaster. The one hope left was American troops in France. The United States stripped its coast lines and the Great Lakes of every available ton of shipping and pressed it into the service of "The Great Atlantic Ferry Company, Incorporated but Unlimited." England took great numbers of boats off her trade routes to South America, Australia, and the East. France and Italy also supplied boats. Of the total number of American troops sent to France from the outbreak of hostilities the United States provided transports for 46.25 per cent, Great Britain for 51.25 and France and Italy for the remainder. Of the soldiers sent over between March, 1918, and the Armistice, American ships carried 42.15 per cent, and British vessels 55.40 per cent. For many Americans service in the war meant sailing continuously across the Atlantic hurrying troops and supplies to France. An idea of their point of view can be gained from the *Song of the Transport Crew.*

Your wife, she's your allotment-girl:
Your kid's your next of kin;
But a mighty close relation
Is the ship that brings you in!
She sickens you; you curse her out;
You call her 'This damned tub';
But you count upon that transport
To dodge the subtle sub!

From New York Town to Quiberon,
'Twixt Hampton Roads and Dover,
There's no one you depend on like
The ship that brings you over!
So when your feet are dry ashore
And she is far awash,
You owe it to the transport that
You lived to fight the Boche.

THE NAVY AND THE TRANSPORT

ONE of the great feats of the combined navies was the protection of the transports which brought more than two million men to France so perfectly that not a single incoming boat loaded with soldiers was sunk. The naval solution of its problem had many aspects. Two great lanes, roughly two hundred miles in breadth, were established for eastward-bound ships. After March, 1918, the bulk of the transports came through the southern lane while the northern lane was full of supply ships, though it, too, saw some transports. The Germans could never in 1918 keep a flotilla of more than ten or eleven effective submarines out at a given time. These generally chose the northern lane because the German command estimated that the submarines could be more useful in attempting to cut the line of supplies of the Allies than in sinking a few transports. The Navy, however, did not depend on the two lanes for the sole protection of the transports. The convoy room of the Admiralty kept the location of every submarine reported plotted on its maps and sent warnings to convoys when U-boats lay in their path.

725 Admiral Henry Thomas Mayo, 1856–, from a photograph by Harris & Ewing, Washington

726 United States destroyer laying down a smoke screen to protect troopships, courtesy of the Navy Department, Washington

THE DESTROYER AND THE TRANSPORT

THE convoys kept up a continual zig-zagging during the time when they were passing through the danger zone. Finally a "convoy of four or five large troopships would be surrounded by as many as ten or a dozen destroyers. Very properly, since they were carrying human cargoes, we gave them an escort at least three times as large per vessel as that given to large mercantile convoys of twenty or more vessels; and this fact made them very uninviting baits for the most venturesome U-boat commanders." A hard grind was the work on the destroyers which brought in one convoy only to turn about and race out to meet another.

"A hundred men in a watchcase ship,
We fellows put to sea,
With a place to sleep (if your foot don't slip!)
And a cargo of T.N.T.
(A place to sleep — when there's time to sleep!)
And we eat when we get the chance —
On a boat that goes
On its toes
And nose
In a dangerous dervish dance;
Dodging subs and the convoy's blows,
We're bringing your boys to France!"

SINKING OF THE *PRESIDENT LINCOLN*

THE *President Lincoln* did experience attack and did go down, but she was on her way home in 15° W, and 48° N. Her crew behaved to perfection. All things considered, the sinkings of United States vessels, during the period of United States hostilities, were surprisingly few, even when we consider the remoteness of her coast and the relative immunity of her vessels in Franco-American waters. The whole number of United States merchant vessels lost was only one hundred and forty-eight; while the number of United States naval vessels was only fifty-six.

727 The Sinking of the *President Lincoln*, from the painting by Fred Dana Marshall, courtesy of the Navy Department, Washington

728   Group of the Yale Unit at Palm Beach (F. Trubee Davison sixth from
         left, back row), courtesy of Mrs. Henry P. Davison

F. TRUBEE DAVISON AND THE "YALE GANG"

"I can pay no finer tribute to American youth than to say that the great aircraft force which was ultimately assembled in Europe had its beginnings in a small group of undergraduates at Yale University. In recommending Mr. Trubee Davison for a Distinguished Service Medal, the commander of our aviation forces wrote: 'This officer was responsible for the organization of the first Yale aviation unit of twenty-nine aviators who were later enrolled in the Naval Reserve Flying Corps, and, in fact, may be considered as the nucleus from which the United States Aviation Forces, Foreign Service, later grew.' This group of college boys acted entirely on their own initiative. While the United States was still at peace, encouraged only by their parents and a few friends, they took up the study of aviation. It was their conviction that the United States would certainly get into the war, and they selected this branch as the one in which they could render the greatest service to their country. . . . In February, 1917, Secretary Daniels recognized their work by making Davison a member of the Committee on Aeronautics; in March practically every member of the unit was enrolled in the aviation service; and their names appear among the first one hundred aviators enrolled in the Navy — a list that ultimately included several thousand. So proficient had these undergraduates become that they were used as a nucleus to train our aircraft forces; they were impressed as instructors at Buffalo, Bayshore, Hampton Roads, the Massachusetts Institute of Technology, Key West and Moorehead City. They began to go abroad in the summer of 1917, and they were employed as instructors in schools in France and England. These young men not only rendered great material service, but they manifested an enthusiasm, an earnestness, and a tireless vigilance which exerted a wonderful influence in strengthening the morale of the whole aviation department. 'I knew that whenever we had a member of the Yale unit,' says Lieutenant-Commander Edwards, who was aide for aviation at the London Headquarters in the latter part of the war, 'everything was alright. Whenever the French and English asked us to send a couple of our crack men to reinforce a squadron, I would say, "Let's get some of the Yale gang."'"
— SIMS AND HENDRICK, 328–29.

KENNETH MacLEISH TO HIS FATHER

ONE of the most remarkable of the human documents that came out of the war was from the pen of one of Trubee Davison's men, Kenneth MacLeish. His ability won him promotion from electrician, second class to lieutenant, senior grade. At the time he was shot down by an enemy plane he was flying with the 213th Squadron of the British Air Force. A destroyer of the United States Navy was named in his honor. "If I find it necessary to make the supreme sacrifice, always remember this — I am so firmly convinced that the ideals I am going to fight for are right and splendid ideals that I am happy to be able to give so much for them. I could not have any self-respect, I could not consider myself a man, if I saw these ideals defeated when it lies in my power to defend them. So I have no fears! I have no regrets; I have only to thank God for such a wonderful opportunity to serve Him and the world. No, if I must make the supreme sacrifice I will do it gladly and I will do it honorably and bravely, as your son should, and the life that I lay down will be my preparation for the grander, finer life that I shall take up. I shall live! You must not grieve, I shall be supremely happy — so must you — not that I have 'gone West,' but that I have bought such a wonderful life at so small a price and paid for it so gladly."

729   N-1 Seaplane taxiing at high speed, from a photograph, courtesy of the Naval
                    Aircraft Factory, Philadelphia

THE DEVELOP-MENT OF NAVAL AVIATION

THE Navy from the outset of the war gave vigorous attention to the development of the aviation arm. Regular naval officers who served with distinction in the building up of this service include Captain T. T.

730   Sea planes at the Naval Air Station, Pensacola, Fla., from a photograph by A. E. Wells, Pensacola

Craven who was aide for aviation on the staff of Admiral Wilson, and Lieutenant Whiting who brought the first naval aeronautic detachment to France in June, 1917. To Captain H. I. Cone was assigned the task of organizing the American naval air forces in Europe. When he was later relieved because of wounds received from an enemy submarine while he was crossing the Irish Sea, his place was taken by his assistant, Lieutenant W. A. Edwards. For his work Edwards received the award of the Distinguished Service Order from King George. When the Armistice came, the Americans had some five hundred planes in commission and a force of twenty-five hundred officers and twenty-two thousand enlisted men. The aviation activities of the Navy included the North Sea, the Irish Sea, the Bay of Biscay, and the Adriatic Sea.

731   Captain David C. Hanrahan (fourth from the left) and officers of the Northern Bombing Squadron, from a photograph in the Navy Department, Washington

THE NORTHERN BOMBING GROUP

THE work of the naval aviators was of many kinds. There was the constant search for submarines and frequent combats with enemy aviators. The Northern Bombing Group under the command of Captain David C. Hanrahan consisting of one hundred and twelve planes, three hundred and five officers and more than two thousand enlisted personnel had for its sole duty the bombing of the German submarine bases at Zeebrugge and Ostend. In the Adriatic, Austrian ports were bombed.

HAMMON AND GATES

THE outstanding heroes among the naval aviators were Ensign Charles H. Hammon and Lieutenant-Commander A. L. Gates. The former in a bombing raid on Pola after being engaged with two enemy planes which shot several holes in his machine went to the rescue of a comrade who had been shot down. With his damaged plane Hammon landed on a rough sea in imminent danger of either drowning or capture. He succeeded, however, in picking up the stricken aviator and in flying back to his base seventy-five miles away. Gates commanded the United States Naval Air Station at Dunkirk, France, which was almost continually under enemy shell and bomb fire. Although it was not within his range of duties, Gates, alone and unescorted, rescued the crew of a British sea plane wrecked off the coast near Ostend. He was later shot down behind the German lines and became a prisoner of war. Sims said of him: "During all his service this officer was a magnificent example of courage, modesty, and energetic devotion to duty."

732   Ensign Charles H. Hammon, from a photograph in the United States Signal Corps, War Department, Washington

733   William Thaw, from a drawing in red chalk by John Elliott, in the National Gallery of Art, Washington

THE ORIGIN OF THE LAFAYETTE ESCADRILLE

TRUBEE DAVISON and his associates were not the first Americans to become interested in air fighting in the war. These were that small group who, on April 18, 1916, reported to Captain Georges Thénault at Luxeuil, France, to form Escadrille No. 124, known for many months as the American Escadrille. The man who had been most active in bringing about this result was Norman Prince, Harvard, 1909. Back of the formation of the Escadrille lay an interesting story. Scarcely had France gone to war when young Americans began volunteering for service in the French army. Some, like Prince and William Thaw, were experienced pilots and applied for aviation. They were doomed to disappointment. France began the war with only eighty planes, not enough machines for the French pilots. The Americans, undaunted, entered the French service as second class soldiers in the Foreign Legion. Many of them were in the trenches soon after the First Battle of the Marne. From the Foreign Legion, one after another, several secured transfers to aviation. Prince had volunteered in October, 1914, but had not succeeded in getting himself accepted until the spring of 1915, when he went directly into aviation. By the spring of 1916 there were many Americans with the French escadrilles. Prince, Cowdin, and Thaw, all recently returned from a winter leave in the United States, together with Captain Thénault, whom they met in Paris, accomplished the organization of the famous flying corps in which practically all the American flyers were gathered together a few weeks after the Germans had started their terrific drive against Verdun. The first members of the escadrille were Chapman, Prince, Rockwell, MacConnell, Thaw, and Cowdin. Lufbery, one of their most famous fliers, joined them a little later.

THE DEVELOPMENT OF FRENCH AVIATION

"AT the beginning of the war fighting aviation didn't exist, and the first machines to be armed were Voisins with a 'pusher' propellor, which were fitted with a Hotchkiss, according to the plans of Captain Mailfert. These machines were masters of the air until the end of 1914. With one of them Frantz had been the first French pilot to bring down a Boche in an air battle near Rheims. The Morane 'Parasol' with a passenger armed with a carbine had held sway in 1915, and an army was considered to be protected as far as the air was concerned when one machine patrolled twenty-five or thirty miles of front. That was the best that could be done owing to the lack of machines. In 1915 little single-seater fighting planes had begun to make their appearance. Then that great pilot Garros had had the idea of armour-plating the propellor of a small Morane so that he could fire his machine gun athwart the whirling blade without fear of its being splintered by a bullet. Should any touch the propellor the armour deflected them and prevented damage. After several successes Garros had been captured in Flanders. The Germans had copied his machine and developed from it the Fokker. Gilbert had gone on working where Garros had left off, and Pegoud had made further improvements on the Nieuport. He had been the first to fix a Lewis gun on the upper plane firing above the propellor. . . .

We [the American Escadrille] were to fly the baby-Nieuport, a machine which had made its appearance four months before, 'the machine of Aces and the Ace of machines' as we called it, the fastest and handiest with its sixteen square yards of surface, eighty horse power Rhone rotary motor and speed of ninety-five miles an hour. For that period it was a tremendous advance. The Nieuport had won its spurs at Verdun, where it clearly outclassed the Fokker."
— GEORGES THÉNAULT, *The Story of the Lafayette Escadrille*, 21–22, 25–26, Small, Maynard & Company, Boston, 1921.

734   The Nieuport 28, from a drawing by Captain Harry Townsend, in the United States Signal Corps, War Department, Washington

THE RECORD OF THE ESCADRILLE

IN all forty Americans served with Captain Thénault and Lieutenant de Laage de Meaux in the Lafayette Escadrille from its formation until January 1, 1918, when it was transferred to the American Army. Its original name was changed in December, 1916, when for diplomatic reasons the Minister of War announced that "the Volunteer Escadrille will henceforth be called the 'Lafayette Escadrille.'" At the battle of Verdun in 1916 the Escadrille had one hundred and forty-six combats bringing down thirteen enemy planes that were confirmed, with only one pilot killed and three wounded. In 1917 it won the following citation: "Escadrille composed of American volunteers who have come to fight for France in the purest spirit of sacrifice. Has carried on ceaselessly, under the command of Captain Thénault, an ardent struggle against our enemies. In very heavy fighting and at the cost of serious losses, which far from weakening it exalted its morale, has brought down twenty-eight enemy planes. Has aroused the deep admiration of the chiefs, who have had it under their orders, and of French Escadrilles, which, fighting beside it, have wished to rival its courage." ". . . the Lafayette Escadrille became the first American fighting Escadrille with the

735 Georges Thénault, from a drawing in red chalk by John Elliott, in the National Museum, Washington

number 103. . . . Lufbery went off to organize another and some months later, setting as always the example, met a glorious death in battle. He fell in Lorraine near Toul. There died there a very wonderful personality and his death was an incalculable loss to the Allies." — GEORGES THÉNAULT. Singularly appropriate for those of this corps who gave their lives were the lines of Alan Seeger who himself died fighting as a volunteer in another arm of the French service.

Yet sought they neither recompense nor praise,
Nor to be mentioned in another breath
Than their blue-coated comrades, whose great days
It was their pride to share — aye, share even to the death,
Nay, rather, France, to you they rendered thanks

(Seeing that they came for honor, not for gain),
Who opening to them your glorious ranks
Gave them that grand occasion to excel —
That chance to live the life most free from stain
And that rare privilege of dying well.

THE SPIRIT OF THE AIR CORPS

WAR aviation produced a type. The service had a point of view and a spirit all its own. Good fellowship and banter went hand in hand with a deep sense of responsibility to comrades and cause. The song of the Ninetieth Squadron sung to the tune of the Cornell "Alma Mater" reflects the temper of the group.

736 Raoul Lufbery, from a drawing in red chalk by John Elliott, in the National Museum, Washington

Flying low o'er Verdun's trenches dodging shot and shell,
Pair o' dice our lucky emblem, we'll give the Huns more Hell.

Far above the noise of battle, dodging "Archie" fire
Taking photos far in Hunland, that's our heart's desire
LIKE HELL (shouted)

Ninetieth ties can ne'er be broken, wherever we may fly,
Friendships formed in face of danger — they can never die.

Chorus

Tails up and flying, any weather, where e'er the call may be,
Happy Landings, Ninetieth Squadron, hail all hail to thee!

This song was always sung by the Ninetieth Squadron, just before the evening mess broke up. All verses were sung standing, with all glasses filled. After the last chorus the following verse was sung (name of tune unknown) and, as the last line was finished, all glasses were drained "bottoms up."

So stand to your glasses steady, and drink to your comrade's eye —
Here's a health to the dead already, and a health to the next man to die!

— Furnished by LT.-COL. WM. G. SCHAUFFLER, JR.

737 Lieutenant Frank L. Baylies, from a photograph
      by Underwood & Underwood, New York

LIEUTENANTS FRANK L. BAYLIES AND
DAVID E. PUTNAM

BAYLIES was another young American who entered the conflict before the United States declared war. He was an ambulance driver from February, 1916, to May, 1917. He then transferred to aviation, went through the training school at Avord and became a member of the Lafayette Escadrille. He chose to remain with the French service and became a member by invitation of a famous French organization known as the Storks. He more than justified his selection. In February, 1918, he shot down his first plane. Then came the great German drive of that year. By June 17 Baylies had brought down twenty enemies though only twelve were officially accredited. On that day while engaging three German triplanes a fourth pounced upon him out of a cloud from the rear. On July 6 a German pilot swooped low over the French lines and dropped a weighted streamer. The message read: "Pilot Baylies killed in combat. Buried with military honors."

Putnam, a descendant of General Israel Putnam of the American Revolution, held a unique record in the American air service. Like Baylies he was trained at the Avord Flying Field. In June, 1918, when the German hordes were driving fiercely toward Paris, Putnam distinguished himself by his attacks on the enemy infantry. Flying low with seemingly complete indifference to the bullets from the ground which riddled his wings the young lieutenant caught the Germans in massed formations and sprayed them with machine gun fire. On June 10 he reached the climax of his career when in two combats behind the enemy lines he brought down five German planes. He was killed September 18, 1918.

THE GREATEST AMERICAN ACES

AN aviator won the designation of ace when he had shot down five enemy machines which had been certified to by observers from the ground. Most aces had on their score one or more machines not accredited. There were sixty-six American aces. The official scores of all who brought down eight or more machines are as follows:

Pilot	Organization	Planes Shot Down	Balloons Shot Down	Pilot	Organization	Planes Shot Down	Balloons Shot Down
Capt. E. V. Rickenbacker	94th	22	3	First Lt. T. C. Cassady	148th	9	0
Second Lt. Frank Luke	27th	4	14	First Lt. H. R. Clay	148th	8	0
Major R. V. Lufbery	94th	17	0	First Lt. L. Hamilton	3d R.A.F.	5	3
First Lt. G. Vaughn	17th R.A.F.	12	1	First Lt. Joseph Wehner	27th	2	6
First Lt. F. Kindley	148th	12	0	Second Lt. S. Donaldson	22d R.A.F.	7	1
First Lt. D. Putnam	139th	12	0	Second Lt. C. Jones	22d	8	0
First Lt. E. Springs	148th	11	0	First Lt. F. O. D. Hunter	103d	7	1
First Lt. Reed Landis	40th R.A.F.	9	1	First Lt. J. B. Beane	22d	6	2
First Lt. J. M. Swaab	32d	10	0	Major J. A. Meissner	147th	7	1
First Lt. C. E. Wright	93d	8	1	Captain H. Coolidge	94th	5	3
First Lt. P. E. Baer	103d	9	0	Second Lt. W. W. White	147th	7	1

A SONG OF THE AIR FORCE

"We're going to blind the enemy, so all the papers say,
We fly the festive Liberty; we're missing the next day.
A bullet in our gas tank; we kiss the world good bye;
They say it's for Democracy, as we fall from the sky.

We like to see the Regular who has a J.M.A. [Junior Military Aviator]
Sit in his cosy dugout with one half extra pay.
He tells us how to fight the war, for he shot on a sleeve [target]
And if we bring down all the Boche, we may get three days leave.

Chorus
For we're the Airmen, the festive Airmen.
Perhaps we never should have flown, but our ships were made at home.
For we're the Airmen, the festive Airmen —
We invite you all to come and fly this crate called Liberty.
Jug-jug-a-jug-jug jug-jug-a-jug-jug C-R-A-S-H"
                              — Furnished by LT.-COL. WM. G. SCHAUFFLER, JR.

738 Insignia of the 168th Aero Squadron, from a photograph in the United States Signal Corps, War Department, Washington

THE AMERICAN AIR SERVICE

WHEN the President delivered his war message to Congress in April, 1917, the United States Army possessed two hundred training planes not one of a type considered fit for service in battle. The air personnel was known as the Aviation Section of the Signal Corps, and it numbered sixty-five officers and approximately eleven hundred soldiers. There is no better illustration of the lack of preparedness of the United States when it entered the World War. On Armistice Day there were actually in service at the front forty-five American Squadrons with seven hundred and forty-four pilots, four hundred and fifty-seven observers, twenty-three aerial gunners and the necessary soldiers. There were in addition twenty-three American balloon companies at the front. On this same day the American Air Service numbered seven thousand seven hundred and twenty-six officers and seventy thousand seven hundred and sixty-nine soldiers. Sixteen training schools, becoming rapidly more and more efficient, were turning out pilots and observers.

739 Student Aviators receiving instruction in magnetos at the Military Aviation School, University of California, from a photograph in the United States Signal Corps, War Department, Washington

740   Field Number 1, Issoudoun, from a drawing by Captain J. André Smith, in the United States Signal Corps, War Department, Washington

THE ACHIEVEMENTS OF THE AMERICAN AIR SERVICE

"OUR air squadrons took part in one hundred and fifty organized bombing raids, and dropped over two hundred and seventy-five thousand pounds of explosives on the enemy. They flew thirty-five thousand hours over the line, and took eighteen thousand pictures of enemy positions . . . they regulated the firing of our artillery, flew in contact with our advancing forces, and from a height of only a few yards from the ground, machine-gunned and bombed enemy batteries, convoys and troops on the march. . . . The American Air Service obtained a total of seven hundred and fifty-three aerial victories, in the accomplishment of which it lost three hundred and fifty-seven airplanes. Seventy-one confined enemy balloons were destroyed by our Air Service and the enemy air service succeeded in destroying thirty-four of our balloons." — SHIPLEY THOMAS, 385–88.

THE AMERICAN SYSTEM

"THIS diagram represents a vertical section of the air as it would appear to one able to see every part of aviation on a good day during our operations of September, October, and November, 1918. The notch in the horizontal line indicates the trench or dividing line between hostile territory. . . . The anti-aircraft machine guns are shown close to the troops, and the anti-aircraft artillery immediately behind them. The heights at which the various types of aviation act are indicated in metres. The special pursuit details, acting at a

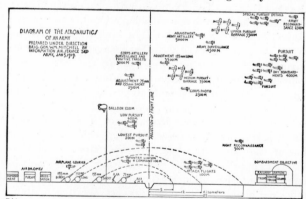

741   From the *World's Work*, Sept. 1919

great altitude (practically as high as they can get) work directly against the enemy's reconnaissance machines. Our own Army reconnaissance, acting up to twenty thousand feet, habitually went thirty or forty miles into the enemy's territory. The Army's surveillance machines kept cruising over the front to report from their own position, by wireless, whatever they could see, so that it could be immediately attacked by their aviation elements. The pursuit and day bombardment elements, shown to the right of the diagram together, indicate the independent or strategical aviation, which acts by itself directly against the enemy aviation and his ground troops." — MAJ.-GEN. WILLIAM MITCHELL in the *World's Work*. New York, September, 1919.

742   Breguet bombing plane used by the United States Air Service, from a photograph in the United States
Signal Corps, War Department, Washington

THE AIR SERVICE IN THE MEUSE–ARGONNE OFFENSIVE

ON October 4, 1918, an American day bombing force was sent out to bomb Dun-sur-Meuse and Landres-St. Georges. It was the opening day of the second phase of the great battle. The aviators dropped a ton and a half of bombs on each objective. Then through the low-lying clouds they were attacked by some thirty enemy pursuit planes. The Ninetieth Squadron got the brunt of the attack while the Twenty-ninth and Eleventh fell upon the enemy's rear. Two German planes had been brought down by the bombers when thirty spads of the American Second Pursuit Group swept to the aid of the bombing planes. The enemy, though he tried desperately to get away, was caught. After the battle thirteen German planes lay in ruins within a space of a thousand feet on the ground. The Americans had lost one plane. In one period of twenty-four hours in the Meuse-Argonne offensive American airplanes dropped sixty-nine tons of explosives on the enemy. As a direct consequence a German counter-attack was frustrated. In the words of the then Brigadier-General William Mitchell: "It was indeed the dawn of the day when great air forces will be capable of definitely effecting a ground decision on the field of battle."

THE CHIVALRY OF THE AIR

ON October 10 near Dun-sur-Meuse occurred perhaps the most remarkable air fight in the history of American aviation. Captain Rickenbacker was commanding eight machines of the One Hundred and Forty-seventh Squadron reinforced by seven from the Twenty-seventh Squadron. Their objective was an enemy balloon. They were suddenly attacked by German planes. Ten Fokkers gave battle to the eight machines of the One Hundred and Forty-seventh, the planes from the Twenty-seventh being off on either flank. Lieutenant Wilbur White, an air fighter of the finest quality, was leading the pilots of the One Hundred and Forty-seventh. Suddenly he saw a German plane dart for the rear machine in White's formation and put himself in a position which meant sure death to the American. White's one thought seems to have been to save his endangered comrade. Rickenbacker, who watched the affair, has left the following account. "Like a flash White zoomed up into a half-turn, executed a *renversement*, and came back at the Hun leader to protect his pilot from a certain death. . . . White's maneuver occupied but an instant. He came out of his swoop and made a direct plunge for the enemy machine, which was just getting in line on the rear *Spad's* tail. Without firing a shot the heroic White rammed the *Fokker* head on while the two machines were approaching each other at the rate of two hundred and fifty miles per hour! It was a horrible yet thrilling sight. . . . For sheer nerve and bravery I believe this heroic feat was never surpassed. No national honor too great could compensate the family of Lieutenant White for this sacrifice for his comrade pilot and his unparalleled example of heroism to his squadron. For the most pitiable feature of Lieutenant White's self-sacrifice was the fact that this was his last flight over the lines before he was to leave for the United States on a visit to his wife and two small children." — *Fighting the Flying Circus,* 1919.

743   Captain Edward Rickenbacker, 1890–, from a
photograph by Harris & Ewing, Washington

CHAPTER XVII

ST. MIHIEL AND THE MEUSE–ARGONNE OFFENSIVE

ON July 15 Von Hindenburg had launched his troops in the Second Battle of the Marne and three days later Foch had struck back with his counter-attack toward Soissons. The comments of General Ludendorff on the events of those days and the fortnight immediately following are significant. In view of the achievements of three American divisions in particular his comments present an interesting point of view. "The [German] losses through the battle had been so heavy that we were compelled to break up about ten divisions and use their infantry as reserves for others. . . . This was the beginning of a vast railway transportation movement. It opened at the end of July and increased considerably at the beginning of August, and from that time onward hardly ever diminished. The troops, who were very much exhausted, had to be brought up to establishment, rested, and given time to recuperate. I had not succeeded in getting any clear idea of the enemy's losses since July 15, but, considering the massed tactics of the Entente, they must have been high. . . .

"The armies of the Entente had also suffered; the battle had cost the enemy as much as it had cost us. The French had sent into action a remarkably large number of Senegalese and Moroccans, and had endeavored to spare their own people. The six American divisions that had taken part in the battle had suffered most severely without achieving any successes. [See Nos. 705 and 749.] One division appears to have been broken up in order to bring them up to establishment. [No division was broken up.] Notwithstanding the gallantry of the individual American soldier, the inferior quality of the American troops is proved by the fact that two brave German divisions were able to withstand the main attack made by very superior American forces for several weeks; and these two divisions, the 4th Ersatz and the 201st, I had up till then considered no better than the average. . . . The attempt to make the nations of the Entente inclined to peace before the arrival of the American reinforcements by means of German victories had failed. The energy of the army had not sufficed to deal the enemy a decisive blow before the Americans were on the spot in considerable force. It was quite clear to me that our general situation had thus become very serious. . . . Early in August I decidedly hoped that we should be able to defeat the imminent attacks and to deliver counterstrokes, though on a smaller scale than heretofore. Even in extremely critical situations we had hitherto always succeeded in discovering a strategical remedy, and I had no reason to suppose we should not do so again." — *Ludendorff's Own Story*, Vol. II, 322–24, Harper Bros., New York, 1921. "When I look back and compare the past," the Crown Prince has said, "that time [the days immediately following the Second Marne] is the saddest of my life — sadder even than the critical months at Verdun or the deeply painful days, weeks and months that followed the catastrophe." — *Memoirs of the Crown Prince*, 240, Scribner's, 1922.

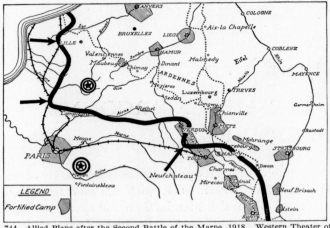

744 Allied Plans after the Second Battle of the Marne, 1918. Western Theater of
Operations, from Brig.-Gen. C. R. Howland, *Military History of the World War*,
General Service Schools Press, Fort Leavenworth, Kansas, 1923

SITUATION AFTER THE DRIVE
TOWARD SOISSONS

THE drive toward Soissons occasioned the beginning of a German retrograde movement which did not end until the Armistice. Von Hindenburg could look to no other fronts for reinforcements. The morale of his troops was low. General Ludendorff considered the situation "very grave." Von Hindenburg estimated that he had lost the offensive and decided to assume the strategical and tactical defensive attitude. He hesitated to issue such orders, however, because of their effect on the spirits of the German troops. He hoped that his enemies would make a blunder which he could turn to his advantage. Foch and his Allied generals, however, made no mistakes. Having seized the offensive on July 18, Foch determined to retain it. This decision was affirmed at a conference of commanders in chief held on July 24. At this meeting the commanding generals planned to retain continuously the offensive until the war was won. They estimated that they had equal combat strength with the Germans on the line and that they were superior in reserves, thanks to the arrival of the Americans, and in artillery, tanks, and aviation. The first phase of the aggressive movement was to be surprise offensives with limited objectives; the second was to be a general offensive to crush the enemy. The first phase was to see blows struck at the Amiens salient, which would free the Paris-Amiens railroad route; at the German positions farther north, to drive the enemy from the mining region of northern France; and at the St. Mihiel salient, which would free the Paris-Avricourt railroad route.

SMASHING THE AMIENS SALIENT

ON August 8 the great blow against the Amiens salient was struck. The British Fourth Army was the weapon used. In preparation for the assault Marshal Haig had issued detailed orders for an attack in Flanders. He had moved Canadian troops into that region. He had maintained a prodigious amount of activity behind the lines of his First Army, building dummy corps headquarters and casualty stations, keeping up a great wireless activity, and maneuvering bodies of tanks when the visibility was good. These efforts were successful in persuading the Germans that the next blow was to be in the north. They were, therefore, quite unprepared when, at 4:20 A.M. on August 8, the British Fourth Army under General Rawlinson without any artillery preparation suddenly left its trenches and moved toward the German lines. It was supported by an intense artillery concentration which silenced the German guns. Accompanied by four hundred tanks the British rushed forward with seven divisions in line and four in support. So swift was the advance of the British that several German division headquarters were taken by surprise. Thirteen thousand prisoners and more than three hundred guns were taken. The enemy was too much surprised to make local counter-attacks. Ludendorff has called this the darkest day of the war. He asked to be relieved and requested an immediate conference with the Government at Spa.

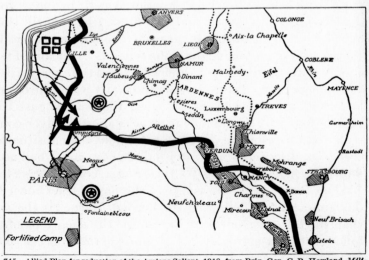

745 Allied Plan for reduction of the Amiens Salient, 1918, from Brig.-Gen. C. R. Howland, *Military History of the World War*, General Service Schools Press, Fort Leavenworth, Kansas, 1923

746 Maj.-Gen. Edward M. Lewis, 1863–, from a photograph in the United States Signal Corps, War Department, Washington

747 Maj.-Gen. George W. Read, 1860–, from a photograph in the United States Signal Corps, Washington

748 Maj.-Gen. John F. O'Ryan, 1874–, from a photograph in the United States Signal Corps, War Department, Washington

THE REDUCTION OF THE LYS SALIENT

THE French First Army and Third Army coöperated with the British Fourth Army in exploiting the success of August 8. Swiftly the Germans fell back before the blows of the Allies. The reduction of the Amiens salient made untenable the Lys salient west of Lille, which maintained control of the mining region. Von Hindenburg decided to evacuate it, having given orders that the mines should be put out of order and the country devastated. The Germans were slowly leaving when Haig struck the flanks of the salient, August 31 – September 2, to expedite their departure. In this enterprise coöperated the American Twenty-seventh Division under General O'Ryan, and the Thirtieth Division under General Edward M. Lewis, of the American Second Corps, commanded by General Read. The Germans were out of the salient by September 6.

ADVANCING ON THE AISNE

THE Allies and Americans continued their work of exploiting the great victories achieved in the reduction of the Amiens and Lys salients. Foch was in general command. Haig directed the operations in the north; Petain in the south. An all-American army was being formed by Pershing to reduce the St. Mihiel salient. By September 25 the Germans had been pushed back to the Siegfried Line. With all hope of victory gone they were fighting desperately to stave off defeat and to enable their Government to arrange a peace by diplomacy. After the Second Marne the following American Divisions participated in the fighting under General Petain between July 18 and September 6: Twenty-sixth, Forty-second, Fourth, Seventy-seventh, and Thirty-second.

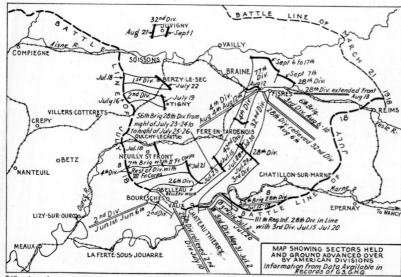

749 Americans at the Second Battle of the Marne, from Brig.-Gen. C. R. Howland, *Military History of the World War*, General Service Schools Press, Fort Leavenworth, Kansas, 1923

750   General Pershing at Chaumont, Oct. 1918, from a photograph in the United States Signal Corps, War Department, Washington

THE AMERICAN FIRST ARMY

THE American First Army was organized by Pershing's order on August 10 with the American commander in chief in direct command. His plans, however, were seriously impeded by the request of Foch for the American divisions already noted to aid Haig and Petain in the work which they had in progress in August and early September. From the first Pershing had been insistent that the American troops could be used most effectively when organized as a unit and when fighting entirely under their own commanders. With considerable reluctance the Allies finally yielded the point. The American First Army was not fully organized before Italy, seeing American divisions going to the aid of the British and the French, had unsuccessfully requested some twenty to twenty-five divisions from the United States. On September 2 Foch finally consented to the concentration of the American First Army as a unit on the fighting front. Such was the background of the St. Mihiel drive.

THE ALL–AMERICAN BASIC STAFF ORGANIZATION

Too long, and far too complex, for description here, this administrative chart shows how all the infinitely varied parts were closely coördinated into one coöperating whole. The date shows how Pershing's plans were pre-arranged, in every detail, five months before he took command of the First Army on August 10, six months before this Army fought its first great fight, seven months before the Second Army came into being, and eight months before the Third Army appeared, just after the Armistice, to occupy surrendered ground. At the upper left-hand corner is Pershing himself, as commander in chief of the whole A. E. F. in Europe. Under him come, first, the commanding generals of "Armies," under these of "Army Corps," and, under these again, of "Divisions." When it is remembered how complex a division was, and that it sometimes numbered nearly thirty thousand men, it can be understood why each Division, as well as each Army Corps and Army, required its own Chief of Staff, who himself required his own subordinates; and also why the divisions, corps, and armies likewise required many general staff officers, as well as many technical officers to deal with the men and material of many highly specialized kinds. Moreover, when it is remembered that Pershing's fighting force had behind it the vast and complex S.O.S., the transatlantic transportation service, and the still vaster "home front," the problems of organization and coordination became almost bewildering.

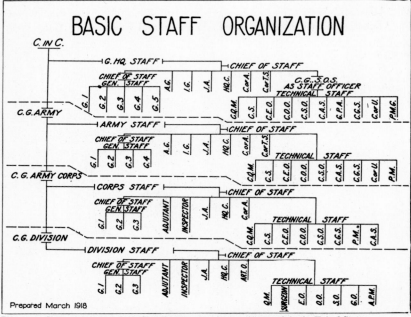

751   Chart of American Basic Staff Organization, from a photograph in the United States Signal Corps, War Department, Washington

THE SITUATION AT ST. MIHIEL

Not without purpose had the Germans held the St. Mihiel salient just south of Verdun since that day in September, 1914, when their offensive in this area had been stopped by the French Third Army. Not far in the rear of these lines lay Metz, a vital railroad center. Close by were the mines about Briey necessary to the Germans for iron. Moreover, possession of the salient interrupted the main Paris-Nancy railroad and the Toul-Verdun railroad. So

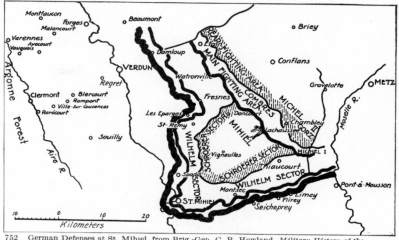

752   German Defenses at St. Mihiel, from Brig.-Gen. C. R. Howland, *Military History of the World War*, General Service Schools Press, Fort Leavenworth, Kansas, 1923

long as the Germans held these advanced lines no important French offensive could be launched from the region of Verdun. When, however, the Amiens salient disappeared in July and August 1918, Von Hindenburg bowed to the inevitable and ordered the evacuation of the St. Mihiel salient. He was contracting his lines to conserve his strength. His order was issued on September 8. But the importance of the positions at Briey and Metz which the salient defended and the strength of the works which the Germans had developed in a terrain highly favorable for defense made the local commanders slow to carry out Von Hindenburg's plan. On September 12 Pershing struck.

753   German dugout in the St. Mihiel salient, from a photograph in the United States Signal Corps, War Department, Washington

754   No Man's Land, from a photograph in the United States Signal Corps, War Department, Washington

BULLARD'S DESCRIPTION OF ST. MIHIEL

General Bullard on October 17 passed through the country over which Pershing attacked in September. He confided the following impressions to his diary. "Yesterday and today I passed through French villages that had been for four years in the hands of the German. A few unfortunate women had been left there during the German occupation. Their stories, their sufferings were sad, unprotected as they were against German brutality and lust. . . . As I passed over quiet areas of beautiful country utterly destroyed by the enemy, as I saw great forests killed as men are killed by shell and shrapnel, as I saw the infinite pains and labor to accomplish all this to hurt his enemy and protect himself, I was tremendously impressed with the German's will to conquer, his great determination and infinite patience. I saw hundreds of miles of trenches rivetted with wood, stone, and cement, thousands of dugouts made almost as great and complete as houses; roads, houses, railroads, and miles and miles of wire entanglements. It looked like the work of a world . . . . — a deeply impressive sight. Villages for many miles, about four miles on both sides of No Man's Land, have been utterly destroyed. . . . They have utterly torn up and desolated all the villages that they have occupied. But to think of the long time that they have held France hard in their grip and to see the ruin they have wrought makes one know that they had France at the throat and would surely have choked her to death but for the coming of the Americans." — *Personalities and Reminiscences of the War*, 286–87.

VII—22

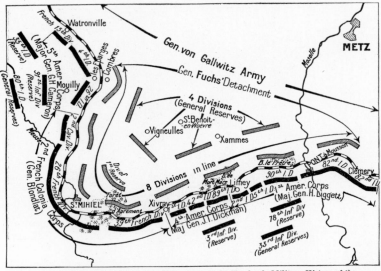

755   Order of battle at St. Mihiel, from Brig.-Gen. C. R. Howland, *Military History of the World War*, General Service Schools Press, Fort Leavenworth, Kansas, 1923

AMERICAN PREPARATION FOR ST. MIHIEL

PERSHING'S plan was to make a diversion against Belfort and then to surprise the Germans holding the St. Mihiel salient by a converging attack on both flanks. The map shows the Fifth Corps on the western face and the Fourth and First Corps on the southern side. These were the assaulting units. The Second French Colonial Corps was to make a holding attack against the nose. Before the attack some five hundred thousand troops, marching at night and resting in the daytime, were secretly assembled. There was also concentrated the greatest aviation force ever engaged in a single action on the Western Front. The French were generous in furnishing guns, tanks, and airplanes. Their staff assistance was also valuable. The preparation for the St. Mihiel attack was a fine example of careful headquarters planning, efficient staff execution, and complete coöperation between allied armies.

OVER THE TOP AT ST. MIHIEL

CAPTAIN THOMAS has described the beginning of the American assault from the point of view of the First Division. "Then at one o'clock in the morning of September 12, the artillery bombardment began. At an instant the sky . . . burst into a sheet of flame when every gun of the American Army fired in unison the opening shot of this, the first American offensive, while platoon leaders who had spent a month looking up at Mont Sec wondered when the Germans from that eminence would begin to pour a deadly return fire into them. . . . Then at 5 A.M., . . . before daylight on that foggy, rainy morning, the rolling barrage began. Up [out of the mud where they had lain for hours] came the stiff infantrymen. The major looked at his watch, then at the barrage, then at his watch again and gave the signal to advance. In the darkness the lines moved forward until the German barbed wire was reached. Here, under cover of the intense American artillery barrage, the infantry cut their way through the belts of barbed wire. These tactics were new. Never before in the whole four years had infantry dared to assault until the artillery had, by heavy concentration, cut the enemy wire. The American artillery, during the five [four] hours' preparation, had not played on the wire, but instead had smothered the German batteries. . . . The wire was soon cut, and the infantry moved forward in wave after wave toward the German front line." — *The History of the A. E. F.*, 213–14. In this artillery preparation twenty-nine hundred guns participated.

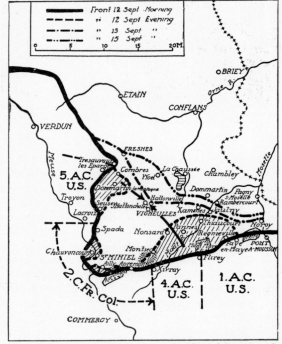

756   American First Army reduction of St. Mihiel Salient, from C. R. Howland, *Military History of the World War*. General Service Schools Press, Fort Leavenworth, Kansas, 1923

AMERICAN GUNNERS AT ST. MIHIEL

THE official caption for this picture reads: "Capturing St. Mihiel Salient. American gunners working at top speed. They did their work well. This photograph shows the speed with which the American artilleryman worked. A shell case flying through the air and a new shell sliding into the breech in the same fraction of a second. (Sept. 12–1918.)"

757 American Gunners at St. Mihiel, from a photograph in the United States Signal Corps, War Department, Washington

758 A tank clearing out a German machine-gun nest, from a drawing by Captain George Harding, in the United States Signal Corps, War Department, Washington

TANKS AT ST. MIHIEL

GENERAL LIGGETT, commanding the American Corps at St. Mihiel, has commented on the tanks. "In this battle tanks were not of much use, due to the softness of the ground. The light tanks helped somewhat, but those of medium weight never got into action. What astonished me more than any other single happening was the way our Infantry got through and over the wire." — *Commanding an American Army*, 68.

759 American troops streaming north in the St. Mihiel Salient, from a photograph in the United States Signal Corps, War Department, Washington

AMERICANS PRESSING THE GERMAN RETREAT

THE photograph gives a vivid picture of the American troops pushing northward, following the enemy who held the south face of the St. Mihiel salient. In the distance may be seen all that remained of a French village battered by American artillery and burned by the retreating enemy. In the foreground is the shell-torn soil of what, a few hours before, was a battlefield.

760 American engineers returning from the front through the town of Nonsard, from a photograph in the United States Signal Corps, War Department, Washington

U. S. ENGINEERS AT NONSARD

ALL night long the veteran First Division marched through the Nonsard Wood, cut the railroad from St. Mihiel used by the Germans and won its way to meet the Twenty-sixth. The United States Engineers did their share with the rest. Road and bridge work in extremely bad weather, and amid the turmoil of the battlefield, taxed their best energies.

THE TWO AMERICAN ATTACKS JOIN HANDS, 7 A.M., SEPTEMBER 13, 1918

THE vanguards of the Twenty-sixth and First Divisions, coming from north and south respectively, joined hands at Hattonchatel, just thirty hours after the great bombardment had begun. The sketch (No. 761) by Captain W. J. Aylward drawn later shows the advance of the American troops.

761   American troops in the St. Mihiel drive, from a drawing by Captain W. J. Aylward, in the United States Signal Corps, War Department, Washington

762   Lieutenant Frank Luke, Jr., next to Rickenbacker the greatest American Ace, from a photograph in the United States Signal Corps, War Department, Washington

AIR FORCES AT ST. MIHIEL

AMERICANS, British, and French: these gallant and experienced airmen maneuvered their nearly fifteen hundred planes with such irresistible force that they completely cleaned the sky of Germans.

GERMAN PRISONERS AT ST. MIHIEL

A FEW of the sixteen thousand captured at St. Mihiel; these Germans are being searched for papers or weapons before being marched to the rear.

763   Pershing entering St. Mihiel, Sept. 19, 1918, from a drawing by Ernest Peixotto, courtesy of the United States Signal Corps, War Department, Washington

764   Americans searching German prisoners for papers and concealed weapons, from a photograph in the United States Signal Corps, War Department, Washington

PERSHING'S COMMENT ON ST. MIHIEL

"AT the cost of only seven thousand casualties, mostly light, we had taken sixteen thousand prisoners, and four hundred and forty-three guns, a great quantity of material, released the inhabitants of many villages from enemy domination, and established our lines in a position to threaten Metz. This signal success of the American First Army in its first offensive was of prime importance. The Allies found that they had a formidable army to aid them, and the enemy learned finally that he had one to reckon with." The picture shows Generals Pershing and Petain arriving with their staffs at the village of St. Mihiel to the unbounded delight of the French townsfolk freed at last from four long years of stern dictation.

CASUALTIES, SEPTEMBER, 1918

"HOMAGE to the nurses. Few motives, and simple, lead men to war. Compulsion, pride, thirst of adventure. But these girls — a thousand adjectives, and the subject not touched. For lives so splendid, one needs an incense of respect more fragrant than any that comes of ink. Eloquent enough, words that came through clenched teeth of one poor devil, writhing in pain: 'By Christ, you gotta hand it to 'em!' Can't evade it — there *is* sublimity in war. Man made in mold of divinity, and more than a flavor of his origin still clinging to his soul. The cheer of these lads, their quiet grave resignation, too beautiful for marring touch of praise. Life has buffeted them sorely: for some it has not yet given its hardest blows. But no quarreling with terms of the game: they carry on." — *Wine, Women and War*, 179.

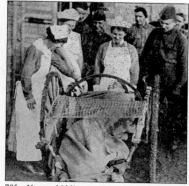

765 Nurses bidding good-bye to convalescent soldier, from a photograph in the United States Signal Corps, War Department, Washington

766 Saint Mihiel, from a photograph in the United States Signal Corps, War Department, Washington

THE CHAPLAIN

THE chaplain's task was to help the soldier to face the mystery of death, so close at hand, calmly and with the assurance which springs from faith. Catholics, Protestants, Hebrews, these religious teachers were men of quality and devotion. They kept the histories of the units to which they were assigned. Theirs was the mournful task of forwarding to relatives the effects of the dead. But their chief duty was to bring faith and healing love to men plunged in the Hell of war.

". . . I tell them of that Man who met
With fearless heart yon despot's cross and sword,
And died, that through his death the soul might live.

They nod their heads; they understand this Christ —
They take him with them to their Calvary!"
— DANIEL M. HENDERSON

SITUATION SEPTEMBER 25, 1918

ON September 25 the first phase of Marshal Foch's offensive came to an end. From July 18 to this day he had directed the mighty armies under his command to the task of reducing particular salients and achieving local objectives. The Germans had been forced back to the line from which they had started that smashing drive in the previous spring which they had confidently expected would win the war. In addition they had lost the St. Mihiel salient, of such vital importance for them. The shortening of the line had given the enemy an opportunity for some rest and for the building up of a reserve. But the German fighting power was rapidly waning as hope of victory faded. Bulgaria was crumbling and on September 25 asked for an armistice. The morale of Foch's victorious legions was high. American troops were arriving in France at the rate of ten thousand a day. On September 12 thirteen million more Americans were registered under the second Selective Service Act. It was clear to everyone

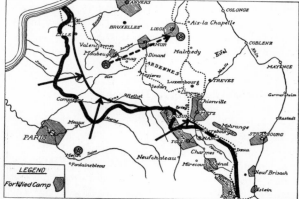

767 Territory recaptured by Foch's offensive (first period), 1918, from Brig.-Gen. C. R. Howland, *Military History of the World War*, General Service Schools Press, Fort Leavenworth, Kansas, 1918

that Germany was destined to go down in defeat. But none of the Allied commanders believed that the war would end in 1918. The spring offensive of 1919 was to be the great thrust that would send the gray hordes fleeing into the Fatherland. Then four million Americans would present a menace against which the war-worn Germans could not stand. In the autumn of 1918 but two million were available.

768 American machine gunners resting during the advance in the Argonne, from a photograph in the United States Signal Corps, War Department, Washington

PERSHING AND FOCH

DESPITE the fact that the Allied generals did not expect to win the war in 1918, Marshal Foch very properly planned to pass without a halt from the first to the second phase of his great offensive. The first had been occupied with the winning of limited objectives; the second was a general assault on the German army with the purpose of driving and harassing it until it was completely defeated. When the American guns opened north of Verdun at 11:30 P.M. on September 25, the final battle of the war had begun. It had been preceded, however, by an episode full of significance. The Americans had come into the lines so fast that they were still inexperienced in the staff work required for the maneuvering of such a large unit as an army. Foch, as already brought out, had somewhat reluctantly approved the organization of the American First Army and had authorized its use as a unit only for the reduction of the St. Mihiel salient. As the first phase of the offensive drew to an end he prepared plans for the second. Foch proposed to reduce the American First Army to ten or eleven divisions and give it a limited objective. The major part of the American forces were to be split up between the French Second Army which was to operate between the Meuse and the Argonne Forest and the French Fourth Army which was to operate west of the Argonne. To this plan General Pershing opposed objections. He pointed out that it was contrary to the idea of a distinctly American army operating on a particular front, for which an immense amount of preparation had already been made. He told the commander in chief that the "older American divisions had encountered so much difficulty, in their service with the French and British, that they were no longer willing to be incorporated in the Allied armies, even by larger units; and, if so incorporated, American morale would suffer further. General Pershing then very frankly told Marshal Foch that the strategical employment of the American First Army would be undertaken wherever Marshal Foch directed, but that the proposal of the latter to disrupt the American army for service with French armies would not be entertained." — HOWLAND, 375. This was a fateful decision from which were to flow consequences of vast importance.

A FATEFUL DECISION

ON September 2 at Foch's headquarters at Bombon with General Petain present Foch and Pershing came to a complete agreement. The French commander not only accepted the contention of his American colleague but handsomely offered General Pershing his choice of two positions on the line, either the Champagne or the Meuse-Argonne sector. Without hesitation the American commander chose the latter. It was indeed the post of honor, for success in this area would cut the vital supply line which served the German army and bring inevitable confusion and defeat to the enemy. Foch in offering this position to his American friend could

pay no higher compliment to the troops from across the Atlantic. Pershing chose the sector for two reasons. His men were still fresh. Already on many battlefields they had demonstrated that offensive spirit which he had sought to instill. The French and British were tired after four years of terrible war. They were bled white. In the record of their achievements on the Western Front were battles which for bravery and skill surpassed anything in the annals of war. Pershing did not believe these weary heroes had the reserve strength to strike a blow that would send the Germans reeling to defeat.

769 The gateway at Verdun, from a drawing by Captain J. André Smith, in the United States Signal Corps, War Department, Washington

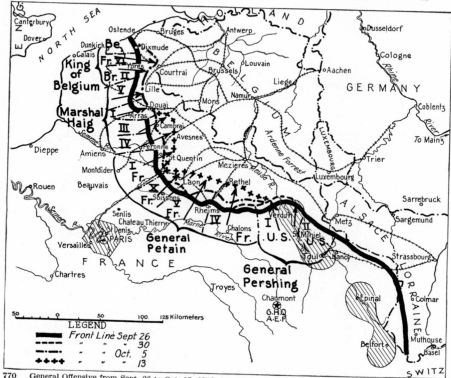

770 General Offensive from Sept. 26 to Oct. 13, 1918, from Brig.-Gen. C. R. Howland, *Military History of the World War*, General Service Schools Press, Fort Leavenworth, Kansas, 1923

THE SITUATION PRECEDING THE GENERAL OFFENSIVE OF 1918

THE German line from the region near Verdun to the sea was in reality a great salient whose base line from Metz to Ostend was nearly one hundred and eighty miles; whose depth from base line to nose was sixty miles; and whose front line was more than three hundred miles long. This vast military area was fed and supplied by three great railroads: the main Paris-Berlin line which passed through Liège and Namur, the Coblenz-Trier-Brussels line which connected with the first at Namur, and the Strassbourg-Metz-Mezières line which crossed the first near Avesnes. This third line supplied not only the region about Metz but the southern part of the great salient north of Verdun. The Germans in this region were totally dependent on it because the Ardenne Forest lay between it and the Coblenz-Trier-Brussels line. The map shows how close to this vital railroad was the German front line from Metz to Mezières. This proximity explains the German willingness to accept the tremendous sacrifices of 1916 in their unsuccessful attack upon Verdun. Von Hindenburg planned an aggressive step-by-step defense against the Allied onslaught. He would fall back slowly from one prepared position to another. He would make the advance so costly to his enemies that they would be willing to make more favorable terms of peace to prevent the further shedding of blood. If forced back to the German border, he would call out all German men in a *levée en masse*. He would fall back everywhere except in the region of Verdun and southward. These lines he would hold at all cost. To be driven back here meant swift and terrible disaster. Here Foch planned to deliver his principal blow with the Americans under Pershing.

771 American infantry entering a German trench, from a wax sculpture group by Dwight Franklin

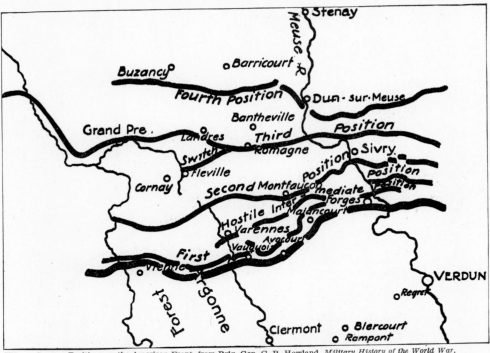

772   German Positions on the American Front, from Brig.-Gen. C. R. Howland, *Military History of the World War,*
General Service Schools Press, Fort Leavenworth, Kansas, 1923

THE PROBLEM THAT PERSHING CONFRONTED

As the American army assembled north and west of Verdun and faced Sedan, the officers and men looked out upon an enemy area which contained great natural obstacles and which, during four years of occupation, had been organized for defense with all that skill and thoroughness for which the Germans were famous. On their left the Argonne Forest stretched its almost impenetrable tangle northward. Before their center towered the wooded heights of Montfaucon, whence enemy observers looked out upon the American area. On their right above the east bank of the Meuse rose other commanding heights perfectly fortified. Between the Argonne and Montfaucon and, in turn, between it and the highland beyond the Meuse, were lower areas, broken by ridges running roughly east and west. North of Verdun the enemy had developed four main positions in front of which was a wide zone of complete devastation which in itself was an important military obstacle. General Pershing confronted a practically continuous maze of trenches and defense positions twenty kilometers deep which utilized to the full the features of a terrain highly favorable for defense. It was as strong an area as the Germans had ever developed, for it defended the pivot upon which their whole step-by-step retirement depended. Seldom had any army ever before faced a task so formidable as this.

773   The Argonne country near Buzancy, from a drawing by Captain J. André Smith, in the United States Signal Corps,
War Department, Washington

GERMAN DUGOUTS

THE perfection of these German dugouts which were taken on the first day of the American advance was the result of their long occupation and the determination of their builders to hold them until France had been beaten down.

774 German dugouts captured by American troops at Cheppy, from a drawing by Ernest Peixotto, in the United States Signal Corps, War Department, Washington

775 Fortified crossroads at Aprémont, from a drawing by Ernest Peixotto, in the United States Signal Corps, War Department, Washington

MACHINE GUN NESTS

THE picture shows the crossroads at Aprémont. The position was in the German front line and was very strongly fortified. The place itself was a nest of machine guns. In the foreground on the right is the entrance to a machine gun emplacement. Such was the country through which the Americans had to fight.

CÔTE 295 OR DEAD MAN'S HILL (LE MORT HOMME) TEN MILES NORTHWEST OF VERDUN

AT the jumping off line of the Meuse-Argonne offensive stood that immortal Dead Man's Hill where the heroic French defenders of Verdun successfully withstood the utmost efforts of the German fury in 1916. At that time this pivotal position was bravely assaulted again and again by the Crown Prince's armies, until the very soil ran red.

776 Summit of Côte 295 showing battlefield of Dead Man's Hill, from a photograph in the United States Signal Corps, War Department, Washington

777 Americans in old French trenches near Verdun, from a photograph in the United States Signal Corps, War Department, Washington

AMERICANS ON HALLOWED GROUND

IN the trenches near Verdun, where the French alone lost more men killed than the A. E. F. lost killed throughout the war, American soldiers paused to scan the horizon over where they, too, must meet the selfsame enemies in the Meuse-Argonne.

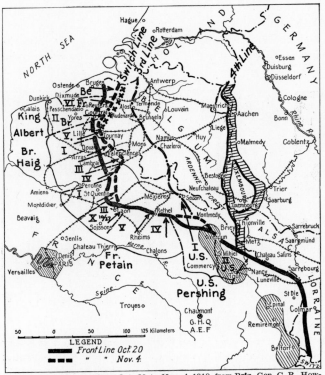

778   General Offensive from Oct. 20 to Nov. 4, 1918, from Brig.-Gen. C. R. Howland, *Military History of the World War*, General Service Schools Press, Fort
Leavenworth, Kansas, 1923

THE GENERAL OFFENSIVE OF 1918

THE swift success of the General Offensive
of 1918 was due primarily to the victorious
thrust on the Meuse-Argonne front because
of the strategic importance of that area. It
should be remembered, however, that from
Verdun to the North Sea, beginning with
September 26, there was a continuous assault
which was never stopped until the guns were
silenced by the Armistice. By November 4
Von Hindenburg had fallen back to his second
line of defense and, in the north, beyond it
to the Switch Line. Only one more line stood
between him and the boundary of the Fatherland. But Von Hindenburg's step-by-step
retreat was not going as he had planned.
His troops were not inflicting these terrific
losses which would make their enemies quail.
The Germans were fighting desperately, but
their ranks were being constantly thinned as
division after division was drawn off and
rushed southward to the Meuse-Argonne
region. American victory here not only would
cut the vital railroad which ran through Sedan
and take the pivot on which the German lines
were turning in their retreat, but would put
the troops in the rear of the entire retreating
German army. So Von Hindenburg in desperation snatched his divisions from the west and north and hurled
them against the American First Army and the French Fourth Army advancing from the south. These two
forces were steadily, irresistibly shutting the door of France against the Germans.

AMERICANS WITH THE BRITISH

THE American Second Corps under General Read fought with the British Fourth Army under General Rawlinson east of Amiens. They were the Thirtieth Division under General Lewis and the Twenty-seventh
under General O'Ryan. On Septem-
ber 29, in the first phase of the general offensive, the American Second
Corps, acting as the spearhead of the
attack in that area, took the St. Quen-
tin canal with its famous tunnel,
which gave the German lines in that
sector almost the strength of a fort.
Then the American corps went to the
reserve and rested. On October 8 the
British Fourth Army with the Second
Corps again as the spearhead struck a
second time and continued fighting
desperately until the German first line
had been penetrated. On the first
day of this movement the Fifty-ninth
American Brigade faced three German
divisions which, during the day, were
reinforced by two more and also by
two battalions.

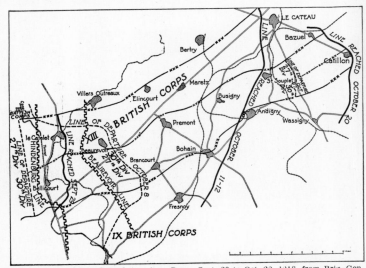

779   Operations of the Second American Corps, Sept. 29 to Oct. 20, 1918, from Brig.-Gen.
C. R. Howland, *Military History of the World War*, General Service Schools Press, Fort
Leavenworth, Kansas, 1923

BREAKING THE "HINDENBURG" LINE

THE painting gives a faint idea of the terrifying realities of an assault upon such a position as the "Hindenburg Line." Yet in spite of the most violent opposition the Americans and the British went forward. Before the infantry, crashed the barrage lifting from point to point. Beside them clattered the tanks armed with one pounders and machine guns. Such an attack as this brings out the rôle of the infantry in sharp relief. The other arms are, after all, auxiliaries; it was the "doughboys" who walked forward to close with the enemy, take his position, and give their lives most freely.

780　From the painting *The Twenty-seventh Division breaking the Hindenburg Line*, by H. C. Murphy, Jr. © 1918

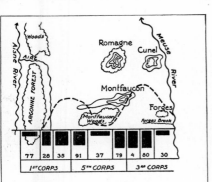

781　Pershing's Plan for attack west of the Meuse, Sept. 26, 1918, from Brig.-Gen. C. R. Howland, *Military History of the World War*, General Service Schools Press, Fort Leavenworth, Kansas, 1923

SEPTEMBER 26 ON THE MEUSE-ARGONNE FRONT

PERSHING'S first problem on the Meuse-Argonne front was the equivalent of forcing two defiles. The Germans from the high ground east of the Meuse, from the wooded ridges of the Argonne Forest, and from the Montfaucon heights could deliver flanking fire. The German artillery knew the exact range to every important point. Pershing planned a double penetration on either flank of Montfaucon. He deployed the divisions in front of the obstacles on a wide front, and those that were to make the penetration on narrow fronts. The attack was a complete surprise. Pershing concentrated his divisions behind a screen of French troops. At 5:30 A.M. September 26 the Americans under cover of a fixed and a rolling barrage moved against the German lines. When the sun set on the first day, the enemy first position had been passed. By noon of the second, Montfaucon had fallen.

A DIRECT HIT

THE caption for picture No. 782 is as follows: "American Advance northwest of Verdun. American artillery scored a bull's eye on a German ammunition dump, which exploded with a terrific uproar at the place from which the cloud of smoke is rolling. The 'jump off' and No Man's Land lie near the crest of the first hill."

782　German ammunition dump exploded by American artillery, from a photograph in the United States Signal Corps, War Department, Washington

783　Loading an American Fourteen-inch Coast Artillery Gun in use in the Argonne, from a photograph in the United States Signal Corps, War Department, Washington

THE A. E. F. BIG GUNS OPEN THE MEUSE-ARGONNE

AT the opening of the Meuse-Argonne, September 26, 1918, this gigantic fourteen-inch gun was manned by United States Coast Artillerymen, whose well aimed shells cut up German troop trains twenty miles away.

784   Observers on the captured hill of Montfaucon, from a photograph in the
        United States Signal Corps, War Department, Washington

AMERICAN ARTILLERY OBSERVATION POST AT MONTFAUCON

ALL through the first long day the Germans held the dominating height of Montfaucon, from which their Crown Prince used to watch Verdun. But on the second, the Seventy-ninth Division resumed its attack, while the guns deluged the top with a tornado of shells. This time the Three Hundred and Thirteenth Infantry reached the top. Then this magnificent position became an American artillery observation post.

ON THE ROAD TO VARENNES

UPON the efficiency of the engineers depended the American advance. "As the attack progressed Northward and the leading elements got beyond supporting reach of our artillery, the advance became slower, and every effort was concentrated upon getting the guns across 'No Man's Land' and into supporting positions. It was a task of enormous difficulty, due to lack of practicable roads and the condition of the ground, which was a mass of shell-holes, wire, and trenches. All during the night of September 26–27 this work was carried on with the assistance of engineers, labor troops, and every other means available. Some guns were brought forward, but not enough to give the infantry the support it should have had. This result was not forthcoming until the 29th of September or later, despite almost superhuman efforts. In

785   Mine crater on the road to Varennes, from a drawing
        by Ernest Peixotto, in the United States Signal Corps,
        War Department, Washington

the Argonne Forest proper the artillery was at all times at a great disadvantage, due to the limited observation, and the tangle of trees and brush covering this complex terrain." — LIGGETT. The illustration shows engineers working to construct a road around a vast crater one hundred and sixty feet wide, the result of a mine which the retreating Germans had exploded in the road leading to Varennes en Argonne.

786   American order of battle, Sept. 26, 1918, from Brig.-Gen. C. R.
Howland, *Military History of the World War*, General Service Schools
Press, Fort Leavenworth, Kansas, 1923

THE MEUSE–ARGONNE OFFENSIVE

GENERAL PERSHING has divided the Meuse-Argonne offensive into three phases. The first lasted from September 26 until October 3. Many of the units used in this phase were inexperienced and some were undergoing fire for the first time. They went forward, however, with a grim determination. The divisions that made the penetrations on either side of Montfaucon suffered terrible losses as a result of machine-gun fire and artillery cross fire from the high ground on either flank. Yet these dwindling divisions carried on, in spite of the fact that Von Gallwitz reinforced his line on September 28 with six fresh divisions, until the Americans had advanced about ten miles and penetrated the German second position. The second phase began on October 4 when more experienced divisions completed the relief of the units that initiated the fighting and continued until October 31. The final phase included the first eleven days of November.

THE SECOND PHASE OF THE MEUSE–ARGONNE OFFENSIVE

In the days between October 4 and October 31 the American troops on the Meuse-Argonne front saw their heaviest fighting — fighting that surpassed anything in magnitude and intensity that the Army of the United States had been called upon to face in all its history. The bare outline of events in that bloody advance is as follows: The assault began at 5:03 A.M. on October 4 well supported by artillery which had been brought up during the latter part of the first phase. By the night of October 5 only small gains had been made with the exception of the First Division which had broken down the opposition on its immediate front and captured Fleville on the edge of the Argonne Forest on a switch of the German third position. (See map, No. 772.) Pershing then carried the fight to the

787 American order of battle, Oct. 1, 1918, from Brig.-Gen. C. R. Howland, *Military History of the World War*, General Service Schools Press, Fort Leavenworth, Kansas, 1923

heights east of the Meuse to drive off the troops that were holding that high ground and to compel Von Gallwitz to weaken his lines west of the Meuse. Pershing ordered the French Seventeenth Corps which was coöperating with the American First Army to attack on the exact spot east of the Meuse where the German army must pivot in order to withdraw from northern France. By the evening of October 9 the French had advanced six kilometers, noticeably relieving the situation west of the Meuse. By October 10 the converging attack on the Argonne Forest of the American First Army and the French Fourth Army was successful and the enemy had been flanked out of the forest. By October 13 Pershing was in front of the third position, the so-called Kriemhilde position, and found the enemy very heavily reinforced. On October 12 Pershing created the American Second Army, giving Bullard the command and putting Liggett in command of the American First Army; Pershing himself retained command of the army group. The zone of action of the American Second Army was east of the Meuse. The attack was continued with the First Army. In spite of the most determined resistance from a perfectly organized position by October 18 Liggett had penetrated the third position taking Romagne, and Cunel. The remainder of this phase was spent in local attacks and in preparing for the assault which was to be the third phase.

788 American order of battle on Oct. 13, 1918, from Brig.-Gen. C. R. Howland, *Military History of the World War*, General Service Schools Press, Fort Leavenworth, Kansas, 1923

THE ARGONNE

789   From the painting *The Argonne*, by
Edward H. Potthast

As Grant advanced into the Wilderness in 1864 so Pershing's men plunged into the deadly Argonne Forest in 1918. Into its tangled thickets fell the hail of bullets from scores of machine-gun nests skillfully hidden and perfectly prepared far in advance. Barbed wire was strung from tree to tree. In this gloomy, treacherous forest where death lurked on every hand the American soldier met a severe test. Units had difficulty in keeping contact with one another. Yet the Americans advanced. Maddened by the fear of the consequences of defeat in this sector the Germans rose to their old-time fighting powers. But step by step they gave way. For the American the Argonne must ever be hallowed ground. Here his kin sacrificed themselves freely that the power of the German war lords might be broken.

THE LOST BATTALION

ON the afternoon of October 2, two days before the beginning of the second phase, the Seventy-seventh Division was carrying out a local offensive in the Argonne Forest. Major Charles W. Whittlesey, commanding a mixed battalion of six companies of the Three Hundred and Seventh Infantry, the Three Hundred and Eighth Infantry, and the Three Hundred and Sixth Machine Gun Battalion was ordered to carry and hold certain positions in a ravine on his front. He accomplished his mission with heavy losses but the units on both his flanks failed to keep pace with him. The Germans quickly filtered in behind him and strung new wire across the ravine through which he had advanced. Having been ordered to hold, Whittlesey made no effort to fight his way back. The enemy surrounded Whittlesey so closely that German artillery did not dare fire on his position. The Germans attacked him, however, with rifles, machine guns, trench mortars and grenades. On October 4 Whittlesey sent back the last of his carrier pigeons with the message: "Men are suffering from hunger and exposure and the wounded are in very bad condition. Cannot support be sent at once?" General Liggett, at the time corps commander in the area, says: ". . . though we tried pressure everywhere, to right and left, day and night, the enemy balked us. For one hundred hours the battalion went without food and virtually without water. Meanwhile, American airplanes had tried without success to drop food within the beleaguered area. Nine men without permission crept out to get food packages that had fallen near by. Of these five were killed and four captured. One of the latter, Private Growell R. Hollingshead, was blindfolded and forced to carry back to Whittlesey the demand for surrender that appears in picture No. 790. The German commander was Lieutenant Heinrich Prinz of the Seventy-sixth German Infantry Reserve Division who had before the war lived a number of years in Seattle. To Whittlesey "no reply seemed necessary." The Battalion was finally relieved by the flanking attack which resulted ultimately in forcing the enemy out of the Argonne Forest. Whittlesey made his attack with five hundred and fifty men of whom only one hundred and ninety-four walked out. Whittlesey, a graduate of Williams College, is an excellent example of the quality of the officers made by the best of the college men.

790   From a reproduction of the original in *Williams College in the World War*, Frederic T. Wood, editor, Williams College, New York

791   Major Charles Whittlesey, from a photograph by Underwood & Underwood, New York

SERGEANT YORK

On the morning of October 8 the Three Hundred and Twenty-eighth Infantry of the Eighty-second Division attacking in the direction of the Decauville railroad, which it took before night, found itself in a ravine under Hill 223 and fiercely assailed by machine-gun fire from its flanks. The then Corporal York was a member of a support platoon (see page 286) and was one of the fifteen men ordered out under Acting-Sergeant Early to silence the machine guns on the left flank. The party without a casualty, though under heavy fire, gained a position under cover in rear of the nests. The Germans in the excitement of battle seem to have forgotten about the combat patrol when it disappeared. Advancing as skirmishers the Americans surprised a German battalion command post and took three officers and some enlisted men. This affair attracted the attention of some German machine gunners less than thirty yards away who, calling to their captured comrades to drop, fired into the Americans, killing six and wounding three, among the latter Sergeant Early. Taking command York ordered his six remaining men to guard the prisoners while he

792   Sergeant Alvin York, from a photograph in the United States Signal Corps, War Department, Washington

attacked the machine gunners single handed. Because of the position of the prisoners who lay between York and the machine gunners the latter could not lay their fire on the ground but kept it very close. York had shot about twelve when a lieutenant and seven men charged him. Laying aside his rifle after one shot York dropped the rest with his service pistol (the automatic pistol fires seven shots). The German major then surrendered all his gun positions, increasing the prisoners to ninety. The situation was extremely dangerous. Putting the major ahead of him and a lieutenant on either side with Early and the unwounded Americans bringing up the rear with the rest of the prisoners, York took a direction opposite from that which the major suggested. As a result he ran into other nests whose men were disarmed and added to the party. A little later York saluted his lieutenant. "Corporal York reports with prisoners, sir." "How many prisoners have you, corporal," gasped Lieutenant Woods. "Honest, lieutenant, I don't know," was the reply. Woods counted one hundred and thirty-two. After the war and his receipt of the Congressional Medal of Honor, Sergeant York returned to his home in the Tennessee mountains to open a school for the betterment of his people.

THE RESERVE OFFICER AT HIS BEST

Henry Blair Keep had been out of college only two years and a few months when he graduated as a First Lieutenant from the Second Officers' Training Camp at Fort Sheridan. From July 18 until his death he saw a great deal of fighting. The following citation and comment portrays the American officer at his best. "The Division Commander cites with pride the conduct of Captain Henry B. Keep, 10th Machine Gun Battalion, during the Meuse-Argonne offensive, from September 26 to October 5, 1918. At the opening of this offensive Captain Keep, though under orders to proceed to Langres for duty there as a student officer, was,

793   American officers watching practice maneuvers, Ballarat, May 9, 1918, from a photograph in the United States Signal Corps, War Department, Washington

at his urgent request, permitted to remain in command of his company to the end that it might have his personal leadership during the ensuing campaign. He thus voluntarily continued in action until killed by shell fire in the Bois de Fays October 5, 1918. . . ." Some time later a hospital worker made a record of a conversation which he had had in a field hospital. "Probably you have heard of the death of Henry Keep. A young Captain who was wounded and in the hospital told me of him. 'A wonderful man, a glory to the regiment, a perfect power with the men, always a fine word to say, always a smile on his face, and he went with the smile still there.' I've set down his words as remembered, but cannot express [his] sorrow." Keep is singled out to represent a type.

HOLED–IN ON HILL 240: 18TH INFANTRY, OCTOBER 11

THE picture (No. 794) shows infantrymen temporarily halted by the enemy, who are protecting themselves in hastily dug excavations on Hill 240, near Exermont, Ardennes, on October 11. The Twenty-sixth Infantry began the day over one thousand strong and ended with two hundred and eighty-five.

794 Holed-in on Hill 240, from a photograph in the United States Signal Corps, War Department, Washington

795 Returning refugees at Hatton-chatel, from a drawing by Captain W. J. Aylward, in the United States Signal Corps, War Department, Washington

GERMAN DEVASTATION

UNABLE to withstand the A. E. F. any longer the Germans retreated destroying the country as they went. Picture No. 795 shows the French folk of Hatton-chatel returning to their ruined homes after the German retreat.

AMID THE DEVASTATION

THE picture (No. 796) of the main street of the little French town of Grand Pré, renamed Kronprinzenstrasse by the Germans, shows the wreck which remained after the tide of battle had receded. Such a scene makes clear as nothing else can do what the war meant to France.

796 German devastation in the town of Grand Pré, from a photograph in the United States Signal Corps, War Department, Washington

797 American machine gunners, from a photograph in the United States Signal Corps, War Department, Washington

AMERICAN MACHINE GUNNERS SHOOTING OUT GERMAN SNIPERS

PICTURE No. 797 shows the machine-gun company of the Three Hundred and Twelfth Infantry turning a stream of bullets on to the cleverly situated hiding places of the German snipers near Grand Pré in the Argonne.

CONDITION OF THE TROOPS

798   Troops resting in a trench, from a photograph in the United States Signal Corps, War Department, Washington

GENERAL LIGGETT has commented on the condition of the American First Army when he assumed command. "I found on my inspection of the army that, due to the hard and bitter fighting which had been continuous since September twenty-sixth, day and night, some evidences of discouragement were beginning to appear among both men and officers, the most conspicuous evidence of which was the great number of stragglers. The weather was cold with continuous rains, the men were without adequate shelter and the difficulties of supply were disheartening. . . . Such endless hammering in bad weather was a tremendous strain on young troops. . . . Divisions were so reduced in strength from casualties and strays that we had to call for replacements from newly arrived divisions. . . . There was a lull of two weeks in the major operation while we tightened up. . . . We established stragglers' posts on all the roads, tightened the military policing of back areas and sent out officers with patrols to search the woods and dugouts, and thousands of strays and hideaways poured in. It is characteristic of the American soldier to scatter the moment he breaks ranks. Like Kipling's British soldier, he is out 'for to admire and for to see.' . . . Too, the Meuse-Argonne was a battle fought under lowering, misty skies in a country so rough and tangled that men without a natural instinct of direction were astray the moment they lost sight of their nearest neighbor. . . . There were others in numbers who were thirty-third-degree brothers in the ancient order of A. W. O. L. [absent without leave], men who had shirked every possible duty from the day they first reported at camp. Our armies — every army — always has had them. . . . The Union Army lost nearly four times as many men by desertion from 1861 to 1865 as were killed on the field. Actual desertion was negligible in the A. E. F. up to the Armistice, in no small part because the Atlantic Ocean discouraged it, but there were other and more gratifying reasons: it was a better army, better led and better backed at home." — LIGGETT AND STOUT, A. E. F. in The Saturday Evening Post, June 18, 1927.

THE CAPTURE OF BLANC MONT

To the west of Pershing's American First Army was the French Fourth Army under General Gouraud. The two armies operated in close coöperation and General Petain had been assigned by Marshal Foch to the special task of overseeing the coördination of their activities. Gouraud and Pershing advanced along parallel lines, and made their initial attack at the same time. The German works were highly developed in front of the Fourth Army. On September 30 Gouraud was stopped on a line just north of Somme-Py. Just in front of it lay Blanc Mont, the key to the whole system of German works in this sector and the strongest point in the lines just west of the Argonne Forest. The French had spent many lives in 1917 in an unsuccessful effort to win this bit of high land. In the advance of September 29 Gouraud had not used the American Second Division which had been in reserve. On October 3 he sent it forward to capture Blanc Mont. With it advanced the whole French line. But the French did not keep up with the Second Division, thus exposing and slowing up both its flanks. After three days of magnificent work not only had Blanc Mont fallen

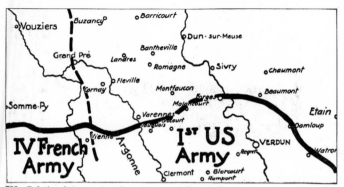

799   Relation between American Army and French Fourth Army, from Brig.-Gen. C. R. Howland, Military History of the World War, General Service Schools Press, Fort Leavenworth, Kansas, 1923

but the line of the Fourth Army had been advanced almost to St. Etienne. General Gouraud reported to Marshal Foch that as a result of the capture of Blanc Mont the Germans as far west as Rheims were in full retreat. The capture of Blanc Mont and the consequent advance of the French Fourth Army made possible the pinching of the Germans out of the Argonne Forest by the converging attack of Gouraud and Pershing. The fight of the Second Division at Blanc Mont was one of the finest American operations of the entire war.

A few iron-souled Prussians—the Boche had such men—stood up to meet bayonet with bayonet, and died that way.

800   From Captain John W. Thomason, Jr., *Fix Bayonets!* Charles Scribner's Sons, New York and London, 1926

THE ADVANCE OF THE MARINES AT BLANC MONT

CAPTAIN THOMASON, who went through it, has painted a vivid picture of the attack upon Blanc Mont. The Marines had started and enemy artillery and machine guns had loosed a hell upon them. "An increasing trail of crumpled brown figures lay behind the battalion as it went. The raw smell of blood was in men's nostrils. . . . There was an officer rapped across the toe of his boot by a spent bullet — the leather wasn't even scratched — who sat down and asserted that his foot was shot off. There was Lieutenant Connor, who took a shrapnel dud in his loins and was opened horribly. . . . There was a sergeant, a hard old non-com of many battles, who went forward beside him. His face was very red, and his eyes were very bright, and his lean jaw bulged with a great chew of tobacco. His big shoulders were hunched forward, and his bayonet glinted at a thirsty angle, and his sturdy putteed legs swung in an irresistible stride. Then there was, oddly audible through the din, the unmistakable sound that a bullet makes when it strikes human flesh — and a long, crumpled, formless thing on the ground turned to the sky blind eyes in a crawling mask of red. There were five men with a machine-gun, barrel and mount and ammunition-boxes, and a girlish, pink cheeked lieutenant went before them swinging a pair of field glasses in his hand. Over and a little short of them a red sun flashed in a whorl of yellow smoke, and they were flattened into a mess of bloody rags, from which an arm thrust upward, dangling a pair of new, clean glasses by a thong, and remained so. . . . In the shadow of the pines were men in cumbersome green-gray uniforms, with faces that looked hardly human under deep round helmets. With eyes narrowed, bodies slanting forward like men in heavy rain, the remnant of the battalion went to them. . . . It was the flank of the Boche column. . . . And now, already shaken by the sight of these men who would not die, it shrank from the long American bayonets and the pitiless, furious faces behind the steel. A few Brandenburger zealots elected to die on their spitting Maxim guns, working them until bayonets or clubbed rifles made an end. A few iron-souled Prussians — the Boche had such men — stood up to meet bayonet with bayonet, and died that way. . . . A great many more flung away their arms and bleated 'Kameraden' to men who in that red minute knew no mercy. Some hid in holes, or feigned death, to be hunted out as the press thinned. And the rest scuttled through the trees and back down toward St. Etienne, while the Marines, lying prone or taking rest for their Springfields, killed them as they ran." — JOHN W. THOMASON, JR., *Fix Bayonets!* 179–84, Charles Scribner's Sons, New York, 1926.

THE SECOND DIVISION COMES OUT

"AND after certain days the division was relieved. The battalion marched out at night. The drumming thunder of the guns fell behind them and no man turned his face to look again on the baleful lights of the front. On the road they passed a regiment of the relieving division — full, strong companies of National Guardsmen. They went up one side of the road; and in ragged column of twos, unsightly even in the dim and fitful light, the Marines plodded down the other side. They were utterly weary, with shuffling feet and hanging heads. The division had just done something that those old masters of the art of war, the French, and the world after them, including Ludendorff, were to acknowledge remarkable.

801   From Captain John W. Thomason, Jr., *Fix Bayonets!* Charles Scribner's Sons, New York and London, 1926

They had hurled the Boche from Blanc Mont and freed the sacred city of Rheims. . . . And they were spent. If there was any idea in those hanging heads it was food and rest." — JOHN W. THOMASON, JR., 191–92.

802   On the edge of Rambrecourt, from a drawing by Captain J. André Smith, in the United States Signal Corps.
War Department, Washington

THE CRUMBLING GERMAN DEFENSE

ON September 30, six days before the capture of Blanc Mont, the German Chancellor, Von Hertling, had resigned and had been succeeded by Prince Max of Baden. The following day General Ludendorff urged the new Chancellor to demand an armistice through President Wilson. On the night before Blanc Mont fell Germany dispatched a note to Washington asking for a peace based on President Wilson's Fourteen Points. On October 1 Von Hindenburg had left the front to be with the Kaiser in Berlin in the event of a revolution.

THE THIRD PHASE OF THE MEUSE–ARGONNE

ON November 1, 1918, General Pershing faced a problem essentially like that which he confronted on September 26. On his left were the dense Bourgoyne Woods, on his right the Meuse highlands, and confronting his right center the heights of Barricourt. His plan, as before, was to take strong places by maneuver rather than frontal attack. His immediate purpose was to help General Gouraud across the Aisne, when the American First Army and the French Fourth Army would make a joint advance against Sedan. Liggett moved his long range army artillery well forward so as to give it maximum effectiveness. On November 1 the Fifth Corps, moving through a mist and behind a heavy and deep rolling barrage, captured Barricourt. The Americans had broken through the Kriemhilde position and were in the open. After helping the French Fourth Army across the Aisne, Pershing, supported by Gouraud, pushed rapidly toward Sedan. On November 2 and 3 the Third and Fifth Corps went so fast that some of its units used motor trucks to pursue the fleeing Germans. The Third Corps turned east, and General Ely in a brilliant operation took the Fifth Division across the Meuse, November 3–5. This forced a general German withdrawal from the strong hill positions so long held north of Verdun. By November 11 the Ninetieth Division of the Third Corps was within artillery range of the German main line of communication. On the same day the Eighty-ninth Division under General Wright, the Second Division under General Lejeune, and the Seventy-seventh Division under General Alexander also had the Strassbourg-Metz-Mezières railroad within artillery range. On November 7 the First Division under General Frank Parker and the Forty-second Division under General Menoher had reached the heights above Sedan and held that fortress and the railroad under easy fire control. The drive from the south had succeeded. The main railroad was cut. The German pivot was about to be captured. The victorious American First Army and French Fourth Army would soon be in the rear of the German host. A *débacle* impended.

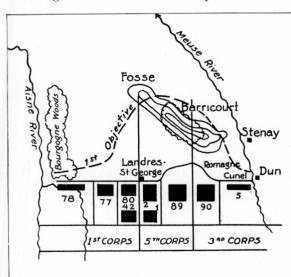

803   General Pershing's Plan for November 1st Attack, from Brig.-Gen.
C. R. Howland, *Military History of the World War*, General Service
Schools Press, Fort Leavenworth, Kansas, 1923

804   German prisoners in the Meuse-Argonne, from a photograph in the United States Signal Corps, War Department, Washington

THE ARMISTICE

On November 6, the day before the Americans reached the heights above Sedan, the German Government sent emissaries to General Foch to request an armistice. They reached him on the following day and received from his hand the terms on which hostilities would cease. The German Government was given seventy-two hours in which to accept. At 5 a.m. on November 11 the emissaries were back and signed the document. At 11 on the same day the guns from Switzerland to Holland relapsed into silence. The armistice amounted to a complete surrender. Germany gave up all her submarines and disarmed her surface men-of-war, which

were ultimately to be taken over by the Allies. She surrendered great quantities of transportation and arms. She renounced the treaties of Brest-Litovsk and of Bucharest. She agreed to repair damage done and to indemnify the Allies in amounts to be determined later. She agreed to evacuate all foreign territory and to permit a neutral zone ten kilometers wide on the east bank of the Rhine from Switzerland to Holland. The Allies and Americans were to hold Mayence, Coblenz, and Cologne and a zone thirty kilometers deep about each center. Seventeen days before the German surrender Ludendorff had been relieved of command by the German Government and charged with responsibility for the defeat. Before the Armistice the Kaiser, from whom had come so many bombastic speeches, had fled ignominiously to Holland. To Holland also went the Crown Prince. So passed the power of the German war lords.

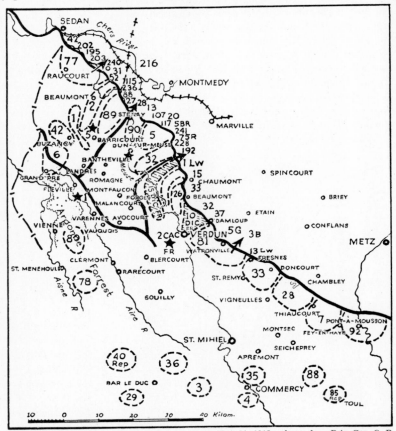

805   Order of battle on American First Army front, Nov. 11, 1918, redrawn from Brig.-Gen. C. R. Howland, *Military History of the World War*, General Service Schools Press, Fort Leavenworth, Kansas, 1923

GENERAL ORDERS NUMBER 232, DECEMBER 19, 1918

"IT is with a sense of gratitude for its splendid accomplishment, which will live through all history, that I record in General Orders a tribute to the victory of the First Army in the Meuse-Argonne battle. Tested and strengthened by the reduction of the St. Mihiel salient, for more than six weeks you battered against the pivot of the enemy line on the western front. It was a position of imposing natural strength, stretching on both sides of the Meuse River from the bitterly contested hills of Verdun to the almost impenetrable forest of the Argonne; a position, moreover, fortified by four years of labor designed to render it impregnable; a position held with the fullest resources of the enemy. That position you broke utterly, and thereby hastened the collapse of the enemy's military power. Soldiers of all the divisions engaged under the First, Third and Fifth American Corps and the

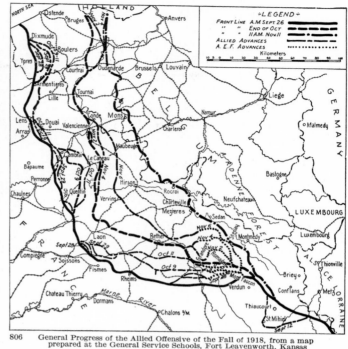

806   General Progress of the Allied Offensive of the Fall of 1918, from a map prepared at the General Service Schools, Fort Leavenworth, Kansas

Second Colonial and Seventeenth French Corps — the First, Second, Third, Fourth, Fifth, Twenty-sixth, Twenty-eighth, Twenty-ninth, Thirty-second, Thirty-third, Thirty-seventh, Forty-second, Seventy-seventh, Seventy-eighth, Seventy-ninth, Eightieth, Eighty-first, Eighty-second, Eighty-ninth, Ninetieth and Ninety-first American divisions, the Eighteenth and Twenty-sixth French divisions and the Tenth and Fifteenth French Colonial divisions — you will be long remembered for the stubborn persistence of your progress, your storming of obstinately defended machine-gun nests, your penetration, yard by yard, of woods and ravines, your heroic resistance in the face of counter-attacks, supported by powerful artillery fire. . . . The achievement of the First Army, which is scarcely to be equalled in American History, must remain a source of proud satisfaction to the troops who participated in the last campaign of the war. The American people will remember it as the realization of the hitherto potential strength of the American contribution toward the cause to which they had sworn allegiance. There can be no greater reward for a soldier or for a soldier's memory. . . ." — JOHN J. PERSHING, General, commander in chief, American Expeditionary Forces.

AT PEACE

Your hands confirm our manhood,
  Your hearts hold women true,
And the wide eyes of children
  Are clean because of you.
Though desperate wars undaunted
  Our future arms retain
Your gift of fear confronted,
  Your gift of conquered pain.
Stronger when foes dispute you,
  Wiser when fools deny,
We who must live salute you
  Who have found strength to die!

— BRIAN HOOKER

807   American Cemetery at Oise-Aisne, France, from a photograph by Underwood & Underwood

NOTES ON THE PICTURES

5. George S. Cook of Charleston, later of Richmond, made photographs of southern scenes and persons. See also Vol. VI.

10. For Gutzon Borglum see Vol. XII.

16. The original bears the notation, "This was the first war sketch received by *Harper's* following the surrender of General Triggs."

24. For an account of Mathew B. Brady see Notes on the Pictures, Vol. IX. Brady followed the Federal Army with a wagon equipped as a dark room in which he developed his wet-plate negatives immediately after exposure. A large collection of these negatives is owned by the United States Signal Corps, having been purchased after the war. A duplicate set by authority of the Massachusetts Legislature was made for the Military Order of the Loyal Legion, Boston, and is on file in the armory of that organization, together with many other Civil War pictures. See 26, 27, 28, 29, 34, 35, 73, 78, 80, 85, 86, 108, 109, 133, 167, 170, 206' 208, 212.

50. Wyeth is a well known mural painter. Specimens of his work are in the Hotel Traymore, Atlantic City, the New York Public Library, the Federal Reserve Bank of Boston and the Peabody Museum of Fine Arts.

64. Hoffbauer, born and educated in Paris, has done much of his work in America. In addition to his murals for the Confederate Memorial Museum he has paintings in Carnegie Institute, Pittsburgh, and Memorial Hall, Philadelphia.

82. Of English birth, William F. Halsall served in the Federal Navy during the Civil War, and afterward devoted himself to marine painting.

96. Before 1861, Edwin Forbes, best known for his stirring etchings of Civil War scenes, was a painter of animals. He was at the front as a special artist for *Leslie's* during the war, and his sketches made throughout the period were preserved in a series of copper-plate etchings awarded a medal at the Centennial Exhibition of 1876. First proofs of these etchings were bought for the United States Government by General Sherman and are now in the War Department, Washington. In later life he again concentrated on animal and landscape subjects. See 128, 129.

97. A pupil of St. Gaudens, Keck is best known for his monuments. See Vol. XII.

99. After studying under Emmanuel Leutze, Julian Scott painted many battle scenes of the Civil War.

100. The third son of Louis Phillipe, duc d'Orleans,

De Joinville sought refuge in England after the French revolution of 1848. In 1861 he placed the services of himself, his son, and two nephews at the disposal of the United States and served with the Federal Army during the Civil War.

101, 106, 111, 112, 127, 134, 160, 163, 214, 215, 323, 336, 379, 382, 386, 387. See Vol. IX, Notes on the Pictures, 80.

107, 119, 308. See Vol. IX.

139. See Vol. I, Notes on the Pictures, 643, also Vols. III, IX, XI.

147. The artist, a Frenchman, made numerous sketches for the works of Guizot, Daudet, Dumas and Verne. With his father, Felix Philippoteaux, he worked on the cyclorama of *The Siege of Paris*, and in 1883 produced the first Civil War cyclorama, *The Siege of Gettysburg*. Other cycloramas which he executed are *Tel-el-Keber* and *The Falls of Niagara* in London and *Plevna* in Leningrad. He also painted many pictures of Civil War scenes, including thirty episodes in the life of General Grant. See 194, 395.

154. See 139.

185, 188. Examples of Nast's early work as illustrator before he became famous as a cartoonist. See Vol. XII. Also Vol. IX, Notes on the Pictures.

194. See 147.

207. Best known as a portrait and figure painter. See Vol. XII.

247. See 139.

252. See 64.

307. Illustrator of Cooper, Dickens and Irving, Darley also delineated scenes of the Revolution and Civil War. See Vols. XI and XII.

341, 363, 368. See 139.

370. See 50.

381. See 307.

388. For a discussion of Nast as a cartoonist see Vol. XII and Vol. IX, Notes on the Pictures.

395. See 147.

396. Ferris is noted for his paintings of events in American history. See Vols. I, VI, VIII and XI.

397. See 139.

400. See 64.

414. Reuterdahl, artist and war correspondent during the Spanish-American and World Wars, was born in Sweden. He was essentially a marine and naval painter, although he also painted industrial subjects. After America

entered the European conflict in 1917 he was appointed the official artist of the United States Navy. Many of his naval paintings are in the Naval Academy, Annapolis, in the Navy Department, Washington, and in the Naval War College, Newport.

416, 417. See 139.

461. An illustrator who in recent years has turned to marine painting, especially of the clipper-ship period. Works in water-color to a large extent.

468, 469, 470. John Elliott was a mural painter whose work is shown in the National Museum, Washington, and the Metropolitan Museum, New York.

482. Louis Raemakers, Dutch cartoonist, bitterly assailed Germany throughout the World War. His powerful cartoons were reproduced in all neutral and Allied countries and were potent factors in swaying public opinion against the Central Powers.

486, 490. The artist is a portrait and figure painter whose early work was notable for its handling of light. See Vol. XII.

495. For Charles Dana Gibson, illustrator and caricaturist, see Vol. XII.

507. Irving R. Wiles is a portrait painter of distinction, whose work hangs in the Corcoran Gallery and the National Gallery, Washington, and in the Metropolitan Museum, New York.

644. Dwight Franklin specializes in miniature wax groups, usually of an historical nature, for museums.

658. Douglas Volk, a pupil of Gérôme, is a portrait painter of the objective tradition. See Vol. XII.

667. See 486.

668. For a discussion of the artist and his work see Vol. XII.

694. See 644.

700. An official artist of the A. E. F., George Harding studied under Howard Pyle and has specialized in mural decoration. See also 707.

711. Cecilia Beaux is a portrait painter whose work is vigorous and characterful. See Vol. XII.

733, 735, 736. See 468.

763. Ernest Peixotto, illustrator and mural painter, was head of the A. E. F. Art Training Center, Bellevue, France, after having been an official artist with the United States Army.

771. See 644.

774, 775, 785. See 763.

INDEX

Titles of books under authors are in italics; titles of ill strations under producer are in quotation marks.